Galician Trails

THE FORGOTTEN STORY OF ONE FAMILY

Galician Trails

THE FORGOTTEN STORY
OF ONE FAMILY

ANDREW ZALEWSKI

THELZO PRESS

Galician Trails

THE FORGOTTEN STORY
OF ONE FAMILY

Copyright © 2012 by Andrew Zalewski

THELZO PRESS

93 Old York Rd., Suite 1-421
Jenkintown, PA 19046

www.thelzopress.com

ISBN 13: 978-0-9855894-0-0
Library of Congress Control Number: 2012943890

All rights reserved. This book or any portion thereof
may not be reproduced or used in any manner whatsoever
without the express written permission of the publisher.

Cover and Interior Design: Peri Gabriel, Knockout Design,
www.knockoutbooks.com

Printed in the United States of America

First Edition

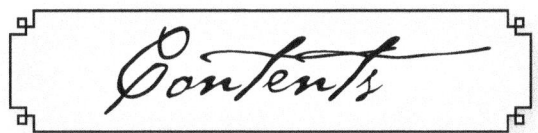

Preface		vii
Chapter 1 — Galicia: A Mysterious Land Somewhere in Europe		1
Chapter 2 — The Lösch and Regiec Families: Taking Chances		25
Chapter 3 — Stanislawow: The Stronghold of Rewera		91
Chapter 4 — Bohorodczany: A World in Itself		131
Chapter 5 — The Sobolewski Clan: Nobles and Farmers		151
Chapter 6 — Helena Regiec Sobolewska		181
Chapter 7 — Gathering Clouds: Trouble at Home		209
Chapter 8 — The Prelude: Troops Are Marching		229

Chapter 9 — The Great War: A Tale of Conflict
and Ordinary Life 245

Chapter 10 — The End in Sight: Is This Time for Real? 273

Chapter 11 — Where to Go? Old Stories Fade Away and
New Ones Are Born 297

Epilogue 321

Acknowledgments 333

Appendix — The Lösch, Regiec, and Sobolewski Family Registers 337

Notes 349

Index 385

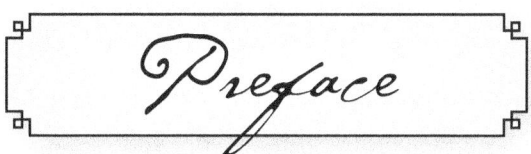

Preface

THIS IS THE TALE OF three very different families connected to the life of my grandmother, Helena Regiec Sobolewska. She was a quiet woman who seldom spoke about herself. When there had been time to ask Grandma questions about her youth, I never did so; like many others, I was unaware that such opportunities would not last forever. Perhaps not that surprisingly, only much later did I begin to realize that I was missing many details about my grandmother's life. Slowly, the thought became clear to me that unless I tried to find out more about the past, her story might be lost forever.

For me, the real quest started inconspicuously on one of those slow Sunday afternoons. The fun of the weekend was almost over, but it was still too soon to get ready for the week ahead. For unclear reasons and not expecting to find much, I typed into a search engine the name of the town where my grandmother had met her future husband. I remembered that it had an unusual name and had been located in a faraway country; other than that, there was nothing in particular about the place that I could really recall. When I pressed "enter," a list of mostly irrelevant links appeared on the screen—but one caught my attention.

It led to an old posting that contained a short list of names, including that of my grandfather. For any reader who was interested in learning more, an email address was provided.

I responded with a short note, and soon someone on the other end was asking for my mailing address. Apparently, a long list of my ancestors was available. Although warning bells rang in my head about a possible scam, I took the chance. A week later, a thick envelope arrived from a retired teacher in Canada, who had painstakingly catalogued several families from that place, located thousands of miles from both of us. Here were many of the names of my newly discovered family; the list stretched from the late eighteenth century to the beginning of the twentieth. Toward the end of this amazing roster, I spotted a detailed entry referring to my grandparents' wedding. I knew immediately that I was on to something unique and could not stop there.

What followed was an incredible journey through the Galicia of the Habsburg Empire, the land where my Austrian and Polish ancestors, both Christian and Jewish, had once lived. Against all the odds of passing time and intervening wars, an amazing window into the past had opened to me. Information that had been buried in archives and collections around the world—personal records, old newspapers, church and school records, early photographs, and more—came directly to my desktop when I learned where and how to look. Without any need for me to travel (to places that might no longer exist or be quite different than in bygone times), a picture started slowly to emerge. Soon, I had the thrilling sense that an imaginary curtain was being lifted. With each new discovery I made, my fuzzy image of the past was slowly becoming sharper. Multicultural Galicia, a place that well deserved the label "melting pot," was unfolding in front of my eyes.

At first, my findings were impersonal in nature; but as the story developed, I realized that this quest was not just about dates and places. It was an intimate journey back to the people who had mattered to my grandmother, and the world surrounding them. My preconceived notions about the past were quickly challenged, as I realized the surprising mobility of some members of my family—those who had been brave enough to take full advantage of opportunities some distance away. Others had remained tied to their ancestral homes for generations. I often thought about the rich and fast-paced lives some of them had led, despite the many imperfections of life in Galicia.

This story starts with Mathias Lösch and his son, who moved to the town of "white gold" in western Galicia in 1809. At first, I marveled at the way this Austrian family had replanted itself in a new land and then made the best of it. Yet two generations later, their descendant Andreas Lösch and his wife, Eleonora, would live in a dizzying number of places throughout Galicia. Then their life stories would suddenly become intertwined with that of Joseph Regiec, who had a different tale to tell.

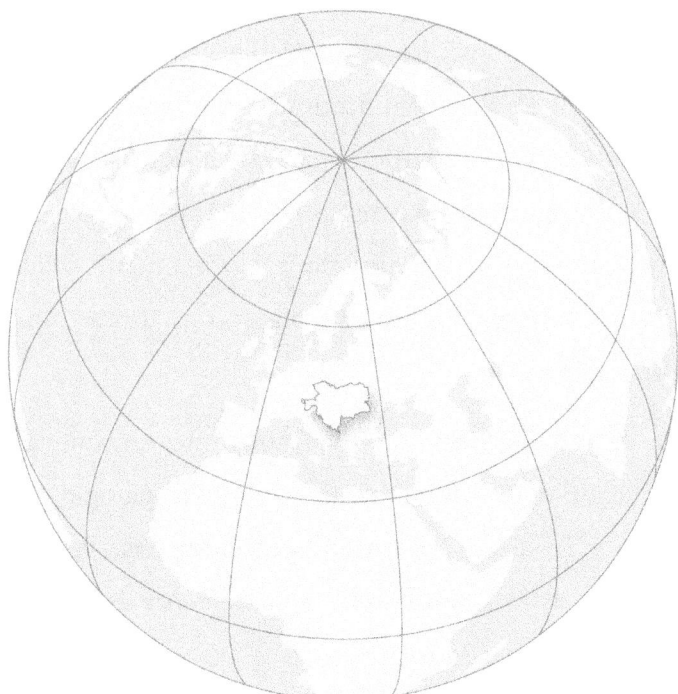

Borders of Austro-Hungary in the nineteenth century.

The saga of the Regiec family stretched from the humble life of a shepherd to the memorable one of the accomplished Joseph. It was he and Stephania Lösch who joined the two families through marriage. Modern people with a deep sense of purpose, they became part of the story of the railroads that were opening the world around them. In time, their daughter Helena Regiec, my grandmother, connected this narrative with a third family through her marriage to Franciscus Sobolewski. The Sobolewskis, nobles turned farmers, had a past very different from that of the Lösches or the Regiecs. My grandmother, an early professional woman, would carry the story forward even when the world around her suddenly moved in unpredictable directions.

When writing about a past with its share of tensions and controversies, it is important to add a few disclaimers. While reading through records of the time, it became apparent to me that some issues had provoked human reactions or official policies that starkly contrasted with the acceptable norms of today. Some readers may find my frequent references to religion, once a much more visible part of people's self-identification, overly intrusive. Others may be surprised to learn about buried tensions that could quickly flare up between different groups, at times with grim consequences. This was, however, the reality of Galicia. There, the many religious, ethnic, and economic differences were indisputably unique, and a strength of the place—but also a cause of painful fractures along those lines.

Whether I'm describing the past or repeating once-prevailing opinions, I must stress that the intent of this book is not to level disparaging judgments at one group or another. Instead, I have tried to carefully observe and record the world as people saw it then, despite what might be considered "politically correct" in twenty-first-century culture.

Preface

This is not a book written by a historian to provide scholarly interpretations. Whenever possible, however, I have thoroughly researched the events I discuss, and have backed up the narrative by references to my sources.

Now that my writing is complete, I realize that my grandmother, grandfather, and those before them had much more fascinating stories to tell than I could have ever imagined. I hope that this record will introduce our forebears to my children and grandchildren as much more than just black-and-white photographs in our family album. Perhaps others will also find this story about the past interesting, and realize that it is never too late to search in their own families for other fascinating and surprise-filled "Galician trails."

Elkins Park, Pennsylvania
May 2012

Chapter 1

GALICIA:

A MYSTERIOUS LAND

SOMEWHERE

IN EUROPE

———❦———

GALICIA, ONCE A PROVINCE OF the Habsburg Empire, was a land where many cultures came into contact with each other, creating fertile ground for unique family stories. The tale of the Lösches, the Regiecs, and the Sobolewskis is one of many such narratives. But despite Galicia's rich past (one not free of controversies), the place has slowly been erased from the world's collective memory. To make matters worse, this land, which once occupied parts of today's southeast Poland and western Ukraine, is sometimes confused with a region in Spain carrying the same name.

Galicia's disappearance into the foggy past was gradual; it started soon after World War I, when Austrian Galicia ceased to exist as a legal entity. Over the next decades, countries that had inherited or conquered parts of it, perhaps insecure about their identities, created their own national narratives in which positive influences from the past were minimized. Today, in many ways, it is difficult to pin down the big historical picture of Galicia, as well as the more complex human dimensions of the place. Eyewitnesses are long gone, historians' views have invariably been colored by hindsight, and diverse personal stories have been lost over the generations. But one thing is clear: Although the Galicia of the Habsburg monarchy was an imperfect place, with many issues ultimately leading to its demise, it was open enough as a society to allow the lucky and the brave to chart their personal courses free from the social strictures found in many other places. The new identities thus forged would leave lasting imprints on generations to come.

The land that would become Galicia had a long and twisted history for several centuries before it fell under Austrian control. The eastern part witnessed struggles for dominance between East Slavic, Polish, and Hungarian kings and princes. It was also subject to repeated Mongol invasions.[1] Its national identity and borders changed many times, and a series of names described this place: the Red Rus' (Red Ruthenia), Kievan Rus', Eastern Little Poland, and today, Ukraine. The first mention of the name "Galicia" dates back to the year 981, when it was one of many principalities under the influence of the grand prince of Kiev. This Galicia, long predating Austrian sovereignty over a small portion of its land, was inhabited by a people known as the East Slavs. Competing claims of influence and frequently shifting control over the territory were a theme repeated time after time over its long history. During those early years, the principality experienced frequent military incursions: from the west by Poles and from the south by Hungarians, with each group trying to enforce its dominance.

Not surprisingly, given this long history, the origin of the name "Galicia" has had more than one explanation. Some believe that the Latinized version of the word *salt* (a well-mined mineral in the area) produced the city name "Halych," which was eventually applied to the entire region, called Halychyna in the native language of the East Slavs. Others argue that the name came from the crow-like bird on the coat of arms of historical and later Austrian Galicia.[2]

The coat of arms of Galicia, the crown land of the Austrian Empire from 1772 until its dissolution in 1918.

In 1141, when Galicia was a dominant force among many principalities of the Red Rus', its capital was established at Halych. Soon it grew further, through union with neighboring Volhynia, leading to the emergence of a new stronghold, the Kingdom of Galicia and Volhynia *(Regnum Galiciae et Lodomeriae)*. Its influence stretched all the way to the Black Sea. But nothing lasts forever, especially in this part of the world, with its competing interests.

That period of greatness was followed by the decline of historical Galicia. New invasions by Poles, Hungarians, and Lithuanians encroaching on the western part of the territory started in the 1340s and would continue for the next four decades. During these turbulent times, Galicia was briefly captured by King Casmir the Great of Poland after his armies successfully repelled Mongol invaders during battles in 1349. Then Hungarians became the rulers of the land, only to be later repelled by Poles and Lithuanians. With such quickly changing masters, not many would notice that the title "Sovereign of Galicia and Lodomeria" was in continued use by a long line of Hungarian kings, even after their expulsion from Galicia. Buried among their many honors, seemingly without real importance, this titular claim to those remote lands would return to the spotlight centuries later.

Soon, another power emerged in this unstable neighborhood; this new player would have a lasting impact on the fate of the East Slavs and neighboring countries. In the north of the Red Rus', the principality of Muscovy was growing in strength. In time, Muscovy adopted the name "Russia," and with its ascent cemented the split of the East Slavs between two spheres of influence: one associated with the Kingdom of Poland and later Austria, and the other with tsarist Russia. This division would continue for centuries.

In 1432, historical Galicia was fully incorporated into the Kingdom of Poland, becoming one of its palatinates (provinces). The next few centuries of Polish dominance introduced not only a new legal system to Galicia but also an influx of Polish magnates, who took ownership of large pieces of land. Others who moved east were members of the lesser nobility and Polish peasants, who continued to migrate there over the next centuries. Among them were the ancestors of my grandfather, the Sobolewskis, members of the rural gentry who established their home in the midst of the majority, the Ruthenians. This period also brought early arrivals of Germans, Jews, and Armenians, who were encouraged by the government to settle there. These changes were felt among the East Slavs, the original inhabitants of the area, and across the entire society.

For the most part, the upper social strata of Galicia—which included landowning families and gentry—were well-assimilated after a few centuries of Polish domination, adopting the language, customs, and religion of that administration. Many of them would become almost indistinguishable from Polish nobles, and would take full advantage of their privileges. The picture of the rest of the countryside was more complex; villages became a mixture of a Ruthenian population preserving its original language and customs; Polonized neighbors; and ethnic Poles, like the Sobolewski family.

Polish rule brought an opening of trade and strong economic dependence on booming grain exports. With this prosperity came the harsh requirement of a steady supply of manual farm labor. Although implementation would vary from region to region, this increased demand for free labor caused the enserfment of the majority of peasants in sixteenth-century Galicia.[3]

The province remained in Polish hands for four centuries, until the First Partition of Poland took place in August of 1772. Three dominant powers of the region—Russia, Prussia, and Austria—divided about 30 percent of Polish territory among themselves. Austria was a somewhat reluctant partner in this escapade; it was more interested in expanding its territory into the Balkans than north of the Carpathian Mountains. The agreement among the three powers stipulated that land that in medieval times had been part of Galicia would now be incorporated into Austria and ruled by the Habsburg monarchy.

The First Partition of Poland. Rulers of Russia (Catherine the Great), Austria (Joseph II), and Prussia (Frederick the Great) are shown dividing the territory of the Polish kingdom. The king of Poland (Stanislaus Augustus Poniatowski) is having difficulty holding on to his crown. *(Engraving based on a drawing by Jean-Michel Moreau in 1773.)*

At first, some wondered if this was only a temporary seizure, with the Habsburgs perhaps ultimately wanting to exchange this remote place for a more valuable territory, in their frequent horse-trading with neighboring Russia. In spite of these speculations, the empress Maria Theresa, the archduchess of Austria and the queen of Hungary, named this possession the Kingdom of Galicia and Lodomeria (*die Königreiche Galizien und Lodomerien*), invoking medieval claims as the ruler of Hungary. As happened many times before and after, ancient titles and myths were repackaged to justify a new political order.

༃

Austrian Galicia now stretched from the history-steeped city of Cracow and a sliver of the Habsburgs' Silesia in the west, to the borders of the vast Russian Empire looming in the east. In the south of Galicia, the Carpathian Mountains rose, forming a natural border with the Kingdom of Hungary, which included today's Slovakia and parts of Romania. In the north, the land became a plateau dissected by rivers, which flowed toward the remnant of the Kingdom of Poland that had fallen under the Russian sphere of influence. Later, some would meekly argue that the name of the new province did not match the historical boundaries of the old principalities of Red Rus', but such details did not really matter to those who were now setting the rules here. From now on, the name "Galicia" would be associated with a new crown land and its people.

The imperial coat of arms of Austria. The Austrian Empire was the successor state to the Holy Roman Empire, which was dissolved by Francis I in 1806. For two years before that, Francis held the unique title of dual emperor of both states.

Within a couple of years, Austria also included within its borders the Duchy of Bukovina (*Bukowina* in German and in the Slavic languages), a territory bordering Galicia that had been acquired from the Ottoman Empire, completing a new administrative structure in the northeast corner of the land.[4] There would be only a few more changes to Galicia's borders, mainly in the western part of the province after the Third Partition of Poland. Final boundaries were set after the Congress of Vienna in the aftermath of the Napoleonic Wars. Galicia was to be governed by the Austrian monarchy until 1918.

Even a brief study of the Kingdom of Galicia and Lodomeria reveals an abundance of stories about its vibrant culture; so it might come as a surprise to the reader that it was a sparsely populated territory. A large majority of its people lived in the countryside, where arable soil was under the control of local gentry who had received ancient land titles from Polish kings and later from Austrian monarchs.[5]

At first, Galicia was one of the poorest of all the provinces of the Austrian Empire; rural church registers and land-census documents display the names of impoverished nobility mixed with those of free peasants and serfs. There were reports of an appallingly low life expectancy, in some places averaging below 30 years of age, although these are difficult to verify. Yet in spite of some reluctance toward dealing with this newly absorbed land and its problems, the Habsburg monarchy became a catalyst that made Galicia an even greater mixture of cultures than in the past. This place would continue to be the fascinating, though often unacknowledged, "melting pot" of Europe.

Soon after taking over Galicia, Empress Maria Theresa of Austria opened its borders to artisans and merchants who were willing to move there in return for a generous, six-year exemption from taxation. Not only Catholics but Protestants were encouraged to settle there, with guaranteed freedom of worship. Although Jews were not explicitly forbidden, they were tellingly omitted from the empress's decree, a sign that the enlightenment of the crown went only so far.[6] Interestingly, the first request for permission to settle in the east came from the Calvinist Swiss, who had petitioned the Austrian government about this as early as 1775. Those early steps were followed by fundamental settlement laws (patents) issued by Maria Theresa's son, the emperor Joseph II, soon after he became sole emperor of Austria in 1780. This led to waves of foreigners moving to the province. Emigration from the south of Germany was especially encouraged, becoming easier with the 1782 Toleranzpatent, which proclaimed full religious tolerance for Protestants in Catholic Austria.[7]

Galician coins with the Austrian eagle.

Many ethnic Germans from Bohemia and Moravia (now part of the Czech Republic) also moved to Galicia with a stream of newcomers that continued until 1820. The trip was quite arduous: They traveled down the Danube River or overland through Prague to Vienna, where they were given final permission and money for travel. Upon entering Galicia from the west over the few available roads, most of them continued to the east. There they were offered generous tax deferments, parcels of former Polish crown lands, and other available farmland. Some of these newcomers settled in existing villages such as Horocholina, which we will visit later in this story; more often, they found homes in newly laid-out agricultural communities.

As part of a grand scheme by Joseph II and his government, such German settlers were welcomed in eastern Galicia in an attempt to modernize the remote, sparsely populated territory. The few maps that have survived show special emigrants' villages (*colonias*) with houses neatly surrounding central points, such as churches or schools. The exact number of emigrant settlers (*colonistas*) is not known, but some have estimated that close to 3,000 families—about 18,000 people—moved to Galicia between the end of the eighteenth century and the early years of the nineteenth. Soon German-named new settlements, like Landestreu, Ugartsthal, and Königsau, started to appear next to Slavic-sounding Galician villages.[8] Other newcomers included soldiers from the Austrian army. Among these were Mathias Lösch and his son, who will become an important part of this story; they too would quickly put down roots in Galicia, adding to its diversity.

Newcomers to this land encountered clear differences between the western and eastern parts. The former was predominantly Polish and Roman Catholic, with pockets of Jewish residents in the cities. The latter had particularly large Ruthenian and Jewish communities coexisting with smaller Polish, Armenian, Slovak, and German groups. Although Ruthenians were the majority in eastern Galicia (with the exception of the capital, Lvov), many more lived beyond Galicia's borders in the Russian Empire.[9] However, the lives of these two populations could not have been more different. For quite a long time to come, Ruthenians living in

Ruthenians (Ukrainians) of eastern Galicia. The countrymen typically wore straw hats and shirttails. In summer months, the women often walked barefoot. *(Photograph taken during World War I.)*

Russia would have no sense of their own identity, language, or religion, often being labeled with the derogatory term *little Russians*. In contrast, their cousins who lived under Austrian rule were receiving official support to form their own organizations and schools; to counterbalance the influence of the Poles, they were recognized as a separate nationality.

The Ruthenians of Galicia were mostly peasants who belonged to the "Uniate" Church, which followed the Eastern Orthodox liturgy but recognized the supremacy of the pope. Under the Habsburgs, their church was renamed the Greek Catholic Church, and the government provided education and seminaries to its clergy to offset the more aggressive Roman Catholic Church attended by Poles. Small, wooden Greek Catholic churches would become a fixture of rural regions in the eastern part of Galicia.

Galician Amazon. Hutsul women from the mountainous regions were excellent horseback riders. *(Maynard Owen Williams/National Geographic Stock.)*

In mountainous areas, travelers through Galicia could encounter enclaves of smaller ethnic groups with exotic-sounding names.[10] In the southeast, beyond the towns of Stanislawow and Bohorodczany, which we will soon visit, lived highlanders called the Hutsuls. The name "Hutsul" is thought to be derived from the word *outlaw* in Romanian. Their tongue was similar to the Ruthenian language, but their origin was the stuff of many legends. The Hutsuls' main occupations were forestry, and sheep and cattle breeding. Their small, sturdy ponies were well-suited for riding through mountainous terrain. Hutsul men and women could often be seen smoking thin, curved pipes; men wore sheepskin jackets and women's garb was adorned with decorative pom-poms.

The story of Galicia is also the story of Jews, who were an important part of Galicia's human mosaic and will be a recurring subject in our journey through time. Their growth in numbers and in contributions to Galician society continued under the Austrian monarchy. High birth rates and waves of immigration from the east, as Jews escaped pogroms in the Russian Empire, outpaced significant Jewish emigration to other parts of the Austro-Hungarian Empire and the United States in the late nineteenth and early twentieth centuries.[11] But the relationship between Vienna and the Jewish population was complex and frequently changing. The government's official instructions to its provincial administrators shifted back and forth from "enlightened" attempts to forcefully integrate Jews into the larger society, to erecting barriers that blocked their full participation. On some occasions, the Jewish population was used to drive wedges between other ethnic groups in Galicia, or blamed for various ills of the society. Importantly, imperial decrees issued between 1781 and 1789 recognized Jews as a free religious minority and members of a civil community. This positive step, however, was quickly contradicted by special taxes levied on Jews, including abusive taxes on Sabbath candles and kosher meat. Starting in 1787, Jews were required to adopt fixed and hereditary surnames; and their congregations were to keep records of births, marriages, and deaths, although not many of these have survived. Other administrative reforms included the division of Jewish Galicia into 140 congregations, each governed by a "kahal" of elders that would represent their communities in dealings with local authorities.

The early nineteenth century brought a step backward in the Habsburgs' policies toward Jews. An imperial decree in 1810 prohibited marriages until the couple had passed a religious examination based on an officially sanctioned Jewish catechism. This was less of an issue for German-speaking Jews living in Austria

Orthodox Jews from Galicia on the Sabbath, wearing the traditional clothes, including black satin coats and fur-trimmed velvet hats. *(Dorothy Hosmer Lee Collection, UCR Sweeney Art Gallery, University of California, Riverside.)*

or Bohemia, but the problem for the Jews of Galicia was that only a few could read German. Then there were other laws regulating marriages among the Jewish communities of Galicia. Suddenly, in the eyes of the law, many Jewish children were proclaimed to have been born out of wedlock when the marriages of their parents, conducted without the purchase of costly licenses, were deemed illegal.

Finally, in 1867, after decades of passing contradictorily liberal and discriminatory laws, the Austro-Hungarian Empire granted all of its citizens equal rights. From that time on, Jews were able to occupy any public position and had the right to purchase real estate. My paternal Jewish ancestors, the Hübner family (whose multigenerational story I am yet to fully discover), were among the recipients of these newly gained rights.[12] Many Galician towns, some of which we will visit on this journey, had clear Jewish majorities. Their vibrant businesses and (often non-monolithic) communities enriched local culture and added important voices to the commonly noisy local politics.

By the 1880s, Galicia's officially recognized religions included the Roman and Greek Catholic, Russian Orthodox, Protestant, and Jewish faiths (with Jews traditionally referred to as Israelites). This ethnic and religious diversity explains not only the Slavic but also many of the non-Slavic names that we will encounter in this story, invariably raising the question, *Where did these people come from, and when?*

Greek Catholic church in eastern Galicia. *(Dorothy Hosmer Lee Collection, UCR Sweeney Art Gallery, University of California, Riverside.)*

When the Kingdom of Galicia and Lodomeria was established under the Austrian monarchy, many trade links were suddenly severed. Borders to the north and west were effectively closed by high fees and taxes. Commerce from the east to other parts of Europe no longer had to pass through Galicia, as the expansion of the Russian Empire further to the north provided more convenient trade routes. From the perspective of Vienna, Galicia was at the periphery of the country, and the province's residents were effectively trapped behind the rugged Carpathian Mountains. Despite a few roads heading southwest from Cracow toward the center of Austria, Galicia was not only isolated from the rest of Europe; its western and eastern parts were cut off from each other.

The arrival of railroads was seen as a modernizing force everywhere in the world. Not surprisingly, for Galicia, railroads had an even greater emotional and physical impact, lessening—if not eliminating—its long isolation. As we will see, the railways also influenced the lives of individuals who will play key parts in our story. I remember hearing snippets of my grandmother's childhood memories that were linked to the railroads in Galicia; to those we will return later.

The first attempts to help Galicia escape its isolation, in connecting different parts of the province and the empire by rail, were painfully slow and not very effective. In 1836, the Austrian emperor Ferdinand granted imperial permission to construct the first steam railway from Vienna to the western part of Galicia. The company and the line were named the Emperor Ferdinand Northern Railway (*der Keiser Ferdinand Nordbahn*). The town of Bochnia was chosen as the terminal point because of nearby commercially attractive salt mines. The project progressed slowly, and the route would never reach Bochnia. Even Cracow, the largest city in the western part of Galicia, had to await the arrival of the railroad for years. Until the late 1850s, when an additional link connected Cracow with the *Nordbahn*, travel from Galicia to the capital of the empire continued to be difficult.[13]

The steam locomotive Austria was the first model that operated on the
Emperor Ferdinand Northern Railway, starting in 1847.

The Emperor Ferdinand Northern Railway, however, only increased people's appetite for more rail lines. Since it reached only the western part of Galicia, it provided almost no relief for the isolation of the capital, Lvov, and the inconvenience of traveling there. An intense campaign was begun by Galician politicians and intellectuals to press for an eastern extension of the railroad. Patrician Prince Leon Sapieha and the famous playwright Alexander Fredro formed an unlikely alliance, and both men apparently became engrossed in studying maps and planning the route. When these efforts did not advance the cause, Archduke Ferdinand d'Este, the supreme governor of Galicia, was petitioned for permission to form a civic organization in support of the east-west line. Delegations were sent to Vienna and, as in modern times, they lobbied not only politicians but the financial powers of the day, including the influential Salomon Myer von Rothschild.

The breakthrough came in 1858, when the Austrian emperor Franz Joseph granted Prince Sapieha a license for extending the railway.[14] In 1861, at long last, the Imperial Royal Galician Railway of Archduke Charles Louis (*k.k. priv. Galizische Carl Ludwig Bahn*), linking Cracow in the west to Lvov in the east, was opened. For years, it would be considered the most profitable line in Galicia.

The steam locomotive Krakow operated on the Charles Louis Railway, linking Cracow and Lvov.

Other lines further to the south followed, including the Galician Transversal Railway (*Galizische Transversalbahn*), which opened in 1884. This was a state-owned enterprise that ran just north of the Carpathian Mountains. It traversed Galicia from the west to the southeast, through many towns that we will visit on this journey, including Mszana Dolna, Nowy Sacz, Jaslo, and Stanislawow.[15] Not by coincidence, the life of my great-grandfather, Joseph Regiec, became connected with these places that were now linked by the new railway. Soon, the east-west lines were joined by a number of extensions, forming additional, shorter links to the north and south, criss-crossing Galicia and reaching beyond its borders. By the end of the nineteenth century, there were seven main routes connecting cities within Galicia and branching further south toward the Kingdom of Hungary and southeast toward the Duchy of Bukovina.

Railway travel in Galicia was considered cheaper than in other parts of Europe. Nonetheless, the trip from faraway eastern Galicia to Vienna cost 30 florins (about 15 kronen) and could be afforded by only a few.[16] There were three and sometimes even four classes available. First-class carriages were lined with velvet and offered the most space, and second class was equipped with spring seats that were considered excellent by visiting English tourists. The third-class travelers were described as "quiet and respectable, and the carriages tolerably clean," whereas the infrequently found fourth class had standing room only. The trains traveled at an amazing speed of up to 25 miles per hour, with stops at railway stations where more affluent travelers could have meals in restaurants.[17]

IN THE MID-NINETEENTH CENTURY, the Austrian Empire was shaken by a crisis that seriously threatened its survival. Hungarians' quest for independence almost split the country in response to real and sometimes imaginary historical claims. This time, however, the crisis was averted with the

The coat of arms of the Austro-Hungarian Empire, formed in 1867. The symbol of the Austrian Empire (Cisleithania), on the left, is joined with the symbol of the Kingdom of Hungary (Transleithania).

Compromise Act, reached in 1867. The concept of a dual monarchy made it possible to preserve the old order under the new name of the Austro-Hungarian Empire. Under this act, the Austrian emperor Franz Joseph was crowned king of Hungary, but his empire was divided into two separately governed parts, one under Austrian rule (Cisleithania) and the other under Hungarian rule (Transleithania). The symbol of a constitutional monarch with only three joint imperial and royal governmental ministries kept the large country together. Galicia continued to be in the Austrian part of the empire, but changes were clearly palpable there as well. Galicia's Imperial Royal (*k.k.*) supreme governors, who represented the emperor, changed from the foreign-sounding Christian Wurmser, Prince Ferdinand Würthemberg, and Archduke Ferdinand d'Este to the Polish-sounding Count Agenor Goluchowski, Count Dr. Alfred Potocki, and Dr. Michal Bobrzynski, to mention just a few.

So what kept this mosaic of lands and diverse people together? Certainly, it was not a language or unifying customs. Paradoxically, it could have been the vast civil administration and judiciary that expanded in response to the industrial revolution of the nineteenth century. As a result, some stated, "For almost all educated people in Galicia, Vienna became a source of promotion, career, favor and honor."[18]

Polish aristocrat Agenor Goluchowski, a governor of Galicia who became a state minister in Vienna and a confidante of the emperor, had the idea of providing a large degree of autonomy to the different lands of the empire. But for years, Count Goluchowski walked a fine line. He was often mistrusted by his nationalistic compatriots, who saw him more as an Austrian than as a Polish statesman; and he was not exactly welcomed with open arms by Viennese bureaucrats, who feared a loss of control. Goluchowski realized that to reform the system, he would have to work from the inside. Appointed Galicia's governor for a record three times, Goluchowski slowly but steadily replaced the province's top administrators with native talent. This was a remarkable initiative, one needed to secure Galicia's much-desired autonomy in a few years' time. But it was not immediately recognized by many Galicians, who were preoccupied with unrealistic dreams of full independence from Austria.

In October of 1860, while serving as state minister in Vienna, Goluchowski issued a directive that would grant broad autonomy to the crown lands of the Austrian Empire. But implementation of these federalist arrangements was not straightforward. An internal power struggle ensued over the best way of moving from absolute rule to a more participatory system. In its wake, Goluchowski was forced to resign. Not surprisingly, the idea of self-government for faraway provinces such as the Kingdom of Galicia and Lodomeria faced stiff opposition from some corners of Vienna. What's more, German-speaking officials feared that they would lose influence if the proposed equality of native languages took hold. The reforms were stalled for a few years, but the seeds of change had clearly been planted, and they bore fruit in a few years' time.

In 1867, an imperial patent called for Galicia and other crown lands to elect regional legislatures. Deputies from the Galician parliament were accorded a large number of seats in the state council in Vienna, second only to Czechs from Bohemia. Another official decree issued in the name of the emperor Franz Joseph proclaimed all citizens to be equal, with their freedom of movement guaranteed as well as the right to assembly and freedom of religion. Even though it was not fully implemented in the provinces, this was a remarkable document, given the time and the place of its origin. But among these progressive ideas, although it may strike today's reader as odd, the emperor was declared to be unaccountable to any branch of the government or electorate. Franz Joseph himself signed that governmental proclamation; clearly, it was still good to be an emperor.[19]

After his return to Galicia and reappointment as supreme governor, Goluchowski effectively negotiated with Vienna to bring increasing autonomy at home. He failed to put Galicia at the level of parity with Austria that had been secured by Hungary, but nonetheless, his actions were unprecedented in scope. Still, his work was not fully appreciated by his compatriots. Goluchowski's efforts to direct Galicia's energy toward self-governance, and his ability to avert brewing internal conflicts, were largely successful. His time in office focused the people of Galicia on attaining their goals through education.[20]

Agenor Goluchowski Sr. (1812–1875) served as the governor of Galicia three times. Although controversial among his compatriots, Count Goluchowski secured a large degree of autonomy for Galicia from the central government in Vienna.

Local newspapers in native languages quickly appeared in several towns that we will visit in our story. Other publications, with audiences throughout Galicia, reemerged after years of suspension by the censors. The tone of one editorial signaled a deeper change when the prior imprisonments of the paper's contributors were only mentioned in passing. Instead, the message was about the real opportunity in sight, arguing strongly against self-serving agitation and the reopening of old wounds.[21]

After 1873, Galicia largely governed itself. The rights of minorities to speak their own languages and a new locally based educational system had been established. Is it possible that two young members of different branches of our family, Bronislawa Lösch and Joseph Regiec, had chosen teaching because of this new climate that took hold in the society of their youth?[22]

The far-reaching autonomy that became a fact of life in Galicia was the main reason that anti-Austrian sentiments were rare there. When, a few years after Goluchowski's death, the emperor Franz Joseph toured Galicia, he was welcomed with genuine gratitude (granted, some of the ovations might be viewed as obsequious by today's standards). His reception could not have been more different from those he had experienced during past visits—in which the monarch had been met with coldness and limited public participation. This time, upon the emperor's arrival in Cracow, 50,000 spectators had reportedly gathered. There were symbolic gestures that underscored the new relationship between Galicia and the Austro-Hungarian monarchy: Franz Joseph's security was entrusted to the citizens' guard, and the Austrian garrison was removed from the old royal castle, which became the emperor's temporary residence.

A week later, a reception in Lvov was also festive; an estimated 100,000 people filled the streets to welcome the emperor, many having traveled from afar. In addition to ceremonies in the local legislature (dominated by Poles) and visits to the Greek Catholic cathedral and the Ruthenian National Institute, the emperor added stops at two of Lvov's synagogues, liberal and orthodox, where he was blessed by the rabbis. At the imperial ball in honor of Franz Joseph that took place one evening in a lavishly illuminated City Hall, pomp was mixed with local politics. Not much interested in dancing, the emperor struck up conversations with members of Polish nobility splendidly dressed in their colorful ceremonial garb—some of them looking a bit like figures from an old, historical painting. Conversations followed with the leaders of three Catholic denominations (Roman, Greek, and Armenian) and the chief rabbi. But the mosaic of cultures and the symbolism did not end in Lvov. At train stations in the eastern part of the province, during brief stops, Franz Joseph was often addressed by local officials in Polish with a few phrases in the Ruthenian language. In response, the Austrian emperor would often reply in French instead of German, so as not to offend local sensitivities.[23]

As a result of the broad autonomy enjoyed by Galicia, only occasionally was Vienna perceived by nationalistic zealots as a source of overbearing trends in literature and music. In vivid contrast to other parts of partitioned Poland, where new rulers made concerted efforts to Russify or Germanize native populations, the Habsburgs only required Galicians to send taxes to Vienna and serve in the imperial army. From 1873 on, all those whom we will meet on this journey would probably have expressed religious and literary nationalism in their mother tongues (including Yiddish), but were generally not antigovernment.[24]

But autonomy did not mean an absence of central government in the crown land. The names of the branches of local administration, as well as the names of other emerging facets of modern life (such as the growing network of railways and civil or post-office buildings), carried the ubiquitous prefix *k.k.* (Imperial Royal). Yet in a less symbolic way, Vienna's perceived role shifted—from being an absolute and foreign power to having a balancing influence that quieted a sometimes conflicted society. The shrewd efforts of the Habsburg Empire to curtail domination of one group over the other led most Galicians to view faraway Austria as a benevolent and stabilizing force.

The figure of a fatherly emperor also provided a sense of continuity. For more than one generation, the image of Franz Joseph transcended ethnic lines and national aspirations, because nobody could remember anyone else at the top of the empire. I recall my grandmother saying that he was viewed less as a ruler from distant Vienna and more as a kind, elderly figure (with a huge mustache). To many, the emperor was seen as a conscientious and impartial force, with the judgment needed to mitigate any excesses of the vast government. His public life was one of extraordinary length; Franz Joseph became emperor years before Abraham Lincoln was elected president of the United States, and died when Woodrow Wilson occupied that office more than 60 years later.

Franz Joseph I (1830–1916) became the emperor of Austria in 1848 and remained at the helm of the country for 68 years, until his death during World War I.

When he died in 1916, in the middle of World War I, the Austro-Hungarian Empire's continuity was broken. It was no longer able to provide the sense of a functioning country, and quickly fell apart into a number of nationalistic and often less tolerant nations.

Chapter 2

THE LÖSCH AND REGIEC FAMILIES: TAKING CHANCES

Austrian Empire and the surrounding countries of central Europe at the beginning of the nineteenth century.

*T*HE LÖSCH AND REGIEC FAMILIES had some similarities. Neither was rooted in the nobility that still, in accordance with the standards of earlier times, valued hereditary titles. Nor did either family claim memorable triumphs on the battlefield. In fact, it is difficult to find any notable historical figure, even one loosely related, bearing one of their names. Yet for some generations, the intrepid Lösches and Regiecs were on the move; they seem to have shared the same unyielding belief that taking chances was essential to making their lives better. Time after time, members of both families took advantage of the opportunities at hand, seemingly rejecting the fear that often accompanies change. The physical mobility of these men and women seems even more remarkable when we remember that in their era, the majority of people grew up, married, and were buried in the villages where they had been born.

Despite these similarities, there were also some obvious differences. Whether in the language their forebears had spoken or in the choices they made to change their lives, they both left behind, through the generations, sufficient small and large clues for us to see their distinct personalities.

The Lösch clan had deep roots in Austria. In the eighteenth and nineteenth centuries, many with that name could be found in Vienna and in the provinces.

Among them was Mathias Lösch, who arrived in Galicia in 1809 with his young son, Christian. Like many of his compatriots, he perhaps had planned to stay for just a few years in this remote land, although many German-speaking administrators ultimately settled in Galicia and made the best of it. Mathias was already 49, a widower whose late wife, Anna Sedlaczek, had likely been from somewhere in Moravia. In multiethnic Austria, a marriage between an Austrian man and a Moravian woman was not considered unusual. Not much else is known about Mathias, other than that he had spent the prior 27 years in the Austrian army. Now his destination was the salt mines of Wieliczka, near the city of Cracow.[1]

These were not ordinary times. Europe was engulfed in the Napoleonic upheavals, its map constantly being redrawn. To the north of Austrian Galicia, with the conflict looming on the horizon, the French had established the quasi-free Duchy of Warsaw. Poles were promised full independence, but for the moment, the mission of the satellite duchy—arranged by Napoleon in a dynastic union with the king of Saxony—was to provide troops and supplies to the French army.

During the year of Mathias's arrival in Galicia, the inevitable happened: War broke out between Austria and the duchy. At first, the Habsburg army advanced to the north and briefly occupied the Polish capital; but then the fortunes of war were reversed. By the fall of 1809, the duchy's forces, with the help of Saxon and French troops, had gained the upper hand. They pushed south and entered the city of Cracow, wresting control from the Austrians. Soon the hostilities were over, and Austrian and French diplomats were busily working in Vienna to resolve territorial disputes. Austria seemed to have no choice but to agree to the many concessions demanded by the victorious French.

Among the contentious issues of the peace negotiations was the fate of Wieliczka. With Napoleon in attendance, the French insisted on unconditional transfer of the salt mines to the duchy. When Austria lodged one strong protest after another, Napoleon finally relented, and a face-saving solution was found.

The parties negotiated a new border passing through Wieliczka, which now found itself between Saxon (in reality, French) and Austrian spheres of influence. Both sides were allowed to keep a small contingent of troops in Wieliczka, but at least in theory, the affairs of the town's citizens were subject to local laws rather than to the national laws of the recently warring states. Most importantly, the mines were to be governed jointly by Polish-Saxon and Austrian administrators, with profits split evenly between the two countries. In a conciliatory gesture to Vienna, the French allowed the Austrians to ship their share of salt free of custom dues through the neighboring territory of the duchy.

Without that long-forgotten clause of the Schönbrunn Treaty, our story could have ended there; the Lösch family would have settled somewhere else in Austria. Instead, Mathias Lösch remained in Wieliczka to become an inspector (*visitationsbeamter*) of the aboveground facilities where the precious salt was stored.[2]

Christian Lösch, Mathias's son, had little time to enjoy his youth. At the age of 14, he started working—first as a helper and then as an associate clerk in the mines' accounting offices. It is one of the quirks of history that Christian's first day of employment came just a week before Polish troops entered Wieliczka on November 11, 1809, in accordance with the treaty signed by France and Austria a month before. A few days later, father and son watched with curiosity—and some wariness—the arrival of the commander-in-chief of the duchy forces. The general, basking in popularity after recent victories against Austria, was greeted with a deafening gun salute. His carriage, surrounded by an escort of cavalrymen, proceeded through town before coming to a full stop in front of the mines' entrance. The administrators, inspectors, and clerks (Mathias Lösch among them) who had been ordered to greet the visitor were already waiting. General Joseph Poniatowski, a future marshal of Napoleon's empire, nodded in their direction and moved quickly to review his troops. Clearly, this was a show of force designed to overawe the Austrians remaining in Wieliczka. After descending

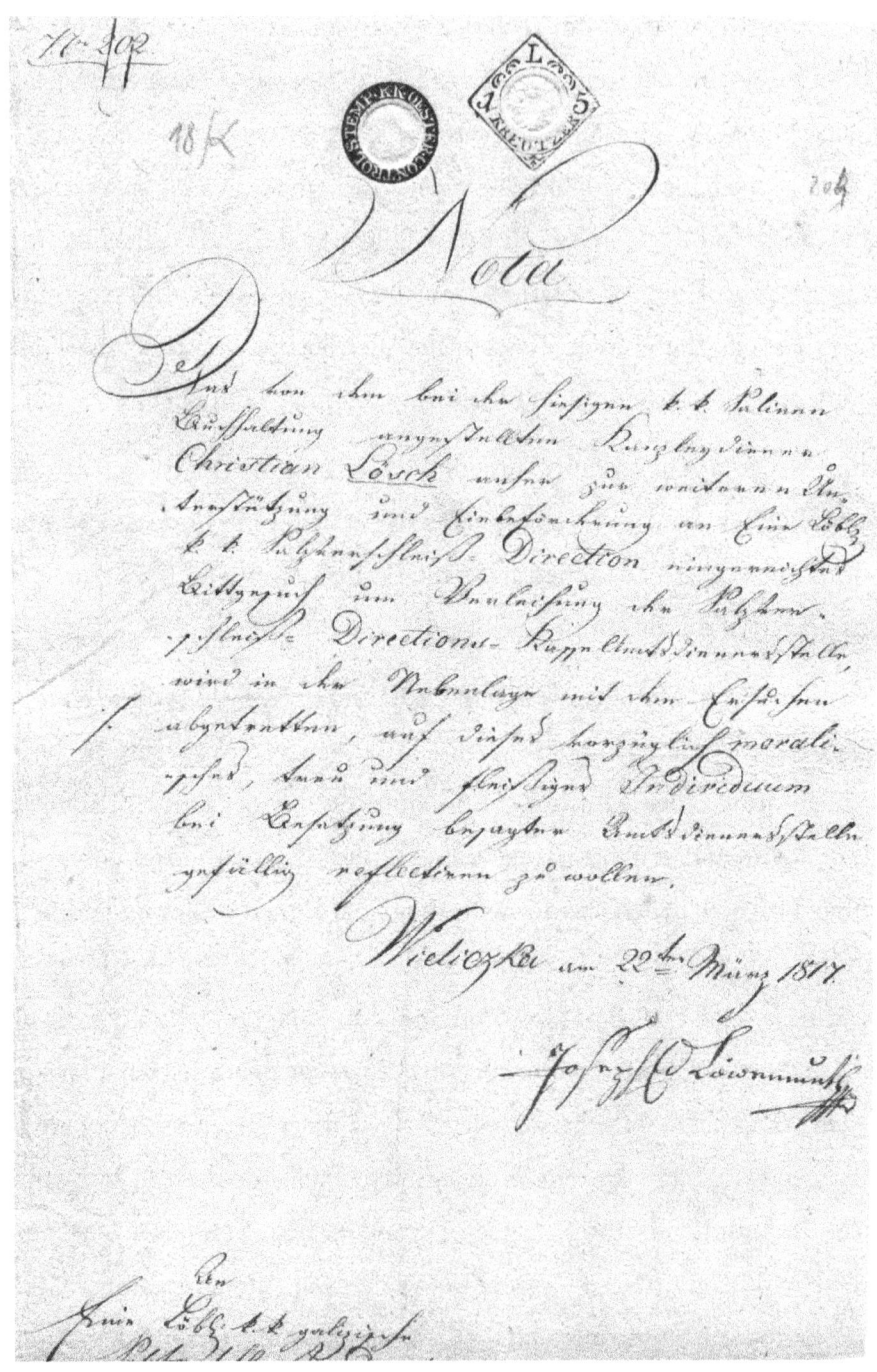

In 1817, Joseph Leo Edler von Löwenmuth wrote this letter on behalf of Christian Lösch to the Imperial and Royal Office of the Director of Salt Distribution. Löwenmuth was the head accountant associated with Wieliczka's mines since at least 1799. His letter ends with the following: "...please give favorable consideration to this particularly moral, loyal, and hardworking individual in filling the aforementioned position of [accounting] clerk."

through the shaft, the general toured the underground area, illuminated on the occasion by countless torches, while the sound of marching music reverberated through the mines' chambers and tunnels. Within a few years, Napoleon's defeat in Russia meant the end of joint administration of the mines; that was quickly followed by the dissolution of the short-lived Duchy of Warsaw. The mines, now officially known as *k.k. Galizische Salzverschleiss* (Imperial Royal Galician Salt Mines), and Galicia would remain firmly in the Austrian Empire until another war redrew Europe's boundaries. For both father and son, this meant that Wieliczka would continue to be home.[3]

The annual yearbooks of administrative bodies in the Kingdom of Galicia and Lodomeria are invaluable sources of information about the Lösches' careers. The Austrians maintained very precise records of their civil administration, allowing us to track thousands of individuals. These and other sources show that in 1814, the 19-year-old Christian Lösch was made an accountant with an annual salary of 200 guldens and full employment benefits. Working for almost nothing for his first few years at the mines had finally paid off for the young man.[4]

With his position now appearing secure, it was time for Christian to start his own family. He had chosen as his bride Antonina Pinkas, and they married in 1819. Their families knew each other well; the Lösch and Pinkas fathers shared a first name, and had worked together in the same department of the mines. Theirs was a close-knit community that intermarried and often shared important family celebrations. In 1820, Andreas Lösch, my great-great-grandfather, was born. But later, he would not have much memory of his mother; when he was only three, Antonina died of what was diagnosed as typhus. His father remarried the following year. Small Andreas was likely well-cared-for by his stepmother, Marianna, and in time he was joined by a number of half-brothers and half-sisters.[5]

The place where Christian Lösch worked and his son, Andreas, grew up was an unusual one. Salt had been mined for centuries in Wieliczka; in those days, it was an expensive commodity. It was used to preserve food in a time when modern forms of refrigeration did not exist. The word *salt* also gave rise to a few common words, such as *salary* (money paid to Roman soldiers to buy salt). With high demand for what was often called "white gold," it should not surprise us that from the first years of Austrian sovereignty over Galicia, the mines had been a profitable business for the crown. Under the agreement signed by the three powers after the First Partition of Poland in 1772, the mines were to provide specified amounts of salt not only to Austria, but also to Russia and Prussia. Indeed, this was a large enterprise; by the nineteenth century, the mines employed about 1,500 workmen. Wieliczka maintained a monopoly on sales of salt in Galicia; trade in the valuable mineral from smaller, private deposits was forbidden, under the threat of severe penalties.[6]

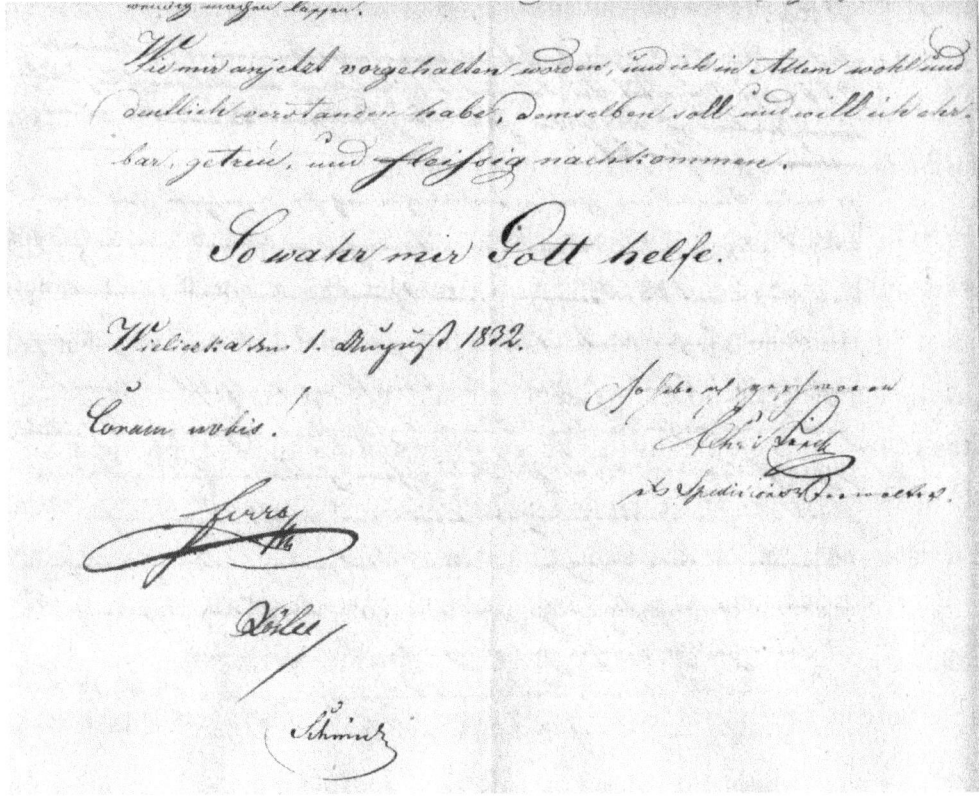

Christian Lösch cosigned (right side) this document in 1832. In sworn statements, inspectors recommended the return to Christian Lösch of 600 florins that he had placed as a cash deposit at the beginning of his responsibilities in the storage and transportation center in Turowka, near Wieliczka.

Bayard Taylor, an early globetrotter from faraway Pennsylvania, wrote about the Wieliczka operation around 1850. He described the solid salt rock and carved-out caves beneath the surface. The American was struck by one underground hall in particular: More than 100 feet high, it resembled an ancient Greek theater, with blocks of rock removed as if preparing for spectators. Salt taken from this section alone, he wrote, was sufficient to meet the demands of all 40 million inhabitants of Austria for a period of one year. Importantly for our story, the visitor also mentioned "large storehouses for the salt, the government offices, and the residencies of the superintendants," providing an eyewitness account, albeit cursory, of where Christian Lösch worked and lived.[7]

Christian's career may have been one of the longest in the history of the mines; over the years, he steadily progressed through the ranks. After working in the accounting department where, along with other junior clerks, he recorded how much salt was brought to the surface, he was put in charge of warehouses located near several mine shafts. Joseph, Janina, and Buzenin were the names of shafts where Christian would work throughout his long career. Because of the value of the salt, those in his position of responsibility were required to pay sizable security deposits, sometimes equivalent to a few years' salary. That should have insured honesty; but not surprisingly, frequent inspections were also the norm. Sworn testimonies of several inspectors have survived, showing support of petitions by Christian Lösch, who was asking for the return of a large cash deposit he had made—apparently because sufficient time had passed to ensure his employer's trust.[8]

Christian's final career stop was in *"Salzverschleis- und Transports- Amt Turowka bei Wieliczka,"* the mines' department of transportation. When in 1850 he was put in charge of these operations, he would have had no way of knowing that he would witness remarkable changes in this position over the next 15 years. This was a critical position in the mines, one that made the enterprise effective and ultimately profitable. There were ever-present concerns, not only about safety but also over the logistics of moving the "white gold" to various places throughout the Austrian Empire and beyond. At the beginning, without railways or other forms of mechanized transportation, the task of protecting the salt from the elements, and hauling approximately 50,000 tons of it per year on horse-drawn wagons, was not a minor undertaking. Believe it or not, despite all such limitations, annual revenues from the mines were then estimated at the astronomical sum of $1,000,000 by Taylor, the inquisitive American. This would equal an impressive $433,000,000 in today's money.[9]

In 1857, the first railroad tracks reached Wieliczka, but not the town itself—only a large warehouse that was under Christian's supervision in neighboring Turowka. Clearly, the purpose of bringing the railroad in was not the traveling needs of the town's citizens but the shipment of "white gold" stockpiled in large warehouses. Three years later, a short stretch of this so-called "saline railway" was extended further, to the entrances of the mine shafts, finally sealing this

The administrative building of the salt mines in Turowka. After being erected in 1811, it housed Christian Lösch's office until 1866. *(Postcard from 1912.)*

transportation link. It was definite progress, although the last part of that railroad was very different from what might be expected today; loaded heavily, train cars were pulled on the tracks by horses to their destination in Turowka. From there, they were transported by coal-fueled steam locomotives; modern times had come to Wieliczka! We can be sure that Christian Lösch knew he was part of history in the making, as he supervised the first transports moving in this radically different fashion.[10]

By that time, Christian Lösch had every reason to feel satisfied with his career; his position in life was a far cry from that of the inexperienced entry clerk who had started on this journey. He was certainly able to provide a comfortable living for his large family. His annual salary of 785 florins was, not surprisingly, lower than that of the head of the salt mines, but the difference was not overwhelming. The Lösch family could easily afford to live in a nice home in the center of town; in those days, the rent of a family house with a small garden (to grow vegetables on the preferred sunny side) would have cost Christian only 150 florins a year. A comfortable amount would have been left for food—cheaper in Wieliczka than in the neighboring city of Cracow—and clothing and education for the children.[11]

With the arrival of 1866, Christian finally retired from the post in *"Salzverschleis- und Transports- Amt Turowka bei Wieliczka."* When the time to leave the mines came, he could have wistfully glanced at the roster of employees; without any trouble, he would have spotted men with familiar names. But they were already the next generation of relatives of his friends, who were long retired. After a remarkable 57 years on the job, Christian Lösch was truly the last of the old guard who had started at the bottom of the ladder during the uncertain times of the Napoleonic Wars. Undoubtedly, this hardworking man was ready for a well-deserved rest.[12]

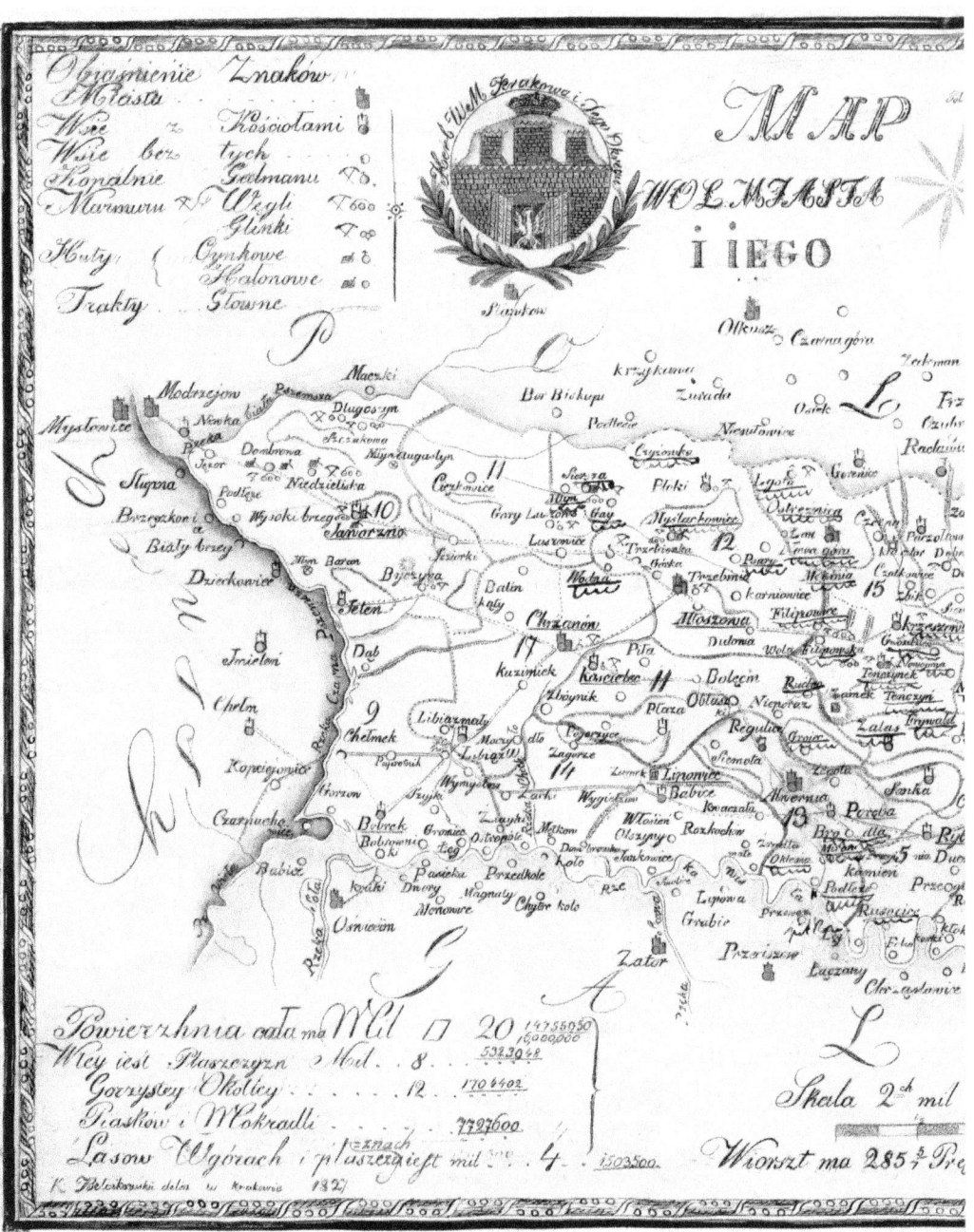

The Free City of Cracow and Its Territory was established in 1815 and annexed to Austria in 1846. Wieliczka,

Chapter 2 — The Lösch and Regiec Families: Taking Chances

marked on the map, was situated just outside the borders of this semi-autonomous city-state. *(Map from 1827.)*

Given the life he was to lead, we can surmise that Andreas Lösch, the oldest of Christian's children, received more formal education than had his father. Certainly, the son did not learn his future craft on the job at the age of 14 as his father had. Raising children in Wieliczka had some advantages; the town had well-established schools that served the families of the mines' employees. For the new generation of Lösches, times were changing in many other ways as well. Soon, it became clear that Andreas would choose to not seek a career in the mines. What persuaded him against following in the footsteps of the well-connected Christian Lösch and both his grandparents is a puzzle. Others would certainly have envied such an opportunity and the prospect of a stable career ahead.

In any case, Christian's stepmother, Marianna Lösch, and her family could have had something to do with this important decision. One of Marianna's young relatives, Adam Kwiatkowski, a possible childhood companion of Andreas's, had recently chosen a career in the civil service of the Kingdom of Galicia and Lodomeria. Shortly thereafter, Andreas Lösch, already in his early twenties, would follow the same path. Was it just a coincidence, or part of the family plan that this young man was first hired for an entry-clerk position (*beedete kanzelipracticanten*) in district offices in the city of Tarnow, joining the relative of his stepmother there? Soon, there would be even more signs that the two young men were indeed close; Adam would later be the witness at Andreas's wedding.[13]

Like his father, Andreas would steadily advance in his career, but with a very important difference. Unlike Christian Lösch, who had remained in the town of Wieliczka through his entire adult life, the son would pursue opportunities in several places in Galicia. After a few years in Tarnow, the time for his first promotion came, and a new position took him to the nearby town of Jaslo. Although this time he relocated only 35 miles away, moving from one administrative post to another would become a distinct pattern in Andreas's early life.[14]

In February of 1846, events in the region intruded on what might otherwise have been a minor step in Andreas's career. Initially, news of an ill-prepared uprising of Polish nobility against Austrian rule was just a worrisome sign of transient instability. The center of lofty speeches and antigovernment agitation was Cracow, which was officially known as "The Free, Independent, and Strictly Neutral City of Cracow and Its Territory." Since Napoleon's defeat, it had enjoyed this unusual status, although it was carefully watched by the three powers (Austria, Russia, and Prussia). As often happens, however, unrest in the city set the entire region on a volatile course.

In nearby Wieliczka, where Christian Lösch had recently remarried, the gentry fired from windows at entering Austrian troops. In no time, house-to-house searches began, and any rebel found was shot on the spot. With small children at home, Christian must have found this time unsettling.[15] The antigovernment insurgency was quickly put down by Austrian light cavalry advancing on Cracow; but in other places, the situation remained tense for longer. Some of the most ferocious battles took place not far from Andreas Lösch's new home in Jaslo. Though the town remained safe due to its large military garrison, it quickly swelled with rumors and with those who were stranded.

Soon the peasants of Galicia rose up, but in a strange paradox, the villagers directed their wrath at those engaged in dreams of national independence. Not unsurprisingly, the serfs had no loyalty to their masters; they must have had in mind the nobles' demands for free labor and their belief in almost absolute control over those living on their estates. Early reports alleged that a district official (*kreishauptmann*) from Tarnow, Joseph Breinl R. von Wallerstern, had encouraged peasants from surrounding villages to attack the insurgents (mainly the local gentry) and ransack their property to prevent the spread of the antigovernment uprising. Coincidentally, von Wallerstern had been Andreas's superior barely a year before.[16]

Galician Slaughter. Rebel peasants are shown bringing the heads of
murdered nobles in exchange for payments dispensed by Austrian troops.
(Painting by Jan Lewicki, 1795–1871.)

In the next couple of months, the rage of the villagers led to the massacre of more than 1,000 noblemen and the destruction of about 500 manor houses by roaming bands of serfs. Horror stories were told of government payments in salt or money in exchange for the heads of rural gentry.[17] The entire Lösch family witnessed this unrest, later known as the Galician Slaughter. Andreas would have seen the reports of violence in the area and may have witnessed defeated rebels brought to town for imprisonment in a former military hospital. In fact, these nobles were probably safer in prison than in the countryside, being hunted with ferocity by local peons.[18]

The Austrian government, which cleverly exercised the principle of *divide et impera* (divide and rule), sent an unmistakable message to the conservative Polish gentry: *Your goals were clearly not supported by a large segment of your own populace.* The feudal rights of the masters of manorial estates, already replaced by modern laws in other parts of Europe, were an anachronism. To bewildered nobles who had thought themselves to be a voice of the nation, Vienna was being viewed as a protector rather than an oppressor by Galician serfs. But when it became evident that the peasant revolt was out of control and bloodshed was continuing unabated, Austrian troops easily restored order.

Future paintings and even staged performances would often depict the brutality of the 1846 upheaval. In its aftermath, Cracow lost its semi-independent status; it was fully absorbed by the Austrian monarchy into the province of Galicia. Only two years later, Count Franz Stadion, then governor of Galicia, finally prevailed over the objections of the landowning nobility and abolished all remaining vestiges of the feudal system.

Despite the turmoil, life in Galicia went on. Perhaps reflecting the return of calm, 26-year-old Andreas Lösch married Eleonora Barbara Wilczek on October 4, 1846. The couple had grown up only 41 miles from each other, but how they met remains a bit of mystery. We can only guess that the two families knew each other through a mutual friend or through the professional activities of the bride's and groom's fathers. As young people at that time, women in particular, generally had limited spheres of contact, the options for how these two met each other would have been few, mainly confined to acquaintances between their parents.[19] At the wedding ceremony in the bride's hometown, a young man who had traveled all the way from Tarnow stood next to the young couple. He was Adam Kwiatkowski, the same civil servant whom Andreas had followed into the profession a few years before. It is not surprising that he was bestowed with the honor of witnessing this marriage, as the links between the two men possibly extended back to their childhood in Wieliczka.

The bride's family, the Wilczeks (literally "young wolf"), traced their roots back to the fourteenth century in neighboring Silesia. From there, their forebears had spread to Moravia, Bohemia, Poland, and even Hungary. Some became counts (*graf*) and statesmen serving the Austrian crown, while others became successful in less prominent roles.[20]

Land purchase document by the "famous Franciscus Wilczek, townsman of Andrychow." The cover page indicates the official nature of the document; the second page describes the boundaries of the property and its price (in old gold coins); and the third page (not shown) provides signatures of local officials, dated 1793 and 1795, certifying to the legality of the transaction.

Eleonora's paternal grandfather, who was from Moravia, had settled in Andrychow at the end of the eighteenth century. Franciscus Wilczek Sr. did not have fancy titles, but he was a wealthy man who came to own 17 houses in town. How he made his fortune is not known, but a clue could come from the fact that Andrychow in the time of Franciscus Sr. was a well-known weaving center, producing, amongst other textiles, decorative tablecloths sought in many countries of the region. He was a trusted member of the community, referred to with respect by his contemporaries in documents that have survived. In time, Franciscus Sr. became mayor of Andrychow and a local philanthropist. The Foundation of Franciscus Wilczek Sr. would operate off and on for years after his passing.[21]

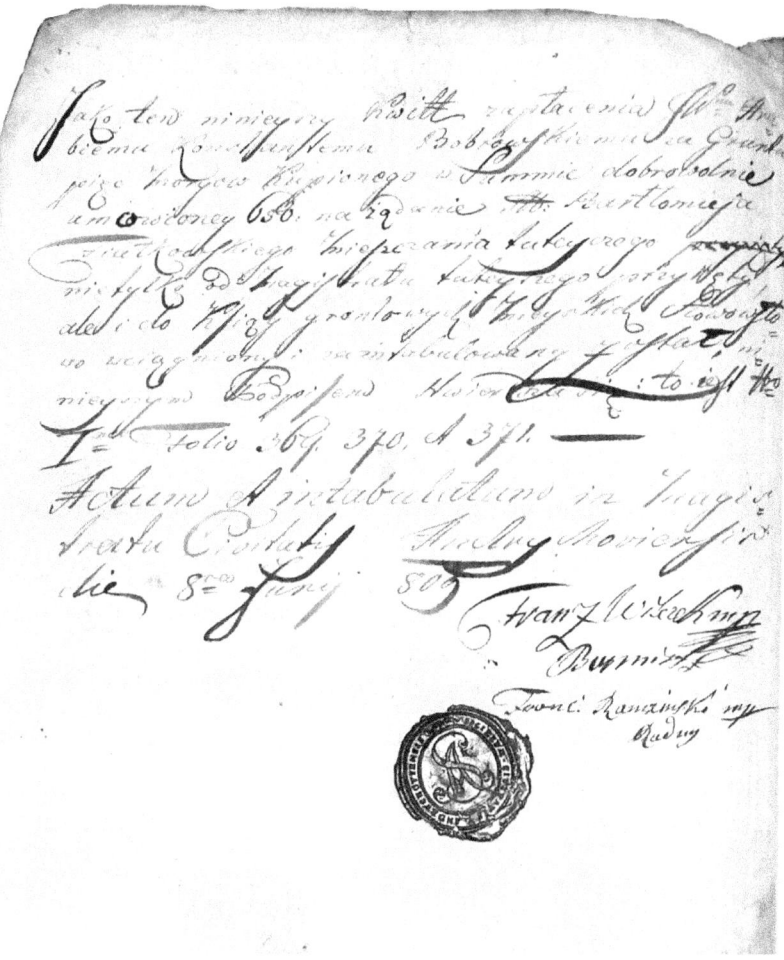

Franz (Franciscus) Wilczek Sr., the mayor of Andrychow, signed this official contract between two citizens concerning the purchase of land in 1809. "*Sigillium Civitatis Andrychoviensis*" on the seal means "Seal of the Town of Andrychow."

Eleonora Wilczek most likely had few memories of her accomplished grandfather, who died when she was a young girl. But growing up, she would have observed many other Wilczek men who had an early preference toward professional careers. Her father, at first a local magistrate assessor, later became a merchant. But his career did not stop there; he eventually returned to public life and was elected mayor of his hometown, the second mayor in the Wilczek family. Eleonora's uncle, Franciscus Jr., also led a fairly visible life as a teacher in the local school and as a notary. Other members of the family sought careers farther away from home. Eleonora's younger cousin, Romualdus Wilczek, only 16 years old at the time of the wedding, would travel to schools in Austrian Silesia and then to Vienna to study medicine. He became a military surgeon. It is safe to assume that being surrounded by a family of professional men prepared Eleonora quite well for her life with Andreas.[22]

The marriage of Andreas and Eleonora also spoke volumes about the fact that the Lösches had no intention of returning to Austria proper; without any doubt, Galicia had become the family's intergenerational home. There were, however, clear signs that Andreas was loosening his ties with the town of the salt mines. Whether it was his search for professional opportunities away from Wieliczka or finding a wife outside the mining community, Andreas's actions exuded the confidence that he could manage his life in a very different way than had his father.

The new family started to grow with a baby girl, Bronislawa, born in 1848. The Lösches were surrounded by a group of friends who would be in their lives over the next 40 years. First Joseph, then Franz and Hieronymus Winkler worked with Andreas. The Lösches also crossed paths with the Jahls and the Telesnickis, who would become part of an extended family.[23]

During these formative years, Andreas made a clear decision about his future career. In contrast to many other young *kreiskanzlisten* (district clerks) who often disappeared from the rosters after a few years of service, Andreas was slowly moving up in the department. Occasional assignments in municipalities outside Jaslo must have been meant to prepare him for more senior positions. In a pattern that would repeat itself in the next generation, there were periods of absence from home that must have been viewed by the Lösches as a necessary compromise for those who aimed higher in life. By the standards of the day, Eleonora, too, was surprisingly mobile. She spent extended periods of time in her hometown, where their second daughter, Wilhelmina, was born in 1852.[24]

By late 1855, Andreas had been transferred to the neighboring town of Biecz. As if being tested in his new role as the county commissioner, he was to oversee civil affairs in more than 30 villages in the surrounding area.[25] Although the town's glory had dimmed over years of decline, Biecz was still considered the pearl of the Carpathians. It sat on a picturesque mountain pass on the road toward the Hungarian border (today's Slovakia), which was just 22 miles away. The remains of medieval buildings along steep streets, and an old City Hall with a slim bell tower dating back to the sixteenth century, became Andreas's neighborhood and workplace. This time, Eleonora accompanied him, and the year's end brought another important event in the family's life. On December 1, 1855, Stephania Maria Lösch, who was to become my great-grandmother and a quiet participant in our story, was born in Biecz.

Biecz. The bell tower and the adjacent City Hall are where Andreas Lösch worked from 1855 to 1856. The town was the birthplace of his youngest daughter, Stephania Lösch. *(Photograph from 1900.)*

Within a year or two, another opportunity for Andreas came along when an administrative position opened in the town of Liszki. This was clearly a bigger change for the Lösches, on several levels. Looking at a map of Galicia, we can see that the family would now move a greater distance compared to the more or less local assignments that had carried Andreas to different towns so far. But there were some bright spots that compensated Andreas and Eleonora for the inconvenience of moving their belongings and three young girls, and finding a home in yet another community. They were moving from a small, rural town to the almost-suburbs of the culturally and historically rich city of Cracow. That town, with its famous royal castle, its old university, and its literary world, was perceived as somewhat snobbish compared with Lvov, the capital of Galicia. But being raised in its proximity was a definite plus for their three daughters, and must have brought back to Andreas many childhood memories of growing up not far from there. Was it coincidence or, more likely, choice that their new address in Liszki placed the family quite close to (the by now retired) Christian Lösch and Ignatius Wilczek? For Eleonora, visiting relatives in Andrychow was an opportunity to share family news. We can safely assume that stories about Eleonora's younger cousin Romualdus Wilczek, a military physician, were not uncommon subjects of conversation. There might have been even brief encounters between now grown-up cousins; a few years back, when a cholera epidemic broke out in the region, Romualdus was deployed to Andrychow to deal with this medical emergency. The records of Dr. Wilczek's other visits to his hometown also survived. But those were only temporary stays; Romualdus was busy serving with different infantry units and in various military hospitals in towns of today's Austria, northern Italy, Germany, Romania, and Hungary.[26]

The lives of Eleonora and Andreas did not remain idle either. Within a few years, Andreas would be joined in the office by one of the Winkler brothers, with whom the Lösches had become good friends more than a decade before. But the professional journey of Andreas was far from over; after 10 years in Liszki, a new opportunity would open. In 1867, he became a commissioner and a member of the treasury commission in Chrzanow, a large district city further west of Cracow. The town had become strategically important with the opening of a new railway linking Cracow with Austrian Silesia to the west, and Vienna to the south.

Despite so many changes, life was not yet to be settled for the Lösch family. By 1875, they had moved once again, this time to the town of Nowy Sacz. Andreas and Eleonora now found themselves in a somewhat familiar place, not far from

Chapter 2 — The Lösch and Regiec Families: Taking Chances

Nowy Sacz. District office where Andreas Lösch worked from 1875 to 1888.
(Postcard from the end of the nineteenth century.)

where they had started their lifelong journey together. Friends from the Winkler and Telesnicki families lived there as well, and the Lösches would maintain close relationships with them and their children for years to come. For the next 12 years, Andreas served as a commissioner in this large district. This was likely his highest professional assignment; the position required oversight of more than 200 villages and three regional courts.[27] For Andreas and Eleonora, there would be no more relocation from one town to another; Nowy Sacz was to be their home for the rest of their lives. This was also the place where the lives of the Lösch and Regiec families would intertwine, making our narrative possible.

THE REGIEC FAMILY HAD quite a different story to tell. Their name suggests deeper roots in Galicia than those of the Lösches; it was not, however, a typically Polish name. The Regiecs were concentrated mainly in the mountainous region of western Galicia, or just on the other side of the highest peaks of the Carpathians—in what was then Hungarian territory and today forms northern

Map of Galicia. The life journey of Eleonora Wilczek Lösch (born in Andrychow) and Andreas Lösch (born in Wieliczka).

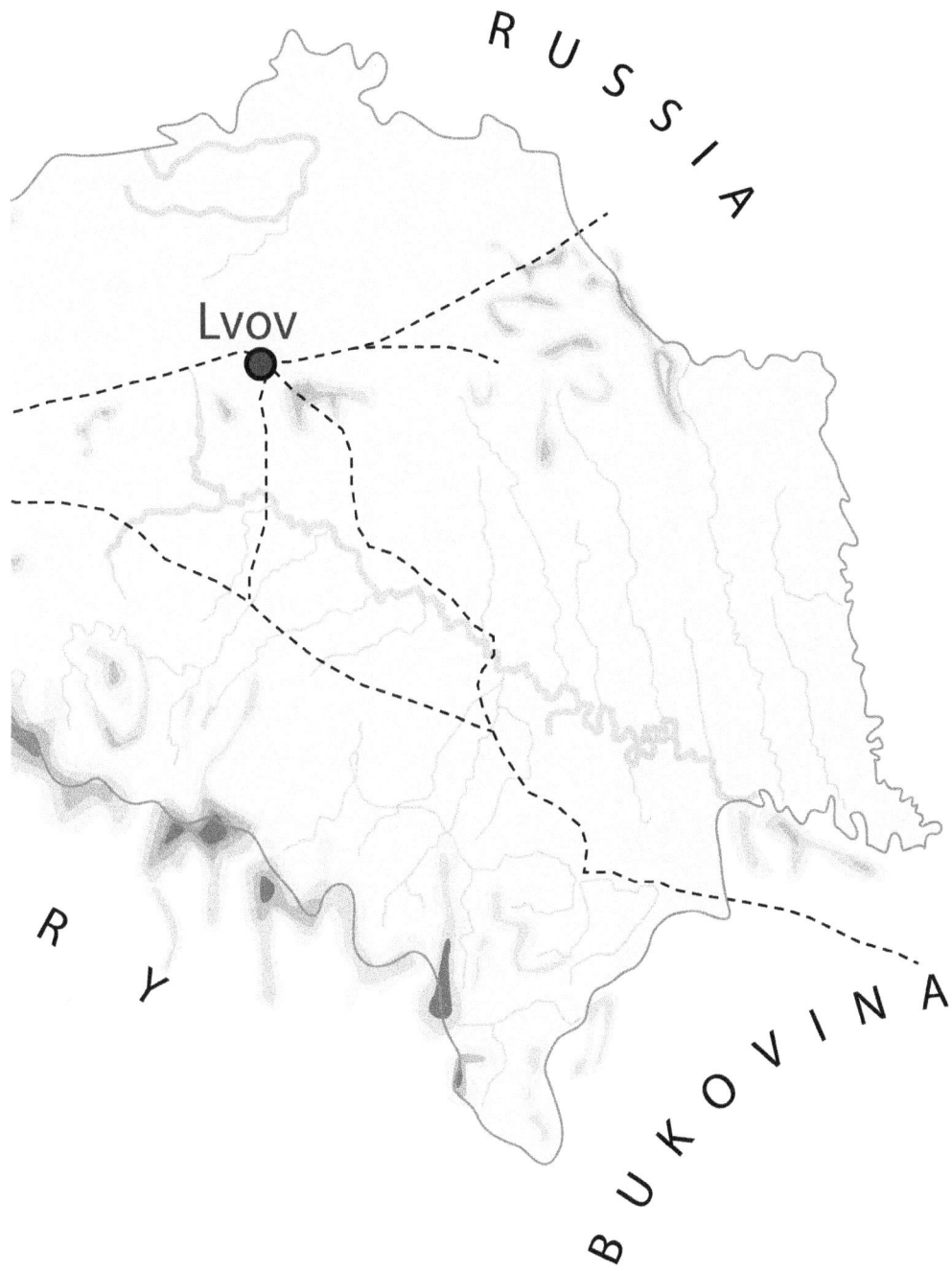

The marriage book from Olszyny parish. Its content included records from the villages of Gierowa and Roztoka, with entries regarding the Regiec family. The cover is from 1717.

Slovakia. The name was often recorded as Regiec or Regec; it bore a resemblance to the Hungarian name "Regetz" that was common further south. Clearly this was more than a phonetic similarity, as one could find some Regiecs living in Galicia who had actually been born in Hungary.[28] A family legend, which is impossible to verify today, claims that some Asian blood was a part of the Regiec heritage. Could it be that this story was linked to the Mongol invasions that swept through Hungary, Moravia, and Poland in the thirteenth century? Or to the Tatars, Asiatic tribes migrating west, who centuries later settled peacefully in areas where Regiecs could have lived? We will never know.[29]

Our acquaintance with the Regiec family starts with Joseph and his wife, Lucia. They were both born toward the end of the eighteenth century, somewhere in the western part of the Kingdom of Galicia and Lodomeria. We first meet them in the small village of Gierowa on the occasion of their wedding in 1817.[30] The 24-year-old Lucia was already a widow, not an uncommon status in those times. The marriage entry in the church record is minimal, with none of the customary references to the parents' names or the couple's birthplaces. We are left to wonder whether this was simply sloppy work on the part of the parish priest or, in his view, the two commoners did not merit additional description.

It is clear that Joseph was a newcomer to that place; village records reveal no one else with the same family name until the births of his own children. There is less doubt about where Lucia was from: Her maiden name was common among country folks in the area. Both husband and wife were simple people. Joseph's profession is later described in the church records as *pastor ovium.* Probably he was a shepherd, although that Latin name could also refer to a sheep farmer. Apparently, caring for sheep was a family craft; Joseph's cousin, who settled around that time in a neighboring village on the other side of the river, is also described as a *pastor ovium*. In the course of Joseph's lifetime, the original family name of Regetz (sometimes recorded as Regietz) would slowly evolve to Regiec, which would be used by all his children and the generations to follow.

Typical village where time stood still. *(Maynard Owen Williams/National Geographic Stock.)*

Michaël Regiec, the oldest son of Joseph and Lucia, was born in 1818. Over the years, he would be joined by younger siblings Petrus, Marianna, Adalbertus, Joannes, Catharina, and Josephus Jr. Michaël's parents raised their children in the tiny rural settlement of Gierowa, between the towns of Tarnow and Nowy Sacz, places that we have already passed on our journey. This nondescript place sat on hilly terrain bordered by the River Dunajec to the west, forests to the south and north, and a natural clearing in the woods to the east. The village, which no longer exists, was a loose spread of 20-odd houses, with fir-forest-covered mountains clearly visible on the horizon. Events in the fall of 1827 underscored the fragility of life there when Michaël's brothers Petrus and Joannes died a mere two weeks apart. The apparent cause was diphtheria, a highly contagious and then-deadly illness that is prevented today through widespread vaccination.

Michaël's childhood was predictably simple; he grew up surrounded by free but dirt-poor peasants and by the serfs living in the village. Sometime during his teenage years or even earlier, he would start working on a large estate that was situated not far from his birthplace, just across the river in the village of Roztoka. As a young man, Michaël was once asked to be the godfather of a child born to local serfs working with him on the estate. As if pointing to the family's place at the bottom of the social ladder, at the baptism, the mother was only able to give the church scribe her first name. Tellingly, she did not know her maiden name; in its place was entered *ignota nominae* (ignorant of the name), leaving us wondering at how different life was then, compared to today. Michaël, who as a free man was standing a notch or two higher in the world of Roztoka, had his full name recorded in the parish books along with that of the child's godmother, the wife of a gardener—without any hint of family affluence.[31]

Today we can only wonder how it was possible that Michaël, but not his brothers or sisters, received some education as he grew up in the village. Not only was there no school in Roztoka, it is also difficult to imagine that his parents had sufficient means to send a young boy to a school somewhere else. But despite his humble beginnings, something in Michaël's early years set him on a trajectory that would clearly define a very different future from that of his parents and even his siblings. Surviving documents bear Michaël's handwriting, rather than the simple cross used as a signature by many of his contemporaries. The ability to write was a rarity at this time, particularly in rural areas, with many—including members of Michaël's family—unable to correctly record their own names.[32]

Like the Lösches, Michaël and his family witnessed the Galician Slaughter. The danger was real and close to home. In a neighboring village, the manor house was ransacked and its proprietor hacked to death by a scythe-wielding group of roaming peasants. The poor man's wife and children were spared, and after braving snow-covered roads on foot, they reached the safety of the nearest town.[33] As far as we can determine today, the Roztoka estate was not overrun by those seeking vengeance in that volatile winter. Was that just luck, or with Michaël's help, had marauding troublemakers been chased away? These questions will have to remain unanswered.

Shortly after these traumatic events, Michaël's father, Joseph Regetz, who still used the old spelling of the family name, would pass away of natural causes. Notwithstanding this personal loss, Michaël Regiec would suddenly be elevated to an important position in his small community, once again illustrating the continuity of life despite its typical ups and downs. What exactly happened is difficult to reconstruct today. Perhaps the old, aristocratic Jordan family, which owned huge swaths of land on the left side of the River Dunajec, was struggling to keep its large holdings profitable. The death of Franciscus Jordan a few years before at the Roztoka estate could be an explanation for why young Michaël Regiec was needed to run the family's enterprise in the village. Other portions of this large landholding were slowly being sold to others.

Roztoka and the surrounding villages [Sukmanie, Milowka, Wielka (Wlk) Wies] all situated on the left side of the River Dunajec. The town of Zakliczyn is seen to the south. *(Section of a map from 1937.)*

Regardless of the circumstances, we can only wonder what skills and what strength of personality propelled the 30-year-old Michaël, who until now had been merely one of many commoners, to become the de facto master of the Roztoka estate in a sort of lease arrangement with the Jordan family. Clearly, this was a major advancement, which must have been achieved more on his own merits than through any hereditary passage of privilege.

The changes in Michaël's life continued. A few years later, on three consecutive Sundays in January of 1850, announcements were read in a local church about his planned marriage. On February 7, Michaël Regiec and Thecla de Bogusz Traczewska were wed in the nearby town of Zakliczyn. The blackened and torn pages of the church record identify Thecla's father as a local property owner; that would have further solidified Michaël's growing affluence. The bride (also known as Magdalena) was ten years younger than her new husband.[34] While growing up, she would have had no difficulty meeting Michaël, as they were living in neighboring villages, but it is unlikely that anyone could have predicted their future marriage.

The Traczewski family traced their roots to a line of minor nobles who used, on rare occasions, the historical cognomen "Bohusz" (or "Bogusz") together with the family name. In more distant times, the family had been recognized by a coat of arms known as Abdank, which was considered one of the oldest in the region. Legend dated its origin to a mythical period when a brave forebear of the Traczewski family had fought with a strange, dragon-like beast to defend a famous castle.[35]

One of the many mysteries of our story remains unsolved: how Michaël not only received some education in a tiny village but earned the personal credibility to lease the estate from the Jordans, and then marry the upper-class Thecla Traczewska, all in the span of a few years. Over the next couple of decades, Michaël would maintain social relationships with the Jordan family—not bad,

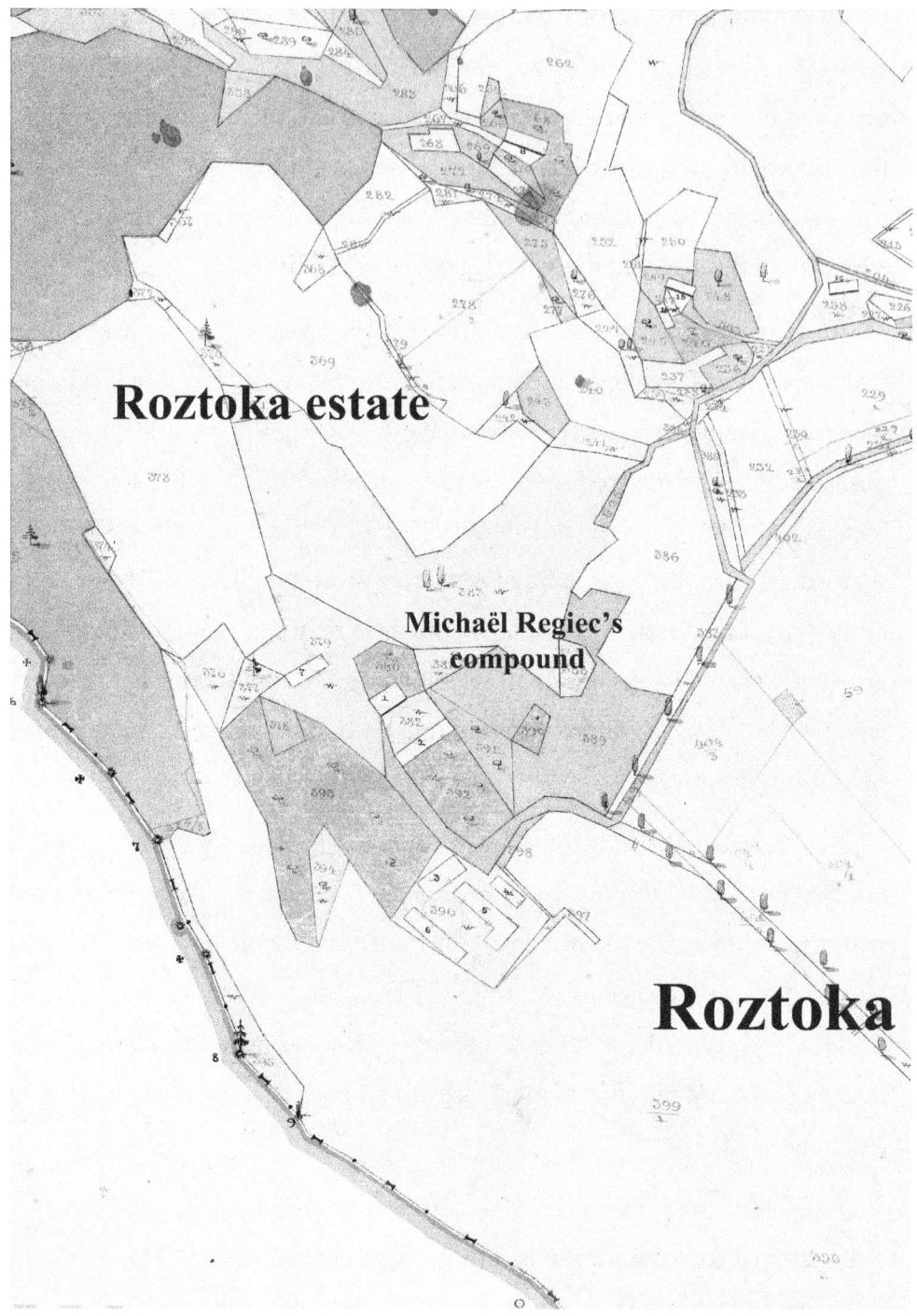

Roztoka. The manor house where Michaël Regiec and his family lived was assigned the number "1." Other buildings (2 through 7) included living quarters for field workers, barns, and stables.

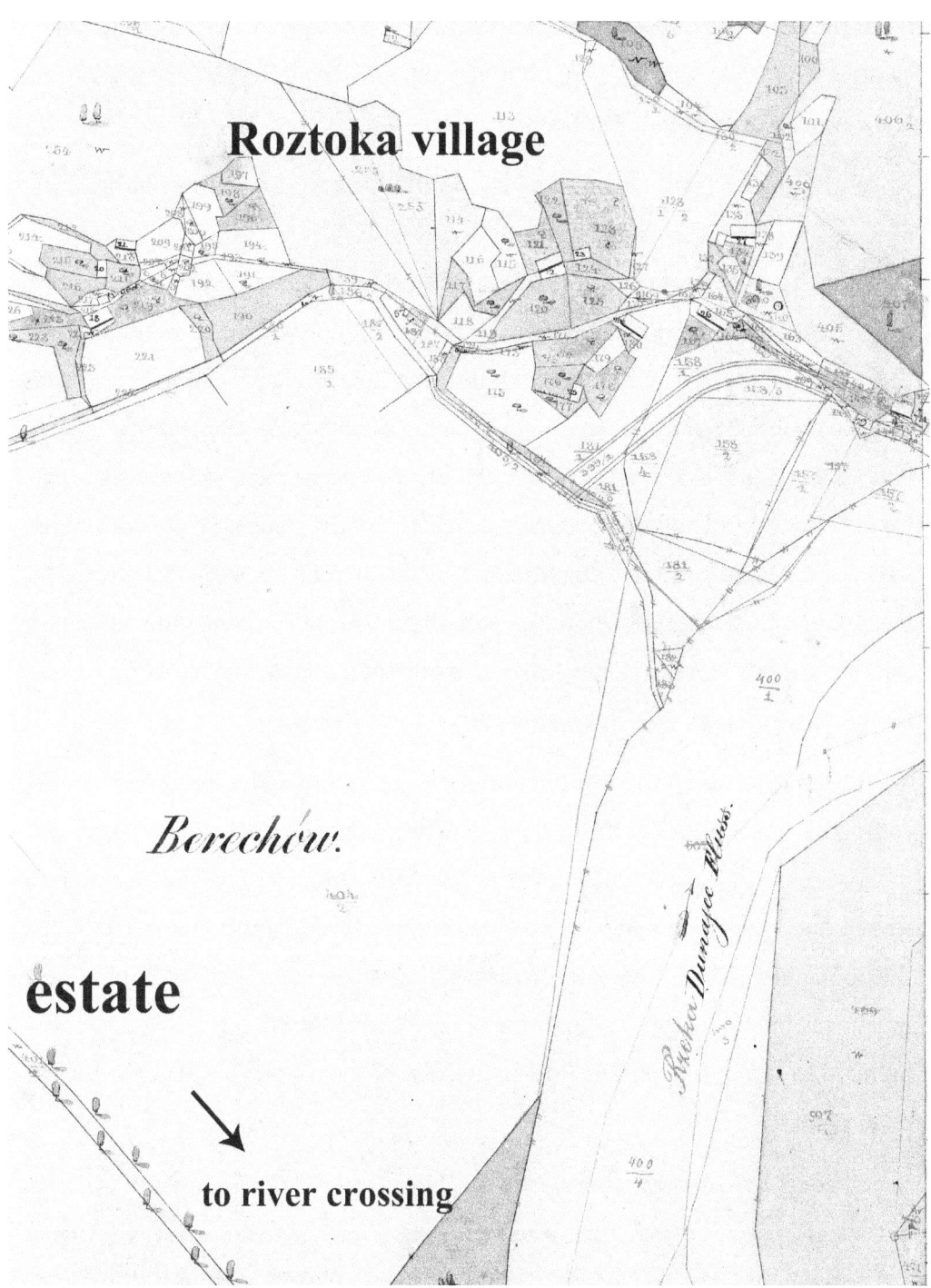

[Based on a cadastral (survey) map from 1848.]

given the structure of society in those days. Some could say that the times were changing; but there was likely more to the story. Michaël Regiec was a man who knew how to overcome many barriers in order to succeed.[36]

With Thecla's family approximately six miles away, the young wife was unlikely to have been considered a newcomer. Roztoka was a small place, with about 180 inhabitants living in 30-odd houses. The center of the village was the manor house, where Thecla joined her new husband. In the vicinity, several buildings that belonged to the estate could be found. The Roztoka landholding at this time covered about 531 acres (an area more than half the size of Manhattan's Central Park), with fields for crops, pastures, and even a few patches of forest that provided firewood and building materials. Just south of the village, the River Dunajec took a sharp turn, forming wetlands along the bend that were often overgrown by reeds. Close by was a spot where three small mills stood. When family members wanted to see the young couple, a river crossing there allowed for a short boat ride for those living in not-too-distant villages on the other side.

Roztoka was a microcosm of rural life in Galicia, filled with almost never-ending hard work but also with the reassuring cycles of births, marriages, and funerals. Glancing at records for the 30 years after Michaël and Thecla married, we see that Roztoka would welcome, on average, seven infants a year. However, the population would not grow too fast as, on average, six deaths were recorded every year, including those of many newborns and children. It is difficult to comprehend today, but not many Roztoka residents would survive beyond the age of 50 years.[37]

Of course, the large manor house was home not only to Thecla and Michaël but also to many of their relatives. Two young women, Thecla's sister Angela Traczewska and Michaël's sister Catharina Regiec, lived there until their own marriages years later.[38] There we also meet Michaël's brother Joseph (not to be confused with their father or with Michaël's son of the same name), who was staying on the estate. He left only when his own marriage to a young widow, Leopolina Granz, made him a small landowner in the neighboring village. Even Michaël's other brother, Adalbertus, and his wife, Apolonia, who remained small farmers, were frequent guests, visiting from the neighboring village of Gierowa, across the river.

Although a few family members living on the Roztoka estate helped Michaël to manage it, this was not enough given the tasks that seemed to stretch from the morning to nightfall. To cope with everything on his farmstead, Michaël employed several villagers; in particular, every pair of hands was needed during harvest time. However, only a few of these would have their own plots of land. The estate provided simple living quarters for those from outside Roztoka—servants, shepherds, and migrant farm workers—who tended the farm animals and surrounding fields. Some of them would marry and have children while employed by the Regiecs, listing the estate as their place of temporary residence.

In stark contrast to his parents, Michaël's family was clearly accorded a special status in his community. Their house was assigned the number "1," signifying its importance. And in accordance with the norms of the day, written records made a very clear distinction between the Regiec family and the others in the village. The names of the Regiecs were recorded with the formal Latin prefixes *Dominus* and *Domina* when referring to Michaël and Thecla, respectively. Michaël's name was followed by his title as the overseer (*possessori allodii*) of the estate, whereas Thecla's name was sometimes accompanied by a notation of her hereditary status (*nobilis*). With the exception of the late Franciscus Jordan, no one else had been addressed in such a formal way in the village.[39] Even Michaël's brothers were not accorded such deference. Despite rural isolation, there were clear social barriers that went beyond such formal titles. It was as if some imaginary curtain now separated Michaël from the rest of the community, for after he became overseer of the estate, his name rarely appeared among the best men or godfathers at family events celebrated among his farming neighbors. We can only wonder why Michaël's younger sister, Catharina Regiec, made an exception when she agreed once to become godmother to a gardener's baby. But Catharina was considered different in the family, as our story will reveal a bit later.

The entry marking the birth of Josephus Blasius Stanislaus Regiec, the son of Michaël and Thecla, born on February 4, 1858. The priest made a mistake in recording his names, with a visible correction: A small "1" is written, with a line pointing to the name "Josephus."

When my great-grandfather was born on February 4, 1858, the Regiecs' was already a busy household, with five daughters and one son milling around. Joseph will become an important part of our story; hence, what happened next could shed some light on his character and the choices he made during his life. The events that unfolded were traumatic to the entire family and without any doubt would have an impact on the boy's life from day one.

It was not uncommon at this time for a woman of 30 or so years, physically strained by five, six, or more pregnancies, to suffer complications from childbirth, which might easily be fatal. With Joseph's birth, Thecla developed severe bleeding and passed away the same day. Two days later, life took a turn that might have been strange and confusing, with the simultaneous celebration of a new life and mourning for one lost. The baby was baptized with the customary hope of a better life ahead, but also with a heavy dose of uncertainty. That same day, Thecla, only 31 years old, was buried.

We can be sure that Michaël's grief was mixed with a deep anxiety about the future of his small children. But life had to go on; a wet nurse was brought in to keep Joseph alive, other Regiec women arrived to help, and the older children took care of their younger siblings. However, these were only temporary measures for a man with an estate to run and a large household. Startling to us, though quite common by the norms of the day, 42-year-old Michaël Regiec remarried after a customary one-year mourning period. It is worth noting that his deceased wife's name was respectfully invoked during the three public announcements made before the wedding ceremony.

Michaël's second wife, Catharina Barbara Stoczynska, came from the neighboring village of Olszyny. In Joseph's childhood, we have another unsolved mystery: We do not know whether he was raised by his father and his stepmother, or was cared for by relatives elsewhere. We do know that Michaël's family continued to grow, with the arrival of an additional seven children over the next 12 years. Ultimately, 11 children would survive beyond childhood. Clearly, this was a household in which a child had to learn to take care of himself or herself, and could not expect to be pampered.

There is another Catharina in our tale, the rather unusual sister of Michaël who was also part of his household. That young woman must have caused quite a stir at the manor when, one year, her pregnancy became apparent. We can only imagine that the otherwise happy news was met with strong condemnation in raised voices, accompanied by the tears of Catharina; all because the sister of the estate overseer was unmarried. Without any doubt, Catharina broke a few rules in Roztoka. Although out-of-wedlock children were not as uncommon as the moral standards of the day would have dictated, most of these were born to poor women; the more affluent had various means to quickly marry off expectant mothers. However, this time, events turned out somewhat differently. When Michaël's sister gave birth, no father's name was recorded in the church register.

Even if the man's name was widely known, prevailing customs and the law would have prevented the newborn from being recognized as his legitimate child. But all seemed to have been forgotten when, three years later, Catharina married a young man from not too far away. As if to stress the importance of the moment, the most senior and accomplished member of the family, Thecla's father, led the happy bride to the altar.[40]

There is more mystery about the Regiecs in Roztoka. Sometime in the late 1870s or early 1880s, the large Regiec family must have left the village; someone else was suddenly listed as the overseer of the Roztoka estate in 1881.[41] Neither Michaël Regiec nor his second wife would be buried there, and none of their many children would start families in the village, either. Even Adalbertus, the most unassuming of the Regiec brothers, would move away. What caused such change in their lives and where the family moved remain unclear. It is evident, however, that ownership of the Roztoka property changed hands. By the late 1880s, it belonged to the Kochanowski family, who in prior years had been well-acquainted with Michaël Regiec.[42]

Despite the long name given to him—Josephus Blasius Stanislaus—my great-grandfather would go through life known simply as Joseph Regiec. He was growing up in times of increasing autonomy for Galicia. When Joseph was nine years old, educational instruction, newspapers, and even official documents of the Kingdom of Galicia and Lodomeria transitioned from the obligatory use of German to use of the languages spoken in that land. There was also a renewed push by the empowered crown land's parliamentary assembly (*diet*) to modernize Galicia, rather than continue with ill-fated bickering and unrealistic dreams of separate statehood. It was becoming clear that to achieve these goals, the society would have to undergo a profound change through education. The modern idea that this was a basic right rather than a rare privilege was ready to be implemented, despite all odds, in Galicia.[43]

At least for now, cooler heads would prevail, and the focus shifted to self-improvement and a desire to look forward with optimism. With these changes, there was a need for many teachers. The first of these from the extended Regiec family was Franciscus Regiec, who became a teacher in 1874. He would teach in a school with a single classroom in the village of Janowice, the hometown of the Traczewski family. But this was only a partial break from tradition. Although he had chosen a different livelihood than working in the fields, Franciscus would remain in the same village school for the next 35 years, leaving the pursuit of bigger opportunities to future generations. During this time, even a few Regiec women began independent careers, to be joined later by many others bearing the family name.[44]

In September of 1879, Joseph Regiec took his place as an educator in the nearby village of Wieloglowy.[45] This must have been his first formal job after his recent graduation from teachers' college. Joseph's new home was a small hamlet of two rural settlements separated by a patch of forest. The church and about 40 loosely spread-out houses formed this community. Classes were held in the home of an organist at a local parish; lessons took place in a single room with a few wooden benches, a teacher's desk, and a blackboard. Joseph was the only teacher there. The work of this young man and many like him must have felt endless; in the countryside, often less than a quarter of the population was able to read and write. Even in Galicia's two largest cities, Cracow and Lvov, barely more than half the inhabitants were literate. The province was clearly trying to catch up after years of neglect.[46]

This young teacher must have had a keen sense of civic responsibility; in any case, something prompted him to write a short chronicle of his tiny school. Speaking with locals and appealing to their memories, he cobbled together its

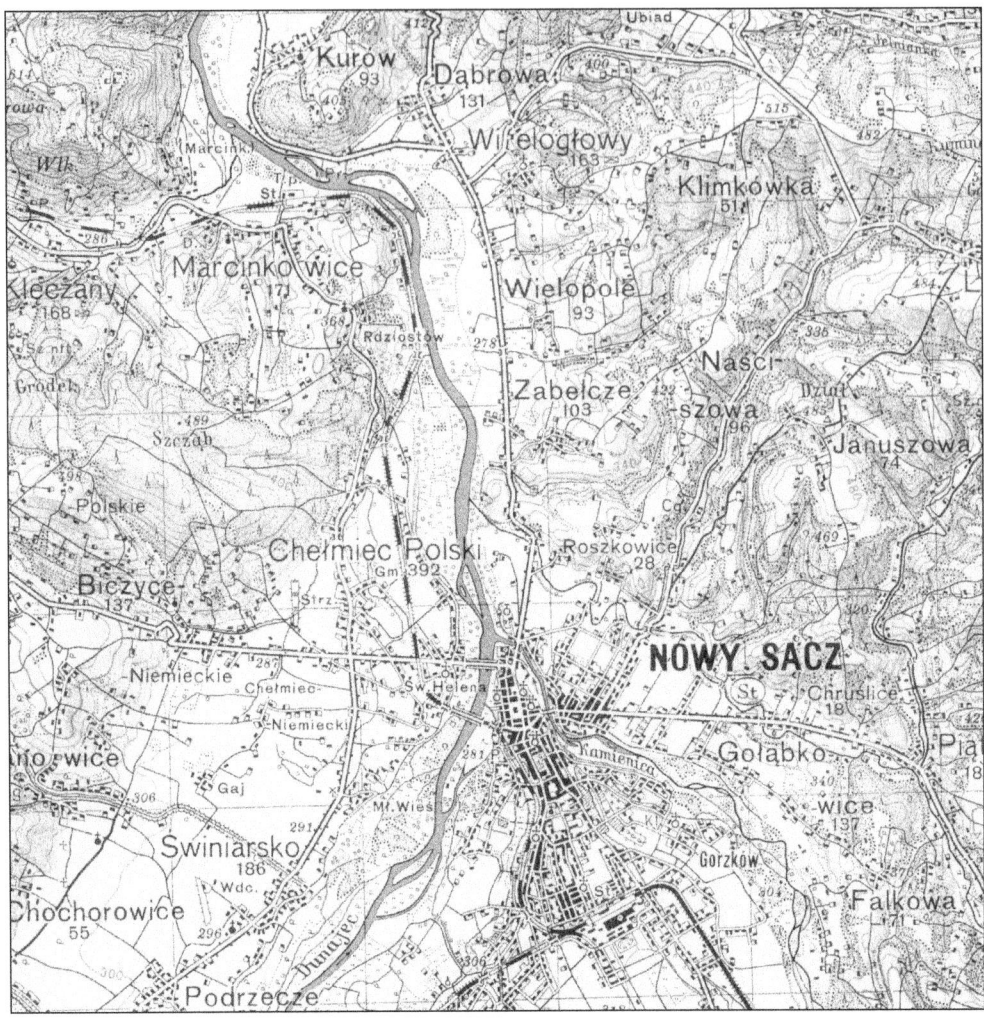

The region of Nowy Sacz. The Lösch family resided in Nowy Sacz from 1875. North of the city are the villages Wieloglowy and Wielopole, where Joseph Regiec taught from 1879 to 1885. *(Section of a map from 1937.)*

history, full of names that went all the way back to 1813. Remarkably, not only would the original document survive in the school library, but it would be fortuitously posted on its website 125 years later. Reading Joseph's words in his own handwriting, we can see his deep concern that so many of his predecessors, who were often liked and considered to be devoted teachers, had left after a short period of service. We begin to see clearly the author's dedication to this small community, which went well beyond simple classroom teaching:

When I arrived in the year 1879, I found the classroom in the organist's house, but no place for me to stay. Luckily, I was able to find a home in the manor house in the neighboring village of Wielopole, where I also taught the children of Mr. and Mrs. Kosterkiewicz [the owners of Wielopole]. For the next five years, I remained determined to make the teacher's position in Wieloglowy one of the most attractive and, thank God, I ultimately succeeded. I don't take credit for this, but I only mention that there was no single day when I would not raise with influential people the issue of living quarters for the teachers and the need to buy a small parcel of land for the school. There were many difficulties...

The cover page of Wieloglowy's school history written by Joseph Regiec. The text reads, "Chronicle of the school from approximately 1813 to 1879 based on only oral testimonies. Józef [Joseph] Regiec, teacher."

Then, Joseph's handwriting suddenly stops. But we are fortunate that one of his successors picked up the task of writing the school's history, some years later. This provides us with a unique glimpse into how Joseph's contemporaries viewed him. As the story was written (about 20 years after Joseph's departure), the young teacher enlisted the help of the owner of the neighboring village.

In the end, Mr. Regiec was able to convince the school board to buy a piece of land for teachers' living quarters and other buildings, including a stable, woodshed, and barn as well as a sports field. I gather, however, that before the construction was finished, Mr. Regiec left his teaching job...for the career on the railroad where he would rise to a high position. Memories of him are still alive in Wieloglowy. As with every teacher, opinions may vary, but most are positive...His former students are unanimous in remembering him as a hardworking and conscientious person.[47]

Unfortunately, the document does not mention details of Joseph's personal life during these five years in Wieloglowy. The village was only five miles north of the district town of Nowy Sacz where, we can only suspect, Joseph met his future wife, Stephania Lösch. What connected the country teacher with the well-established Lösch family will have to remain an untold story. Even if the young lady and Joseph had lived in the same town during their teenage years, they would have attended separate schools for boys and girls. Was it just a coincidence that Stephania's older sister, Bronislawa, was a newly appointed teacher as well?[48] Or was a promising young man introduced to the family by other relatives and mutual friends (who will be reappearing in our story on important occasions)?

The entry marking the marriage of Joseph Regec [sic] and Stephania Lösch on February 3, 1886, in Nowy Sacz.

Stephania and Joseph's courtship led to a marriage ceremony in Nowy Sacz on February 3, 1886. The 28-year-old groom and 30-year-old bride were accompanied by longtime friends of the Lösch family, Wilhelm Winkler and Vincent

Telesnicki Jr.[49] Perhaps reflecting a somewhat distant relationship with his own family, none of Joseph's many brothers or sisters were official, recorded witnesses at the exchange of marriage vows, although some of them certainly might have attended the ceremony.

As if foretelling a future of searching for new opportunities, the young couple did not stay in Nowy Sacz or in Wieloglowy. Instead, they established their first home west of there, in Mszana Dolna, a small town of approximately 1,800 inhabitants.[50] To the south of the town, mountain peaks could be seen, with pine forests that supplied material to nearby lumber mills. Surprisingly, Joseph's name was not to be found among staff at the local school. Although it is not impossible, it is unlikely that he would have taken a job as a private tutor to some well-to-do family. Instead, the recent opening of a train station in the town, an event that connected this place with a larger world, could be the clue to Joseph's move there.

This was a time when railroads were becoming a symbol of new engineering feats. As we will soon see, this technology of speed and power was not without risk, but it was an irresistible career opportunity to many—not unlike the way aviation would be viewed some 50 years later. Perhaps with the help and influence of Andreas Lösch or Vincent Telesnicki Sr., Joseph had developed a clear ambition to go beyond teaching and build his future around these new and exciting opportunities. Although railway jobs were few and always in high demand, both families had early personal connections with the railroads. Among the Lösches' friends from the old times was Wilhelm Winkler, the stationmaster in Nowy Sacz; for the Telesnickis, the link was even closer, with one of their sons working as a railway engineer. Undoubtedly, Joseph's decision to persevere in an untested profession would have a longlasting impact on his and Stephania's lives. Joining the railroads meant a new way to live, and the Regiecs were poised to become an intrepid family that was often ahead of its times.[51]

Baptismal certificate of Helena Wanda Regiec, born on November 16, 1886, in Mszana Dolna.

On November 16, 1886, Helena Wanda Regiec, my grandmother, was born in Mszana Dolna. Five days later, she was baptized in a local church. Besides the names of the parents, Joseph and Stephania, and the grandparents from the Regiec and the Lösch sides, the baptismal certificate lists the names of Julianus and Wilhelmina Telesnicki, who took part in the ceremony as Helena's godparents. Once again, members of the Telesnicki family were present at an important event in Joseph's and Stephania's lives.

It is remarkable that the original baptismal certificate survived in my grandmother's possession and later in her daughter's papers, despite the many relocations that followed—let alone the destructive forces of two world wars, in which so many other personal documents were to perish. I vaguely remember my grandmother heading to Mszana Dolna approximately 70 years later to obtain a birth certificate from the civil authorities, based on this document. The priceless church-issued slip of paper was no longer considered sufficient.

Within a couple of years, Joseph Regiec moved with his young family back to Nowy Sacz. There were plenty of reasons behind this decision; Stephania was expecting another child, and for Joseph, new career opportunities had conveniently opened in the town. The Regiecs settled in an apartment provided by the railway. Other members of the Lösch family lived not too far away; Joseph's father-in-law, Andreas Lösch, now retired, was well-known in the town, due to his former position as district commissioner. Bronislawa Lösch, Stephania's oldest sister, was living with her parents, focused on her flourishing activities as a teacher. By then, Wilhelmina, the middle Lösch sister, was in Stary Sacz, just a few miles away.[52]

Joseph Regiec (1858–1920). This picture was taken in Nowy Sacz in the late 1880s or early 1890s.

Paradoxically, of the three Lösch sisters, the person we know the least about is Stephania, the youngest and my great-grandmother. As far as we know, she remained a homemaker, with her hands full looking after a growing family.

In 1888, Wanda Regiec, Helena's younger sister, was born in Nowy Sacz. Possibly the older Lösches were smiling, having three daughters themselves and now welcoming to the family two girls as their grandchildren. Undoubtedly, the Regiecs were happy when, a few months after Wanda was born, a published list of the railway administration included Joseph's name; as of January 1, 1889, he had officially been given a coveted permanent position in Nowy Sacz. For the first few years, he would work there as a clerk and later as assistant to the stationmaster.[53]

Nowy Sacz. The train station of the Galician Transversal Railway, where Joseph Regiec worked from 1888 to 1894. *(Postcard from the end of the nineteenth century.)*

At that time, Nowy Sacz had about 11,000 citizens, including a large Jewish population of approximately 5,000. Jews had been established there at least since 1699, when plans for the first synagogue had been laid out.[54] As in many towns of the region, the city center featured a large square, on which stood a

City Hall topped with a tower. Not far from there, Andreas Lösch's former office was located in a small but handsome building that housed the district administration. Nowy Sacz was becoming a busy place, with several judicial courts and rapid growth as a transportation center. There were two railway stations in town. An older one was for the north-south railway that had been established soon after the Lösches moved there in 1875; a newer station had opened on the city outskirts and served the Galician Transversal Railway (*Galizische Transversalbahn*), which linked towns between the east and west of Galicia. The newer train station would remain Joseph's workplace for the next few years.

Not unlike today, progress had its vocal critics. At times, locals claimed that railroad construction was causing more frequent seasonal flooding; these torrents could certainly be violent at times, with the river carrying away trees or even large farm animals caught in the swelling current.[55] But notwithstanding these accusations, the railway was a real boon for Nowy Sacz, and a number of jobs and businesses opened as the result of these changes.

With Joseph soon absent on assignments far from home, we can assume that Stephania was the one firmly in charge of the Regiec household. The family continued to live near the Galician Transversal Railway, so Joseph could walk to work when in town. On Sundays, the family could choose from a few different spots for recreation. At the city outskirts was an old castle with a partially preserved tower and thick defensive walls. By the time the Regiecs moved there, the buildings housed an armory and a warehouse for the military garrison. Not far away, a wooden bridge, passing high over the River Dunajec, connected the town with a governmental road heading further west. The bridge was a popular spot; many walked there and paused to look down at the swift currents roiling beneath them. On the other side was an area described as a favorite place for family strolls, under many poplar trees alongside a picturesque road. We can only wonder if Joseph and Stephania, with two little girls hopping up and down, once walked amongst the many Sunday visitors.

The decade of the 1890s turned out to be quite eventful for the Lösch and Regiec families. It brought both expected and unexpected events in their personal lives and in the world around them. As with generations before and after, as time passed, the losses of family members were felt deeply; but this was accompanied by a real sense of better opportunities ahead for the young people. The next generation of Lösches and Regiecs pushed hard to have meaningful lives, whether in Nowy Sacz or soon, far beyond. Undoubtedly, for many of those whose stories we will follow, this was a time of contrasts and impactful decisions.

ॐ

The year 1893 was definitely not a good one; first, Andreas Lösch died of cancer after only five years of retirement. From then on Eleonora, widowed after 47 years of marriage, would be looked after by her three daughters, with the oldest, Bronislawa, remaining closest to her. Bronislawa taught in the girls' school at 32 Jagiellonian Street, just a few steps from where she herself lived.[56] For many years, this five-grade school remained the only place that offered formal education to girls in this not-so-small city.

Nowy Sacz. The section of Jagiellonian Street not far from the schools where Bronislawa Lösch taught. *(Postcard from the end of the nineteenth century or early twentieth century.)*

Bronislawa Lösch's signature as the temporary school principal, dated June 26, 1889.

Handwritten entries in the school's records show Bronislawa's rapid rise to department head, then deputy principal, then principal. She continued to have a successful career in this modern institution, soon to be named after Queen Hedwig from Silesia. In time, Bronislawa would become a permanent fixture there. The story of her success could have stopped with that, but make no mistake: Bronislawa had a very busy life beyond the daily routine of going to and from classes. Although she would never marry, her life could not have been busier and more fulfilling. The causes she would champion were a great testimony to her deeply held belief that education was the key to independence in Galician society. When, year after year, the state failed to open a badly needed women's teachers' college in Nowy Sacz, Bronislawa and others succeeded in establishing a private school that tried to fill the void. This was a work of perseverance, as the school did not have its own building and classes were initially taught in private homes. Once the college opened, Bronislawa focused on her next idea: how to prepare girls for universities. Within a few years, a private, women-only *gymnasium*—the equivalent of today's high school but with an emphasis on classical education in Latin and Greek—was established. Bronislawa became responsible for its first admissions office.[57]

Minutes of the meetings of an educational association, the Folk School Association, active in Nowy Sacz, give a closer glimpse of Bronislawa. Almost always present during evening discussions held in various places, she continued to report to the executive committee on work done, or tirelessly plead for new causes. At various times, she expressed her views as a member of the executive committee, trusted and respected by others (as evidenced by the large number of votes she received during annual elections). Then, she served as deputy chairwoman, an unusual feat in that male-dominated society; as secretary of the association, taking meticulous notes of evening deliberations; and as the treasurer or delegate to national conventions.

Bronislawa exhibited boundless energy, embarking on many initiatives that might look a bit trivial or even patronizing by today's norms. Nevertheless, these were important in her time, and required not only her personal dedication but also quite a bit of ingenuity. Through the association's records, a picture emerges of a person speaking in a thoughtful and measured voice, but at the same time not afraid of taking on new responsibilities. She was involved in obtaining books and newspapers for reading rooms in rural communities, and fundraising for chairs or lamps needed for libraries; she even managed to oversee amateur theatrical performances in her free time (these would have provided a type of entertainment that was otherwise available to very few). On other occasions, she served as a voluntary librarian for the association, cataloguing and packing books for small libraries—including one in Wieloglowy, where Joseph Regiec, her brother-in-law, had taught years before.[58] When she is reported to have been in contact with a local teacher there, we can only wonder if a few words were not exchanged between them about Joseph, by then on a new career path.

As with any voluntary organization, there were small disappointments, such as her associates' loss of interest in good causes and a constant lack of funds, but there were also many small triumphs that gave her satisfaction. She must have been liked by her colleagues, as she was often asked to represent them at openings of new chapters or small libraries, or to carry out honorary duties. One year during carnival season, Bronislawa, accompanied by a visiting member of the national parliament in Vienna, led an impressive number of 80 couples in a polonaise, the opening dance of a festive evening. As reported by the newspaper, the ball turned out to be both fun and a successful fundraising event for the causes she cared for. From time to time, Bronislawa was also asked to address public gatherings during national holidays in Nowy Sacz or in the countryside. But she was not a fiery activist; the topics she chose for her speeches reveal her softer side, focusing on stories about the theater and music or her favorite topic, how to give girls a practical education.[59]

Bronislawa was a remarkably modern woman who understood the emerging influence of the press and successfully argued for sharing news of the association with local and national newspapers, thus gaining wider support among the citizens of Galicia. She was convinced that lofty goals were not enough to attract donations for education. In meeting after meeting, she petitioned her colleagues with her own ideas: for instance, offering patrons of confectionary shops or restaurants an opportunity to add a few cents to their bills in return for small postcards with nicely printed views of Nowy Sacz. The proceeds of this imaginative campaign were, of course, to benefit the association.[60]

Bronislawa Lösch (1848 – 1912). This picture was taken in Nowy Sacz in 1908.

In later years, Bronislawa Lösch would become publicly recognized, not just for her ideas but also for her actions in addressing the educational needs of women. Among her many activities, she was a quiet but effective champion of teenage girls and those young women who were already working. Her idea was simple: to provide them with a place to congregate that was both educational and entertaining. To this end, she was instrumental in finding and arranging a spacious women's reading room for a self-support group that formed in Nowy Sacz. Under Bronislawa, the place offered not only a wide range of newspapers and magazines, but also chances to attend lectures and seasonal concerts. She was clearly ahead of her time; at the opening of the reading room, the executive committee of the association unanimously approved a resolution thanking Bronislawa for her "extraordinary efforts." We can only surmise that the late Andreas Lösch would have felt proud seeing his daughter so recognized for a good cause. With time, the reading room for women even turned a small profit, which was used to buy clothes for impoverished children.

Toward the end of her life, Bronislawa would direct her energy through her organization in seeking support to build a teachers' retreat. At the time of her last public appearance, her educational association was consumed by a debate over who would lead it into the future. One evening, the committee seemed to reach an impasse, with no easy solution in sight. The handwritten minutes of the meeting tell of her calming influence: "Then Miss Lösch rose, explaining that, as the oldest among those gathered, she would humbly venture a motion for the unanimous vote for..." offering the name of someone she felt was the best qualified. Her opinion seemed to matter; despite the bickering just minutes before, the candidate was quickly confirmed without a single dissenting vote.[61]

To those who knew her and even to those of us who have read the meeting notes today, Bronislawa's absence in subsequent gatherings clearly signaled trouble ahead. When she passed away the following year after a long illness, her obituaries were generous in praise of her life, not only as a distinguished teacher but also as a selfless person. To keep her legacy alive, fellow teachers and friends opened a local kindergarten that year, named after her.[62]

Bronislawa Lösch's obituary. Under the heading "From the grieving page," the text reads, "Bronislawa Lösch, retired teacher from Nowy Sacz, died after a long illness 9th of [September] at age of 64. The deceased worked continuously in her profession for 35 years in Nowy Sacz, where she taught two generations [of students]. The funeral procession attended by many was the telling testimony of the feelings shared by local citizens for her tireless work in the educational and civic fields. Hail to the esteemed employee! Hail to our good colleague!"

In contrast to Bronislawa, her sister Wilhelmina was often away from Nowy Sacz. She had been widowed very young but remarried in 1879, when she was in her late 20s. Her second husband was Vincent Telesnicki Jr., well-known to her entire family. Vincent Jr., employed by the railroad as a mechanical engineer, continued to move from one post to another, taking Wilhelmina and their young family to different places in western Galicia—not unlike the early lives of Andreas and Eleonora. However, these waystations were familiar to the couple and not too far from Nowy Sacz. The young family spent a few years each in several towns, including Tarnow, Stary Sacz, and Jaslo, some of which we have visited before.[63] Ultimately, the couple would have two boys and two girls.

Vincent Jr. and Wilhelmina remained close to Stephania and Joseph Regiec. As already mentioned, Vincent was the witness at their wedding, and Wilhelmina became a godparent to their first child, Helena. We can only wonder if Joseph Regiec and Vincent Telesnicki Jr. had something to do with each other's fledgling careers in the railroad. But the young Telesnicki couple's journey together came to a screeching halt the same year that Andreas passed away. In 1893, during a routine inspection of repairs on a steam engine, an explosion occurred. Vincent, who had the misfortune to be standing high up on the black locomotive, was thrown to the ground by the massive blast. The impact was deadly. In the second blow to the Lösch, Regiec, and Telesnicki families that year, Wilhemina's husband died tragically at the age of 38, and she found herself a widow for the second time.

Few early pictures of Helena Regiec survive from the time when she, as a young girl, lived with her family in Nowy Sacz. Photography was still at an early stage then, and taking a picture was a serious affair that required an appointment with the only studio in town, owned by Mr. Friedman. But that photograher's luck at having no competition lasted only a few years. Soon, that gentleman would face the arrival of others who were skilled in the new art.[64] In any case, one visit by the Regiec family to the Friedman atelier is documented; it must have been considered a splash of luxury, reserved for special occasions by those who could afford it. Not surprisingly, young Helena looks rather serious in her photo. Smiles were not considered appropriate, even if they had been possible to maintain—given the time that was required to stay still in front of the camera.[65]

More dramatic events touched the extended family around that time. Around noon one Tuesday in April of 1894, fire broke out in Nowy Sacz on the roof of a bakery by the market square. Within minutes, a strong gust of wind had spread the flames from one structure to another (many were covered with wooden shingles). Soon, the post office and the telegraph station were consumed, which only delayed requests for help. Local firemen arriving on the

Helena Regiec (1886–1977). This picture was taken in Nowy Sacz in Michael Friedman's atelier in the early 1890s.

scene were helpless, as there were only a few wells in the city center. To make matters worse, the horse-drawn fire trucks turned out to have empty barrels; the water had been used just a few days before when the streets were cleaned for an official visitor. The tragic irony was that, in a city squeezed between rivers, there was suddenly no easy way to put out a raging fire. Among those who deserved praise in the chaos of heat and choking fumes was a Mr. Winkler, referred to as the railway commissioner and possibly a Regiec family friend. As was later reported in several newspapers, he was one of the very few with a cool head. He quickly arranged help from his employees and, seeing the local firemen in disarray, began to direct them. We can only wonder today if Joseph Regiec was one among many men who rushed from the train station to the rescue.[66]

Despite such efforts, almost all the buildings around the central square burned to the ground. Within hours, the old City Hall, with its priceless archives of the past 600 years, perished. As if this was not devastating enough, the fire had spread quickly to nearby churches, causing roofs to collapse and heavy bells to fall inside. Then, the Jewish district went up in flames. With sparks flying through the air, fires started to erupt as much as a few miles away from the city center. Flames even began to light up some straw-covered buildings in the village of Wielopole, where Joseph Regiec had tutored the children of his mentor years before. To the despair of one respected citizen from Nowy Sacz who had quickly evacuated his belongings to the safety of Wielopole, one of the stables he was using for temporary storage caught fire in the evening. The man's possessions literally went up in smoke; it seemed that for some, there was no escape from the tragedy.

In the end, hundreds of houses were destroyed in the fire, and up to 5,000 citizens were made homeless. Downtown Nowy Sacz smoldered for hours, with ghostly looking, blackened chimneys standing among the ruins. The central square was littered with broken furniture, pots and pans, papers, pillows, and whatever else the victims had been able to save from the fire.

In spite of the misery surrounding them, the Lösch family probably considered themselves extremely lucky. Just a few years before, after Andreas's retirement, they had moved to an area that was miraculously spared on that fateful day. Perhaps Eleonora and her daughter Bronislawa wondered what would have been their fate had they stayed in their former house just south of the central square. That building was now gone, and the area was surrounded by ruins.[67]

The Regiecs were also safe. Joseph and his family lived toward the city outskirts in the south, in another of the few districts that were unaffected by the fire. Many others were less fortunate, and a number of empty lots were apparent in the downtown area even a few years after the disaster.

In the fall of that eventful year, my grandmother began attending the elementary school on Jagiellonska Street. Helena Regiec was a good student; one

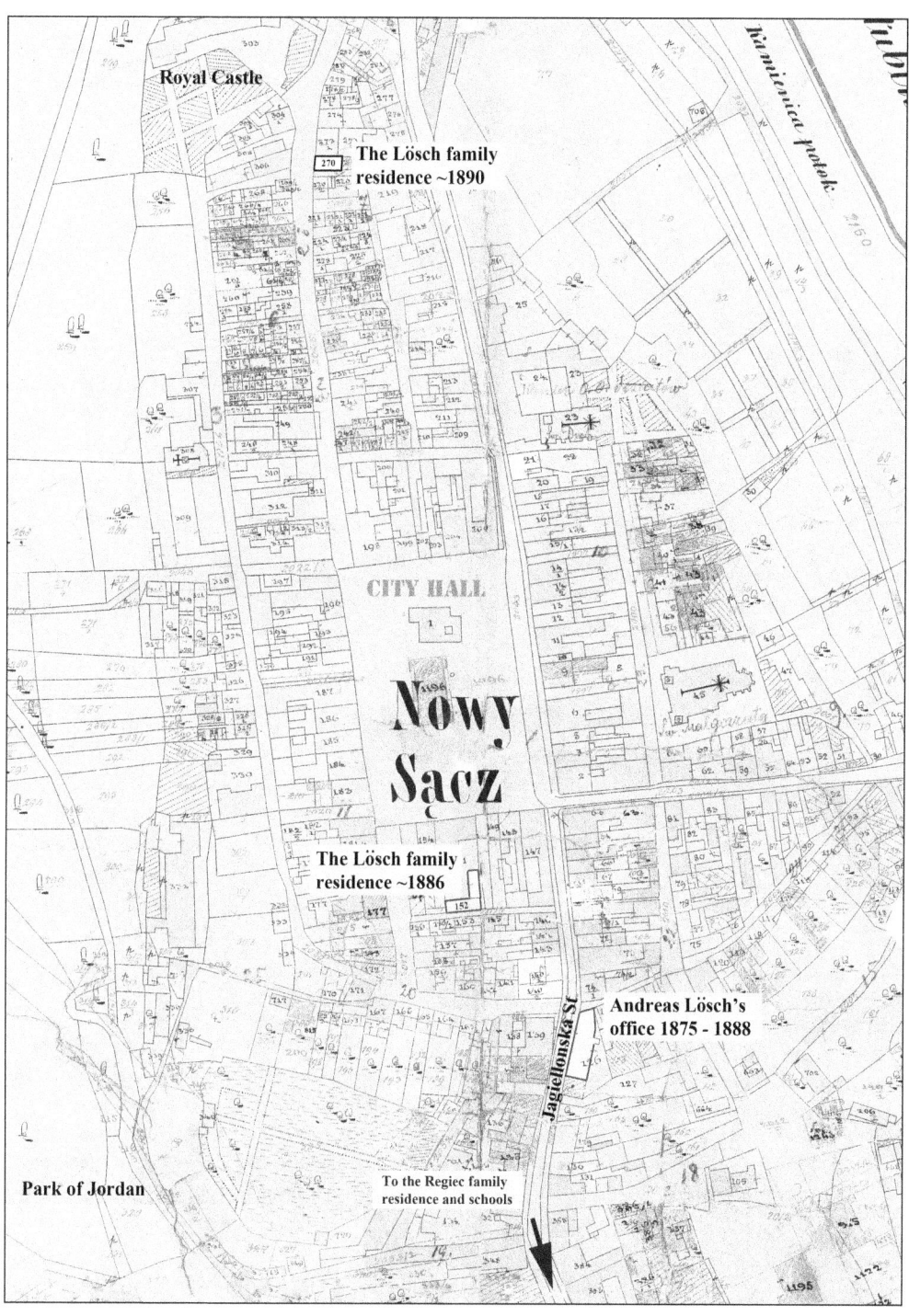

Map of the downtown in Nowy Sacz. *(Map from 1899.)*

Nowy Sacz. The elementary school attended by Helena Regiec in the 1890s.
(Postcard from the end of the nineteenth century or early twentieth century.)

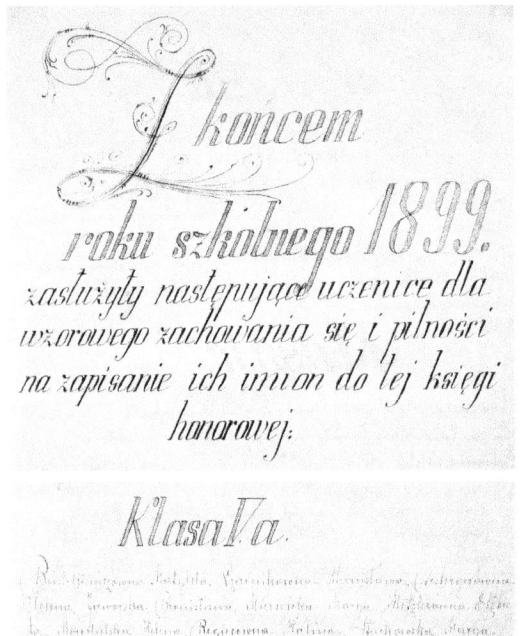

Page from the book listing honor students from Nowy Sacz. The heading reads, "At the end of the school year 1899, the following pupils earned that their names be recorded in the honor book for exemplary behavior and hard work." The entries below include fifth-grade student "Regiecówna, Halina [Helena]." Helena's last name is written in an old Polish style where the ending "-ówna" denotes an unmarried woman.

can still find her name carefully calligraphed in a commemorative book, among honor students deserving special recognition in the fourth and fifth grades.[68] Whether she was on the way to school or going to visit Eleonora, we can picture Helena walking through streets that still bore the scars of the fire's destruction.

In the city center, houses were rebuilt quickly. A new City Hall, with its Parisian facade, would bring a sense of recovery and optimism for many; but for others, it became a focus of anger, its construction criticized as extravagant and poorly planned. Undoubtedly, this was the reality of local politics: It was impossible to satisfy everyone.

For the young Regiec family, as it had been earlier for Andreas and Eleonora Lösch, life was not to become entirely settled yet. Joseph was advancing in his career, and with this came the choice of whether to remain in the familiar surroundings of Nowy Sacz or take advantage of new opportunities with some strings attached. The opening of a new Railway Directorate overseeing the growing network of railroads in the eastern part of the province created new positions for those who were not afraid of changes. Not surprisingly, Joseph was one of the first to sieze on this opportunity. By 1895, he had made the choice to accept a

Helena Regiec. This picture was taken on the occasion of Helena's first communion in Nowy Sacz, in 1894.

position on the railways at the edge of the Austro-Hungarian Empire. With this came a few job-related perks and steady pay; not a lot of money but still amounting to approximately half of what a city mayor would earn in those days. More importantly, the prospect of future advancement in the ranks of the expanding railroad administration was something not to be ignored.[69] For the next few years, Joseph's work in the regional railways took him to the Duchy of Bukovina, a province located further east and south in an area split today between Ukraine and Romania.

Although situated just beyond the historical boundaries of Galicia, the Duchy had been linked administratively off and on with the Kingdom of Galicia and Lodomeria during Austrian rule. The name of the region was derived from beech trees that had apparently covered the territory in distant times. The population there differed greatly from that of western Galicia, where Joseph was from. In the south, Romanians were a majority, speaking a language much

Nowosielica (Austrian Nowosielitza). The border town's train station, where Joseph Regiec worked from 1897 to 1899.

different from German or any Slavic language he knew. In the north, Ruthenians and their mountain-inhabiting cousins, the Hutsuls, were more prevalent. In population numbers, these groups were followed by Germans and much smaller groups of Jews, Poles, and Hungarians.

The town of Nowosielica was Joseph's first posting in Bukovina. This was one of those unusual places where, by chance or by the verdict of history, the borders of three nations (the Austro-Hungarian Empire, tsarist Russia, and Romania) came together, making it a busy trading center. As this was the last stop of the railway on Austrian soil before it continued further south to Romania, large customs fees were collected on goods moving in and out of the empire. Even the River Prut was put to work, with large logs flowing on its current toward trading posts. In this rugged territory, Joseph would stay alone for a few years; Stephania Regiec continued to care for not only her young daughters, Helena and Wanda, but also her ailing mother in Nowy Sacz, approximately 350 miles away from Joseph.

The next stop in Joseph's professional journey came soon; this time, the railroad took him to administrative tasks in Czerniowce, capital of the Duchy of Bukovina. Knowing that these fast-paced relocations were simply stepping stones to a more desirable position somewhere else, and/or considering Stephania's likely wish to stay behind in Nowy Sacz, Joseph was not accompanied by his family there. How often his young daughters were able to see their father, we do not know for sure. From the stories my grandmother told, however, I know that Joseph was always on the move, inspecting various parts of the constantly expanding railway network and likely visiting home more often than other fathers who worked far away. The young sisters also went to see him, and Helena was able to travel with her father south to Romania. This was, however, only a small prelude to more exciting trips to come.

With the nineteenth century coming to a close, troubles of a very different sort erupted back in Nowy Sacz. In the course of pre-election agitation, the region witnessed civil unrest, with peasants attacking and looting Jewish merchants. With the perspective of time, it is apparent that poor and uneducated Galician peasants were easily manipulated by shrewd politicians when no real solutions to their poverty were readily offered. Prior concerns that the demagoguery of one populist leader would one day spark real violence, this time materialized. The instigators turned the temperature up further by spreading false rumors that the emperor Franz Joseph had given tacit permission for them to attack Jewish property.[70]

Undoubtedly, the Lösch and Regiec families were acutely affected when such violence paralyzed their town, with its large Jewish population. The press described groups of rowdy peasants stirring up trouble on the streets and in open markets. A number of Jewish taverns were set on fire, stalls overturned, Jewish possessions and liquor supplies stolen. There were injuries and property damage not only in Nowy Sacz, but also in other towns in the western portion of Galicia. The subtext was clear, reminding all about the dangerous events that had occurred about 50 years earlier. Although the targets of the violence were different this time and no loss of life was reported, there was a collective memory of the Galician Slaughter, and fear of what could happen if the situation was not brought under control. We can only wonder if Eleonora, by now one of the few remaining individuals who had lived through those events of 1846, saw ominous parallels.

This time, the government acted decisively and with no ambiguity. The governor of Galicia quickly arrived in Nowy Sacz to support local government and oversee the situation. To quell unrest among those who ignored warnings, troops (including cavalry) were sent in, and a brief but effective martial law was declared in 33 counties of western Galicia.[71] The police instituted preventive incarceration of more than 1,800 of those who were suspected of taking part in the unrest, with the courts issuing summary judgments against looters. The public was sternly warned that death sentences could be carried out within hours of

Nowy Sacz. Saving Bank. *(Postcard from the end of the nineteenth century or early twentieth century.)*

court verdicts, with no right to appeal by those found guilty of capital offenses. Although some decried these methods as medieval, order was quickly restored, and calm returned within a few weeks.

One postscript to these ugly incidents was somewhat theatrical. A few months later, the *New York Times* reported that the instigator of the unrest had been taken into police custody but had managed to escape by jumping from a Vienna-bound train moving at the "amazing" speed of 25 miles per hour.[72]

⁓

The year 1900 started on a sad note. In February, Eleonora Lösch died at the age of 81. With her passing, the generation that had witnessed monumental changes in their daily lives, such as the transition from uncomfortable horse-drawn carriages to travel by train, was fading away. Eleonora and Andreas Lösch had belonged to a generation that once brightened their evenings with flickering

Map of Galicia. The life journey of Stephania Lösch Regiec (born in Biecz) and Joseph Regiec (born in Roztoka).

candlelight or kerosene lamps, and then experienced the popular gas lighting that opened new ways for self-education and richer social interaction. When Eleonora died, electricity was still a new invention with a somewhat uncertain future. Just a few years before, a well-publicized failure of electric lighting during a theatrical performance had been accompanied by mocking arguments in the press, insisting that gas lamps were a better means of reliable illumination.[73] Despite twists and turns in the journey toward modern life in their world, the older Lösches had clearly been ahead of their times. This urbane and multilingual couple's life story evidenced an openness to change, a still uncommon attitude in their fairly conservative society. By the norms of our times, they were a middle class family that first embraced the fast-paced career of Andreas and then the successful professional life of Bronislawa, not out of financial necessity but as a new way of life for women as well as men.

With the passing of her mother, Stephania no longer had any reason for living apart from her husband. Fortuitously, around that time, Joseph was promoted to a position in the Department of Revenues in the Directorate of Railway Administration. For the Regiec girls and their mother, it was equally exciting that the office was located in the city of Stanislawow, a town that offered many opportunities for the family. As before, without Joseph's personal drive and his eagerness to take chances, the next part of this story would not have happened.

Chapter 3

STANISLAWOW: THE STRONGHOLD OF REWERA

WHEN, LATER IN LIFE, MY grandmother was asked where she was from, her answer was always, without hesitation, "Stanislawow." Although the Regiec family moved there when Helena was in her early teens, this was the town where she went to high school, made her first plans toward adult life, and later kept returning with her young daughter. Even when going back was no longer possible, she maintained a special bond with Stanislawow through correspondence with her younger sister, Wanda, who remained there for several decades to come. But these are stories that we will touch on a bit later.

When the Regiecs moved there in 1900, Stanislawow (*Stanislau* in German, *Станиславів* in Ruthenian, *Stanislaopolis* in Latin) was considered a desirable place to live in Galicia; it ranked just behind the somewhat rundown but historic Cracow and Galicia's vibrant multicultural capital, Lvov. Like many places in that part of the world, its long history blended facts with myths. Stanislawow had grown from a village on a large estate of the Potocki family (an old aristocratic line in the Kingdom of Poland). Initially, this nondescript village became a simple fort, surrounded by defensive walls constructed of tree trunks. These were built to defend the population against repeated attacks by Tatars, Ottoman Turks, and other invaders from the east. In 1662, the settlement became a town that was most likely named by its founder, Count Andreas Potocki, after his young son, Stanislaw (*Stanislau*). Soon thereafter, the name "Stanislawow" could be found in an edict issued by the Polish king, Casmir the Great; in the writings of a foreign traveler passing through the area; and in many documents issued by its founder, Count Potocki.¹ But the origins of places are usually subject to more than one explanation, and this was true for Stanislawow. Later some argued that the town had been named in honor of Andreas's father, also called Stanislaw, who was a viceroy of these lands. In any case, the older Potocki, a man hardened in numerous battles, was known to frequently repeat the Latin phrase *re vera* (in truth); hence, the town also acquired the honorific description "The Stronghold of Revera."²

From its inception, Stanislawow was a multicultural place. Initially, Count Potocki issued an edict permitting Poles, Ruthenians, and Jews to settle within the town walls, and decreed the right of each group to govern its internal affairs. Soon, small groups of Armenians, Hungarians, and Germans had moved there as well. Armenians, in particular, would be remembered in the town with remarkable fondness. Perhaps warm memories of them reflected the gratitude of the townspeople, because the Armenians had often acted as intermediaries to gain release of hostages taken by the Asian invaders who frequently pillaged these lands.

But for the most part, townspeople looked back on the Armenians as large-scale, colorful merchants, who on occasion traveled to the steppes surrounding the Black Sea, leasing land for a dozen or so years to raise cattle and horses. They were true cowboys long before their counterparts in the American West earned their fame. In a ritual that would be remembered for generations, the Armenians ran herds of steppe-raised cattle and horses west through Bukovina and Galicia to destinations in Austria and Germany. These were operations on a massive scale; a merchant once reportedly delivered an astounding 19,000 horses to a Bavarian court. Upon returning home to Stanislawow, these traders would bring gold, silver, and pearls. Then they would stay for a few years with their families, attending to local businesses of leathermaking or the grain trade, before going east again.³

A description by a Dutch visitor passing through the region gives us a glimpse of early Stanislawow. The wooden castle of the Potocki family, churches of various denominations, a synagogue, and a school of higher learning with five professors all come to light in this report from 1672.⁴ However, good stories were mixed with bad. During the next hundred years, Stanislawow suffered at the hands of foreign invaders; Tatar and Russian armies on a few occasions breached the defensive walls and plundered the city. To make matters worse, Stanislawow also suffered from the internal squabbles that plagued the eighteenth-century Kingdom of Poland.⁵

With the first partition of Poland in 1772, the city became part of the Kingdom of Galicia and Lodomeria. The new rulers in Vienna quickly abolished some antiquated ethnic- and community-based ways of resolving local conflicts, by establishing a common civil administration for all citizens of the city. Edicts issued in the name of the empress Maria Theresa flooded the land. Everything seemed to be touched by the new administration, from rulings requiring an oath of allegiance to the new sovereign, to detailed instructions as to how the courts should function, to pronouncements that sound exotic today—such as those forbidding citizens to resolve their disputes through duels. At least on paper, there were even to be free public lectures in German and Polish for those wishing to learn about medicine, surgery, and midwifery.⁶

With the death of Maria Theresa in 1780, her son became the undisputed ruler of all her lands. He continued with even greater vigor to remake the country. In 1782, not long after his ascension, the emperor Joseph II visited Stanislawow. The heiress of the Potocki family, Catharina Kossakowska, greeted the emperor

1. Potocki's Castle
2. City Council Tower
3. Armenian Gate
4. Tysmienicka Gate
5. Halicka Gate
6. Roman Catholic Church
7. Greek Catholic Church
8. Armenian Church
9. Synagogue

Map of Stanislawow in the early 1800s. The spread of the city beyond fortification walls is evident.

Chapter 3 — Stanislawow: The Stronghold of Rewera

(Based on a map from Kriegsarchiv in Vienna.)

in richly decorated apartments in the castle. For the next three days, for reasons that are shrouded in mystery, the emperor chose to have his headquarters in the home of a Jewish family rather than in the more opulent castle.[7] But let us not forget that Joseph II was a prolific reformer and often a social contrarian when dealing with Jews or the Catholic Church, once he no longer felt constrained by his more conservative mother.

Despite what was viewed as a successful visit, strong-willed Catharina Kossakowska quickly ran into troubles with less prominent Austrians. The next few years brought frequent disputes with local government officials steadily chipping away at her rights as the owner of Stanislawow. In a game of tit for tat, when the military once requested delivery of a small supply of lumber from her dominion, she refused. Instead, the feisty heiress promised, tongue in cheek, to donate the entire forest if the purpose was to build gallows for nagging bureaucrats. Verbal skirmishes, however, could not prevent the unavoidable from happening when Catharina ran out of money. In a letter to a relative, she summed up her situation with usual flair: "I gave away Stanislawow and I am moving from Halychyna [the name of the region]. Oh! Damn it! I wish the lightning strikes down on my nemesis. Sincere good-bye."[8]

By 1801, the aristocratic Potocki family was no longer able to manage Stanislawow and the large nearby landholdings on its own. A map from the period shows the castle and the inner city surrounded by defensive walls, with the main entrances (the Halicka and Tysmienicka gates) and the smaller Armenian Gate used by pedestrians. But the town's expansion beyond the city walls was clearly visible, signaling the need for further change. Ultimately, Stanislawow and the Potockis' lands were bought by the Austrian government, and the modern era of the city began. Within a few years, the castle had been converted to a hospital, and the defense fortifications were demolished. With the instability of the region receding and the quarrels among major powers in the area settled (at least for a while), the moats, no longer needed to thwart invasions, were filled with stones and dirt, allowing the city streets to expand.

Stanislawow. The aftermath of the big fire of 1868. *(Postcard from the nineteenth century.)*

There were, however, problems plaguing the city that even the new administration could not prevent. Fires erupted repeatedly in Stanislawow over the next decades. The worst struck the city with devastating force in September 1868 when, under innocent circumstances, a blaze started one early afternoon on Lipowa Street. During the annual ritual of making preserves for the winter, an open flame had been used in a small backyard. Suddenly, a strong gust of wind spread a fire that would ultimately consume the entire downtown, including City Hall, an old Armenian church, two synagogues, and many other surrounding buildings.[9] With fires still smoldering late into the night, the first counts of the losses were shocking. Ultimately, 260 buildings were found to have been destroyed. Many people, now homeless, gathered in an empty market square to escape burns or choking fumes.

Almost immediately, the magnitude of this calamity raised doubts as to whether Stanislawow could ever be rebuilt. By November of the same year, however, the national *diet* had guaranteed a large loan for the reconstruction. The central government in Vienna followed suit and created a special lottery, with proceeds reserved for payment of the city's debt. Over the years, there would be other signs of support. A visit—albeit a mere stop with speeches at the train station—by the emperor Franz Joseph reassured residents still wondering whether the town would regain its prior status. The emperor, speaking in French, inquired about local affairs, startling those greeting him with questions about the workload of Stanislawow's courts. But regardless of the topic of conversation on the platform, for the reported 3,000 spectators who gathered around the train station, Franz Joseph's visit seemed to be the best evidence that their town was not forgotten.[10]

Over the next few years and then decades, a city of wider streets, with stylish public buildings designed by Galician and Viennese architects, would slowly emerge, adding to the architectural originality of the reborn Stanislawow. Construction soon began in the town's center on one of the first Reform synagogues

Stanislawow. New City Hall after its construction was completed in 1872.
(Postcard from the nineteenth century.)

in Galicia. Its model, based on a design by a Viennese architect, was prominently displayed in the window of a local bookstore, arousing public interest. From time to time, the press reported on accidental findings during construction, which included a few ancient human bones and a foundation stone covered with old Cyrillic letters placed there more than two hundred years before. Once completed, the synagogue would be an impressive building with towers rising at the four corners of the *Templum*, topped by cupolas.[11] There were renovations of churches, including the Roman Catholic collegiate, the Greek Catholic cathedral, and the blue-roofed Armenian church. A new City Hall with a high tower was built; its picture would become a hallmark of early postcards with greetings from the town. A period of modernization followed, with Stanislawow becoming the first city in Galicia to begin installation of gas street lamps, in 1876. By the time the Regiec family arrived in 1900, modern street lighting covered almost the entire city. With thinly veiled satisfaction, a local paper proudly reminded its readers that in contrast to Stanislawow, in some parts of Lvov, antiquated kerosene street lanterns were still in use![12]

Further to the south, the city laid out new parks where families could stroll while military bands entertained with Viennese waltzes or Hungarian marches. In the summer, these parks were the places to see and be seen. A local reporter described smartly dressed young men there wearing fashionable Panama hats and high, starched collars; my grandmother later remembered that the latter were jokingly called *"vater mörder"* (father's murderer) in German. I wonder if she heard occasional complaints from her father, Joseph Regiec, at putting such stiff contraptions around his neck. In any case, the men strolled, holding box-like cameras in one hand and decorative walking canes in the other, with ladies walking a few steps behind in long dresses with trailing trains. Such photo opportunities were ones that nobody wanted to miss. From time to time, young boys in their then-popular navy outfits caused mischief by stepping on the women's trains. Less "urbane" ladies, as the story was told, could easily be

Stanislawow. One of many city parks. *(Postcard from the early twentieth century.)*

spotted wearing skirts that just covered the knees, with scarves on their heads instead of the more fashionable hats.[13]

By the beginning of the twentieth century, Stanislawow was gaining a reputation as a healthy place to live. The town boasted low rates of tuberculosis, the disease that ravaged the lives of many in Galicia's crowded cities. For those who required medical care, there was a choice of 37 physicians, who often saw patients from their own homes; but it would not be until 1918 that the first woman opened a medical practice in Stanislawow. A public hospital employed 5 doctors and 10 nurses, who were quite busy, reportedly performing over 1,000 surgeries per year. With medical

The photographic camera frequently advertised in the early 1900s. *(Sport & Salon April 1, 1905; ÖNB, Vienna.)*

practice quite different than it is today, the average hospital stay of 21 days was considered short! It may come as a shock to us now, but when the hospital became full, less-ill patients were required to share beds. Apothecaries in the town prepared mostly herbal medicines but were also required always to keep fresh supplies of leeches for medicinal emergencies.[14]

Most of all, Stanislawow was busy with trade and manufacturing businesses connected to agriculture, the leather industry, and fine ceramics. Business, government affairs, and frequent military inspections were bringing in more than 5,000 travelers a year, who would register at one of several fine hotels in the city. The best was the Union Hotel, with its 35 rooms generally reserved for dignitaries or the rich and famous of the day, who could afford to pay for reportedly impeccable service and accommodations with private baths.[15]

Among the citizens of the town, Jews always played a unique role. With the passage of time, they became an important force in commerce, ultimately replacing the Armenian community in dominating trade. When the Regiecs settled there, most local craftsmen were already Jewish. This group formed the majority of the population in the downtown area, where they owned real estate, retail stores, and a number of larger enterprises engaged in wholesale trade. The Jews' relationship with Poles, who sometimes lamented a somewhat imaginary loss of influence in business, was not always easy; but for the most part, it was

Stanislawow. A view of the Reform synagogue, which was completed in 1899. *(Postcard from the early twentieth century.)*

free of the open anti-Semitic hostility that flared up on occasion in other parts of Galicia.

Several distinguished Jewish families resided in Stanislawow, including a long line of Horowitzes. Generation after generation, members of that family held influential positions in the rabbinate of Stanislawow. Another highly regarded family went by the name of Halpern; they were recognized for their charitable work and support of local development. Among their contributions, the Halperns established the Jewish hospital and founded other institutions, including those for the general public, such as the first theater building. Several mutual aid societies were helped by the Halperns' generosity in assisting the poor of Stanislawow, including citizens of all faiths. At times, this aid included free meals, dowries for poor Jewish brides, and subsidized wood for heating homes. Equally remarkable is that the Halperns were early organizers of charitable activities on a global scale, providing help to Jewish families escaping repression in tsarist Russia, and establishing an orphanage in Stanislawow with not only their own money but an endowment they had secured from German Jews.

To a large extent, the Jewish community of Stanislawow was spared from the sort of disruptive internal disputes between Orthodox Hasidic leaders that were common in other towns of Galicia. In the latter part of the nineteenth century, Stanislawow had a large Maskilin movement, with its secular Jewish members advocating full integration into society. From time to time, the city would host meetings of Zionist organizations arguing, for instance, against Jewish emigration to Uganda or in favor of Palestine's remaining under Ottoman rule. Increasingly, local high school graduates were from Jewish families, a noteworthy fact since finishing school was an unusual accomplishment in the life of a young person at the time. On rare occasion, the Yiddish weekly advocated the opening of a separate high school for Jewish children, with German and Hebrew language instruction; but for the most part, these appeals did not receive much support from the Jewish majority of Stanislawow.[16]

Jews not only played visible roles in trade-related occupations, they were also noted members of other professions, such as medicine and law. From the end of the nineteenth century, they gained a presence in local government. Among these, the most notable was Dr. Arthur Nimhin. As a young lawyer, he cofounded and then edited a successful weekly paper before going into politics. Focused on debating ideas rather than attacking the motives of those with opposing views, Nimhin clearly saw the future of the Jewish majority in Stanislawow as fully integrated into the political life of Galicia. In 1896, he became the city's mayor, and despite the quarrelsome nature of city politics (which were no different in Stanislawow than anywhere else), he ran the city for more than two decades. He was a cautious but effective administrator who was able to produce budget surpluses, an uncommon feat for any city mayor. Less prone to the rhetorical exaggeration common in politics, and more of a technocrat, he must have been doing something right. Nimhin would continue in his post through the upheavals of World War I some years later. His ability to increase investment in parks, street paving, and school buildings without adding to local taxes or resorting to budgetary gimmicks was mentioned by the press as far away as the Galician capital of Lvov.[17]

Mayor Nimhin also built a reputation as an honest broker with his impartiality during the potentially explosive situations that sometimes bubbled up in the multiethnic city. One year, the Catholic Church made a formal complaint that, during the carnival-like celebrations of the Jewish holiday of Purim, a few revelers had dressed as priests and driven through the city in an open carriage, holding fake religious symbols. If true, this would not have constituted just a minor act of impersonation; it would have been regarded as a highly disrespectful situation with grave consequences, having the potential to aggravate religious

Stanislawow. The Armenian church as seen from City Hall. *(Photograph from the 1930s.)*

tensions. In response to these charges, an investigation by the mayor proved the allegations utterly false, demonstrating step by step how gossip had distorted the truth. In the end, the conclusions of the mayor's commission were accepted by the city council, and Nimhin's personal adherence to facts rather than emotions was acknowledged by the city's religious leaders, including those who had made the initial accusation. At a time when religion was often hijacked for other-than-spiritual purposes, this was not a minor accomplishment by the mayor.[18]

With the skill of an attorney who became a politician, Nimhin was not afraid to tackle sensitive issues in the community. One year, in preparation for a national census that would determine future subsidies for education in the city, he certainly must have raised eyebrows among some conservative Jews of Stanislawow when he publicly appealed to them to identify Polish rather than Yiddish as their primary language. The mayor's purpose was actually to increase the chances that the census would fully account for the Jewish population of Stanislawow; government bureaucrats tallying the census had been instructed to throw away entries noting the use of "unofficial" languages. Undoubtedly, Dr. Nimhin knew that he was walking a fine line; for many Jews, the recent rejection by the highest court of the Austro-Hungarian Empire of Yiddish as a recognized language was surely seen as unfair.[19] But whether that was right or wrong was beside the point for the pragmatic mayor—uncounted entries would simply mean fewer resources for the city.

The year 1901 began, of course, with newspapers celebrating the new century. The customary retrospectives included nostalgic looks at Napoleon Bonaparte of France, despised by many in Europe but cherished by Poles. Others wrote about the Spring of Nations (the wave of revolutions that almost broke apart the monarchies of Europe in 1848) and many technological advances that had come to life in the past century. Predictions of what the new century would bring were amazingly vague, with not a hint that the twentieth century would ultimately mean the end of Galicia. The new year brought news of a brutal war in faraway South Africa; the passing of the long-lived symbol of the British Empire, Queen Victoria; and the death of the famous Italian composer Giuseppe Verdi.

Stanislawow. The Greek Catholic cathedral. *(Postcard from the early twentieth century.)*

On a local level, Stanislawow newspapers reported the results of the census, which revealed a population of more than 30,000. The number would be even more impressive if the proposed widening of the city limits—which meant inclusion of a suburban town within its boundaries—could finally be implemented. In contrast to today, when the rapid growth of a city's population might be viewed with mixed feelings, the newspapers of that time heralded the growth of Stanislawow with pride, as a measure of its emergence from provincial obscurity.

Every 10 years, when the census data were reported, Stanislawow's public paid close attention, not only to its prized place as the third most populous city of Galicia but also to its ethnic composition. With just minor changes, the town maintained roughly the same multiethnic fabric for several decades. Approximately half of the city dwellers were Jewish, followed by Poles (constituting about 30 percent) and a smaller group of Ruthenians.[20]

Around the time that the Regiec family moved to town, new technologies were making slow inroads into the ways people communicated. The city still had only 41 registered telephones, a far cry from the mind-boggling 697 in Galicia's capital. Those were also times of innocence, when privacy was not the issue it is today. Not

Horse-drawn carriage (fiacre), a frequent topic of complaints by the citizens of Stanislawow. *(Die Muskete March 7, 1907; ÖNB, Vienna.)*

surprisingly, the local newspaper was able to print all telephone subscribers on a single page, but somewhat surprisingly, number 56, the home phone number of the mayor, Dr. Nimhin, was included.[21] Perhaps those less influential who did not have this luxury were not too despondent, because there were so few opportunities to use this new invention. Only years later would it become possible to make a phone call from Stanislawow to Vienna, rather than resorting to a telegram or the even slower mail service. But this was not a major issue for most citizens of Stanislawow, who instead complained of too many horse-drawn carriages for hire crowding the streets, along with rude service and overcharging by whip-wielding cabbies. Solutions to this were already on the horizon, with plans for the first electric tram recently submitted to city hall.[22]

But not all matters could be resolved locally. And just as it is today, not everyone welcomed new businesses. All four of Stanislawow's pharmacists, upset about competition, unsuccessfully appealed to the governor of Galicia in protest of the planned opening of new apothecaries in town. Another newspaper article complained that the central government in Vienna was not raising the salaries of railway staff in line with growing revenues from Galician rails, which had amounted to 22 million kronen the previous year. It is safe to assume that Joseph Regiec was in full agreement with the latter argument.[23]

Then there were highly charged rumors, only to be denied days later, that Stanislawow might lose its status as headquarters of the Third Directorate of the Railway Administration, in favor of Czerniowce (which Joseph had left just a year previously). Not long before, the city had made major investments in buildings needed for the railroad administrators, and now the possible loss of prestige along with several well-paid jobs constituted an unnerving threat.[24] Wrangling among politicians and anxious petitions behind the scenes began in Vienna. Not unlike today, newspaper pundits quoted unnamed sources, who pontificated that moving the railway's regional headquarters to the Duchy of Bukovina would be a grave security mistake—owing to the Duchy's proximity to Russia, a potential enemy of the Austro-Hungarian Empire. Then, as suddenly as it had begun, the anxiety abated when the government announced unambiguously its need to retain Stanislawow as the communication hub. As though to make both sides happy, plans for future expansion of railway administration offices in Bukovina were disclosed at the same time.[25] This was typical of the way the government bureaucracy resolved contentious issues in the empire. We can be sure that Joseph and Stephania were relieved at the outcome of this debate, which could have threatened their plans for many years to come.

There were other kinds of news to be read about as well. Violence was rarely reported and, if mentioned, it was seldom with today's attention to gruesome details. But occasionally there were exceptions, as when both local and national newspapers reported sensational crimes from nearby Old Bohorodczany, which we will visit later in our story. One man in this quiet village town, it was reported, fell gravely ill and asked that the neighbors be invited to hear his final good-byes. When they gathered, he garnered his strength and insisted on having a "last" game of cards. This turned out to be quite an unusual game; as it was not going to his liking, the "frail" man grabbed an axe and managed to decapitate one of the guests.[26]

WHEN THE REGIEC FAMILY moved to Stanislawow, they settled in a spacious apartment at 1 St. Joseph Street. This recently completed building was conveniently situated within walking distance of a number of schools and the city center. In the summer of 1901, my grandmother, Helena, graduated from Queen Sophia's Middle School. For most 14-year-old girls, this would have marked the end of education. But Helena would continue to an all-women teachers' school, the equivalent of today's high school and junior college. She was considered lucky for at least two reasons. Perhaps Joseph and Stephania Regiec had been influenced by the successful career of Helena's aunt in Nowy Sacz, or perhaps they just saw the opportunity to help their daughter become an independent woman; in any case, they belonged to a then small group of parents who encouraged the education of girls beyond simple skills. My grandmother was also fortunate to live in Stanislawow, which was one of only a few cities in Galicia to offer such education—the highest level of learning then available to young women.

Stanislawow. The women's teachers' school that opened in 1893.
Helena Regiec graduated from this school in 1906.

Her new school had been established for less than a decade; it was under the able direction of Monsignor Franciscus Skarbowski, who ran a large institution by the standards of the time. Approximately 140 girls studied there for four years before taking final qualifying examinations. This education was not free, but the monthly tuition of up to 16 kronen (the equivalent of U.S. $85.00 today) was affordable.[27] Girls who aspired to education beyond middle school but did not want to become teachers had to wait a few more years before a school for them would open in Stanislawow.

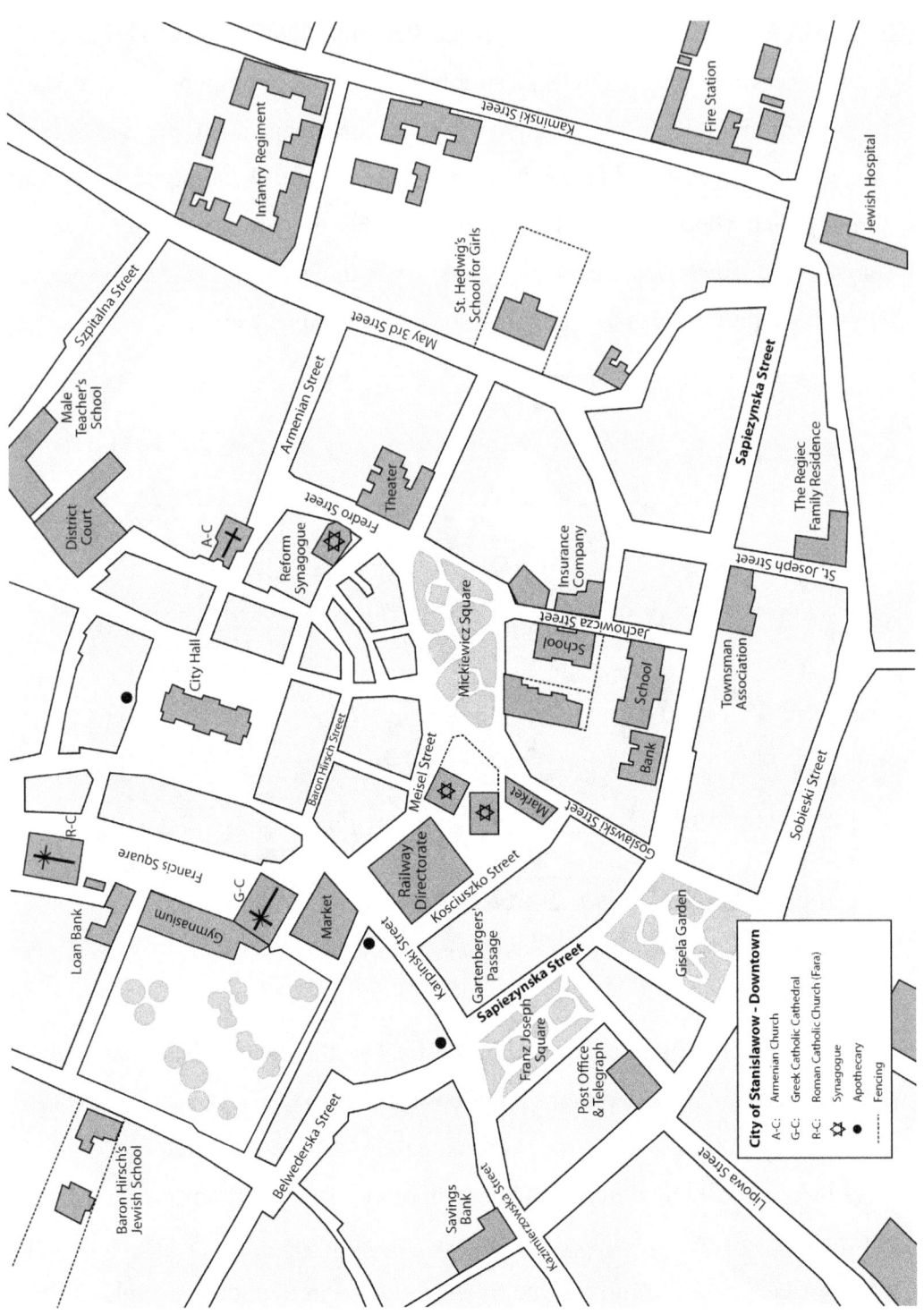

Map of Stanislawow. The city center with the Regiec family residence on St. Joseph Street and Joseph Regiec's office on Karpinski Street. *(Based on a map from 1904.)*

In late fall of the same year, unscheduled vacations came along when Stanislawow's schools closed for four weeks due to an epidemic of scarlet fever. Although the Regiec girls must have enjoyed this break, the city was clearly on edge. Scarlet fever was a highly contagious disease and still deadly in the absence of modern antibiotic therapy. Local apothecaries quickly advertised new home machines that were said to disinfect indoor air, for those who could afford such contraptions.[28] Lists of those affected by the illness, with their home addresses, were published weekly, as if to warn everyone away from visiting those with the disease. Clearly, privacy laws and customs differed from those today. As luck would have it, no one in the Regiec household became ill, and with the arrival of colder weather, schools reopened.

Wanda, Helena's younger sister, pursued a different type of education. Sometime during these first years in Stanislawow, she was enrolled in music school. Within a few years, she became a gifted pianist who, in due course, was repeatedly praised in the press for her talent. Surely, these references to Wanda's performances, during annual gala concerts at the end of each academic year, would have made her parents proud.[29]

Looking at a town map from the period, we can easily trace Joseph Regiec's daily routine. The walk from home to his office took no more than 20 minutes. This was surely a pleasant way to start the day; Stanislawow was considered a clean city with nice-looking streets.[30] Just after leaving home, Joseph, no doubt wearing a suit and the customary hat, would turn right. On the opposite side of the street were a few stores, including one with famous glass products from Bohemia and another offering warm quilts for sale. St. Joseph Street was a short one, with no more than six buildings on each side of the street, so after a minute or two, Joseph would turn left onto the much larger Sapiezynska Street, lined with numerous shops. This was considered a perfect place for shopping, meeting friends, or just watching others. By evening, the entire stretch of that street, from the apothecary on one end to

Stanislawow. Sapiezynska Street, the place to shop and stroll. *(Postcard from the early twentieth century.)*

Karlsbad's porcelain store on the other, would become the city promenade, with men and women enjoying a leisurely walk. Some gentlemen would comment, only half-jokingly, about having a busy time with repeated tipping of their hats while strolling back and forth on Sapiezynska Street.[31] Those with more time on their hands could stop to eat or drink and read a newspaper in one of the many cafes or confectioneries. On occasion, someone would lament that the waiters spoke German rather than Polish, and that too many Viennese newspapers were offered, but for the multilingual city, this was the reality.[32]

On weekday mornings, however, Joseph would not have had time to linger. Instead, he would walk toward the building of the Townsmen Bank and a few tailors' establishments with fine fabrics, in sight just ahead. At the first intersection, he would turn right onto Jachowicza Street. There were two schools along his path and, on most mornings, boys and girls in their mandatory school uniforms would have been rushing past Joseph to get to their separate schools on time. After cutting through a small square with a statue of a poet in the middle,

Stanislawow. Jachowicza Street, with buildings housing high schools and an insurance company. *(Postcard from the early twentieth century.)*

Stanislawow. Mickiewicz Square, with the towers of the Greek Catholic church and City Hall seen in the background. *(Postcard from the early twentieth century.)*

he would approach two small synagogues. Just a few more steps through Potocki Square, bearing the name of the city founder, and Joseph Regiec would have arrived at the entrance of his office, facing busy Karpinski Street.

On the building's street level were upscale stores: one with Swiss watches and another selling binoculars and microscopes. On the opposite side, an open market, an apothecary, and a few other stores could be seen. The railway administration headquarters were on the square, at the site of old city fortifications. The large building had been designed in Vienna but built by a construction company from Lvov. When completed, it had been leased to the railways for the next 20 years, earning a healthy profit for the city. My great-grandfather would work there at various administrative positions for the next several years.[33]

The first years in the city were surely exciting for all members of the Regiec family. Stanislawow offered various types of entertainment that Joseph, Stephania, and the girls had never had the opportunity to enjoy before. In 1902, a famous Viennese orchestra directed by one of the members of the musical Strauss family gave concerts in the city, albeit to mixed reviews. The public loved the sound and rhythm of the famous waltzes, especially *An der schönen blauen Donau,* although a local newspaper critic was quite upset with Maestro Strauss's undignified jumps up and down, with violin in hand, while directing the orchestra. In a scolding tone, the paper would mention that such behavior on stage might have been appropriate for Vienna, but not for properly behaving Stanislawow.[34]

There was no permanent dramatic company in Stanislawow, but the city was frequently visited by touring actors from Lvov or Vienna, and even by more exotic troupes from as far away as Japan. Dramatic and musical performances by amateur players were also common on the local stage. On such occasions, artistic tastes and prevailing fashion trends often collided with remarkable ferocity. Not uncommonly, post-performance reviews decried, "LADIES, HAVE

Chapter 3 — Stanisławow: The Stronghold of Rewera

Stanislawow. A picture of the theater building, which was erected in 1891. In later years, Wanda Regiec had her musical performances there. At times, the offices downstairs were rented (the sign over the entrance reads, "Trade School"). On the opposite site, the Reform synagogue is visible. *(Postcard from the early twentieth century.)*

MERCY." But this was not about the talents of female actors. Instead, theatergoers were complaining of the giant hats worn by the fashionable women of Stanislawow, which made watching a play or concert a strenuous exercise of neck muscles for those seated behind them. Men remarked on the wall of "colossal hats" resembling, in their words, "a hedge or a collection of flora from various climates." When the appeals to women to either take off their hats in the theater or purchase more expensive seats in the theater boxes went unheeded, some frustrated male theatergoers threatened to publish the names of the ladies who stubbornly wore such gigantic arrangements on their heads.[35]

Theatergoers. Fashionable, huge hats worn by women were the subject of frequent complaints by those trying to watch performances from behind. *(Die Muskete July 12, 1906; ÖNB, Vienna.)*

It is safe to assume that the young sisters, Helena and Wanda, were more likely interested in seeing a popular *Fotoplastikum* that showed images from around the world. These shows, an hour long, included three-dimensional pictures viewed by guests staring into a special apparatus. Before and after the shows, patrons relaxed in a comfortable waiting room lit by gas lamps, making comments that the views were so realistic that you could almost hear the sounds of those faraway places. Every week, a new show was introduced, and with a bit of imagination, we can envision the Regiecs among the audience when highly recommended shows about Philadelphia or New York City were on display.[36]

Newspaper advertisements for *Fotoplastikum* show (top) fifty pictures from Philadelphia, Baltimore, and Washington D.C.; (middle) "sightseeing" of the World's Fair in Chicago; and (bottom) sightseeing of New York [City] (as described in the ad, "the capital of the New World and the heart of American culture"). (*Kurjer Stanislawowski* 1903, 1904.)

Soon, other innovations arrived. The first of these, a so-called "electric theater" or cinematograph, started presenting short moving pictures on occasional visits to the city. In the summer months of 1905, two showings a week were given outdoors; these were described without much enthusiasm in the local press as "in focus and interesting."[37] By 1907, the first permanent movie theater, able to hold up to 200 patrons, had opened on elegant Sapiezynska Street. This was the first theater in all of Galicia to show the new invention, silent movies.[38] In just a few years, three movie theaters were operating in town; a weekly dose of these pictures was available to those interested. The films were received from Vienna after review by censors. They had to first pass a rather benign police review, and then be rated by the much stricter Viennese School Commission, which considered their appropriateness for younger audiences. The ratings were then made public, and subtitles in local languages were added. Not surprisingly, pictures deemed risqué were soon the most popular.[39]

These were also the years when automobiles began to appear on the roads, although they would remain beyond the means of the average person for a long time to come. We can only wonder what Joseph or Stephania would have thought about these horseless carriages; but it is safe to assume that some of the loud engines must have captured their attention on leisurely strolls. There were deeper signs of the changing times: The public was amazed at press reports of a

Cars were seen with increasing frequency on the roads, although during the snowy winters, horse-pulled sleighs were still considered more reliable means of transportation. (Die Muskete *May 17, 1906; ÖNB, Vienna.*)

commoner suing the Belgian king after being hit by an automobile the monarch was driving.[40] Clearly, a new era had arrived, and not only from a technological standpoint. Soon, there was talk of a city steam- or gas-powered omnibus service. Initially, its route was planned between the bustling train station and Stanislawow's downtown.[41]

There were related announcements that didn't seem to be taken seriously. Automobile drivers were not to exceed three miles per hour in busy urban places; this was reasoned to be appropriate because it was comparable to the speed of a pedestrian. They were permitted to move at nine miles per hour in other places, matching the pace of a trotting horse. Only in open spaces were cars allowed to drive at their full speed of approximately 30 miles per hour. The police also reminded citizens that these new machines required license plates—no exceptions.[42] In winter, however, there was no competition from such relatively untried inventions. Horse-drawn sleighs still ruled the roads, and residents of Stanislawow demanded that bells be attached to the harnesses to warn passersby.[43]

The city's original train station soon became too modest for this proud town that aspired to become the third metropolis of Galicia. Thus, a few years after the Regiec family settled there, an ambitious reconstruction of that building began. Tour books of the period described the refurbished terminal, completed in 1908, as one of the most elegant in Galicia; it had been built at the cost of 600,000 kronen (equivalent to U.S. $2.4 million today).[44]

In the summertime, Stanislawow was a convenient location for brief excursions. A short trip by carriage would have brought the Regiec family to the banks of the River Bystrzyca, a frequent spot for bathers and a nice place for a picnic. At times, members of the public would complain that cabbies refused to take city dwellers to this popular spot, wanting to avoid a long wait until their passengers were ready to head back to town. Young ladies were warned not to go there without a family escort; "horror stories" were published about pranksters throwing

Stanislawow. The original train station from the turn of the century (the town was linked with local and later national railways since 1866). The building underwent major reconstruction, with the new train station opening in 1907. *(Postcard from the early twentieth century.)*

girls' clothing into the river when they were in the water. We can only imagine the embarrassment of the unfortunate young ladies in long undergarments, looking for ways to get home unnoticed.[45]

There were other places for the family to go, particularly as Joseph's affiliation with the railways provided them with discounts on train travel. Early on, before Bronislawa Lösch's passing, there might have been a few trips back to visit her in Nowy Sacz. Or they could have taken a shorter train ride, only an hour or so, to the village of Jaremcze. Since 1894, when the railroad had connected this secluded village to the wider world, Jaremcze had become a favored summer destination for residents of Lvov as well as Stanislawow. With many villas, restaurants, and small hotels along the main road, it was considered the perfect place to relax, socialize, or just escape one's own dusty town. Well-marked trails through a pine forest brought visitors to a waterfall or led up the surrounding summits to the best places to view an impressive bridge spanning a deep mountain valley. By the time the Regiec family would have visited Jaremcze, its local attractions drew as many as 1,500 summer visitors every year. As today, however, vacationers complained of the increasing prices of rental accommodations; two-bedroom apartments for the summer were offered for the outrageous price of 200 or even 300 kronen (the equivalent of U.S. $1,020 or $1,530 today).[46]

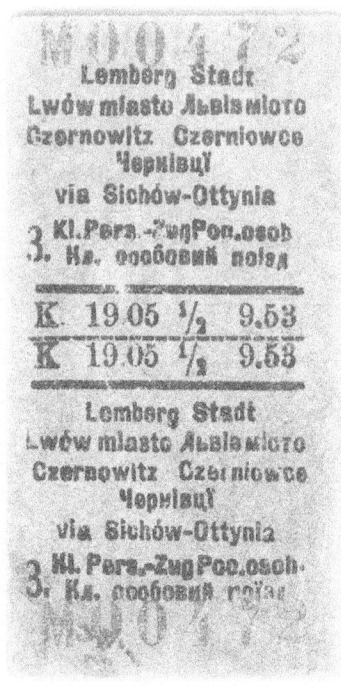

Train ticket printed in the three languages most commonly spoken in Galicia. The line connecting Lvov with Czerniowce (Bukovina) was passing through Stanislawow.

But the highlights of those years, for Helena, were trips taken with her family to faraway places within and even outside of the borders of Austro-Hungary. My grandmother would always remember her visits to Vienna and Venice. By the standards of the day, it was rare for a young woman to venture so far; only a few affluent people could afford to send their daughters on such eye-opening trips. The journey would start with a ride in a horse-drawn cab, which would carry the four, with their many pieces of luggage, to the train station about a mile from the city center. Once there, passengers could purchase tickets printed in Polish, Ruthenian, or German. For the average person, a ticket to Vienna cost about 46 kronen (equivalent to U.S. $245 today). But as my grandmother described it, Joseph Regiec and his family traveled at a special rate and in a special car furnished with separate bedroom compartments and an office to conduct business. At times, the car would be detached, so official duties could be completed at a particular location, to be reattached to the next train heading toward the capital of the empire.

Even if Joseph had no work to be done along the way, the journey from Stanislawow to Vienna could take up to 36 hours.[47] First, the train headed west via the Galician Transversal Railway or through the more northern route of the Galician Railway of Archduke Charles Louis. After traveling 410 miles in about 24 hours, passengers arrived in a west Galician town, where they changed to the Emperor Ferdinand Northern Railway. Those with more time could have a brief visit to the nearby city of Cracow. The last leg of the trip, 256 miles, took travelers beyond the borders of Galicia on a journey of up to 12 hours. First the train passed through Austrian Silesia and then, after taking a sharp turn south, it went through a mountain pass and parts of today's Czech Republic before finally reaching Vienna's Nordbahnhof station.

Despite the name "Austro-Hungarian Empire" and the country's dual monarchy, Vienna retained an undisputed role as the empire's splendid capital. Budapest, the Hungarian seat of govenment, was a great city; but old Vienna could not be matched. There were many attractions for visitors, including stately palaces, museums, the opera house, and frequent concerts. For the young Helena, there were a few images that stayed in her memory for years. The Ringstrasse, as she later recalled, was a broad avenue encircling the city center, with elegant buildings along its way; it was considered one of the finest streets in Europe. There was a variety of trams in town—some were still pulled by horses, others were powered by steam; and then there was the most recent invention, powered by electricity.

As they would have done today, Helena's parents surely took their children to the city's famous museums and galleries. Years later, however, Helena would not mention Vienna's paintings or sculptures. Instead, it was the Museum of Natural History that made the biggest impression on her, with its displays of rare rocks, precious gems, and even meteorites. She also remembered a collection of medical curiosities, including one jar that was said to contain a preserved human stomach full of fingernails. Many years later, this would become the highlight of my grandmother's scary warnings about what might happen to children who bit their nails.[48]

Helena Regiec as a student in the women's teachers' school in Stanislawow.

Another place that Helena would remember was the Prater. This public park, on the grounds of a former imperial hunting retreat, featured many coffeehouses and fine restaurants; broad avenues were lined with chestnut trees for leisurely strolls or rides in horse-drawn carriages. But the main attraction for the Regiec girls was the amusement park, which had even more enjoyable activities—in particular, the Viennese Giant Wheel (*Wiener Riesenrad*), which had been erected for the golden jubilee of the emperor Franz Joseph. The Regiec family could sit in one of the large gondolas attached to its rim and, in just a few minutes, they would enjoy a breathtaking panoramic view high above Vienna.[49]

∽

Back home, Stanislawow also offered attractions. In June of 1905, an exciting trade show was in town. This touring exhibit displayed various new products manufactured in Galicia. The city was blanketed with posters announcing free admission; schools arranged trips for their students, and the press asked the public to support Galician businesses by attending. In two days, 8,000 people saw the show. A broad range of products was on display, from a precursor of decaffeinated coffee (called "healthy coffee") to trendy tiled stoves that offered homes both warmth and a decorative touch. Locally made sweets in elaborate wrappings were said to compare well with similar products imported from Paris.[50]

Some complained that not enough men from Stanislawow were in attendance—in any case, a few of the immediate needs of local businesses were being addressed when speakers appealed to visiting women to demand Galician merchandise when shopping. In the long run, however, the exhibit was seen as a way to convince the younger generation that there were many professions waiting for them in Galicia. But despite all the novelties on display, local newspapers mockingly reminded the public of a paradox: The interior of the main post office was still lit by antiquated kerosene lighting, while the city prison would soon enjoy modern gas lamps.[51]

Regardless of this fact, a construction boom was definitely visible around Stanislawow. Opening early in 1905 was the Parisian-style Gartenbergers' Passage, an elegant shopping arcade where the public strolled from one shop to another under a high glass ceiling. A previously unattractive inner courtyard squeezed between buildings had been transformed into a chic place, allowing passersby to enter through one of five enticing gates. Inside, large windows displayed attractive merchandise under gas lights, adding not only convenience but extra ambience. For those interested in technology, the Norbert Ehrlich store was the place, offering a new American invention, the typewriter. Just next door was the even more popular Cafe Edison, with live music by a military band or Hungarian gypsies, and a quieter reading room. The Passage quickly became the spot to meet other shoppers, take a quick shortcut from one street to another, or just have a break in the cafe. It isn't difficult to imagine two young sisters, Helena and Wanda Regiec, on occasion with their mother, Stephania, walking through the Passage, glancing through the windows at the many items on display.[52]

Several other buildings, with large apartments boasting the most desirable addresses, were being erected around this time on Sapiezynska Street, so often frequented by the Regiec family. Some hoped that with all this construction, apartment rents would soon become more affordable for railway employees. However,

Stanislawow. Gartenbergers' Passage was an enclosed shopping area with elegant shops and the popular Cafe Edison.

in May of the following year—the traditional month for lease renewal—many were described as "suspended between heaven and earth" (or between dreams and reality) wondering what had happened to those more affordable places to live. In the end, such hopes turned out to be only wishful thinking.[53]

In the summer of that year, quite a different event took place. Stanislawow, not to be outdone by other European cities, witnessed a bit of Americana. The famous Buffalo Bill's Wild West Show visited the city for two performances. This complex enterprise included 800 people and 500 horses, which arrived in three specially designed trains. Thousands of spectators lined the streets to watch the horse-drawn covered wagons and performers of "The Congress of Rough Riders of the World" in their native costumes, riding magnificent steeds through town. After this exotic procession reached a large field next to the military grounds, stables and a huge tent containing an arena with 12,000 seats were erected within only three hours. The kitchen, powered by an electric generator and with cooks in white uniforms, was quickly ready to serve meals

Stanislawow. The corner of Kazimierzowska and Sobieski streets in the downtown.
(Postcard from the early twentieth century.)

to the performers. With crowds from surrounding areas descending on the city, the atmosphere could be only compared to today's rock concerts. But the unaccustomed audience was a bit taken aback by assaults on their wallets when Buffalo Bill programs, Buffalo Bill drinks, Buffalo Bill souvenirs, and other items were incessantly offered for purchase.

The performance itself featured riders and marksmen from around the world. Certainly it was the first time that Stanislawow had witnessed Native American, Mexican, Gaucho, Arab, Cossack, and Japanese riders all in the flesh in one place! There were many re-creations of the sort of cowboys-and-Indians tales that had shaped Europeans' views of the American frontier. A happy ending was always a must—although ferocious-looking Indians attacked a settler's cabin, they were quickly repelled by Colonel Cody (Buffalo Bill himself), who dashed to the rescue on horseback with a group of mounted cowboys.

Only 45 minutes after the last spectator had left the big tent, the field was emptied; and the show left Stanislawow that night. Later, some wondered which had been more exciting: the show itself or seeing this amazing operation appear and disappear without a glitch. Press reviews were mixed, but the event was a success for the Buffalo Bill enterprise, reportedly bringing in more than 40,000 kronen (equivalent to U.S. $202,000 today).[54]

The year 1908 began for Stanislawow with a heavy snowfall; many roads were closed, and railway transport was canceled for days. The city felt like one under siege, cut off from the rest of the world without even mail or newspaper deliveries. Heroic efforts had to be undertaken to rescue unfortunate train passengers; some had become stranded between cities, their tracks buried under massive amounts of snow.[55] Nonetheless, winter brought good news to the Regiec family. In early January, there was the announcement of a long-anticipated promotion for Joseph. His new position as commissioner in the Department of Revenues for the Regional Railway Directorate meant an increase in annual salary to 2,600 kronen (equivalent to U.S. $72,400 today). Surely, it must also have been welcome news at 1 St. Joseph Street that the new rank carried four paid weeks of vacation per year, a rare benefit in those days. And contrary to the family's earlier experiences with Joseph's advancements, there was no need for them to relocate.[56]

Toward the end of the year, a different type of celebration took place in Stanislawow and far beyond its boundaries. The entire Austro-Hungarian Empire was rejoicing at the 60th anniversary of Franz Joseph as emperor. News traveled fast about a spectacular light show in front of the Imperial Palace in Vienna, attended by 1.5 million spectators. In Stanislawow, a 24-gun salute and a military parade started the day; the downtown was decorated with flags, and commemorative pictures of the monarch were displayed in many windows. But the occasion was likely welcomed in the Regiec household for other reasons as well: First, Railway Directorate employees were given the day off. Second, Joseph Regiec was awarded the Jubilee Cross and the commemorative medal for civil administration; no doubt, those were reasons for a small celebration at 1 St. Joseph Street.

Many other citizens would be recognized by the state with honors and decorations, and commentaries in the raucous Galician press were unusually polite and respectful toward the emperor, who was generally depicted as a wise, elderly man. Some noted that he had begun his rule as an absolute monarch in a time of great crisis; 60 years later, he was a respected constitutional monarch, presiding once again over what was described as a weakened Austro-Hungarian Empire. Hopes were expressed by many that, with the passage of time, Galicia would evolve even further toward a federal model of increasing self-governance.[57]

The cartoon "Older Statesman" carried the caption, "My ladies, don't worry about Austria! I've been declared dead so many times!" It was published on the 60th anniversary of Franz Joseph's becoming emperor. (Die Muskete *December 3, 1908;* ÖNB, Vienna.)

☙

With the first decade of the twentieth century coming to a close, Joseph had many reasons to feel a bit of satisfaction. He was much closer to that place in life where he had so wanted to be when starting his career in a small school in the countryside. Not much is known about Joseph's and Stephania's married life, but no stories of trouble at home were ever recalled by my grandmother. Their union had given them two daughters, now in their early twenties, who were approaching a time of decision about their own lives. Professionally, Joseph's perseverance had paid off, and he was feeling secure in the career that had brought him to a comfortable existence in Stanislawow. News of this hard-earned success even traveled back to some of the places that he had passed through along his path.[58]

More important than his own professional success, or even despite it, Joseph was a good man who remained interested in the welfare of others. As a former teacher, he always retained a keen interest in education. On top of his professional obligations, Joseph volunteered in some of his spare time, becoming active in an association that supported Galicia's schools and aimed at improving their curricula. By coincidence or by choice, this was the same civic organization, the Folk School Association, in which his sister-in-law, Bronislawa, had been active; Joseph was elected to the executive committee of Stanislawow's chapter out of more than 600 members. On their behalf, he and others were empowered to provide financial help to six schools in the area.[59] Perhaps with Joseph's vision and support, the group thought of attracting more people to their reading rooms by offering more than newspapers, magazines, and books. They also began to provide free legal advice, a service that was initiated in 1910. Apparently, this campaign turned out to be very successful, not only helping to raise the educational level of Stanislawow's citizens but also, in a more immediate way, aiding those who had to deal with the town's sometimes overwhelming bureaucracy.

Over the years, Joseph would often contribute to projects that educated the less fortunate, indicating that he was a man of conviction who had stayed his course—even though his current profession took him away from the classroom. He also joined an organization providing financial assistance to a local boys' orphanage. Looking at this from afar, his small contributions to this noble cause might be seen as a mere matter of paying annual dues, hardly worth mentioning. But to us, knowing Joseph Regiec's life story, it seems that this more likely had a deep personal meaning for a man who knew what it was to grow up without a mother.[60]

Chapter 4

BOHORODCZANY:

A WORLD IN ITSELF

---❦---

Map of Bohorodczany and the surrounding communities. To the northwest of town on the other side of the river, a cluster of farms and fields in Old (Stare) Bohorodczany is visible. To the southwest, the village of Lachowce stretches along the River Bystrzyca. *(Based on a map of the region from 1880.)*

*O*UR JOURNEY THROUGH TIME NOW takes us to a different place, one that will play a special role in this story. In the town of Bohorodczany, two families would cross paths—one that we have already met and another, yet to be introduced. Even a cursory look at the origins, aspirations, and life experiences of both families would show that the Regiecs and the Sobolewskis were quite different. For the old Sobolewski family, Bohorodczany was an ancestral home. A livelihood centered on the land had defined the family from one generation to another. But for young Helena Regiec, coming from a family that thrived on change and the steady pursuit of opportunities, the town must have felt a bit strange at first—perhaps more like a brief stop than a permanent home.

Bohorodczany, a district town in eastern Galicia, was only about 9.5 miles south of Stanislawow.[1] It lay in a beautiful spot at the foothills of the Carpathian Mountains, near the River Bystrzyca, which took its name from rapids rushing through stony riverbeds. The place was a microcosm of the rural society of Galicia, now long gone—with its strengths but also its prejudices. It forms one more example of the complex, easy-to-misinterpret, and quite amazing human diversity of Galicia, which constitutes an important part of our story.

The origin of the town's name is not entirely clear; it may reflect what the Virgin Mary was called in the old Slavic languages (Bohoroditsa). It was sometimes known as Brotchin or Brodshin in Yiddish or Bogorodchany (Богородчани) in Ruthenian. In any case, it was an old settlement dating back to 1441, when it had belonged to a royal official.[2] From the latter part of the fifteenth century, Bohorodczany and the surrounding region became part of the estates of the aristocratic Potocki family, the same clan that founded the city of Stanislawow.

For centuries, the town's main connection with the outside world was by a government road. This was an ancient trans-Carpathian thoroughfare, originating far west in Silesia and then, like a thread through fabric, traversing the western part of Galicia, passing through many towns and over many rivers to reach its eastern segment. From there, it continued to Stanislawow, where it took a sharp turn to the south, as if avoiding the borders of tsarist Russia. Advancing further south, it crossed the Carpathians, finally arriving in Bukovina, a far-flung province of the Austro-Hungarian Empire that we have visited before.

By 1880, the population of Bohorodczany had grown to 4,597; census information on religious affiliations and spoken languages gives a clear picture of the place's diversity at the time. The largest group in town was the Jewish community of 2,009 people. Jews had lived in Bohorodczany and the surrounding area for as long as anyone could remember. In written records, they are mentioned for the first time when they paid a head tax of 756 gold coins in 1717. Over the next 200 years, the community of Israelites continued to grow, at one point accounting for at least half the local population. Under Austrian rule, census after census shows a large number of Jews, living mainly in the town with only a few in the surrounding villages. They were engaged in leasing, innkeeping, the lumber trade, and manufacturing of linen from locally grown flax.[3] Thus, it will not be surprising when we meet several Jewish merchants a bit later in our story.

Chapter 4 — Bohorodczany: A World in Itself 135

Bohorodczany. The interior of one of the town's synagogues.
(Photograph from the beginning of twentieth century.)

This was also a community that looked after its members in need. A local Jewish charity for the poor and sick had operated there since 1870.[4]

Not far from the town's center was the synagogue courtyard (*shulhoyf*), where several places of worship were found, including the "Great" Synagogue (*Groyse shul*) with its study hall (*Beit Midrash*), and the "General" Synagogue (*Algemayner shul*), as well as the Vizhnits and Stretin Hasidic synagogues. Every Sabbath, the place was filled with people coming to worship and to exchange local news and gossip.[5]

Next in size was a large population of Greek Catholics, consisting mainly of Ruthenians. In the census of 1880, these totaled 1,788 inhabitants, who belonged to the archdiocese of Lvov. At the beginning of the twentieth century, their wooden church, in outward appearance much like other churches in the countryside, attracted visitors from many places in eastern Galicia who admired its famous wall of old icons (*ikonostas*). This unique work of religious art, which some thought bore resemblances to works of the Flemish masters, had been created elsewhere between 1699 and 1705, and had later been bought by the Ruthenian community of Bohorodczany. On occasion, the town hosted high dignitaries from the Greek Catholic hierarchy arriving to see the *ikonostas*.[6] The Greek Catholic parish also served inhabitants of the small rural settlements of Pochowka and Skobyszowka. By 1880, this extended parish, including not only the town but surrounding villages, numbered 2,807.

Roman Catholics, 800 altogether, were mainly Poles and a few families of German or Bohemian origin; they were clearly the smallest group, although not necessarily the weakest when it came to local influence. Their parish had been established in 1691 by Constantia Potocka, remembered as the widow of the king's treasurer. (As the owners of small towns and villages, many Potockis donated money and land so that churches could be erected in the region.)[7] Over the years, the parish grew, and with this growth came many changes to the appearance of the building, which would become a landmark of the town. In 1742, the original wooden church was replaced with a brick structure, followed by the addition of a Dominican cloister in 1762. From then on, friars in their distinctive white robes became a permanent fixture of the parish, not only tending to religious matters but working in the surrounding fields.

Entries in the church's books from the early eighteenth century mention rare visits by "*Illustrissimo Magnifico Dominus* (Illustrious Magnificent Master) Josephus Potocki." A son of the founder of neighboring Stanislawow and a colorful magnate, he was the owner of these lands. Powerful but often betting on the wrong horse in the Kingdom of Poland's confusing alliances, Joseph Potocki was also the overseer of the eastern Kiev province and was the crown's grand hetman. He was deferentially referred to as *Palatinus Kieviensis* and *Duci Regni* (Crown Duke).[8] Since he was frequently away on military campaigns, his daughter, Sophia (married to Dominic Kossakowski, another noble), and other members of his

Chapter 4 — Bohorodczany: A World in Itself

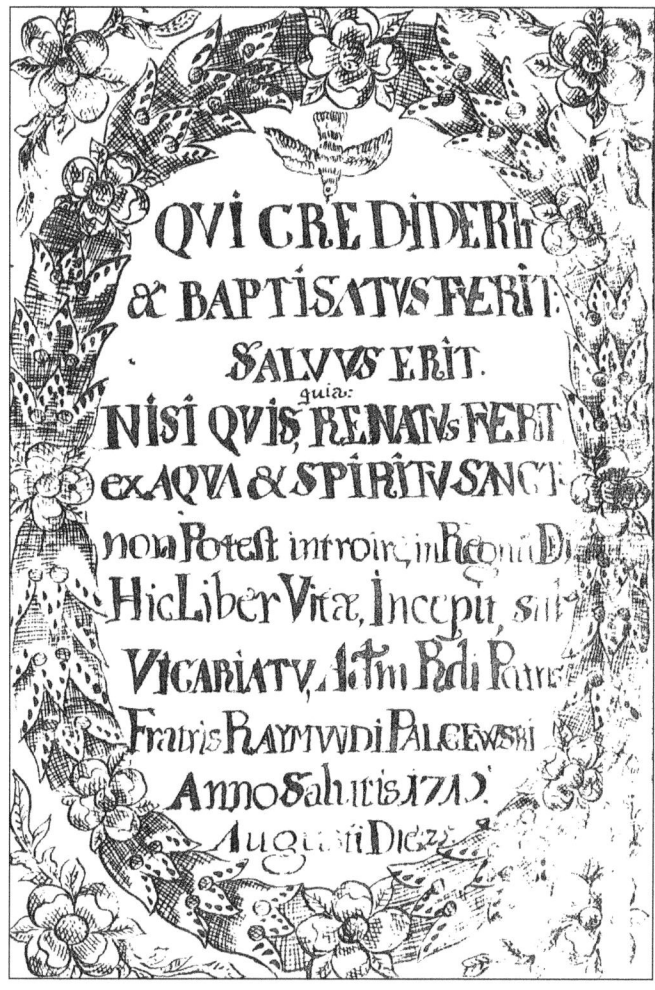

The book of baptisms from the Dominican church in
Bohorodczany *(dated 1715).*

family were more often mentioned in local records.[9] We can only assume that on their visits, the Potocki and Kossakowski families stayed in a small fortress castle that stood in Bohorodczany at the time.

Although this small, provincial town was far from the capitals of Europe, it once welcomed a group of very high-ranking celebrants. There must have been a big commotion in town when on June 6, 1744, a series of esteemed visitors related to two royal families arrived in their carriages. With many members of the powerful Potocki clan also in attendance, twin boys newly born into the Leszczynski family were baptized, with much fanfare, in Bohorodczany's church. The Leszczynskis were not an ordinary family; the infants' father was closely related to the former king of Poland, Stanislaus Leszczynski, who during his struggles to hold on to the throne, had always had an ardent supporter in Joseph Potocki.[10] We can safely suspect that the grand hetman's steadfast defense of the king's cause was not only a matter of his own convictions; perhaps the influence of his wife, Victoria, contributed to his political choices as well. Indeed, this would not be surprising, as some claimed that Victoria was Stanislaus Leszczynski's sister. But the links with royalty did not end there. Upon marrying the French monarch Louis XV, King Leszczynski's daughter Marie had become queen of France, reigning from 1725 to 1768. Thus, for a brief moment, and with a bit of imagination, a baptism in remote Bohorodczany brought the place closer to two royal courts of Europe.

Over the next 170 years, Bohorodczany's Roman Catholic church continued to evolve; ultimately, it would become the highest structure in town. From the beginning of the twentieth century, its characteristic facade with two belltowers would be featured on postcards. Record books from the church have survived, offering us a unique glimpse of this community; they show that the parish eventually extended to a series of

Bohorodczany. The Roman Catholic church, with its distinctive towers. *(Postcard from the beginning of the twentieth century.)*

smaller villages with names like Old Bohorodczany, Grabowiec, Horocholina, and Lachowce.[11]

Bohorodczany was primarily a farming community. Its boundaries included more than a market square and the surrounding houses; there were also large farms, meadows, apple and pear orchards, and pastures, all not far from the town's center. Some of the less wealthy residents cultivated small farm plots scattered throughout the area. During Austrian times, undoubtedly Count Franz Stadion, and later his brother Rudolph, were the largest property owners. They owned arable land, several mills, and a large forested area outside of Bohorodczany.

Bohorodczany. Manor house from where the Stadions' estate was administered.
(Postcard from the beginning of the twentieth century.)

Over the decades, the members of the Stadion family had distinguished themselves as bankers and politicians, serving the Austrian crown in many posts, including the governorships of Galicia and Moravia.[12] They had purchased big swaths of an old property in 1837, after the government took possession of Polish crown lands from the Potocki family. Ownership of the estate remained solidly in the hands of the Stadions until the end of 1918.[13] Running it was a big business, requiring a steady supply of local contractors and farmworkers. Within the town's boundaries was a self-governing manor house occupied by those administering and working on the estate, with more than 50 listed inhabitants.

The Stadion family oversaw their huge estate from afar, probably not living in the town for any notable period of time. At the beginning of the twentieth century, advertisements for bids to manage, among other holdings, the forests of the estate, originated in Chodenschloss, Bohemia, rather than from a local address.[14] Despite their impact on the community as an employer and an occasional benefactor to civic causes, the Stadions did not have a single member born, married, or buried in the district.

Bohorodczany was also the district seat. It had a local commission to regulate land taxation and a collection office, probably not much appreciated by

Bohorodczany. The district offices are seen in the foreground with the Roman Catholic church visible in the background. *(Postcard from the beginning of the twentieth century.)*

those being taxed. There were a few other institutions, including a district court, a notary, and a gendarmerie headquarters occupied by just a few men. A small post office in town was not too busy, being staffed by a single contract postmaster. Every few years, the male citizens of Bohorodczany elected not only a representative to the Galician *diet* in Lvov, but also one deputy to the national parliament in faraway Vienna.[15]

At the beginning of the twentieth century, Bohorodczany grew to a town of more than 600 houses, two elementary schools, and two registered Jewish schools. The official statistics also noted several religious institutions. Bohorodczany at this time had a stable population of approximately 4,700, dominated as in prior years by Jews and Greek Catholics. Most of the rest of the inhabitants identified themselves as Roman Catholics, with just a few others of less common faiths.

In those times, one's religion often determined one's spoken language. It comes as a surprise that German was listed as the primary tongue of approximately 2,000 people, which would have been nearly half the population. However, the apparent predominance of German, in fact, reflected the Jewish majority in town, which spoke mainly Yiddish. As in the rest of Galicia, Yiddish was not officially recognized as a separate language; thus, it was frequently, though incorrectly, designated as German.

BOHORODCZANY ALWAYS STRADDLED TWO worlds: one connected to its self-contained pastoral heritage and the other requiring a degree of entrepreneurship. In 1870, it was hard to find many businesses there—just three tanneries processing animal hides, a small distillery, and a couple of breweries. Those who did not own land were employed in leather processing, in shoemaking, or on farms as seasonal workers. But the picture started to change with the

Bohorodczany. The market square was surrounded by one-story townhouses. On the left side of the main road, there was a Greek Catholic church (*Heil. Dreyfaltigkeit*, Church of the Holy Trinity*)*, with the Roman Catholic church (*Maria Heimsuchung*, Church of the Visitation of the Blessed Virgin Mary) situated →

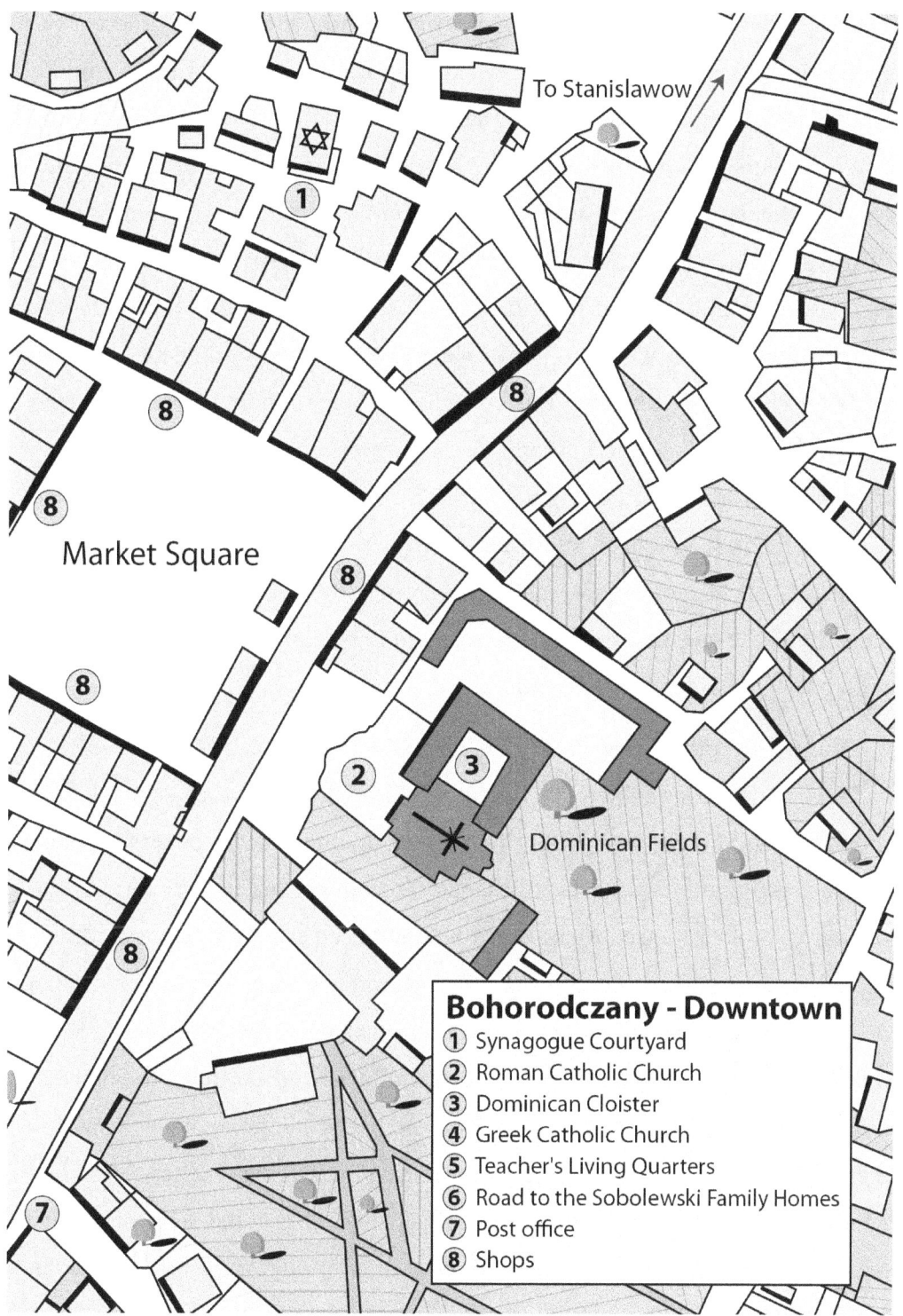

across the road. Several synagogues were located just north of the market square. The agricultural fields are clearly visible within the town's boundaries. *(Based on the section of a cadastral map from 1878.)*

dawn of a new century. As if slowly shifting its profile to address the changing needs of its population, Bohorodczany in the first decade of the twentieth century had many more businesses than before. Small retail or manufacturing establishments were mainly owned by Jews, with a few Polish stores and only a few Ruthenian owners. There were two simple restaurants, owned by Leib Klarberg and Franciszek Swietlik. In the absence of modern plumbing and running water, an important institution was the public bathhouse, run by Simon Meyer Rubin. As there was no gas or electricity, the firewood needed by residents for cooking and heating was brought from surrounding forests and sold from several lumberyards.[16] There was a barbershop for haircuts, trimming stubborn mustaches, or getting a good shave for big occasions; it was owned by Mendel Barci. For those interested in leather saddles and various pieces of harness, Chaim Bauch's store was in town. These items came in quite handy if one wanted to ready a horse for a quick gallop to a neighboring village or go for a more leisurely ride in a small carriage.

There were other, more complex businesses as well. The busy town now had several tanneries owned and operated by Jewish proprietors. Aron Geller's shop applied different dyes to fabrics, making among other products the thin, decorative ribbons bought by Ruthenians to adorn Sunday dresses. If you wanted to build a house, bricks could be purchased from a brickyard administered on behalf of the Stadion family. A chimney service was offered by Jan Bednarczuk, and lumber came from a mill owned by Herzel Halpern. There was a small savings bank and, for the more affluent and cautious, the office of insurance agent Michal Polluk offered life and fire protection policies as well as crop insurance against occasionally devastating hailstorms. The town also had a local "garage" for renting or repairing carriages. One could send or receive telegrams at a telegraph office, but there were no public or private phones in town as late as 1912.

Chapter 4 — Bohorodczany: A World in Itself

Bohorodczany. The courthouse. *(Postcard from the beginning of the twentieth century.)*

Health and safety issues seem to have been well-covered in Bohorodczany. The town had three local physicians, a veterinarian, and four midwives.[17] The local apothecary was owned initially by Simon Edelmann and later by Henryk Löwner, both from the Jewish community. The nearest hospital was in the larger city of Stanislawow, but it was seldom considered as an option. Order in town was maintained by four policemen. The district court in Bohorodczany was situated in a small house by the main road; the appellate court was in neighboring Stanislawow. The district court's jurisdiction extended over the town and the surrounding villages; it grew from an office occupied by a single judge and a few clerks in 1907 to one with five judges, seven clerks, and two court messengers in 1912. But despite their provincial location, these judges could impact the lives of the townspeople in very unforgiving ways, as will become apparent later in this story.

A small road and a bridge linked Bohorodczany with the village of Old Bohorodczany, situated just one-quarter mile to the northwest. As described in 1880, the town and the village were separated by the River Bystrzyca. Old

Bohorodczany was mainly an agricultural place, dotted with numerous small farmers' plots, a few orchards, pastures, and a forest. As in the neighboring town, the largest property, far surpassing all the peasant lands taken together, belonged to Count Stadion. The population of 3,551 was mainly Ruthenian, with 3,106 Greek Catholics, 415 Jews, and only 30 Roman Catholics. There was a local Greek Catholic parish, a small school, and a loan office for farmers. By 1907, Old Bohorodczany had grown to 4,029 people, with approximately 3,900 of them self-identifying as Ruthenian based on their primary spoken language. By that time, the village had more than 650 farmhouses and two manor houses with 122 people living on their premises.[18]

In the opposite direction was Lachowce (Ляхівці in Ruthenian), situated about two miles southwest of Bohorodczany. The village was another simple farming settlement that will also become important in our story.[19] This was more or less a rural suburb, with inconspicuous mounds marking its boundaries. In the center of Lachowce, the small St. Nicholas Greek Catholic Church stood, entirely surrounded by fields. There were no other places of worship in the village; the few residents of the Jewish and Roman Catholic faiths belonged to congregations in Bohorodczany. The River Bystrzyca, which flowed from the mountains south of the village, divided itself into many tributaries in and around Lachowce. On the river's east side, a stream called Dzwiniacz emptied into it; on the west side, simple farm buildings could mainly be seen.

Despite its seemingly obscure location, the village had first been mentioned in local records as early as 1441, when its then owner agreed to pay a large sum of money to the governor of Lvov.[20] Prior to the First Partition of Poland in 1772, Lachowce was part of the crown lands, and was owned and administered by the Potocki family. But with changes taking place in the region, the Austrian government took full possession of large landholdings there in 1787. At the time,

Chapter 4 — Bohorodczany: A World in Itself

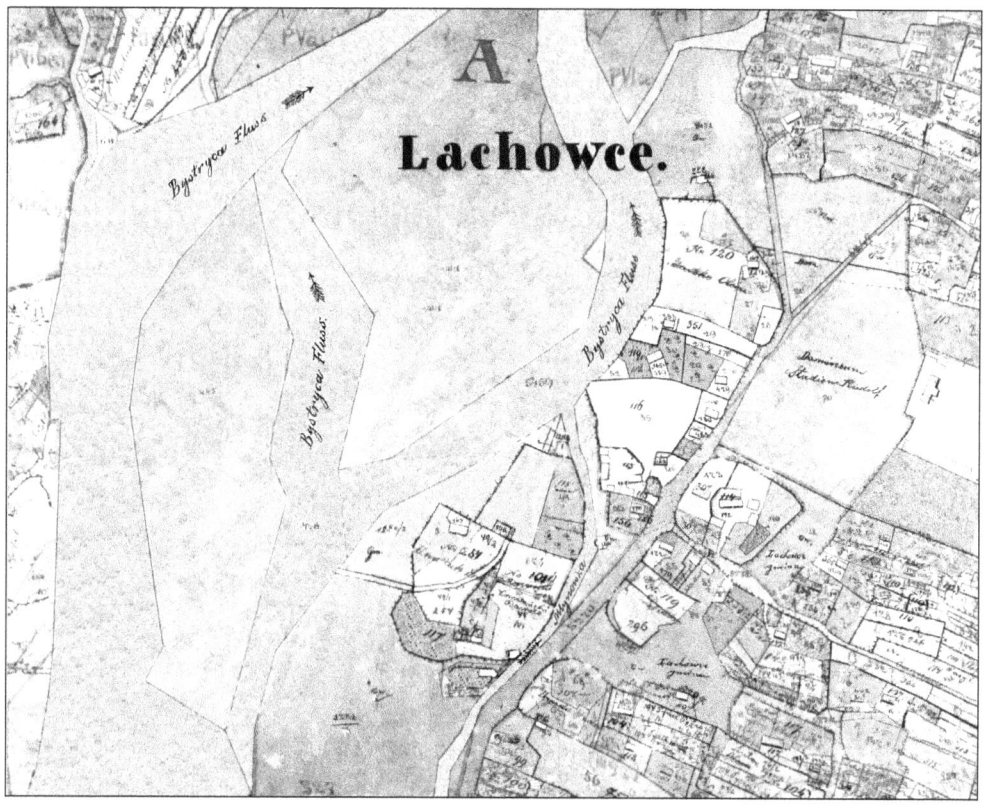

Lachowce. Map of the village south of Bohorodczany situated by the River Bystrzyca (Bystryca Fluss). *(Section of a cadastral map from 1848.)*

Lachowce was a collection of mostly small farming plots, with characteristically narrow strips of land to allow access from the few simple country roads. By 1837, the unoccupied land in and around Lachowce had been bought by the Stadion family, which established ownership over a large estate in the village as well. The contrast could not have been greater between the tiny plots, many of them farmed by peasants who were still serfs, and the large expanses of territory belonging to the Stadions.

In 1880, nearly 2,000 people lived on 414 small farms spread throughout Lachowce. Not much would change there over the years; a quarter-century later, the census recorded 2,337 inhabitants, the vast majority of them identified as Greek Catholics (2,195), followed by Jews and a small minority of Roman Catholics. Most lived in simple huts; only a few affluent inhabitants occupied six

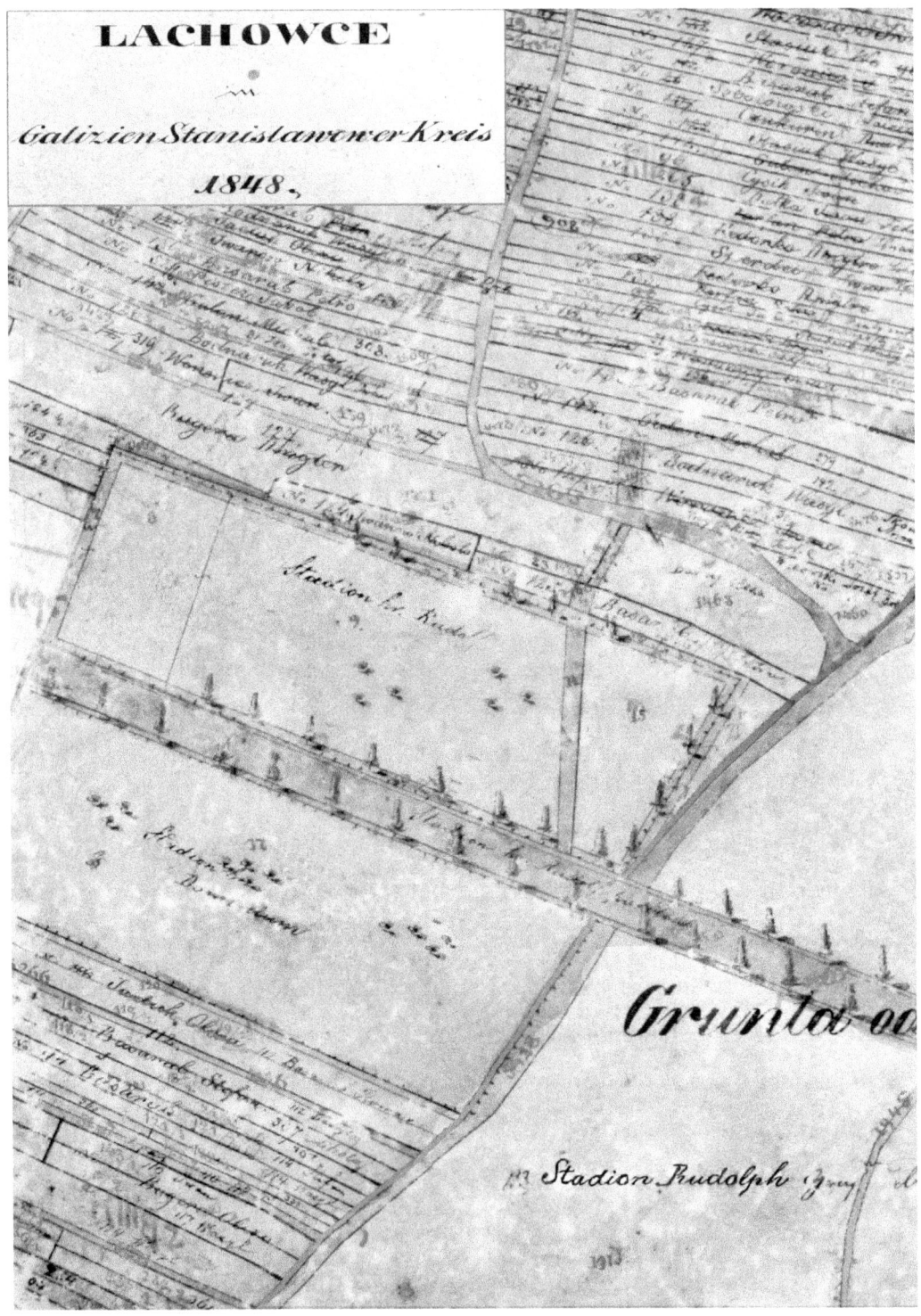

Lachowce. Map showing the Stadion estate that straddled Lachowce (left) and Bohorodczany (right).

Its size contrasted with narrow strips of land owned or leased by local peasants.
(Section of a cadastral map from 1848.)

small manor houses. The most common language spoken there was Ruthenian, probably followed by Yiddish. There were only a few public institutions, namely a simple school and a savings bank. To the village's southeast, there was a settlement called Horocholina. To the west were other rural hamlets, Hlebowka and Sadzawa. Forests covered a nearby summit that rose to the height of 1,332 feet.[21]

Finally, there was Starunia, a village approximately 11 miles south of Bohorodczany and not far from the neighboring district town of Solotwina.[22] As in the other places around Bohorodczany, there were several small streams joining larger rivers flowing from the mountains. The landscape here was hillier, with the highest point, 1,899 feet, on the village's southern border. Starunia was mainly known for its natural resources; since at least 1881, oil had been pumped from shallow deposits. The discovery of petroleum there led to a short-lived boom and a few dreams that reached beyond reality. Some considered global trade in these newly discovered riches; one of the boldest plans was put forward by a merchant from Shanghai, who had actually approached a local Austro-Hungarian consul about exporting Galician oil all the way to China. When the news arrived home, those involved in the business entertained this idea for a time; but after a great deal of heated deliberation, the scheme was dismissed as impractical because of the distance and transportation issues, not to mention punishing tariffs imposed by Austro-Hungary on its own exports.[23]

The Starunia area yielded occasional reminders of strange creatures that had roamed the region eons before. Time after time, geologists accidentally discovered bones and mummified fragments of ancient animals. These were dug up and slowly made their way to the museums of Galicia. In October 1929, the village of Starunia made a big splash in the news when land surveyors discovered the almost intact remains of an ancient woolly mammoth. Pictures have survived of the mummified giant with a large trunk.

Chapter 5

THE SOBOLEWSKI CLAN:

NOBLES AND FARMERS

The statement under oath by the representatives from Lachowce attesting to the accuracy of the census that was completed in their village on March 28, 1787. The signatures of the witnesses from Bohorodczany and other neighboring settlements are also recorded. The Josephine land census carried out across the entire Austrian empire was a massive undertaking. It provides today unprecedented description of small towns, villages, individual landholdings, and locally grown crops.

*T*HE SOBOLEWSKI FAMILY WAS AN ancient one that had been recognized as nobility for centuries. Over time, however, it became a matter of debate who had been the first of record in their long line of ancestors. Some said that the earliest known forebear had been a simple man named Kula from the village of Sobolów. That would have given Kula's descendants the original spelling of the name Sobolo(e)wski. The village was a small place not far from Cracow, in the south of the Kingdom of Poland; it was known to have existed for centuries, having first been recorded as early as 1105.

Others believed that the Sobolewski family could trace its roots to Paul (*Pawel*) Kula Sobolewski, who had taken part in a provincial council, the details of which had long been forgotten. Regardless of the true origin of the family, the name "Sobolo(e)wski" first surfaces in tax records from the Cracow region dating back to 1564. That year, a man by that name paid a tax as part-owner of a village called Janowice.[1] By amazing coincidence, the Regiec family would be living in and around that same village centuries later. But let's not get too far ahead in time.

An early document, from August 1616, with the name "Sobolo(e)wski." Albertus Sobolo(e)wski is mentioned as a godfather to children born in the village belonging to Tropie parish.

I also stumbled across another early member of the family while looking through barely legible records from a small parish in the same area. The name of Albertus Sobolo(e)wski appeared as godfather to many local children born between 1616 and 1620. We can only presume that his popularity in the village was a testament to his character and generosity.

Like seeds carried on the wind that become seedlings on fertile soil, in time the Sobolewski name could be found further and further away. Soon, the family would emerge in Cracow. Some members of this branch of the Sobolewskis would be knights in the service of the crown (*miles auratus*), their names recorded in official rolls in 1633.[2] Others, however, pursued quite different interests. Young Michael Sobolo(e)wski was an educated man who became close to an influential family by the name of Stocki. Alexander Stocki, as *burgraf* of Cracow, was a king's official in charge of an old royal castle; he wielded considerable power. As a friend of the family, Michael was immortalized in a panegyric published on the occasion of the wedding of the *burgraf*'s daughter in 1679.[3] In the next century, the most accomplished members of this branch of the Sobolewski family would serve as electors of future kings. Among them, Joseph Sobolewski from Cracow province cast his vote during a contested election of the last king of Poland, Stanislaus Augustus Poniatowski.[4]

Other Sobolewskis pressed east from very early times. Among them, Fabian Sobolewski distinguished himself for bravery in the service of the Hungarian-born King Batory, who ruled the Commonwealth of Poland and Lithuania in the latter part of the sixteenth century.[5] Although details of the military adventures of family forebears, and the names of battlefields where they fought, have been lost in the mists of history, they were most likely gallant warriors. Perhaps in recognition of their valor, the Sobolewski men received the right from the sovereign to the honorary use of the cognomen "Cyrus"—the name of the legendary ruler of the Persian Empire. Many of them added this symbolic distinction of their character between their first and family names beginning in 1649.

The coat of arms, called "Łada," used by the Sobolewski family.

There was an even better way to recognize Sobolewskis, regardless of where fate took them. Their coat of arms, called "Łada," underscored their noble status and distinguished them from others carrying a similar name. Łada illustrated the virtues espoused by the Sobolewski clan, and it had all the key symbols that counted in those times. There were a lion holding a sword for strength and a shield for effective defense. Two arrows in the picture implied speedy and precise weaponry, as if to warn any potential attackers. Finally, a horseshoe with a golden cross, as carried by the knights of the day, symbolized the always needed luck.[6]

Exactly when the Sobolewski family settled in Bohorodczany will have to remain shrouded in mystery. What is known, however, is that they came to this area long before the First Partition of Poland. In the neighboring fortress city of Stanislawow, a few families carrying that name could be found not long after the city was established. Among them were a soldier (*militis*) who, in 1738, was likely serving in the forces of the omnipotent magnate Potocki, and others working in non-military professions.[7] Whether one of these Sobolewski families bought land in Bohorodczany or whether, perhaps, a brave soldier was rewarded with an estate after many military campaigns, is not clear. Let us not forget that despite nominally owning a large portion of this eastern province, the Potocki family urgently needed to populate the countryside with loyal nobility.

Well into the eighteenth century, Bohorodczany and the surrounding area were considered wild territory, plagued not only by foreign forces but by internal ones as well. In particular, Ruthenian bandits, *opryshky*, spread fear in many when they would suddenly descend from the mountains or emerge from dense forests to attack traveling merchants and pillage settlements. At times, even receiving a piece of a paper with burn marks on its edges was enough to exhort ransoms from owners of isolated manor houses, who feared losing everything to arson. For some, these bandits were local heroes who would be later romanticized; but for many others, they were simply cruel criminals who often targeted Jews and local gentry.[8] At times, these troublemakers were even bold enough to target small towns, and in one such surprise attack, Bohorodczany was briefly taken over in the summer of 1744. Its small fort was plundered, and pricey objects were stolen from coffers of the Kossakowski family, who had married many of the Potocki daughters.

Despite this setback, the town quickly recovered; and at the violent death of a leader of *opryshky* a year later, some of the stolen jewels, found sewn into the man's clothes, would ultimately be returned to their rightful owners. In due course, *castellanus* (governor of the castle) Stanislaus Kossakowski, grandson of Grand Hetman Potocki, would sign a death warrant for the next leader of these Carpathian thugs, while residing in Bohorodczany's citadel.[9]

Whether male members of the Sobolewski family enlisted in the armed militia, which was stationed in a number of towns to defend the region, is not

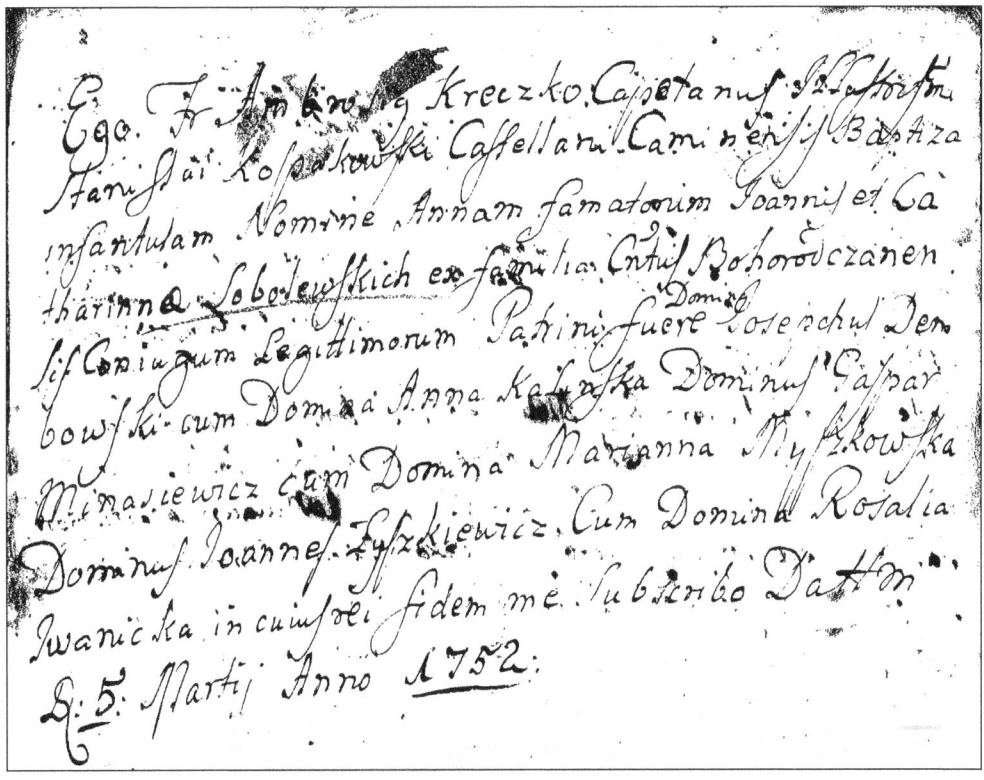

The first record of the Sobolewski family in Bohorodczany. The entry refers to the baptism of Anna, daughter of Joannes and Catharina Sobolewski, on March 5, 1752.

known. But certainly they could have witnessed these struggles. Around this time, the family name first appears in records from Bohorodczany. On March 5, 1752, a short note was written by Dominican friar Ambrosius Kreczko, a chaplain to the powerful *castellanus* Kossakowski. In a few lines written with a quill pen, ink smeared here and there on the page, he noted the early spring baptism of Anna, infant daughter of Joannes and Catharina Sobolewski from the county of Bohorodczany, with several witnesses in attendance.[10]

Certainly, a new era began when Austria took possession of the territories that had been lost by the Polish crown in 1772. How fast the news of the change in regime spread, and how the daily lives of Sobolewski men and women were affected by this historical event—if at all—remains unknown. But the changes were real and a long time in the making. Not surprisingly, the transition was remarkably peaceful, with many breathing a sigh of relief and hoping that the turmoil of the past would now diminish. The names of the old magnates Potocki, Kossakowski, and Leszczynski who, with their long, elaborate titles, had previously dotted many pages of Bohorodczany's records, started to fade away. In their places, other names would grow in number. For the Sobolewski family, what started as a trickle, with an occasional entry, became a stream of births and marriages producing brothers, sisters, and cousins all living in Bohorodczany.

Putting down roots there, the family responded to a government call to confirm their ancient claims to noble status under the Austrian administration. For unknown reasons, however, they seem to have done this with some hesitancy; it would be a few years before any formal certification process was started on their behalf. In part, these official proceedings were done for the sake of tradition and pride, as if to mark the difference between old honors and the more recent shower of titles granted by the new regime to secure loyalty. But certainly there were also less sentimental reasons, with noble status guaranteeing hereditary ownership of land and other privileges. Although the Austrian Emperor Joseph

II fought the tradition of serfdom with a new edict, the old system passed down from Polish times was recalcitrant, and it still guaranteed nobles cheap or even free labor by local peasants.[11]

At last, in 1796, the Galician State Council (*Collegium Staatum*) appointed by the Austrian emperor officially acknowledged the hereditary titles of three men: Joannes, Ludovicus, and Ignatius Sobolewski of the Łada coat of arms.[12] But make no mistake, despite their long and proud past, the Sobolewski clan clearly now belonged to local gentry rather than the landowning aristocracy. Thus, not surprisingly, the records reveal interesting paradoxes or, more likely, realities of their lives. Most entries about key family events would continue to have the Latin *nobilis* attached to the Sobolewski name, increasingly reflecting respect for tradition, as opposed to pointing out special status. In fact, who they really were can be much better gleaned from meeting the people around them.

The Sobolewskis' friends and distant family members, especially those invited to be witnesses at their weddings or christenings, were a motley group. They included not only other members of the agrarian nobility but also shoemakers (*sutor*), blacksmiths (*ferrifaber*), and farmers (*agricola*) without fancy hereditary titles.

෴

Our story is connected back through the generations to Ludovicus Sobolewski. He was the oldest of three men who were probably brothers living in the village of Lachowce, just outside Bohorodczany. When and where they were born remains unknown, but it is certain that they grew up before the annexation of the region to the Austrian Empire. By 1787, the family already lived in Bohorodczany. Around that time, Ludovicus married Magdalena Krechowiecka, from a neighboring village. Given his age, this was likely not his first marriage; and the ties between the two families would continue, including later marriages.[13]

The Sobolewskis' was a large farming household, with Ludovicus and Magdalena ultimately having five children, all born in the same family house. Not surprisingly for their times, Ludovicus's parents and at least one brother, Joannes, lived with them as well. Although early records are spotty, the elderly *nobilis* Sophia Sobolewska, who was noted as living in the same house, was likely the mother of the three Sobolewski brothers. Who her husband, the patriarch of the family, was is lost in the dust of history. But Sophia was described as the owner of a large farm (*fundi in heredi*) before passing it on to the next generation. Sophia lived long enough to see at least the beginning of Galicia, as part of the Austrian Empire, before dying in May 1799.

The extended Sobolewski clan was a well-to-do family compared with other inhabitants of the area. Although they were far less affluent than the Potocki and Kossakowski families of the bygone era, Joannes and Ludovicus Sobolewski owned a large piece of land. It was second in size only to properties belonging to local churches and the municipality of Bohorodczany.[14] With the passage of time, their homes became incorporated into the boundaries of the town and no longer would be described as situated "*in de villa de Lachowce*," although they were still living away from the town's center, with some of their land straddling the unmarked border between the two municipalities.

Standing on a narrow country road, a visitor could enter one of the three family compounds. The house where Ludovicus's family lived was identified by the number 26, and it was certainly larger than those of the other relatives. Whether or not the Sobolewskis had built their home when the family settled there, or had moved first into an old country house that once stood in the area, is not known.[15] On both sides of the property were vegetable gardens, and further to the left of the house, a small orchard had been planted. In addition to the main house, three other buildings stood on the property: most likely a barn, an animal shed, and a little woodshed or outhouse. After passing a few of the apple

Map showing the Sobolewski family compounds on the border between Bohorodczany and Lachowce. The houses were occupied by several generations of Sobolewskis. The house numbered 26 was to the left of a small road, and houses 25 and 246 were both to the right of the road. *(Section of a cadastral map from 1878.)*

and pear trees that were commonly grown in the area, one would have reached the edge of a stream. Locals called it Millbrook (Mühlbach or Młynówka), as it powered a small watermill that stood further north in Bohorodczany. On the other side of the stream, Ludovicus and his family owned a pasture that transitioned to marshes by the River Bystrzyca, which flowed further west.

Walking back through Ludovicus's courtyard and crossing the small road, a visitor could enter two other compounds occupied by members of the Sobolewski family. First was house 25, which belonged to Ignatius. Later, his son Adalbertus's large family would fill every available space there. This was a busy farming place, with several buildings standing in an open courtyard. Next to it, Martinus Sobolewski and his family lived in the smallest house, with a vegetable garden tucked behind. Oddly, it was numbered 246, suggesting that it had been built in more recent times than the other two houses. The proximity of these households meant not only living in a tight community of large families; it also reflected a less desirable economic reality. Repeated subdivisions of original landholdings into smaller and smaller plots with each generation were a fact of life. This is quite apparent today when looking at old cadastral maps.

Farmland that the Sobolewskis tilled themselves and would later lease to others was found in a few locations spanning the boundaries of Bohorodczany and Lachowce. One was just behind Ignatius's family compound in an area called Lachowce Fields (Lachowce Łany), which could easily be reached by going through a small gate and crossing a working area behind the house. The soil there was rather poor, and it allowed mainly the planting of oats, which were grown on several rectangular fields.[16] Additional plots of farmland belonging to the family sat on the other side of a small country road, in Lachowce. There were also other, smaller fields owned by the Sobolewski brothers further west, in the area that locals called "Beyond the Stebnik," denoting a stream of that name that passed through the area.

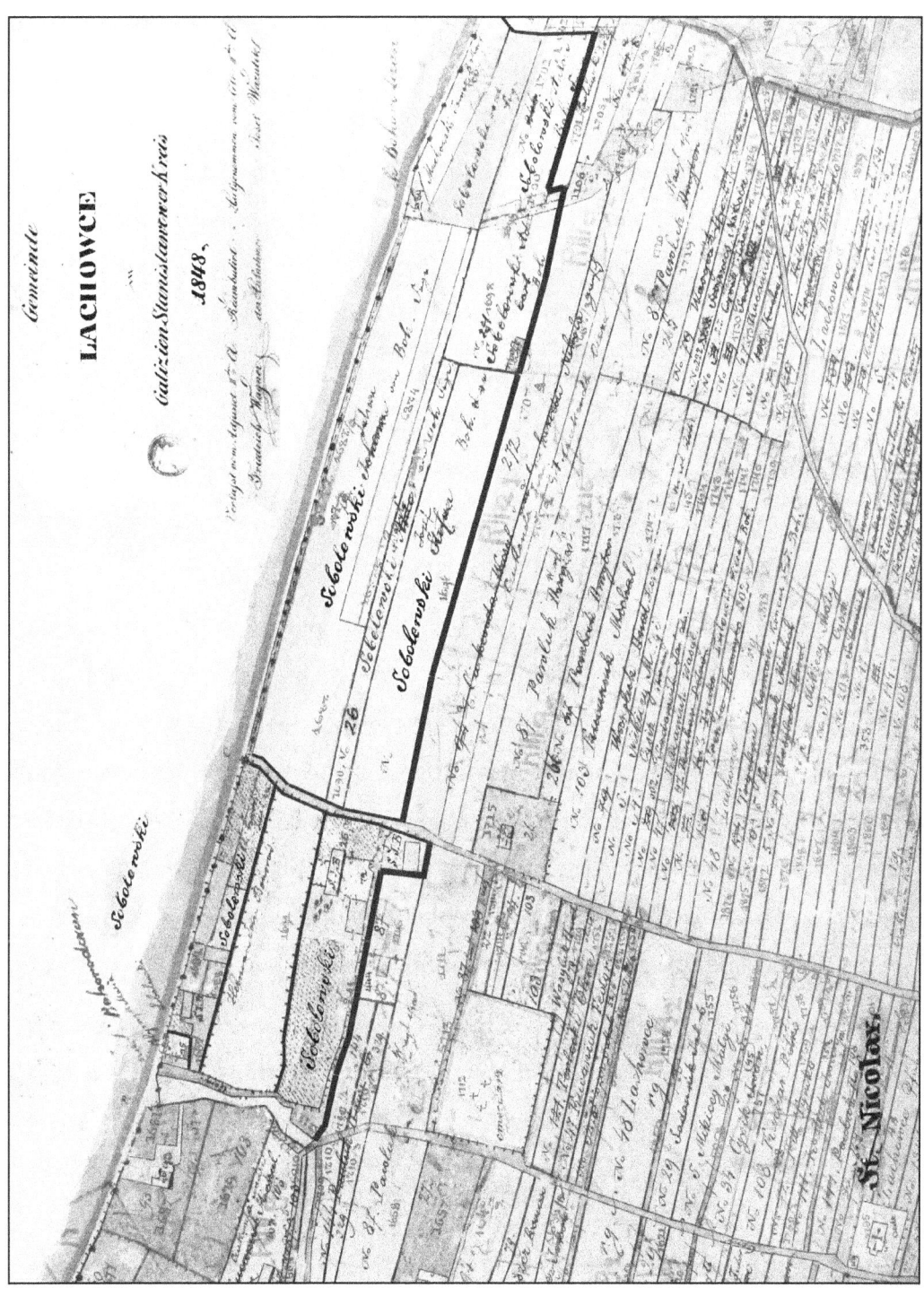

Map showing the Sobolewski family fields in Lachowce, near their domestic compounds in Bohorodczany. *(Section of a cadastral map from 1848.)*

Sobolewski men, for the most part, married early—around the age of 20—and a string of children usually followed, implying that most of these men had somehow been able to avoid long military service. Did some members of the clan seek other career opportunities in those times? If they did, these attempts must have been rather sporadic, and any resulting positions, at best, temporary. We will have to wait approximately one hundred years before seeing a sustained break of any Sobolewskis from their ancestral lands.

Of the three Sobolewski brothers whom we have mentioned, Ignatius died first, in 1817. A few years later Joannes, who had never married (*caelibis nobilis*) and had continued to live with Ludovicus's family, passed on in 1822.[17] Without getting too far ahead of our story, let us note that the last of their generation to go was Ludovicus, who died in 1835.

In an era without modern healthcare, this was an unusually strong and healthy family. All of them seemed to live to a very old age; Sophia's and Ludovicus's records have each of them more than 100 years old at the time of death. But we should quickly be reminded that the sense of time and the perception of age were certainly different then than they are today. The documents we take for granted now were nonexistent; thus, it is quite possible that a decade or two were added to actual ages after a death, either by a distraught family member or by a less-than-inquisitive Dominican friar making entries in official records.[18]

Despite Bohorodczany's location in the far eastern part of Galicia, the Sobolewski family came into contact with many newcomers who arrived in the area from other parts of the Austrian Empire or even from beyond its borders. There were German-speaking farmers (*colonistas*) coming to town from their nearby settlements, which bore foreign-sounding names such as Landestreu and Ugartshal. Even the village of Horocholina, which bordered some of the Sobolewskis' land, had a sizable population of farmers from Bohemia or Germany. Over the course of a few generations, many of them became Polonized and integrated into the local society, like the Schüssel family, with roots somewhere in Bohemia, who lived next to the Sobolewski compound. In contrast to future xenophobic attitudes that would fuel ethnic tensions, those were times of friendly contacts between the new arrivals and their neighbors—including the Sobolewskis.

Living in a small community also meant that the Sobolewskis became linked through marriage with several other families from Bohorodczany. Expectedly, when going over years of records, we can easily find Polish-sounding names for young brides marrying Sobolewski men (Kaszubinska, Machowska). But the diversity of this place is quickly evident when we notice other sorts of names, both those of new brides and those of friends recorded as witnesses. Names of German origin (Ernest, Herman, Kühn) mix with Ruthenian names (Semianow) and, on rare occasion, Jewish-sounding ones (Feyerl and Baumann, from Bohemia). These were all new spouses joining the extended Sobolewski family in the early part of the nineteenth century. The same was true for daughters of the Sobolewski clan. Thus, it did not come as a surprise when one year a young woman, Theresia Sobolewska, married her next-door neighbor, Mathias Schüssel, a weaver (*textoris*).[19] Others wed men with Ruthenian-sounding names (Halawaj, Martyniec) and then, on occasion, followed Greek Catholic religious rites. Daily interactions among neighbors, intermarriages, and frequent participation in each other's family celebrations speak of a remarkable harmony between Poles, such as the Sobolewski family, and the larger group of Ruthenians living in Bohorodczany. This was in stark contrast to the real or sometimes inflated (for political reasons) ethnic tensions that would later surface in eastern Galicia.[20]

There were other visitors and new settlers in the area. From time to time, a soldier from a Hungarian military regiment was stationed there; or a newcomer born in the province of Moravia, on the other side of the Carpathian Mountains, was married in a local church with members of the Sobolewski family as witnesses.[21] With its multiethnic composition, the Austrian Empire had brought a

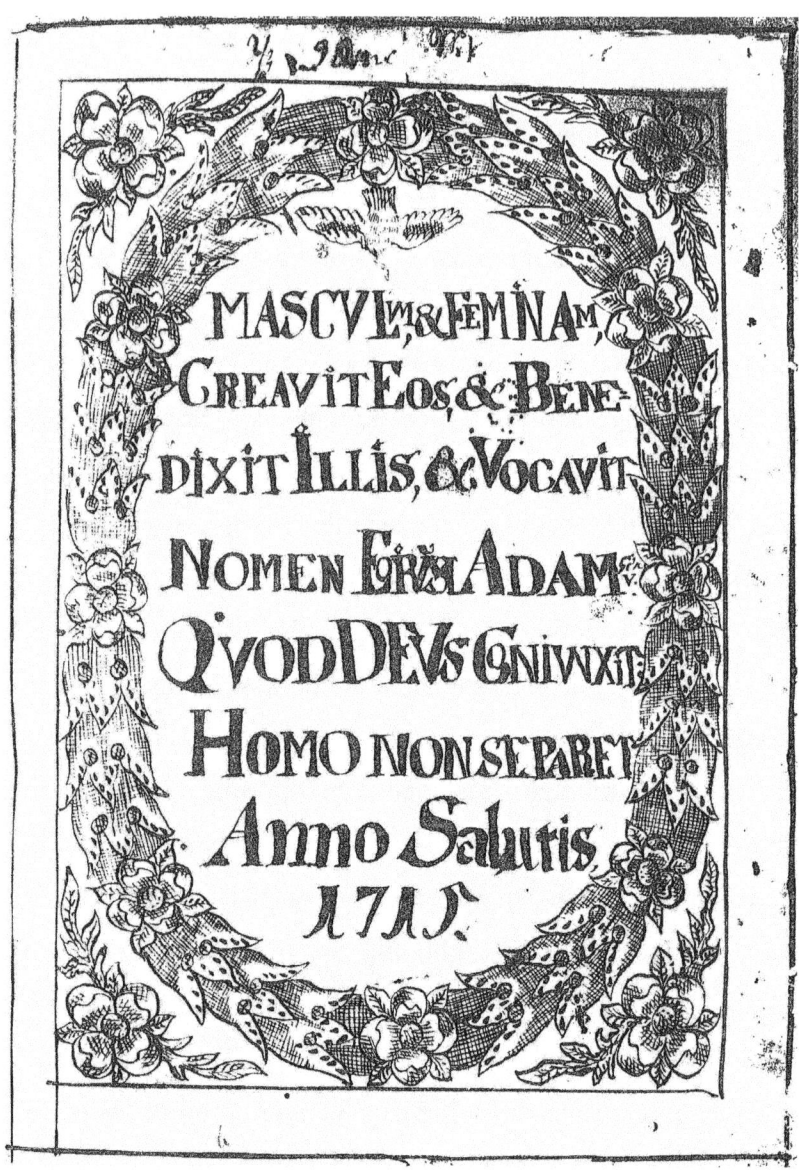

The book of marriages from the Dominican church in Bohorodczany (dated 1715).

period of tolerance that allowed for even such unusual events as the marriage of a Lutheran couple in a Catholic church. Perhaps an inconspicuous note about this particular wedding, buried among other more typical entries in Bohorodczany's church register (*liber copulatorum*), signaled that a broader acceptance of different faiths was making slow but definite inroads in Galicia.[22]

At many of these important events, Sobolewskis signed their full names in their own hand. Others, however, must have been less comfortable with writing, as they depended on clerks to register their full names. On those occasions, "occupation" would be entered in the record books as rural gentry (*nobilis agricola*); but that term was slowly giving way to a more general description of who they really were—small, independent landowners (*possessori liberi fundum*). Times were changing; young men from the farming nobility were tying the knot with daughters of shoemakers and blacksmiths, with much less attention being paid to titles. With the exception of Jewish neighbors who, until the next century (with rare exception) remained off-limits for marriage, ethnic background seems not to have been particularly relevant. Certainly, the completely free choice of a husband or wife was still generations ahead; but a healthy dose of pragmatism was part of the social fabric that helped people manage the land and raise families in this farming community.

A tumultuous time surrounded the birth of Antonius Sobolewski, Ludovicus's son, in March 1805. Within a few years of that event, Napoleon and his armies had pushed east, marching through the land that had formerly belonged to Poland. This was the same year that Mathias Lösch arrived in Wieliczka, in the western part of Galicia, as part of Austria's wider attempt to respond to Napoleonic expansion near its borders. But the ultimate prize for the French armies was the conquest of Russia. War came closer to Bohorodczany in 1809 when nearby Stanislawow was overtaken by a small detachment of cavalry loyal to Napoleon's cause. Without much fighting, the Austrian garrison laid down their arms and fled in haste.

Suddenly, in towns of the region freed from Austria, calls for citizens' militias were coupled with a grandiose plan for establishing the first Galician-French military unit. Over the course of a few weeks of patriotic fervor brought by dreams of statehood, mounted and armed members of the rural nobility were to arrive for active duty. Those unable to serve were expected to furnish foot soldiers in numbers corresponding to the size of their landholdings. Every man counted, and free peasants were called into scythe-armed regiments. But after less than two months, local plans for joining Napoleon came to a screeching halt when Austrian troops retook the area.[23] Even with Austrian sovereignty quickly reestablished in Stanislawow and the surrounding area, the period of tension must have lasted for months. The military garrison that was stationed in Bohorodczany suffered losses; its young soldiers were dying under suspicious circumstances that year. Whether this reflected the simmering of the pro-French insurgency or rather common but deadly military accidents will most likely never be known.

Were Sobolewskis directly affected by these events? Perhaps because they lived in a small town south of the major theater of war, they may have remained (except for the few months of the "Galician-French" dream) for the most part shielded from the storm that engulfed other parts of Europe. We do not know the answers to these questions, but we can notice in passing an officer with the surname Sobolewski who served gallantly in a squadron of Napoleon's Guard. Fighting against charging Cossacks somewhere on the eastern front, he distinguished himself for bravery against an overwhelming enemy force. Unfortunately, not much else can be said about this man, as neither his first name nor his place of birth was recorded.[24]

A few years later, when Napoleon's threat to European order had been eliminated, life in Bohorodczany returned to its rural rhythm. House 26 was full of growing children. In time, the girls moved out to follow new husbands, whereas married Sobolewski boys tended to remain in the family compound with their wives and children, at least for a while. Once again, house 26 became a multifamily nest; it must have benefited from plenty of helping hands but offered much less privacy than we expect today.

Chapter 5 — The Sobolewski Clan: Nobles and Farmers

Sometime in 1824, 19-year-old Antonius Sobolewski married local girl Anastasia Kaszubinska. An unusually long gap between their wedding and the birth of their first child is surprising at first; it is likely explained by Antonius's misfortune of being drafted into the Austrian army. In those days, a long military service, generally starting at age 20, could keep men away from their homes for up to a decade. Ultimately, however, Antonius and Anastasia would have nine children between 1838 and 1853. Like the offspring of prior generations, most of these would remain in Bohorodczany. In due course, they would establish their own families, which would join scores of cousins in the quickly growing extended Sobolewski family.

Antonius's and Anastasia's son Andreas Sobolewski had been born in 1848. This was another period of turmoil in the empire; this time, the country would be shaken by troubles both inside and outside the borders of Galicia, threatening the very survival of the regime. But Bohorodczany would be again shielded from many of these events. Even the violence of the Galician Slaughter, which had taken place a couple of years before, would for the most part be considered a faraway event. Yet life did not spare the Sobolewski family from adversities closer to home.

Tragically, records suggest that Anastasia, Andreas's mother, died not long after her last son was born, in late December 1853. As in the life story of Michaël Regiec of western Galicia, who lost his wife in similar circumstances, the widowed Antonius, with so many children, remarried quickly, in 1855. This was most likely a marriage of pragmatism rather than passion; Antonius was 51 years of age and his second wife, Anna Ernest, was a 45-year-old widow. Anna's family had been established for a long time in Bohorodczany. They had emigrated from Germany in the eighteenth century, and some of their men had been involved in the construction of the Dominican church.[25]

Predictably, Andreas's childhood was spent in the family compound, and at the age of 25, he married young Anna Machowska. Hers was one of the oldest families in Bohorodczany; their names are found in records dating back to the early eighteenth century. Anna was only 16; in accordance with local tradition, she was ready for marriage, but the couple required special permission from her father, Joannes Machowski. The church rolls contain the text of the approval, written by a Dominican friar and signed by the father of the bride with only an *x*.

This turned out to be a long and fertile union: Andreas and Anna had 12 children between 1875 and 1900. Many of their offspring were born in the ancestral home, number 26; they were the last generation that would be. Their parents must have had a special fondness for the name Ludovica, after Ludovicus Sobolewski, who had started this large branch of the family. Unfortunately, two girls given that name, born almost 20 years apart, did not survive beyond the first few years of life. As happened in almost all families at that time, several of the children (four altogether) would die shortly after birth.[26]

In the records of new arrivals in the Sobolewski family, Andreas's occupation is noted as either farmer (*agricola*) or baker (*panifex*). The godparents at baptisms of his children, and the witnesses at weddings of the next generation of Sobolewskis, included local cousins, his wife Anna's relatives, and numerous others. For the first time, the next generation of the Sobolewski family can be seen by us with greater focus—often through pictures, and records other than entries in church registers. Paradoxically, however, the lives of some of them will become more difficult to describe, as we try to understand not only their journeys through time and place but also the reasons for the many changes that were to come.

With a quickly growing household, the Sobolewski family eventually came to need more space. We also suspect that the wooden house 26 that had stood for more than a century and had been home to four generations was coming to the end of its useful life. Sometime after 1898, Anna and Andreas and their many children moved to a new dwelling, given the number 546. A couple of surviving photos show a wooden house with a small porch and a few steps in the front. Modest by the standards of today, this house was nevertheless a symbol of the family's financial independence. When a few years later arson fires would plague the wealthy families of Bohorodczany, apprehensive discussions must have filled many evenings around the Sobolewskis' dinner table. Whether due to luck or some well-planned preemptive steps, this family house would remain safe.[27]

AMONG THE MANY CHILDREN of Andreas and Anna Sobolewski, Franciscus, my grandfather, was their sixth. He was born on November 15, 1885. We might wonder if his parents were concerned about his health; if so, that might explain his recorded baptism on the same day as his birth. Or perhaps there is a simpler explanation: a friar's simplifying the records, as all newly born children on this particular page of the *liber natorum* have baptismal dates that match their birthdates. The register identifies as godparents of the infant Franciscus Alexander Swirski, a blacksmith; and his wife, Apolonia, related to the boy's maternal grandmother. Alexander must have been a good friend of the parents, as over the years he was asked to be godfather to several of their many children.

Like his brothers and sisters, Franciscus received a basic education at the local elementary school. His early years were apparently uneventful, but soon an important decision was to be made about his future. It was something like reaching a fork in the road. There was a real possibility that Bohorodczany would remain Franciscus's entire world, as it had for Andreas, Antonius, and Ludovicus Sobolewski before him. Or would he have a chance of turning in a new direction? The signs were clear that living off the land was becoming less attractive for the Sobolewski children, and new opportunities were opening up. Sure enough, in 1901, Franciscus and his cousin Stanislaus went on to high school and teachers' college in Stanislawow. These boys were lucky, because Franciscus's older

Stanislawow. The teachers' college attended by Franciscus Sobolewski from 1901 to 1904. *(Postcard from the early twentieth century.)*

brother Antonius had recently moved to that town after being hired by the railroad. This must have provided some sense of security for the two country boys.

Surviving pictures of Franciscus's siblings provide a glimpse that an intergenerational change had been set in motion. The Sobolewski family's long tradition of earning its social position from owning and leasing ancestral lands was fading away. The pictures show smartly dressed and sophisticated-looking young people who clearly no longer worked with the soil. Rather than repeating patterns of the past, two Sobolewski sisters would marry men who earned their livings in new professions. Franciscus's brother Michael was poised for a career in civil service; other siblings also tried their luck far beyond their familiar fields.[28] Soon, Sobolewskis from various branches of the extended family would appear on the scene, occupying new professions—including accountant in the magistrate office of neighboring Stanislawow and physician in a different part of Galicia.[29] One can only wonder if Andreas and Anna, the parents of

Franciscus, were supportive or apprehensive about their children's chosen paths—into adulthoods that would be so different from their own life journeys.

The month of July 1904 turned out to be quite important for the entire family. Happy news arrived first: Franciscus and his cousin had successfully passed their oral and written examinations and graduated from the teachers' college.[30] Franciscus could now return home, but in a break from tradition, he was no longer expected to tend to or even administer family land. And there was other news of concern to

Michael Sobolewski (1883–1907) in a picture from 1904.

the family. During that same month, Antonius Sobolewski, the oldest of the Sobolewski brothers, petitioned a local court in Bohorodczany about a minor legal matter. Not surprisingly, the papers were filed in Polish; but when the court reply came in Ruthenian, Antonius's emotions flared up.

In those times of growing ethnic sensitivities, language was often used to impose national identity or signal dominance of one group over another. Despite its status as one of the official languages of Galicia, German was often frowned upon by Poles when it was used in public. Ruthenians, in turn, had tried to assert their rights by increasing the use of their own language when interacting with the Polish-dominated civil administration. Yet Poles growing alarmed about the prospect of loosing ground in eastern Galicia jealously guarded against any

Antonius Sobolewski (1875–after 1954) with his bride, Catharina, in an undated picture.

attempts of making their mother tongue less relevant. In this context, Antonius viewed the court reply in a "foreign" language as an affront. As often happens when emotion overtakes reason, the initial legal matter became irrelevant and was quickly forgotten. The imagined slight became the issue, harsh words were said, complaints were made, and judicial reports were hastily written. Suddenly, a judge in a small court in Bohorodczany perceived all the protests and the manner in which they'd been raised as contempt of court by a member of a rabble-rousing Polish family. Without wasting any time, he sentenced Antonius to three weeks in jail for offending an officer of the court. This, of course, only added to the minority Poles' sense of victimization.

News of what was perceived as injustice to those who, like "patriotic" Antonius Sobolewski, were simply asserting their rights, spread quickly. Alongside military developments in Asia and large strikes erupting in the oil-rich region of Galicia that summer, the "case of Mr. Sobolewski" was brought into the spotlight by several newspapers from Stanislawow and Lvov. In the excitement of the moment, nobody seems to have remembered that the opposite "offenses" had happened many times before. The feelings of Ruthenians or Jews, who so often were forced to use Polish when dealing with the national Galician administration, were not even mentioned in passionate commentaries about "Mr. Sobolewski." But there was no time or inclination then to exercise more balanced judgment. A respected lawyer, Salomon Leser from Lvov, was promptly hired by the family, and the verdict was appealed to a higher court in Stanislawow just before the jail term was to be served. Initially, the outcome was only partially successful. The higher court sensed a potentially explosive situation that might reverberate beyond Bohorodczany and touch the sensitivities of more than one family. The contempt-of-court verdict was retained, but the jail term was replaced with a fine. Antonius was ordered to pay 105 kronen (approximately U.S. $1,100 in today's money).

For most, this would have been the end of the story; however, the Sobolewski clan was of stubborn stock. Antonius's lawyer appealed to the prosecutor's office in Vienna, arguing the injustice of the lower court's decision. In its Delphic wisdom, deciding to remain above the fray, the judiciary of the central government only asked the lower courts to review the case. In the end, a judicial inquiry established that while speaking in anger, Antonius had not mentioned the judge's name or that of any other officer of the court, and the case was thrown out. Thus, a potentially explosive affair (albeit one that some today might view as a tempest in a teacup) reached its final resolution.³¹

Theophilus Sobolewski, the youngest of the Sobolewski brothers, was not involved in any explosive events as far as we can tell. Like his older brothers, however, he was set on breaking with family tradition by seeking opportunities in the outside world. At the age of 22, Theophilus took his youthful desire to a new level by leaving Galicia. Like thousands of other potential emigrants from his homeland, he had to make a crucial decision about where to test his luck. In 1908, emigration to the New World was the most chosen path; 338,000 people arrived in the United States from the Austro-Hungarian Empire in that year alone. Migrants from Galicia included Poles, mainly from the countryside, and impoverished Jews from many towns in the eastern region.³² Every few years, there would be additional waves of Jews who were only passing through Galicia on their way to the United States, escaping pogroms in tsarist Russia. Other groups included large numbers of Ruthenians, many from Bohorodczany, who often headed for Canada. Argentina was another destination for those seeking a better future. That country had a booming agricultural sector and largely unpopulated but fertile plains, called *pampas*, that needed farmers. In fact, at the turn of the century, some wondered whether Argentina, rather than the United States, would become the new center of the world.

Theophilus Sobolewski (1890–after 1954). Theophilus emigrated to Argentina before World War I.

To move thousands of people across the ocean, many of them illiterate and unfamiliar with anything beyond their own villages, required well-run operations. Would-be emigrants were recruited by special agencies that transported them from Galicia by train to the key European ports of embarkation. In general, there were two routes advertised: the northern one was more popular, taking brave passengers to Bremen or Hamburg in Germany, where they boarded steamships bound for North America on a passage that took a week or longer. The southern route included a change of trains in Vienna and further travel to the port of Trieste, which today is situated in Italy but then belonged to Austro-Hungary. From there, travelers boarded ships that would reach Buenos Aires or New York in about two weeks, after ports of call in Naples, Barcelona, and the Canary Islands. Each ship could transport up to 800 passengers in three classes of service. But make no mistake: most emigrants, of necessity, traveled on the cheapest ticket, third class.

The latter route was the one that Theophilus Sobolewski chose, in order to seek adventure and opportunities in Argentina. Nothing is known about why he chose Buenos Aires as his destination; was it just one of many possibilities, or did some acquaintance await him there? We can only wonder whether, boarding the train in Stanislawow at

Steamship routes to North and South America. The passage on "Magnificent Fast Steamship Marta [sic] Washington" to Buenos Aires lasted "only 16 days."
(Kurjer Lwowski *January 1, 1905;
and* Kurjer Stanislawowski *December 7 and 24, 1911.*)

the outset of the trip, Theophilus suspected that this would be the last time he would see the members of the Sobolewski family who stood on the platform bidding him good-bye.[33]

⁂

In the fall of 1904, Franciscus Sobolewski, my grandfather, resurfaces in our story as a teacher in the boys' elementary school in Bohorodczany. He and his cousin Stanislaus, who were two of the many Sobolewskis living in town, most likely had no difficulty immersing themselves in their new responsibilities; this was still familiar territory. The next year, one of the Sobolewskis spoke at a regional school conference held in Bohorodczany. There, routine appeals for better teaching materials and financial support were mixed with a more controversial proposal to remove German from the school curriculum. From the perspective of today—when early exposure to several languages is often considered a strength—it is strange to hear arguments about how difficult it was for schoolchildren to learn the three officially recognized languages. Rather than a genuine concern about too much homework, this was more likely a thinly veiled reflection of the nationalism that was on the rise in Galicia.[34]

Within a few years, Franciscus's name would temporarily disappear from the roster of local teachers. Like many young men his age, he was eligible for compulsory military service, although deferrals for teachers were common. Franciscus, however, opted for a voluntary service in the imperial army that lasted only one year.[35] This option was generally reserved for graduates of schools of higher education, who had to pass a proficiency test clumsily called the "intelligence examination."[36] For young men from Bohorodczany, the most likely place for military service was Stanislawow, where the 58th Infantry Regiment was quartered. But that would not be Franciscus's destination; like his brothers, he was looking for new experiences. Perhaps seeking adventure, he enlisted in the 7th Infantry Regiment, stationed in Graz, in Austria proper. Franciscus served as a cadet, and after his training was completed, he was discharged back into civilian life as a noncommissioned officer in the reserves.[37]

After spending this short time away, Franciscus resumed his teaching career at the end of 1907. The names of his contemporaries on the school staff are noteworthy as they reflect, once again, the diverse community of Bohorodczany. We see there the Polish name of Julian Fialkowski (the school principal) along with the Ruthenian-sounding name of another teacher, Mikolaj Denysiuk, and a Jewish teacher, Hersh Krammer. Among his colleagues, Franciscus would have no problem quickly noticing a new teacher, a young woman with red hair from neighboring Stanislawow. But this story is yet to come.

The Jubilee Cross. On the occasion of the 60th anniversary of Emperor Franz Joseph's reign, Franciscus Sobolewski and Joseph Regiec were the recipients of this decoration in 1908.

This was still a period of peace, and soon, with thousands of others, Franciscus celebrated the emperor's 60th anniversary at the helm of the Austro-Hungarian Empire. By an official decree of 1908, all active and former military men registered on the day of the emperor's birthday, December 2, were to receive the Jubilee Cross. This would become Franciscus's first decoration, although not for valor on the battlefield. His life was becoming stable and, to some extent, predictable. By 1913, after successfully passing the required examinations, he became a permanent teacher in the Bohorodczany school.[38] Everything suggested that this would be his career for life, but events that loomed ahead would permanently alter his trajectory.

Chapter 6

HELENA REGIEC SOBOLEWSKA

$\mathcal{B}$OHORODCZANY, HER NEW HOME, was not too far from the old one. Still, Helena Regiec must have felt some anxiety; the young woman was about to make her first step into adulthood. However, by virtue of her character and the modern upbringing she had received, there was no place for too much fuss. Her parents, Joseph and Stephania Regiec, had wisely encouraged their daughters to seek professions so they could become independent in life. It is also likely that Bronislawa Lösch, her aunt and an accomplished teacher, had had some influence on Helena's chosen career and offered a few words of advice from her own experience.

The beginning of the twentieth century was a time when most young women in Galicia still left their parents' homes only after they were married. Few held outside jobs or lived alone by choice; roles for them beyond those of supportive spouses and mothers were still far from accepted. However, times were beginning to change—albeit with some hesitancy. Only a few years before, women in the empire had been granted permission to be doctors or pharmacists (upon fulfilling the same educational requirements as men), although not too many were yet choosing those paths.[1] Teaching was a more accessible profession that allowed women to accomplish a measure of independence, at least prior to marriage.

As in other parts of the Western world, women's suffrage was a matter of great debate in Galicia. Interestingly, women themselves may have been somewhat ambivalent about their right to vote; one advocated in a local newspaper that the process should be advanced step by step over a period of some years, with educated women (e.g., teachers) or independent women (e.g., widows) allowed to vote first. One female correspondent's cautious advice was that married women should always follow their husbands' political instincts, in order to avert domestic quarrels. Of course, these opinions may have simply been conciliatory gestures toward those with more conservative views, calculated to gain in the long run by not rocking the boat too strongly.[2]

Such controversies were probably not at the front of Helena's mind after she passed her examinations in September of 1906. Her first assignment as a teacher-in-training came quickly, in the following month. Why my grandmother was given her initial appointment in Bohorodczany rather than Stanislawow will remain unclear; but we can guess that this would not have been her first choice. Helena certainly knew of the town because it was so close to Stanislawow. And, as in later generations, newly minted teachers were probably pressured to move to rural areas, where schools were few and often inadequately staffed. Perhaps there were other, more practical reasons she moved there; possibly her parents had some acquaintances in the town who could help Helena get established in her new home.

The trip from Stanislawow to Bohorodczany was not arduous, but it certainly was quite different than it would be today. There was no train or bus connecting these towns, and the only automobile service, which had opened with much fanfare that same month, was solely dedicated to mail delivery.[3] Certainly one could bicycle, as the road was considered a good one. But it would have been unlikely for a young woman in an ankle-length dress, wearing a wide-brimmed hat and with some baggage, to bike so far from the city alone. Instead Helena, her sister, and their parents must have taken a carriage, so they could look over the town and living quarters for the young teacher-to-be. Undoubtedly, Joseph Regiec reminisced along the way about his own experiences some 27 years before, when as a new teacher he had arrived at his small, single-classroom school and found no lodging place waiting. There must have been a few bits of advice from father to daughter, who was of course anxious not to make any mistakes in her first job.

Although Bohorodczany was nearby, the trip from Stanislawow would not be cheap. The cost of a carriage with coachman and two horses could be up to 10 kronen (about U.S. $105 today). After one or two trunks were loaded into the carriage, they would have left behind the elegant city center and traveled along Kazimierzowska Street, watching large buildings give way to simple, single-story houses. They would have passed the city hospital, and likely caught glimpses of cavalrymen from the Austro-Hungarian regiment that was stationed nearby. A few parks were briefly seen on their left, and soon they were outside the city, heading southwest.

The right side of the valley was hilly, with a mountain range called the Black Forest rising up on the horizon. A bit closer to the road, they could see the river (Bystrzyca Solotwinska) curving this way and that, its rapid current being joined by a number of smaller streams. In a few places, the river was split by boulders and even some small islands. On the left side of the road, the terrain was flatter, with pastures and a few meadows. After two and a half miles, the carriage would have passed through the small village of Krechowce, with the Greek Catholic church visible from the road. Then, just to the right, by the river, there was another village, with the long name of Drohomirczany.

Roughly halfway between Stanislawow and Bohorodczany, Helena and her family would have reached a small town, Łysiec. In passing, they would have seen City Hall, and caught glimpses of an old Roman Catholic church established by the founder of Stanislawow in 1669. The crosses of the Greek Catholic, Armenian, and Orthodox churches were also visible.

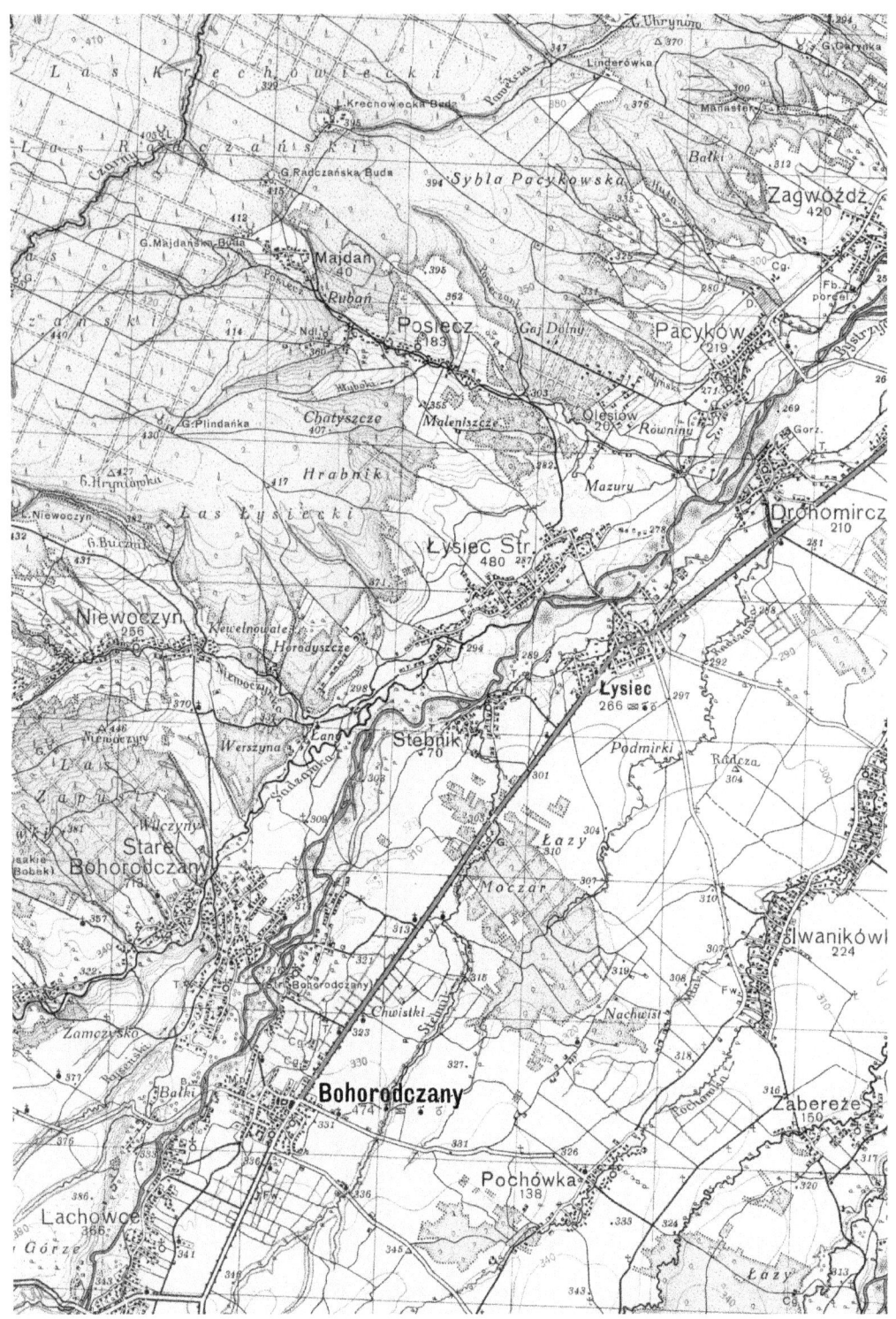

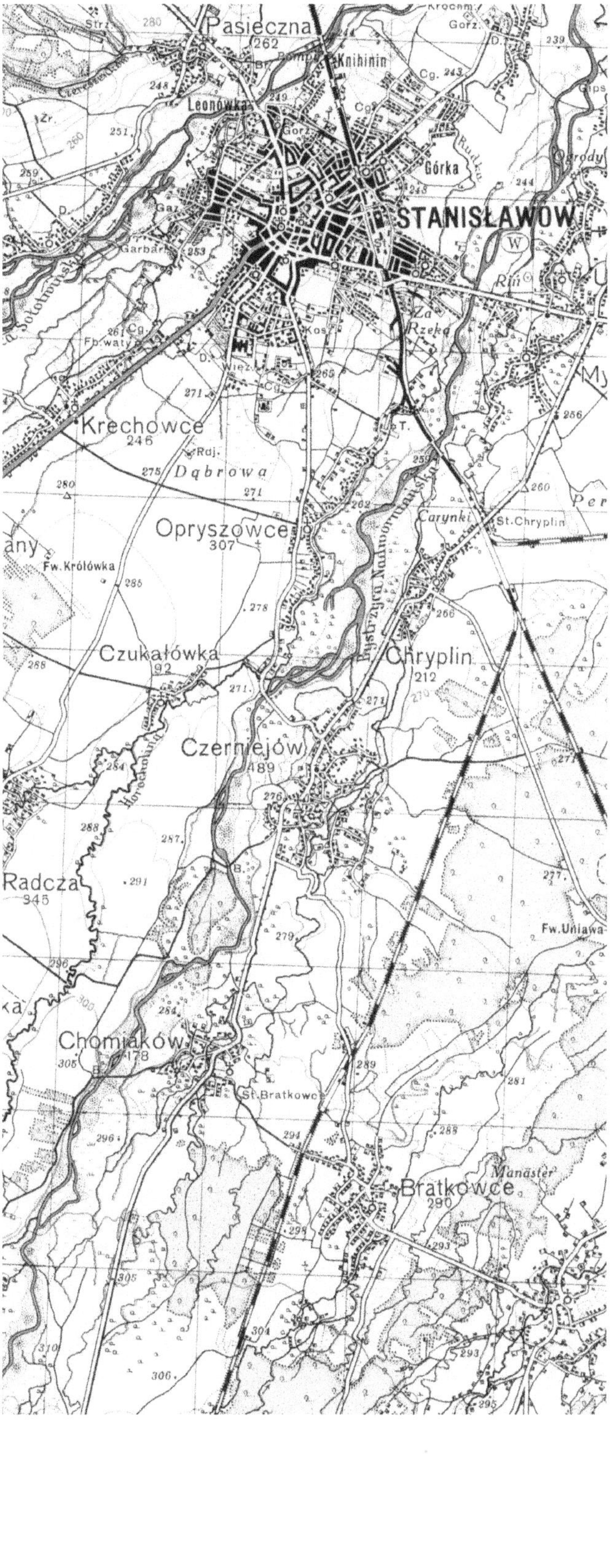

Stanislawow-Bohorodczany area. Leaving Stanislawow, a traveler passed through Krechowce, Drohomirczany, and Łysiec before arriving in Bohorodczany. The mountain range is visible to the west of the valley.
(Section of a map from 1932.)

The seal of Bohorodczany from 1820.

On the way to Bohorodczany, they were almost certainly passed by horse-drawn wagons (frequently driven by Jewish coachmen) or by a group of Hutsuls bringing their wares to local markets. On their left was a stream called Stebnik, with some adjoining small cattle farms.

About half an hour after leaving Łysiec behind, the family's coach would have approached their destination; the towers of the Dominican church were clearly visible to travelers from some distance away. The school where Helena was headed was on the left, almost opposite the courthouse. After crossing a small stream that ran under the road, the family's carriage could have turned sharply right; that would have had them passing several of the synagogues of Bohorodczany. Exploring a bit further in that direction, the Regiecs could have seen a wooden bridge across the River Bystrzyca, leading to the village of Old Bohorodczany, which was clearly visible on the other side. Turning around, the family would have noticed a small manor house, which belonged to the Stadion family, just outside town. Back on the main road, they would find themselves next to the market square, with its many shops and stalls. Looking further south, they would see the wooden roof of the Greek Catholic church and a small post office on the other side of the road.

After a ride lasting a bit more than an hour, the family would have stretched their legs and strolled around, inspecting the town and perhaps looking for an appropriate place for Helena to stay. Whether it was the family's choice or an arrangement already made by the school, the new teacher's lodging would consist of a simple room in a house near the center of town, allowing Helena to easily walk back and forth from work.[4] Surely, there were a few final words of advice from her parents. Perhaps to cheer Helena up, her family reminded her that it wouldn't be long before she would visit home to tell them all about her new life. It was already fall and the days were getting shorter, so the three Regiecs would not have stayed too late. Perhaps after a bite to eat, they said their good-byes, climbed into the carriage, and went back to Stanislawow.

Bohorodczany. The scene from the downtown. *(Postcard from the early twentieth century.)*

On November 1, 1906, Helena started her new job, beginning a professional career that would take her through many twists and turns until retirement 43 years later. In her understated way, she would always remain proud of being a professional woman. Thus, let's pause for a moment to see how the schools of Bohorodczany developed over time, and what welcomed this aspiring teacher there.

The town had had a variety of schools since the end of the eighteenth century. From that time onward, there were separate institutions for Jews and Ruthenians, as well as state-sponsored ones that were theoretically open to everyone. A German-Jewish school opened in Bohorodczany shortly after the Austrian government took over Galicia in 1772; it was part of a wider network administered by the secular Jewish educator Naftali Herz Homberg. These schools provided instruction in German but also offered limited classes in Hebrew. Where exactly they were located in Bohorodczany, and how many students attended, is not known, except that Mr. S. Bland was one of the first Jewish teachers there. As in other places in Galicia, however, local rabbis despised the idea of secular education functioning outside the religious community, and the system ultimately failed. Herz Homberg's schools, as they were called, were shut down, and the last teacher left town in 1806. But in later years, a number of smaller schools would open, this time run by the local Jewish community with instruction given in Hebrew, to complement state education for Jewish children.[5]

Bohorodczany's first public school had been established by a decree of the governor of Galicia in 1789. At the beginning, it was a single classroom where local kids were taught basic reading and writing. Sometime after 1837, the school gained an early benefactor, Count Rudolph Stadion. We can gain a glimpse into its life by examining records from the year 1865. At that time, there was a single teacher, Mr. Przeslakiewicz, who had been teaching for the previous 37 years and would remain in this position for another 10 years. The poor man, who was already 67 years old, oversaw 95 boys and 33 girls in a single classroom. These kids were considered extremely lucky; at the time, approximately three-quarters of all children of school age living in Bohorodczany never enrolled at even a simple classroom. Besides his annual salary of only 42.5 Austrian kronen (about U.S. $12,600 in today's currency), Mr. Przeslakiewicz was also compensated with a few bushels of wheat, barley, and rye, not to mention some firewood and hay, all coming from the Stadion estate. We can guess that these items came in quite handy, in light of his rather small income.[6]

*

By the time Helena arrived in Bohorodczany, the town had separate public schools for boys and girls. Nonetheless, even basic education continued to be a luxury. No doubt, some progress had been made over the past 50 years; but approximately one-third of children in Galicia still had no formal instruction at all.[7] The boys' school where she was to teach was a far cry from the earlier single classrooms or the smaller wooden schoolhouses still common in the countryside.

No longer were teachers compensated with a few bushels of wheat or rye. By the standard of the day, Helena's school was considered quite modern. The boys were taught in a recently built, two-story brick building containing six classrooms and an apartment for the principal. Behind the school was an open field where the children could play, and there was an adjacent orchard to pick apples and pears in the fall. The school for girls was down the street, in a building that was part of the Dominican cloister.[8]

We can safely assume that Helena's father had been pleased when he compared his daughter's new teaching conditions with his own experiences. She would not have to struggle to find support for herself and her school as he had. As the county seat, Bohorodczany had a regional school commission with the mandate to oversee school policies. Besides mundane responsibilities like those of any other school board, it had the challenging task of navigating sometimes contentious religious and ethnic sensitivities. To avoid control by Polish administrators who used state-sponsored education for cultural dominance, the commission included members of the main religious denominations. Thus, the records from Bohorodczany show a Greek Catholic priest representing Ruthenians, a member of the Jewish community, and a Roman Catholic priest all working alongside civil administrators on school budgets and regulations. They seem to have been aware of how critical it was to use schools for the purpose of teaching, rather than as a means to encourage tensions or preferences.[9]

The next two years of Helena's life were occupied with her work as a teacher-in-training at the elementary school for boys, which provided lessons through the fifth grade. After joining the school's staff, she must have heard a few stories about another teacher, Franciscus Sobolewski, who had recently left Bohorodczany for his military service. Undoubtedly Helena met, even if only in passing, other members of the large Sobolewski family, including Franciscus's brothers

Wilhelmina Sobolewska, (1892-1972), the youngest sister of Franciscus Sobolewski.

and sisters. As often happens, those initial interactions could not have foretold the romance that would blossom later.

Helena's days were filled not only with work but probably with frequent biking trips to surrounding villages, and occasional visits to Stanislawow. On her teacher's salary of 78 kronen per month (about U.S. $2,090 in today's money), she could not afford an expensive ride in a hired carriage whenever she wanted to see her parents and sister.[10] Instead, on occasion, she would share a ride with others heading to Stanislawow. It would be four more years before a public, horse-drawn "omnibus" would provide regular service between the two towns, offering four trips daily. Motorized buses would appear on the roads of Galicia a little over a year later.[11] Unfortunately, there was no longer time for Helena to take extended trips abroad with her family.

As for fun, I remember my grandmother telling me that she had always liked to read and that, like most young women, she enjoyed dancing. Her preferences, however, were not popular waltzes or a later arrival, the fashionable tango. Instead, she liked the quadrille, a dance that can be seen as a dignified precursor to square dancing. Very popular in the Austro-Hungarian Empire, the quadrille had elaborate steps and involved at least four couples, with men bowing to the ladies and constant changes of partners. There were other dances, such as the boisterous mazurka or the more formal polonaise. Did Helena in her early 20s have the opportunity to dance the quadrille in Bohorodczany, or was that only possible in Stanislawow during carnival balls, under the watchful eyes of her parents? The latter was a more likely place to get an invitation to a ball; these were popular in Helena's time, with young and old eagerly awaiting the arrival of the season every year. But even the small town of Bohorodczany once boasted five dancing parties in a single month!

It is not too difficult to imagine young Helena enjoying herself at a dance in the company of her fellow teachers, perhaps young Franciscus Sobolewski among them. On at least one such occasion, a reporter described the music (by a military band) as excellent; the atmosphere was said to be full of light humor, and local ladies were praised for their elegant evening gowns. The rivalry between two local beauties, discreetly identified only by their initials, was noted in good spirit; what woman would not like to be crowned the queen at such an event? But perhaps trying not to sound too frivolous, the reporter quickly lamented that gatherings devoted to wholesome patriotic causes could never attract such big crowds.

For those interested in formal entertainment in Stanislawow, the success of a ball would be judged by the quality of the orchestra and the master of ceremonies, who directed the order of the dances and movement on the floor. Seeing "only" 20 or 30 dancing pairs was considered a disappointing evening. By 1907, some had complained that the elegance of these balls was in decline, with younger gentlemen often unable to dance properly; the clumsy male partners would be described unflatteringly as "jumping sparrows on a clothesline." Not to mention the criticism directed at those who dared to smoke in ballrooms! Ladies of society were difficult to please; some scathingly remarked that tails, as opposed to the now more frequent tuxedos, were the only appropriate dress for true gentlemen at carnival balls. But comments like those would have been unlikely from the Regiec women, who were much more grounded in reality.

Despite their presumed flaws, the men present at balls were still surveyed carefully by mothers and daughters, as this was the season for at least some romances to ignite. We can only imagine the dashed hopes among young ladies of Stanislawow when two female observers opined one carnival season that there were many officers and students at evening parties but very few single men with "appropriate" employment.[12]

After a couple of years as a teacher-in-training, Helena was ready to take the next step in her career. To become a permanent teacher, she had to submit her high school diploma, her certificate of training for the past two years, and a list of books she had used to prepare for the required examination. In January 1909, she sat before the qualifying commission in Stanislawow and received a certification (*patent*) that allowed her to assume a teacher's position in elementary school, using Polish as the language of instruction. As required, Helena also passed examinations in other languages commonly spoken in Galicia, such as Ruthenian and German. Without knowledge of these, teaching in eastern Galicia would indeed have been quite a challenge.[13] Although instruction was given mostly in Polish, schools must have been a cacophony of conversation in Ruthenian, Yiddish, and German.

Our newly minted permanent teacher, with credentials in hand, soon began giving classes at the elementary school for girls in Bohorodczany. The teaching staff there included seven women, including the Jewish teacher Jetti Seinfeld. Every Friday, Jewish girls were brought to the boys' school, where Hersh Krammer provided religious instruction for both girls and boys.[14] The school week was long, lasting from Monday through Saturday, with the exception that Jewish children were excused from attending school on Shabbat. Class days were short by our standards, however, starting at 8:00 a.m. and finishing by 1:00 p.m.[15]

Being a teacher and an independent woman meant that Helena became increasingly involved in other aspects of life in the Bohorodczany community. For instance, she helped to organize artistic performances by a youth group in town. This would not have been entirely surprising for a teacher, but I discovered that

Helena Regiec's teacher diploma (*patent*) issued in January 1909 in Stanislawow.
It qualified Helena to teach in the elementary schools.

my grandmother had talents beyond just helping with logistics. A short newspaper report from one such January evening described the gathering: After a choir sang and someone recited a poem with feeling, "concert performances followed, with Miss H. Regiec playing on violin a melancholic piece with great success, accompanied by a cytra." Next, a few solo songs were sung by another young teacher, and a short play capped the evening.[16]

Not long after Helena moved to Bohorodczany, she joined the Folk School Association. Its local chapter was much smaller than the chapters in Nowy Sacz (where her aunt Bronislawa was active) and Stanislawow (where her father had made his mark). Nonetheless, this group of approximately 40 people was truly on the front lines; support for education was needed even more in small towns than in large cities. Knowing my grandmother's fondness for reading, it does not come as a surprise that she actively promoted the use of the local reading room and library as a way of improving literacy in Bohorodczany.

The association's reading room carried only a couple of Galician magazines, but it had a rather large collection of books (630 titles). Despite a tight budget, apparent when we see in the records a small year-end deficit, the local chapter sponsored musical and theatrical performances as well as a few popular discussions. In 1910, young Helena was chosen to be on the local executive committee; there she would come into contact with a few members of the Sobolewski family. In 1912, the volunteers were joined by fellow teacher Franciscus Sobolewski, who became secretary of the organization. In a surviving publication of this group, we can see hundreds of members, photographed as they gathered in Lvov for their national convention. We come close to catching a glimpse of Helena, but the picture is, disappointingly, too grainy to pinpoint her in the crowd.[17]

FOR MANY REASONS, the year 1912 would be very important in Helena's life. During the previous fall and the first two months of 1912, she spent time studying for another important examination. After six years in Bohorodczany, Helena was to become a fully accredited teacher in the grammar school, the next step in her professional journey. In February, she headed first to her parents' home in Stanislawow. Then, after an additional three or four hours by train, Helena arrived in Lvov. This time, the 26-year-old probably had little time for sightseeing in Galicia's capital city. Instead, she took oral and written examinations in front of an official imperial and royal (*kaiserlich und königlich*)

Helena Regiec's teacher diploma (*patent*) issued in March 1912 in Lvov.
It qualified Helena to teach in today's equivalent of middle schools.

educational commission. Besides assessing her qualifications in reading, writing, and math, these tests included hand drawing, calligraphy, geometry, and technical drawing. In addition, she was required to show her ability to provide practical instruction to schoolgirls. We can be sure that Helena and her parents rejoiced one month later when the official certificate, with its omnipresent likeness of Emperor Franz Joseph, arrived, stating that Helena Wanda Regiec was now fully accredited to teach in the next level schools, and qualified to teach all of the above subjects.

By now, Helena was eager to move on, since the town of Bohorodczany did not offer teaching positions beyond those in the elementary schools. Her new diploma gave her the opportunity to follow in the steps of her aunt Bronislawa, and to pursue a career in schools that focused on an academically oriented curriculum, the equivalent of today's middle or junior high schools. Where would

Franciscus Sobolewski and Helena Regiec.
This photograph was taken in the winter of 1911 or 1912.

she use her new skills? We can only surmise that she was thinking about that and trying to decide upon her own path, experiencing a restlessness similar to what her father had felt in his early professional years.

This time, however, Helena's plans were put on hold—not by a lack of opportunities or the notorious bureaucracy of the Austro-Hungarian Empire but by matters of the heart. At some point, her collegial relations with fellow teacher Franciscus Sobolewski had ripened into love. A picture of them taken early in their relationship gives us a glimpse of how their courtship might have advanced. In the photo, Franciscus looks passionate and determined; based upon that and what we know of the customs of the time, he must have pursued her with some eagerness. Yet looking at Helena in the photograph, we see a young woman also with a good amount of determination, albeit in a softer form. Can we make a guess that Helena would have reined in her suitor's eagerness, insisting that they discuss the practical aspects of marriage—listening to their heads as well as their hearts?

We cannot be sure how long the courtship between them lasted, but we know that young couples in that time and place were traditionally expected to have long engagements. Although the customs of courtship were much more formal than ours today, contacts between the two were likely less restricted than for most of their contemporaries. They were teaching in the same school, and perhaps there were times during their workdays when they could slip away from their duties for a few moments alone together.

At some point, Franciscus Sobolewski must have visited Joseph and Stephania Regiec at 1 St. Joseph Street in Stanislawow to ask for Helena's hand. Even if the Regiecs already knew him from prior visits to Bohorodczany, a young man was expected to reassure his beloved's parents that he was indeed the right match for their daughter.

Once the Regiecs had approved of Franciscus, his parents, Andreas and Anna Sobolewski, would have met with them to formally talk about wedding plans and the couple's future. Those families could hardly have been more different: the Sobolewskis, with deep roots in their ancestral land and traditions; and the Regiecs, exemplifying the urban and upwardly mobile part of Galician society. Notwithstanding this disparity, the introductions must have gone well, because a date for the wedding was agreed on. Undoubtedly, the families debated where it should take place. Would it be better to follow custom and have the ceremony in Stanislawow or, given the size of the Sobolewski family and the couple's place of residence, should the event be held in Bohorodczany? Finally, this was decided in a somewhat surprising way.

On Friday, July 17, 1912, Franciscus and Helena walked down the aisle, not in the old Dominican church in Bohorodczany or the church attended by the

Kochawina. Helena and Franciscus got married in a new church, visible on the left, on July 17, 1912. *(Postcard from the early twentieth century.)*

Joannes Trzopinski, rector of Kochawina parish, who married Helena and Franciscus.

Regiecs in Stanislawow. Instead, a town approximately 50 miles northwest of Stanislawow was chosen for their marriage. With a bit of imagination, we can envision the wedding party—Helena, Franciscus, and their guests—boarding a special train car arranged by the father of the bride. That splash of luxury during the short trip from Stanislawow to their destination would have seemed quite appropriate for the occasion, even by the standards of the usually modest Regiec family.

The church in Kochawina and its parish rector, Joannes Trzopinski, were quite famous in eastern Galicia; it must have been quite an honor to be married there.[18]

Despite the need to travel, we can surmise that the church was full of the Sobolewski clan: not only the parents of the groom and Franciscus's many siblings but some Sobolewskis from other branches of the family. The Regiec crowd was most likely smaller, including Joseph and Stephania and Helena's sister, Wanda. Perhaps a few relatives on Stephania's side, the Telesnicki family, also traveled to witness the joyous ceremony.[19]

As required by law, the young couple registered their marriage in the Dominican church of Bohorodczany soon after returning home. The records identify Helena as *magistra scholae* (female teacher), a finding that made me very proud. Few women were identified in local registers as having professions. Even in large cities, women's progress was sometimes met with ridiculous resistance in Galicia's still male-dominated society. Rambling and patronizing arguments were put forward by self-appointed experts that education might hurt young girls' health and should not be encouraged to go too far.[20] Franciscus was listed in the marriage record as *magister scholae* (male teacher). The official entry was made days after the ceremony had taken place; hence, it is not surprising that the two

Entry in the marriage book marking the wedding of Franciscus Sobolewski (*magister scholae*) and Helena Wanda Regiec (*magistra scholae*).

official witnesses were Antonius and Andreas Sobolewski rather than members of the Regiec family, who would have already returned to Stanislawow.[21]

No wedding pictures, or stories about the celebrations following the ceremony, have survived. There is, however, the aforementioned picture of Helena and Franciscus, taken a few months before or after their wedding. Helena is wearing an elegant hat, with a bit of her carefully arranged hair to be seen underneath. Although it is not obvious in the picture, she was a tall woman with thick reddish locks.[22] Franciscus is looking intensely at the camera, wearing a top hat and a high-collared shirt just barely visible beneath a heavy overcoat. They were, indeed, a handsome couple. Unfortunately, only two pictures of my grandparents together survived.

The newly married pair moved to house 560, located a bit further from the town's center than Helena's prior home but next door to her in-laws. As in every new marriage, this must have been an exciting time for them, as they discovered and created together those little things that constitute a family. Undoubtedly, this was also time of dreaming and planning. Were they considering staying in Bohorodczany, or were they determined from the beginning to move on? Any sort of planning would soon become perilous for this generation, as time after time events around them began to dictate the course of their lives.

Bohorodczany itself was changing. As it had for centuries, the town still had strong links with the surrounding farms. There were busy cattle, horse, and poultry trading yards not far from the central square. During weekly market days, this was a busy place where farmers could sell or buy any imaginable agricultural product. But in the six years since Helena's arrival there, Bohorodczany had grown to be more than just a place for the farming community to gather. The town's center, with its one- and two-story buildings, had just been rebuilt after a recent fire.[23] There were 120 registered businesses and many shops. Eleven blacksmiths produced horseshoes, nails, hooks, and other metal items;

Market day in a sub-Carpathian town in Galicia. *(Dorothy Hosmer Lee Collection, UCR Sweeney Art Gallery, University of California, Riverside.)*

among them was a shop that belonged to Alexander Swirski, Franciscus's godfather. These shops were mainly owned by Poles and Ruthenians; in contrast, the leather business was firmly in Jewish hands. Busy tanneries situated closer to the river were receiving hides and providing dyed leather to 22 shoemaking firms and 20 furriers. But the latter certainly did not produce the fancy furs expected in large cities. Rather, they made tailored sheepskin coats, with the warm fleece inside; these came in handy during long, cold winters. There were also weavers spinning flax yarn into linen, and small shops selling the popular ribbons or lace to adorn clothing.

Even on Sundays, the sounds of blacksmiths forging wrought iron and shoemakers tapping leather soles with different types of hammers were heard along the main road, where several small shops were located. To the chagrin of pious passersby on their way to church, the market square, with its display of housewares on sale, piles of fruits and vegetables, and bundles of wrapped goods ready to be hauled away, conveyed an image of a busy trading day rather than the customary day of rest. When a few complained about the "unholy" atmosphere in Bohorodczany's center, the town's official laconically stated, "It is what it is"—making it clear that nothing would be done to slow the pace of work in order to pacify a few unhappy citizens.[24]

Bohorodczany was clearly opening to the world, with three transportation companies where one could hire wagons or carriages with coachmen to transport people and goods as far away as Stanislawow. Two inns and five restaurants were now in town, but Helena more likely visited Eizyk Rothstein's bookstore; she liked reading novels and popular books about exotic lands. Nearby, she could purchase groceries at Joseph Schmerler's delicatessen, or buy meat from a couple of butcher stores. Fresh dairy products could easily be bought in town, and just a bit further away in Old Bohorodczany, Helena could buy a tasty sharp cheese made of sheep's milk (*bryndza*) that would always remain her favorite.

Back in the town center, there was a lamp store that also sold mirrors, porcelain, and glass. From time to time, Helena purchased kerosene from either Izrael Engelberg's or Feiga Lanczer's shop—without this, evenings at home would have been dark. (Kerosene was cheap; the region around the nearby village of Starunia and further south was dotted with oil rigs, pumping the petroleum from shallow deposits.) Bohorodczany had six clothing stores, including those selling accessories, stockings, and linens. There were shoe stores for men and for women, and for those needing professional tailoring, one could choose from five tailors. If Helena wanted something fancier, Stanislawow, with its many stores, was not too far away, though her teacher's salary likely limited such extravagances.

Carolina Sobolewska Kubas (1888-1964), Wilhelmina Sobolewska (standing), Franciscus Kubas (Carolina's husband), and Mania Kubas in a photograph from the beginning of the twentieth century.

Sometime in the spring after her marriage, Helena discovered that she was pregnant. Certainly this was a happy event, but one often approached with some apprehension because childbirth killed so many women at that time. However, everything turned out all right, and on October 5, 1913, with the help of a midwife attending her at home, Helena delivered a baby daughter. "Irka," as she would be later called by her mother, was the first grandchild of Joseph and

Stephania Regiec; it is uncertain whether the infant was the first grandchild of Andreas and Anna Sobolewski, who already had a number of married children.

In a move somewhat unusual for the times, the traditional family celebration that marked the birth was delayed. We can only guess that both parents wanted to allow for the arrival of family members from faraway places. Times were clearly changing, and as we have already noted, many of the Sobolewskis' siblings and cousins no longer lived in the same town. A lovely, hand-written postcard from one Sobolewski sister to another spoke of coming home soon and the opportunity to share gossip about their large family. Between the lines, the sender was asking how Helena, her sister-in-law, and the baby were doing at home in Bohorodczany.

Bohorodczany. The winter scene.
(Postcard from the twentieth century.)

At last, with the arrival of the holidays and everyone gathered, Irena Maria Sobolewska was baptized on New Year's Day, 1914, in the same Dominican church in Bohorodczany where Sobolewski children had been baptized for generations. It is not difficult to imagine a frosty day in this sub-Carpathian region, with roofs and roads covered by snow. Although normally the family walked to the town center, Helena and Franciscus most likely arrived at the church in a sleigh, holding their daughter tightly bundled up against the cold.

Franciscus Kubas, Carolina Sobolewska's husband (top row, middle) is pictured with his coworkers in Czortkow. The picture was sent by Carolina to Wilhelmina Sobolewska in Bohorodczany in the fall of 1913.

Records of this event identify parents and grandparents from the Regiec and Sobolewski families. But these names, already familiar to us, were joined by entries of two other individuals who played special roles in the ceremony. Ladislaus Sobolewski, the second among Franciscus's brothers and a sergeant major in the Austro-Hungarian cavalry regiment of Czerniowce, was chosen as Irena's godfather. The other person was Carolina Kubas, who was the aforementioned postcard-writer, longing just a few months before for a visit home. Carolina was Franciscus's sister; she lived with her husband further east in the town of Czortkow and had been chosen as Irena's godmother.[25] Unlike the Sobolewski

Ladislaus Sobolewski, older brother of Franciscus, in the wedding picture with his bride, Helena Guminska, and her brother. The photograph was taken in Czerniowce in 1910.

men, her husband, Franciscus Kubas, was a rather slim individual who sported an impressive mustache, its tips carefully curled up (a very trendy fashion statement of the time). We can be sure that the gathering also included Stephania and Joseph Regiec with their younger daughter, Wanda, who would have made the short trip from Stanislawow for this joyous occasion.

Chapter 7

GATHERING CLOUDS:

TROUBLE AT HOME

———⁂———

For some time, a palpable sense that Galicia's old order was about to evolve into something different had been in the air. Since the beginning of the twentieth century, speculation about impending change had become frequent, in both conversation and newspaper commentary. Initially, the ideas put forward were somewhat unclear: exactly what this change might be, how it might happen, and what sort of country would ultimately emerge, no one could really say. What was clear was that with this uncertainty, different elements of Galician society were gravitating toward disparate goals. The tensions that built up among them seemed to bode trouble for the years ahead. This climate was right for a proliferation of political parties, with some becoming increasingly nationalistic, populist, and even anti-Semitic.

Poles of Galicia had always agitated for more autonomy and continued dominance in civil affairs, while trying to wrest more fiscal control from the central government in Vienna. They were increasingly supported by assimilated Jews who'd had successful careers in Polonized society. Other members of the Jewish community tried to remain neutral, aware that taking sides could bring about a backlash. At the same time, large numbers of them were leaving Galicia for other parts of the empire and, often, the United States.

Ruthenians (by then often called Ukrainians) had split into three groups by this time.[1] The so-called Old Ruthenians, the smallest of these, had a sense of belonging to a distinct group of East Slavs but largely advocated cultural and literary activities within the boundaries of Austro-Hungarian Galicia, without much animosity toward Poles. The second group, which was increasingly vocal, was often called Ukrainophiles; its members saw their future as very distinct from the current status quo. This populist movement voiced, in no uncertain terms, aspirations for a separate statehood extending from the Carpathian Mountains (covering eastern Galicia) to the Caucasus Mountains (including the territory of tsarist Russia, where most Ruthenians lived). Members of the third group, the Muscophiles, dismissed the Old Ruthenians' cultural aspirations within Galicia and the statehood aspirations of the Ukrainophiles. They considered all Ruthenians as part of a common Russian nationality. Given Polish hostility toward tsarist Russia, and Austrian wariness of its eastern neighbor, it is not surprising that the Muscophiles were viewed with suspicion by everyone, including Poles, Ukrainians, and the central government, and were often accused of sedition.

Relationships between Ruthenians and Poles ranged from relatively calm and cooperative through the 1890s to increasingly polarized in the first decade of the 1900s. Some of the views expressed by Ruthenian politicians ignited emotional fears in the Polish-dominant administration of Galicia. Whether they were lobbying Vienna for a division of Galicia along ethnic lines or demanding a separate Ruthenian university in Lvov, their demands were viewed with hostility by Poles. The Ukrainophiles, in particular, argued with some merit that the eastern part of Galicia was predominantly Ruthenian, with Poles exercising a disproportionate dominance over the poorer majority. Their proposal was to split Galicia along the River San, roughly separating the Polish majority in the west from the Ukrainian majority in the east. From time to time, newspapers in Galicia ran speculation about possible support for this plan by the government in Vienna and

The agrarian strike in Galicia in 1902. The economic conflict about unfair wages escalated to tensions between Ruthenians (Ukrainians) and Poles.
(Wiener Bilder *August 6, 1902;* ÖNB, Vienna.)

even alleged secret efforts of Ukrainian politicians to reach foreign powers, including Germany, in order to bolster their pleas.[2]

Demands for equality for the Ruthenian language—in both education and public affairs—were slowly accommodated through the creation of Ruthenian schools, newspapers, and published literature. Still, feelings that progress toward a multilingual society was inadequate, on the Ruthenian side, and that too many accommodations had been made, on the part of Poles, poisoned any attempt at constructive debate on the subject in eastern Galicia.

Another fracture point was the economic inequality of the Ruthenian population, who lived mainly in rural communities. Waves of agrarian strikes for higher wages were common in eastern Galicia in the first decade of the twentieth century; year after year, they were suppressed with force by the Polish administration.

Initially, these were mainly isolated disturbances, but they became particularly widespread in 1902. In the middle of that summer, protests by farm laborers paralyzed what would otherwise have been a busy harvest season. This time, however, their actions were better organized than before; more than 100,000 farm hands went on strike, with over 200 villages affected. Within days of this event, it was apparent that economic losses would be huge, as crops lay rotting in the fields.

Owners of large estates, who were mainly Poles, called for help, and the government sent in the army and police. In some villages, the officers were met with throngs of women, throwing themselves on the ground to block their passage. This only served to add more drama to the workers' cause, and what had started mainly as an economic conflict was quickly recast along ethnic lines. Where it was still possible to save some of the harvest, the government then resorted to the explosive step of bringing in laborers from neighboring Bukovina. Martial law and arrests followed in several districts. Some newspapers cautioned the government with headlines such as "Careful with Fire." With the end of the harvest season, the storm quickly passed—only to recur in subsequent years. A deep-set polarization of eastern Galicia was becoming a reality.

Bohorodczany, although tense, remained fairly quiet through all this. We can only speculate that the Sobolewskis' farmland had already been sold or leased to others, most likely their numerous Ruthenian neighbors. If there were any problems with the harvest on the few fields supplying their personal needs, those must not have risen to a level that warranted newspaper reports, and may have been resolved peacefully. Even the Stadion family's landholdings, although large by Bohorodczany standards, were probably too small to trigger the ire of the strikers—and the Austrian heritage of their owners would have also been a mitigating factor. Over the next years, however, the town would witness its share of Ruthenian discontent, with passionate speeches and demonstrations in its center. Yet even the threats of a boycott did not escalate to violence; local ties between the neighbors, often extended families, seemed too strong to be easily broken in the heat of the moment.[3]

Adding to the atmosphere of mistrust were constant grievances over election law. The old system of voting was based on non-proportional representation that favored large landowners, mainly Poles. In effect, sometimes less than one hundred votes were sufficient to elect a deputy among landowners, whereas tens to hundreds of thousands were required to choose a parliamentarian from other voting blocks, called *curiae*.[4] By 1907, however, universal male suffrage had been introduced for the national parliament; that increased the number of Ruthenian deputies sent to Vienna. Yet not long after the election, debate erupted in that body about alleged voting irregularities in Galicia. Predictably, Ruthenian representatives accused the provincial administration, largely in Polish hands, of election fraud. Stories about pre-printed ballots, with only the name of a candidate set to "win" the vote, were told during heated arguments. The testimony of the internal affairs minister of Austria did not assuage the situation. After reassuring those present that the governor of Galicia attested to the legality of the elections, he was met with ridicule by Ruthenian deputies.

In the end, these claims of fraud were rejected in a parliamentary vote. In protest after the ballot, Ruthenian politicians rose and sang national songs, and government ministers were forced to abruptly leave the chaotic scene.[5] But an additional problem had to be solved in Galicia. After a protracted debate in the province among politicians of many stripes, Poles demanded modification of the plurality law. Concerned about the future composition of the provincial legislature, they wanted some guarantee of their seats, in order to preserve their influence in the east, where they were a minority. Not surprisingly, Ruthenians interpreted these demands as another example of the political shenanigans of the more powerful Poles. During a time in history that we often imagine was gentler than today's, surprisingly vitriolic language on this subject was common in the

The campus of the University of Lvov was a frequent flash point of skirmishes between Polish and Ruthenian (Ukrainian) students. (Nowosci Illustrowane *December 21, 1907.*)

press. Political discourse in Galicia was becoming ruthless, full of accusations of political mischief and, often, the trading of personal insults between individuals.[6]

The University of Lvov was one frequent hotbed of unrest. This old and venerated institution had had its share of troubles when shelled by Austrian troops during a brief uprising in 1848. After reopening, the school had become a symbol of Polish identity in eastern Galicia. In a spirit of accommodation, the Austrian government had agreed to make Polish the university's official language, with German and Ruthenian as auxiliary languages. At least in theory, examinations in Ruthenian were permitted as long as Polish professors had proficiency in that language. But times were changing and, increasingly, this concession was viewed as insufficient by nationalistically leaning Ruthenians, who made repeated demands for a separate university.[7] In hindsight, we can see that the climate was set for an inflation of internal differences to something far worse than loud exchanges. Yet despite such tensions, this was still an age of innocence; nobody expected the heated debates to escalate to murder.

 — Gathering Clouds: Trouble at Home

COUNT ANDREAS POTOCKI, OWNER of mines, estates, and factories in Galicia, Russia, and elsewhere, was a lawyer by education, a diplomat by training, and a former member of the parliament in Vienna who had been the supreme governor of Galicia since 1903. At this time, almost anyone could approach the governor during one of his Sunday audiences, to express a grievance or request assistance. These meetings were entirely private, with no scribes or security personnel present.

On April 12, 1908, as in previous weeks, there were only a few scheduled visitors waiting in the foyer of the governor's office. A pharmacist from a small provincial town wanted to ask for help against the bureaucracy preventing him from opening a shop; a young man with an unknown petition waited in front of a mirror, checking to make sure his hair was in order; and the final petitioner, who was about to graduate from Lvov's Polytechnic College, was hoping to plead with the governor for a job in civil administration. First, the clerk ushered the pharmacist into the inner office. The governor quickly assured him that he could return home with no worries, as his case would be simple to resolve. Next was the turn of the young man who had been concerned about his grooming. Surprisingly, that petitioner had left the waiting room, but he was quickly found in the adjoining coatroom, where he seemed to be looking for something. He rushed into the governor's office and closed the door behind him. Almost immediately, three or four shots rang out. When the visitors and clerk hastily opened the door, they saw the governor, wounded in the head and arm, still conscious but kneeling on the floor just a few steps from the door, as though struck when going to greet the visitor. Count Potocki pointed at his attacker and said "Catch him!" The assailant, gun still in hand, calmly stated that he would not attempt to escape.[8]

The assassination of Andreas Potocki (1861–1908), governor of Galicia, by Miroslaw Siczynski is depicted on the front page of a Viennese newspaper. (Wiener Bilder *April 15, 1908;* ÖNB, Vienna.)

Potocki was bleeding from his head wound and, when someone assured him that physicians had been called for, he said that he most likely needed a priest rather than a doctor. The governor was able to dictate a brief telegram to the emperor Franz Joseph and lost consciousness shortly thereafter. Two hours later, he was pronounced dead.

News of the assassination spread quickly throughout Galicia. A telegram with a brief account of the events reached Stanislawow by three o'clock that afternoon. In Lvov and Vienna, special Sunday evening editions of the newspapers were quickly printed and distributed. Theatrical performances were canceled, and crowds quickly gathered in front of the governor's mansion.

The next day, newspapers in Vienna, London, and New York provided shocking details.[9] Headlines in the Galician press read "GOVERNOR'S ASSASINATION" and "BLOODY TRAGEDY" but were strictly factual and did not exploit the situation, which would have heightened current political tensions.

At the state funeral in Lvov, dignitaries from all over Galicia paid last respects to the governor and gave their condolences to his widow, Countess Cristina Potocka. Ministers from the central government and representatives sent by the emperor were also in attendance. After the official ceremonies, a dignified funeral procession accompanied the casket through the streets of Lvov to the train station. Some worried that unruly crowds might disrupt the event and further fuel ethnic divisions, but luckily this problem did not materialize. A special train transported the casket to the Potocki estate in Krzeszowice, near Cracow in western Galicia.[10]

In Stanislawow, as in all other towns of Galicia, public offices were draped in black. The Jewish organizations of the city strongly condemned the act of violence, and an impassioned service by Rabbi Horowitz in the main synagogue was noted by many. In Bohorodczany, memorial services were most likely attended by Helena Regiec and Franciscus Sobolewski. These turned out to be the ceremonies that spoke volumes about the mood of the moment. After a mass in the Dominican church attended by schoolchildren, teachers, and local citizens, the crowd walked to the synagogue, where the choir sang and speeches by the local rabbi followed. At least for the moment, grievances were put aside, with both services attended by Poles, Jews, and Old Ruthenians.[11]

The assassin was Miroslaw Siczynski, a radical Ukrainophile and a student of philosophy at Lvov's university. His motive was clearly political; other acts of violence were said to have been committed or at least talked about by other members of his family. There was never a question of Siczynski's guilt; later attempts to use an insanity defense were meek. He wanted to be a martyr, stating from the very beginning that he would not attempt suicide but would await death by hanging.

The raucous Galician press was unusually restrained in this case. Although a few commentators complained that Ruthenian politicians should have condemned the assassination with greater vigor and made fewer excuses for the criminal, there were no appeals for revenge. The local and Viennese presses both pointed out, however, that this was the first time—not just in Galicia but in the entire Austro-Hungarian Empire—that an assassination had been directed at a representative of the emperor.[12] With some sadness, it was noted that this event signified the crossing of an unmarked Rubicon. At least until then, acts of terror had been common in tsarist Russia but not in Austro-Hungary, which was generally believed to be more tolerant and more cultured. Some were perplexed why such a thing would have taken place in Galicia. Certainly, they pointed out, it was an imperfect place; but it offered much more freedom than did Russia, where the Ruthenian language was banned, and there was a total absence of schools, theaters, literary publications, and political parties for the vast majority of Ruthenians.[13]

Siczynski's initial trial came to an end in June of 1908. After the prosecutor (who, as it was underscored, was Ruthenian himself) and the defense completed their statements, the 12 jurors deliberated for only 30 minutes. The unanimous verdict was guilty, to a single count of the indictment. The jury found that the defendant had committed a premeditated act of violence, with intent to murder the governor. The same day, the court sentenced Siczynski to death by hanging.

But there was no jubilation on the streets. Instead, there were frequent appeals for commutation of the death sentence; it was believed that this would prevent further bloodshed.[14] Even the widow, Countess Potocka, wrote to ask Emperor Franz Joseph for mercy toward the killer. The deep meaning of her letter was noted not only locally but also by those in Vienna who remained critical of the political squabbles in Galicia. The press considered this a magnanimous act of tolerance, a striking plea for peace and the hope of a better future in Galicia.[15]

There would be appeals, but neither claims of insanity nor allegations of juror misconduct changed the verdict. The highest court in Vienna was clear in its opinion, rejecting all arguments of the defense: It ruled that the crime was murder, with no mitigating circumstances. Then, in a dramatic climax, the emperor commuted the death sentence, replacing it with a prison term of 20 years. There was a collective sigh of relief in Galicia, mainly among Poles who felt they had achieved a moral victory with the unambiguous court opinion but were reassured by the emperor's decision. That wise man had effectively prevented irrevocable damage to their reconciliation efforts with Ruthenians, which by then seemed elusive but still possible.[16]

But the story did not end there. Soon, Siczynski would be transferred to Stanislawow to serve his prison term. At first, suspicions were raised when news of a supposedly secret transfer of the prisoner was leaked; a few supporters actually turned out to welcome him at the train station.[17] With time, however, the attention of the public shifted elsewhere, occasionally to return to the inflammatory affair when reports that Siczynski's compatriots at home and as far away as Allentown, Pennsylvania, had petitioned the emperor for his release.[18]

For the next few years, Siczynski's life was divided between working in the prison's carpentry shop and reading, including a few books for the study of English. This rather boring picture of the assassin turned out to have been misleading when the headlines returned to this sad affair one autumn a few years later. In November 1911, out of the blue, news spread throughout Galicia that Siczynski had managed a spectacular escape. There was no tunnel dug underneath his cell, no bars had been removed from his window, and there were no signs of a forceful departure. The next days and weeks brought stunning headlines: Allegedly, a bottle of wine had been given to his unsuspecting cellmate to make him sleep soundly that fateful evening; and clothes had been folded into a body shape under a blanket, to mislead guards who checked the cell every few hours through a peephole.

Later, a police investigation revealed that Siczynski, dressed in a guard's uniform, had simply walked through the gates in the company of an accomplice. The plan had been well-executed, and to the embarrassment of prison officials, the escape had not been discovered until the next morning![19] Soon, rumors were swirling everywhere: that the fugitive had been taken in a speeding carriage, under cover of darkness, to the Romanian border; that he had traveled by train under a false identity toward Budapest; or that he was hiding somewhere in the vicinity of Stanislawow until the storm passed. At times, unconfirmed stories of Siczynski sightings on foreign soil were greeted with skepticism, as potential misinformation by sympathizers to persuade police to halt their investigation.

Ultimately, the mystery of this bold escape was solved, and two prison guards admitted that they had helped Siczynski escape. They were sentenced to prison terms of two to four years each; other conspiring guards were subjected only to administrative dismissals. The fugitive himself first surfaced in Sweden, and ultimately ended up in the United States, where he died decades later, apparently never showing any remorse for his senseless crime.[20]

In the tense atmosphere that now existed in Galicia, troubles were instigated by the Polish side as well. On December 12, 1908, Dr. Bobrzynski, the new governor and an educator himself, attended an annual celebration at the University of Lvov. The occasion was the ceremonial entry of new students into the university register, with professors in full faculty regalia in attendance. As in prior years, the governor was to present a rare honor (*sub auspiciis imperatoris*) to a doctoral student who had demonstrated exceptional academic achievement.

Just days before, information had been leaked to the press that the central government in Vienna, with the knowledge of the governor, was to provide funding for the creation of two new departments at the university. Under normal circumstances, this detail in the annual budget would have been ignored or, at best, viewed with some satisfaction by a few school administrators. But this was not a case of routine educational support; the government stipulated the opening of new departments solely staffed with Ruthenian faculty, and specifying Ruthenian as the language of instruction.[21]

In Galicia at this time, language and education could easily have become a volatile mixture; so during the ceremony, the atmosphere was visibly tense. Some expected walkouts or shouting by Ruthenian or Jewish Zionist students, who often used this type of occasion to express their grievances against the Polish administration. The ceremony was uneventful, except that a larger-than-usual attendance by Polish students caused an overflow of spectators. The governor made a short speech and presented the honored young man with an engraved ring on behalf of the emperor.

The ceremony over without the much-feared outbursts, the governor, his small entourage, and the rector of the university made their way toward the exit. Suddenly, shouting and scuffles began in the crowded hallways. The governor

Governor Michael Bobrzynski is assaulted by Polish students in the hallways of the University of Lvov. (Nowosci Illustrowane *December 19, 1908*.)

was pelted with rotten eggs by Poles enraged by the prospect of "their university" allowing the formation of Ruthenian departments. In the narrow corridors, the governor's military aide was quickly overpowered; his ceremonial sword was bent by defiant students, rendering it useless. Governor Bobrzynski was pushed and shoved in the hallways, and once he reached the staircase that was to lead him outside, he was unceremoniously pushed downstairs with egg smeared over his face and clothing.[22] After the governor's hasty departure, an angry petition was presented to the university senate, and hundreds of enraged students marched toward the governor's mansion. As if security lessons from earlier that year had been quickly forgotten, a single mounted policeman at the gate was easily overtaken by the crowd. Before reinforcements could be sent, stones and small bottles of ink were thrown at the building.

Initial reactions to this uprising were clear. Several student organizations quickly distanced themselves, although their high moral ground had been lost. The press condemned a fringe group of Polish students for the attack on the governor and the street outbursts that had followed. In a veiled comparison to the recent assassination, the papers decried the fact that violent unrest had never before been attributed to Polish students. But this fuss was more about the means of protest than the appalling absence of a solution to the recurring tensions.[23]

Less than two years later, another outburst at the university turned even more violent. In hindsight, there had been signs of something to come when, on one day, hundreds of telegrams were sent from Lvov throughout Galicia, calling on Ruthenian students to travel to the city. By no coincidence, troubles erupted the next morning when a unilateral deadline set by Ukrainophile deputies for the decision about opening a separate Ruthenian university passed without any response from the central government. This time, Ruthenian students and their supporters, armed with handguns and sticks, staged a protest in one of the buildings on campus. When Poles barricaded some of the hallways, piling up desks to

Tense days in Lvov after the death of a Ruthenian (Ukrainian) student shot on the university campus. *(Nowosci Illustrowane July 9, 1910.)*

keep demonstrators from other sections of the university, insults were traded and several shots were fired. Sadly, flying bullets left one Ruthenian student dead, shot from behind by one of his colleagues; several others were wounded.

News of the bloody unrest traveled fast, with crowds of several thousand on both sides of the dispute gathering within hours on the streets of Lvov. Mounted police were called in, and the army, with bayonets on their rifles, quickly restored order. The university and key government buildings were cordoned off and the campus was locked down, with more than 200 demonstrators briefly detained for police questioning. Who shot whom would be debated for days, but in the end, an official inquiry put the blame on Ruthenians.[24] In the aftermath, there would be condemnations of violence from both sides but, predictably, for very different reasons. In what became a recurring theme, Poles and Ruthenians each assigned culpability for the unrest to the other party, but no one was able to put forward a constructive plan on how to break this cycle.[25]

Increasingly, both sides were using not just heated rhetoric but physical violence to advance their causes. Trying to deflect the issue, some Poles wondered aloud why no demands for a Ruthenian university had been heard from Kiev, the heart of the emerging Ukrainian nationality that still remained under the absolute control of tsarist Russia. As always in recalcitrant issues, historical arguments were used (or more often, misused) in the debate to justify actions. Ancient claims going back to the founding of the university by the Polish king Casmir the Great were coupled with inflexible arguments that Polish was the legal language of instruction, guaranteed by modern laws passed in Galicia.[26] Despite Galicia's multiculturalism, Poles viewed the university as a hard-won symbol of their cultural identity, which had been long suppressed after the partition of their country. The future appointment of a few Ruthenian professors and then the opening of Ruthenian departments were viewed as a step-by-step retreat under pressure rather than as a needed path to reconciliation. Ruthenians could not have had a more opposite view. Being a majority in eastern Galicia, they saw only Polish dominance in the denial of their rights to use Ruthenian at the university.

In the end, in a somewhat disingenuous way, the central government was blamed for meddling in what were considered local affairs.[27] Slowly, it was becoming apparent that rather than attempting to change an old institution, forming a separate Ruthenian university might be a better way forward—even though this might take a long time to accomplish. A few suggestions by some in the Polish press to place a future Ruthenian university in the backward provincial town of Halicz (Halych in Ruthenian), rather than in Lvov, did not help the dialogue.[28]

Next, the city council of Stanislawow and a few other Galician cities joined the fray by grudgingly passing resolutions supporting the idea of a separate university but stating that its home should be somewhere else. Finally, a compromise was reached between parliamentarians from both sides who gathered in Vienna, far from local, often inflammatory, rhetoric. It was decided that the long-awaited Ruthenian university would become reality no later than the autumn of 1916.²⁹ Thus, both sides would be able to claim victory. Poles could say that Polish remained the University of Lvov's language of instruction; there would be no need now for either linguistic or cultural accommodation. Nor would there be any threat of dividing the university campus. Ruthenians finally saw the realization of their dream of a separate institution of higher learning; although it most likely would be situated outside Lvov, it would have the financial support of the state. To cement the deal, the emperor Franz Joseph, in a public declaration from Vienna, instructed the government of Galicia to implement the compromise. This wise man, who knew his subjects well, also said in no uncertain terms that if the bickering continued by the time of his deadline, the University of Lvov would be divided after all.³⁰

History, however, had a bitter surprise for both of the sparring sides. The events that would soon engulf the region with such force made the entire discourse about the university irrelevant. Ultimately, neither group would ever know whether this compromise could have made a real difference; whether it might have helped heal the rift between the two cultures living side by side in eastern Galicia.

Chapter 8

THE PRELUDE:

TROOPS ARE MARCHING

AT THE BEGINNING OF 1904, tensions between major world powers had been on the rise for some time. But as often happens before a major catastrophe, those early signs did not immediately feel ominous, at least to the citizens of Galicia. In early February of that year, Russia and Japan became locked in an armed conflict. The tsar's empire, its expanse extending from formerly Polish territories in Europe to the Far East, needed a warm-water port in southern Manchuria for its navy. Recently modernized Japan viewed the Korean Peninsula and the adjoining province of Manchuria as part of its strategic sphere of influence. Their seven-month struggle over this territory came to be known as the Russo-Japanese War.

In Galicia, such troubles seemed far away; public attention was still focused inward. But the Austro-Hungarian Empire, and Galicia in particular, did take notice when news of Russia's humiliating defeat uncovered its vulnerabilities. First, the Russian navy suffered losses in a surprise attack by Japanese destroyers. A relentless land and naval campaign, with the Russians on the defensive, followed. Throughout that year, illustrated Viennese magazines featured gripping scenes from the battleground, which consistently showed the weakness of the tsar's forces. In this respect, the perspectives of Vienna and Lvov were perfectly aligned; and both met Russia's troubles with a bit of satisfaction, since their big neighbor to the east had always been viewed with apprehension at best. Recurring news of Russia's harsh treatment of ethnic minorities, regardless of whether they were Jews or Poles, had only added to Galicia's unfavorable view of that vast country. The Galician people were well aware that compared to life under the tsar, they enjoyed a large degree of autonomy in their internal affairs; their noisy but generally free political climate was largely accepted by the Austro-Hungarian authorities. The partitioned Polish lands under Russian control were not so lucky, as most Galicians knew.

So both the Poles and the Jews of Galicia welcomed reports of the Japanese army's advances. Perhaps because of the anti-Russian sentiments so close to the surface (not to mention skillful manipulation of news by the victors), no one noticed the cruelty of the Japanese forces that would come to light much later. Instead, the occupying Japanese army was portrayed as uniquely sensitive to local

Japanese attack on Port Arthur during the Russo-Japanese War. Port Arthur fell into Japanese hands in January 1905. The humiliation of the Russian army was on a grand scale, with its commander subsequently court-martialed.
(Wiener Bilder *September 28, 1904*; ÖNB, Vienna.)

populations, avoiding ruthless military confiscations of property and even limiting the use of the Japanese language when dealing with natives in occupied Korea. Ironically, nobody questioned the veracity of reports about POW physicians who were allegedly being released by the Japanese, with expressions of gratitude for running hospitals during their brief captivities.[1] In January of 1905, spontaneous celebrations broke out in Stanislawow and other Galician cities at news of the Japanese takeover of Port Arthur, the ultimate prize of the conflict. Marching youths shouted "Banzai Japan!" and "Down with tsarist Russia!"[2] Nevertheless, these events, far away in Asia, were viewed more as a diversion than any kind of threat.

When the Russo-Japanese conflict came to an end, with the help of diplomatic intervention by the United States under President Theodore Roosevelt, the peace treaty signed on American soil was clearly favorable to victorious Japan. What was perhaps not apparent at first was that this meeting was more than a diplomatic gathering about resolving a regional crisis. Early signs

Theodore Roosevelt and Franz Joseph meeting in Vienna.
(Wiener Bilder *April 20, 1910*; ŐNB, Vienna.)

were appearing of what would soon become clear: The United States would increasingly assume the role of a global power. Theodore Roosevelt's efforts to bring the combatants to the negotiation table were lauded by many in the world, and he would be rewarded the Nobel Peace Prize the following year.

A few years later Roosevelt, already out of office, passed through Vienna during one of his European tours. A newspaper drawing of the large, self-assured, gesticulating American visiting the elderly emperor Franz Joseph, who leaned forward in his chair as if hard of hearing, showed more than the physical differences between the two men. It expressed visually a new vitality and an old frailness that could easily be applied to the countries that those men represented.[3]

Soon, public opinion in Galicia was riveted by another hot spot—one that raised concerns of possible instability, but this time much closer to home. For a short time in 1908, news of the Austro-Hungarian annexation of Bosnia and Herzegovina in the Balkans was viewed with concern. A broader conflict was feared, not just with local forces from neighboring Serbia vying for the same territory, but with Russia, wounded in Asia yet holding tight to its European aspirations. After a few weeks of dramatic headlines asking "War or Peace?," news from the Balkans was relegated to the back pages of the newspapers, and Galicia quickly became preoccupied with itself again. With tensions seemingly over, a visit by Emperor Franz Joseph to Sarajevo, capital of the troubled province, was considered a success. He was welcomed by representatives of various faiths—including an Eastern Orthodox metropolitan, a Roman Catholic bishop, a Sephardic rabbi, and a chief imam.[4] But the harmony could not have been more deceptive.

A couple of years later, the situation in the Balkans was again on the front pages of Galician newspapers. This time, it was a conflict between the weakened Ottoman Empire, retreating from its European possessions under pressure from the Balkan countries of Serbia, Bulgaria, Greece, and Montenegro. But that was only a backdrop to a dangerous struggle between the superpowers. A dance of diplomatic formalities was soon on full display; this was an age when international custom demanded formal exchanges of declarations of war, delivered by formally dressed ambassadors. The Balkan nations, united in their purpose, had delivered notes announcing impending hostilities to the Ottomans before armed conflict commenced. Real battles ensued, and it was clear this time to everyone that this Balkan war could easily explode into a much wider conflict. With no other access to the sea than through its Adriatic ports, Austro-Hungary saw this struggle as potentially threatening to its survival as a superpower.

Indeed, the news soon became alarming. In 1912, Russia massed troops on its border with Austro-Hungary, sending a clear signal to Vienna to stay away from the Balkan conflict. To add to the message, the Austrian consulate in Kiev was ransacked by unruly crowds under the noses of tsarist police. In return, waves of suspected Russian spies were arrested in Galicia. Reports of general mobilization in Austro-Hungary, coupled with subsequent quick denials, only added to the uncertainty. In any case, military units from all over the country, including one from Stanislawow, were soon being transported closer to the troubled Balkans. Each of these superpowers was warily watching the other, ready to pounce at the first sign that it might exploit a local conflict. There was now no doubt in the minds of anyone that Galicia could easily become a theater of war if events got out of control.

The Poles of Galicia were leaning toward supporting Austria, should any military conflict arise with Russia. This was seen by them as a way to build Galicia's strength, and to move it toward its hoped-for (although somewhat undefined) independent statehood. In Stanislawow, nerves were already frayed; with all the talk of war, the public rushed to withdraw savings from local banks. The pretext was a widely circulating rumor that Vienna would have to tap the personal accounts of its citizens to cover its growing military expenditures. A real run on the banks was not eased by the government's increase in interest rates on deposits and repeated reassurances that citizens' assets were safe. There was even a statement from the governor of Galicia saying in no uncertain terms that the government was not secretly raiding private bank accounts to finance the military. But that did not help much. Despite all these measures, the main savings institution in town would default, with losses estimated at more than 2,000,000 kronen (U.S. $9,160,000 today).[5]

Slowly, after three months of international tension, calmer news started to emerge. By the beginning of 1913, a global conflict seemed to have been averted. The Ottomans had effectively retreated from the Balkans and lost sovereignty over most of their former European territory, with the new country of Albania emerging in the aftermath.[6] Deceptively, as it turned out, the so-called First Balkan War appeared to be over; but recurrent flareups would punctuate the headlines for months to come. The Balkan nations had turned from being allies in a common struggle against the Ottoman Turks to enemies attacking each other. For the moment, however, the threat of global conflict had receded again, and Galician troops were finally beginning to come home from the Austrian part of the Balkans, including Carniola (today part of Slovenia and Italy), Dalmatia (today part of Croatia), and Bosnia and Herzegovina.

When a military train with soon-to-be demobilized reservists from the local 58th Infantry Regiment arrived in Stanislawow, thousands of people were gathered at the railroad station. A military band played the Radetzky March, always popular with soldiers, and the customary tributes and ovations for Emperor Franz Joseph were called for. Then the troops, with the officer corps at attention and a ceremonial guard in place, were welcomed home with three speeches. A colonel spoke first in German and a captain gave a short address in Polish, followed by a lieutenant greeting the returnees in Ruthenian. The symbolism of the scene could not have been greater; this was yet another reflection of the ethnically and linguistically diverse Galician world.[7]

Chapter 8 — The Prelude: Troops Are Marching

ALTHOUGH A GLOBAL STORM had been averted, the price for these instabilities was felt acutely at home. For the first time since Dr. Nimhin had become mayor of Stanislawow, the city coffers were empty. To make matters worse, neither Lvov nor Vienna was able to come up with money for the public works that might address growing unemployment. There were hotly contested arguments about whether the city should take out loans to stimulate its economy, thus quickly running up a previously unheard-of budget deficit. Fiscal prudence, which in former times had been considered a virtue, would be criticized the following year as the mayor's passivity or lack of imagination. The engine of antiestablishment sentiment was a weekly publication, *Rewera*, which repeatedly traded insults with another weekly newspaper, *Kurjer Stanislawowski*. A war of words for and against Dr. Nimhin's administration escalated. At one point, the arguments became so heated that the journalists involved were ordered in court to apologize to each other—only to trade new insults a week later. The opposing

Warring weeklies from Stanislawow. *Kurjer Stanislawowski* was supportive of Mayor Nimhin, whereas *Rewera* was the antiestablishment paper. The vehement debate about local politics spilled over to insults traded between the editors of the weeklies.

newspaper constantly railed against unsanitary conditions and against bureaucracy in local government offices, even offering the tongue-in-cheek advice that a stranger should "ask a fiacre [carriage] to proceed quickly to a morgue in case of medical emergency" rather than pointlessly look for any help in town.

More ridiculous charges followed, often implying Dr. Nimhin's guilt by association. This was a testament to freedom of speech in Galicia, but the mayor's vocal opponents saw nothing right in Stanislawow any more, and the tone of their invective moved from cynical to vicious at times.

Despite his critics, Dr. Nimhin was overwhelmingly reelected for another six-year term in 1912.[8] Putting the rancor of the press aside, the reality was that the construction of a new public hospital and much-needed improvements to the city's infrastructure would have to be put on hold. Plans that had been realistic a few years before, such as installing a modern sewer system and constructing a town water system to replace local wells, were suspended. Laying tracks for the long-awaited electric tram, a symbol of urban innovation in those days, suddenly became an unrealized dream. Construction of the elegant apartment buildings that Stanislawow was acclaimed for also slowed. Suddenly, the city went from a scarcity of apartments for a growing population to a glut of apartments that no one could afford. As if this was not enough, food prices rose; some blamed this on bad weather.[9]

But as always, life had to go on, and these challenging times also brought lighter topics of conversation. Toward the end of 1913, Stanislawow's press proudly announced that the first cabs (called motorized carriages) with fare meters had started operation in town. The public was told that those few taxis could be found in front of the Union Hotel and could carry more than three people, and even packages for an additional charge.[10]

Despite the financial crisis, there was a fair share of excitement on the social scene. Some wondered what the tango mania that was sweeping Europe would mean for the upcoming balls. One newspaper columnist sternly opined that no mother should allow her daughter to learn this morally questionable dance which, in any case, was merely a fad and would never make it to the ballroom. Apparently, he was not alone in this criticism; local authorities banned the tango during the next carnival season. The ban caused some consternation not only among young, home-grown enthusiasts; to the disappointment of some ball organizers, a tango-performing couple who had been invited to come all the way from Paris had to yield to that moral verdict.[11]

Stanislawow also witnessed more than its share on the stage that year. Surprisingly, there were no longer complaints that the public was not interested in the performing arts; most shows were sold out. What could explain this apparent paradox? One can only wonder whether attending classical music concerts, operas, or the theater was the population's subconscious refusal to submit to gloomy forecasts; or was it just a coincidence that the townspeople, like the local government, were living beyond their means?

Wanda Regiec (1888–1960s).
This undated photograph was taken in Stanislawow.

Among those who got high marks for their talent was my grandmother's sister, Wanda Regiec. By now in her early 20s, she continued to live with her parents and support herself by giving piano lessons. But Wanda also had other artistic interests. Not long after visiting Helena, who had just given birth to my mother in neighboring Bohorodczany, Wanda would perform in two plays reviewed by the press. The first, entitled *The Mill Owner and his Daughter*, was one of those traditional dramas considered appropriate to see but not necessarily the most exciting choice. Nonetheless, Wanda's acting caught the attention of the public, and she was described by a critic as "quite good and well-prepared."

A month later, it was Wanda's turn for a comedy, one that brought many laughs to the audience. But this turned out not to be the typical humor that was seen each year in the weeks before Christmas. Instead, the young actors pushed the boundaries of acceptable entertainment. The subject matter, which included prostitution, was considered risqué by the standards of 1913. (Earlier in the year, the drama had been made into a silent film, which attested to its popularity and could have contributed to the sold-out stage performances.) Despite the grumblings of a local critic, who lamented that the talented playwright had not delved into a more wholesome subject, Wanda's acting in a supporting role was again praised on the pages of a newspaper.[12]

The end of the year also brought a much-needed hilarious moment when Stanislawow suddenly welcomed two unexpected visitors. One evening, a large balloon with a gondola below it landed outside the city. It was quickly surrounded by perplexed peasants, who looked with bewilderment at the two travelers who emerged, speaking a language that no one in the village could understand. As it turned out, they were neither celestial creatures nor spies. Just a couple of days before, the visitors had set out from Paris to beat the world record, an uninterrupted balloon flight of 1,490 miles. In falling darkness, the hapless aviators had mistaken a blanket of fog and a bright, flickering light for the edge of the sea and a lighthouse. Instead of reaching their ultimate destination, the port city of Odessa some 400 miles further east, they spent the next few days in Stanislawow's Union Hotel. Their gear was thoroughly searched, and police were finally convinced that they had no nefarious intent. While the Parisian press was trying to salvage the reputation of the famous balloonists—by alleging that the embarrassing landing was due to gunfire aimed at them—all of Stanislawow was laughing.[13]

Chapter 8 — The Prelude: Troops Are Marching

With the start of 1914, at least in the view of some, the Balkan drama was finally coming to an end, with the major warring parties exhausted by the conflict. Helena was certainly quite busy with her infant daughter at home in Bohorodczany. It would have been no surprise if she and Franciscus had been preoccupied with plans, like many young parents, about how to care for the baby in the months to come. But if Helena had had time to glance at commentaries published on New Year's Day, she would have likely found a glimmer of hope. If the rumors were true, they would herald the possibility of sustained peace at home.[14]

In Galicia as a whole, reasonable voices were being heard more often. Even the somewhat paranoid Polish fears about the spread of the Ukrainian language in education were slowly receding. With the university debate largely behind them, pragmatists advocated more study of Ukrainian in Polish schools as a way to foster better understanding between cultures. Others voiced a belief, not necessarily backed by the facts, that Ukrainians had greater support for their national cultural events than Poles did for their own fragmented and often competing civic organizations.[15]

However, hopes for calmer, more reasonable times were quickly dashed when the archduke Franz Ferdinand, heir apparent to the Austro-Hungarian throne, was assassinated on June 28, 1914, in Sarajevo during a visit to the troubled Balkan province of Bosnia. There could be no doubt that the murder had been committed by Serbs. This act not only threatened Austro-Hungary's presence in the Balkans, it signaled the aspirations of Serbs to build a Greater Serbia at the territorial expense of the aging Autro-Hungarian Empire. When their expansion south had achieved success during the Balkan Wars, Serbs, with the tacit approval of Russia, had turned their attention north. Their aim was to trigger unrest among Slavic minorities in the southern part of Austro-Hungary. This was a threat to the very survival of the multiethnic empire.[16]

Gavrilo Princip, a Bosnian Serb, captured shortly after the assassination of the archduke Franz Ferdinand of Austria and his wife on June 28, 1914, in Sarajevo. (Wiener Bilder *July 5, 1914*; ÖNB, Vienna.)

In many places, news of the assassination arrived by telegraph on the evening of the day it had occurred. In Stanislawow and many other cities of Galicia, government buildings were soon draped in black. Galicians now had to grapple with the uncertain outcome of a risky geopolitical game involving many nations of Europe. During official gatherings, the people of Galicia expressed not only their support for Austro-Hungary but a genuine sympathy for Emperor Franz Joseph. There was a sense of sadness that the emperor, now a man in his mid-80s who had previously mourned the loss of his only son to an apparent suicide, suffered this new blow that prevented him from transferring constitutional powers to his successor in the face of increasing complications.[17]

However, not all grasped the gravity of the situation. Amazingly, a leading Polish monthly reported the assassination, an event which would trigger unparalleled conflict, on its fourth page without any recognition of its importance. While the drama of diplomacy unfolded in the capitals of Europe throughout July 1914, the Stanislawow public read in its weekly papers about promotions in civil administration and obscure proceedings of the city council. Perhaps with a slower pace due to annual vacations, the antiestablishment paper wondered, with much less than its customary vitriol, if Dr. Nimhin would run in the next mayoral election. Those staying in the city during the summer months must have been disappointed to read that the military band would not play in the city park for six weeks, observing a period of official mourning.[18] Indeed, this turned out to be true, and no alternative entertainment would be offered in Stanislawow, but for very different reasons. Cataclysmic events that would mark the end of one era and the beginning of another were about to erupt.

Chapter 9

THE GREAT WAR:

A TALE OF CONFLICT AND

ORDINARY LIFE

IN THE NAME OF HIS MAJESTY the Emperor and Apostolic King Franz Joseph, the government of Austro-Hungary declared war on Serbia on July 28, 1914. The diplomatic note delivered to the Serbian government was simple in its message: "In light of the unsatisfactory answer of the Serbian Royal Government to the note of July 23, the Imperial and Royal Government [of Austro-Hungary] is forced to protect its rights and interests. To this end, the government [of Austro-Hungary] appeals to its military [to respond to the conflict]. From this moment, Austro-Hungary considers itself in a state of war with Serbia." It was signed "Foreign Minister of Austro-Hungary, Berchtold."

There is never a right time to go to war, and this was certainly true in the summer of 1914. For a few days after the declaration of hostilities, many speculated—or indulged in wishful thinking—that the war might turn out to be just another local conflict in the Balkans.[1] But such commentary in the press was rather unconvincing, and news from Russia about partial troop mobilization, which soon became a full call to arms, was ominous. Within days, the failure of diplomacy was apparent across the European continent. Polite but unyielding notes exchanged between ruling cousins, the German kaiser and the Russian tsar, were portrayed as last-ditch efforts that failed to avert the crisis. At first, there were only two countries at war, Austria and Serbia; but within days, Germany declared war on Russia, and then more than a dozen countries announced hostile actions against one party or another. The situation had evolved into a domino effect, becoming increasingly out of control.

On August 5, the most anticipated event happened: The ambassador of Austro-Hungary delivered a note to the tsar's government in St. Petersburg. It read, "In light of the aggressive stand taken by Russia in the conflict between the Austro-Hungarian monarchy and Serbia, and as the result of hostile actions [by Russia] against Germany, resulting in a state of war [between the two powers], Austro-Hungary also considers itself in a state of war with Russia."

The next day, headlines in Galicia screamed, "AUSTRIA IN WAR WITH RUSSIA." As a brief, front-page editorial in one paper put it, now that the almost unbearable uncertainty of the past few days was over, there was a feeling of some relief that the war had finally started. In a major case of false prophecy, the paper reassured its readers that this storm almost certainly would be followed by a long period of calm. History would show that nothing was further from the truth.[2]

At first, nobody knew what to call this war; somewhat confused newspapers initially reported each conflict as a separate event, although everyone quickly realized that what was unfolding would be very different from anything in the past. Soon, a somber feeling descended; this would not be a collection of unrelated shots or artillery fire in the east, west, and south of Europe. The General War, as it was sometimes referred to during those pregnant summer days, would become known as the Great War, a title that would underscore more than its geographical scope.

My grandmother's recollection of World War I was later diminished by the even more horrific events of the other war that erupted in Europe some 25 years later. In a sense, the experience of two world wars in the lifetime of a single generation was too much. No one's memory could be expected to put them on an equal level, as the escalated carnage wrought by the second conflict tended to overshadow the suffering of the first. What Helena remembered about the Great War was repeated marches of big armies back and forth around Bohorodczany and Stanislawow. She spoke of the heavy use of artillery and the intermittent bombardments that, as we will see, came so close to home.

When the order for general mobilization came, the scope of preparations reached a massive scale. Facing war with Russia, with its almost limitless human resources, Austro-Hungary called out army, navy, and auxiliary forces that would soon grow to more than 1.5 million. This figure, as high as it might seem, was only a prelude to the greater and greater numbers who would serve.[3] Besides young men of draft age and military reservists aged 19 to 42, in some circumstances, men up to age 60 were called. Those qualifying for service were to start their journeys to military posts no later than 24 hours after seeing an announcement in a newspaper or on display at a public square. In addition to the throngs of men, great numbers of horses were collected from villagers. The army needed all the power it could get to move troops, and pull heavy artillery and other equipment.[4]

General mobilization in Austro-Hungary on July 31, 1914.
(Wiener Bilder *August 9, 1914*; ÖNB, Vienna.)

Franciscus Sobolewski, my grandfather, was one of those who responded to the general mobilization order. A junior officer in the reserve, Franciscus was leaving behind a new wife and a daughter less than a year old. To make matters worse, Helena, my grandmother, was pregnant with their second child. We can safely assume that, in the tense moments just before Franciscus left Bohorodczany, he and Helena privately whispered their hopes that the war would soon be over. It would not be a surprise if, like many in those days, they thought that this conflict would last only a year or so. On August 1, 1914, the couple said their final good-byes either in Bohorodczany or in Stanislawow, where Franciscus reported for military service. The sights around them would have been like nothing they had seen before; all the roads were packed, and Stanislawow was overflowing with soldiers or soon-to-be soldiers, camping on public squares while awaiting orders. The army barracks on the city outskirts were simply too small to accommodate everyone. Within days, Franciscus Sobolewski, now a second lieutenant in the 58th Infantry Regiment, was deployed to the front line with thousands of others. As he headed toward the Russian border, he had no way of knowing that it would be not a few months or a year but many years before he and Helena would be reunited. Even then, they would find themselves in a very different world than the one Franciscus was leaving behind.

At first, crowds of onlookers in Stanislawow watched, with curiosity, the movement of the troops and their equipment across the city; but soon that became the norm. The railroad station was a place of apprehension and some chaos, and not just for departing troops. Many of those staying behind worried whether the few still operating trains would be able to bring back family members hastily returning from summer vacations, or take on board civilians who were stranded in the city. Within a few days of the declaration of war, local schools and the railroad terminal had been converted to field hospitals, staffed by an increasing number of Red Cross personnel in their characteristically marked armbands.[5] It was no illusion that, with the Russian border so close, it would be only a matter of time before many wounded would start arriving. But nobody suspected that the red cross on a white background would remain a common sight for years to come, signaling not just the availability of medical help but the real danger of injuries and loss of life.

For a brief time, many believed in the argument that modern methods of troop transport favored decisive military actions. Others mentioned the unsustainable cost of any global conflict—which, it was said, could only shorten the war.[6] In any case, initial news from the front lines was good. In the north, German allies fighting in the Masurian Lakes region of East Prussia inflicted real damage on the Russian army. In the south, Russia was retreating from the part of Poland previously in its hands; the void was filled by Austrian troops from western Galicia marching north. But the optimism quickly turned out to be premature. By mid-August, the Russian army suddenly poured from the east into Galicia and Bukovina. Along a quickly moving front, their attack was fierce; battles engulfed many towns and villages, including Bohorodczany. Swirling suspicions about Russian sympathizers and spies added to rising tensions among civilians. In Stanislawow, under extraordinary military powers, preventive arrests of Greek Catholic clergy, Ukrainian teachers, and peasants (all suspected of being "Muscophiles") were recurring news in August.[7]

Whether Helena and her 10-month-old daughter stayed at home or went to Stanislawow to join her family is not known; in any case, the larger city would not offer much protection. Certainly, the situation did not look good in Stanislawow when the savings bank shut its doors and evacuated all its assets to the safety of Budapest. On September 2, Austro-Hungarian troops withdrew from the city; the sound of explosions marked their intentional destruction of bridges as they fled. That only added to an atmosphere that was growing ever tenser, as residents anxiously awaited whatever would come next. At first, the vanguard unit of the enemy galloped hurriedly through the main streets without stopping. By the following day, however, the feared Cossacks had settled in for good, extracting ransoms in the form of watches or money at random to ensure free passage.[8]

Next in the line of fire was Galicia's capital, Lvov. Under the rules of military censorship, newspapers could freely report events from the western front; but any news around the city was conspicuously absent, even though the sound of nearby artillery was quite audible. In the closing days of August, fierce combat took place as the Russian army quickly encircled Lvov. On August 30, headline read, "BIG BATTLE. Vienna. Official reports from the war press headquarters: Big battle that started on August 26 continues. Situation of our troops is favorable. The weather is warm and sunny." The outcome, however, was all but favorable, with 30,000 soldiers and hundreds of officers taken prisoner by the victorious Russians. On September 2, Lvov was declared an open city to avoid its destruction at enemy hands. The next day at seven o'clock a.m., one-page fliers were everywhere; the appeal by city officials read, "CITIZENS! The Army of [the Austro-Hungarian] Monarchy has suffered serious losses and retreated west. In a short time, the winning Russian army is expected to enter Lvov." In hopes that the city and its stunned population would remain safe, a plea for calm followed. On the same day, mounted Cossacks trotted through the center of Lvov.[9]

The bad news would continue for several weeks, if not months. The Russians pressed hard west, taking over not only eastern but also large parts of western Galicia. There would even be talk of their army soon attacking Cracow, effectively ending Austro-Hungarian sovereignty over the province. The threat seemed so real that the evacuation of Cracow was ordered; many left the city for temporary stays in Moravia or joined thousands of Galician refugees already descending on Vienna. Although Cracow would ultimately remain safe, Austro-Hungary suffered losses in the south of Galicia as well. By the end of September, Russians were approaching the Carpathian Mountains. Here the prize for the tsar's army was a quick push toward the Hungarian plains, the soft underbelly of the empire.

Chapter 9 — The Great War: A Tale of Conflict and Ordinary Life

Feared Cossacks crossing the Carpathian Mountain passes to Hungary. Only the arrival of winter halted their conquest of Austro-Hungary. *(Nowosci Illustrowane October 3, 1914.)*

The Cossacks, a highly mobile and brutal force, were probing for weak points in the front line; they soon started to appear on the other side, having crossed through a few unmanned passes. Despite the military censorship put in place in Galicia, there was news of panic among those in the path of this advance force.[10] Luckily, however, high mountain peaks with heavy winter snowfalls halted the Russian army; its infantry units were unable to surmount this natural barrier, which separated Galicia from the center of Austro-Hungary.

The Russian occupation of Galicia was harsh, and not just in a physical sense; it also became an example of clumsy political judgment. Dealing with strands of a multiethnic society that were often at odds with each other, the occupiers would have found no shortage of supporters—had they not managed to alienate everyone. As it was, there were food shortages and curfews in the cities. The salaries and pensions of teachers and railway employees were not paid for months, under the pretext that money had been evacuated to the western part of Galicia. Then anxiety was heightened by swirling rumors that the Russians were not committed to the obligations of the prior government, although for the moment they required all members of the civil administration to report to work. In a small conciliatory gesture, the first military governor allowed schools to open, which was good news for Helena, among many others. She was then able to return to the classroom, providing at least some support for her and her daughter.

The illusion that life was returning to normal did not last long. Soon, it became evident that the victors had very different ideas about running Galicia. Tight censorship was introduced, with stern warnings to owners of bookstores, libraries, and theaters about fines and the risk of imprisonment in case of anti-Russian publications or performances. The few lucky newspapers allowed to circulate were smaller in volume and bland in content but devoid of any openly pro-Russian stance. Occasional empty spaces on their pages served as reminders of military censors.

With the arrival of a new military governor by the end of September, the Russification of Galicia went into full swing.[11] An unidentified Russian officer allegedly summed up the occupiers' prevailing view of eastern Galicia: "A strange country [with] Russian land, Jewish money, [and] the Polish language. Making it [truly] Russian means getting rid of the Jewish capital and uprooting the Polish language. That is our purpose."[12] (Although the authenticity of this statement cannot be confirmed, the message does chillingly presage what happened after World War II in those territories.) Within a few months, schools all over the province were shut down until new teachers, able to provide instruction in Russian, could be brought from the east. Troubling reports started to trickle in that one hundred elementary schools, staffed solely by Russian teachers, were to open in the near future. That prospect certainly meant more financial hardship for Helena who, like many other teachers, would now be unable to receive a salary.[13]

In Stanislawow, there were already many layoffs within the civil administration. The mayor, Dr. Nimhin, was suddenly portrayed as a crook who had collected a salary advance in the waning days of August only to appear later in the safety of Vienna. To make matters worse, troubling reports surfaced of a large, newly discovered deficit in the city finances. Under the circumstances, it was certainly difficult to distinguish truth from the misinformation being used to justify hardships. There would be an additional period of anxiety for Joseph and Stephania Regiec, Helena's parents, who must have wondered whether Russians would replace Galician railway administrators with their own. Even if Joseph was fortunate enough to retain his position as superintendent, he would certainly not receive his salary until well into the next year. The civilian government of the occupied city appealed to Vienna to help pay the railway employees. But these pleas fell on deaf ears. It was, of course, unrealistic to expect a belligerent country to honor any payment to those now behind the front line."[14]

Autumn was punctuated by other signs of troubled times, mixed with fleeting glimpses of hope. Toward the end of October 1914, a vanguard of Polish riflemen from the Austrian military reached the streets of Bohorodczany in a surprise counterattack. Later, stories would be told about the bravery of boys turned soldiers, and even surprising gestures of compassion on the part of the Russians, suddenly facing what was not exactly a seasoned, professional army. A stunned nurse at the hospital in Stanislawow recalled a Cossack carrying in a lightly wounded 13-year-old who had charged him with a bayonet. The fierce warrior, it was said, walked in with the attacker in his arms and murmured "Вот какой солдат" ("What a soldier"). But as uplifting as this might have been to those living further away, we can safely assume that to Helena, the sound of gunfire in town only added to her sense of insecurity. In any case,

Cossacks in Stanislawow. With every new wave of Russian occupation and retreat, Cossacks plundered the city. (Wiener Bilder *August 1, 1915;* ÖNB, Vienna.)

hopes for the liberation of Bohorodczany and Stanislawow were quickly dashed, as the Russians easily pushed back the inexperienced attackers. In just a few days, captured young soldiers started to arrive in Stanislawow before being sent to prison in Russia.[15]

On a grander scale, the Russian government was intent on speeding up Russification of the conquered territories. In the zeal to remake eastern Galicia into part of the tsar's empire, many poorly educated and incompetent Russian workers were dispatched there, replacing members of the prewar bureaucracy dominated by Poles. As a result, the province was brought almost to a standstill. And the hostility of the victors was directed at others as well. Surprisingly, most of the Ukrainian population was suspected of being disloyal and was frequently targeted with deportation and imprisonment in Russia. Use of the Ukrainian language was discouraged, if not forbidden, in some areas. The Greek Catholic Church, which had embodied the awakening of a national identity among Ruthenians, was now under attack, with parishioners forced to convert to the Orthodox faith. The metropolitan, head of the Church—a generally revered and conciliatory figure—was deported to Russia. To further discredit him, a story about his transfer under humiliating military escort was reported in the press, along with disparaging remarks.[16] The *New York Times* would publish an emotional protest by Ukrainian parliamentarians in Vienna decrying the loss of all the freedoms that their constituents had been able to gain under Austro-Hungarian rule. These people refused to be labeled "Little Russians," insisting on their linguistic and cultural differences from the new masters of Galicia.[17]

Finally, the Jews of Galicia were the objects of harsh repression as well. Because of many cultural links, as well as the emancipation they had received under the Austro-Hungarian monarchy, Jews felt generally loyal to Vienna. Many, like the family of my paternal grandfather, Joachim Hübner, spoke German at home and would later send their children to Austrian universities. These factors, in combination with the traditional anti-Semitic policies of Russia, were enough to make the arriving occupiers treat this segment of Galician society with suspicion. Jews, often accused of spying, were soon forbidden to send any mail in Yiddish—under a military order excluding it from the list of "officially" sanctioned languages. The post office, which accepted only unsealed letters, simply destroyed any that were written in a language not on the official list. Suspicious articles with questionable intentions started to appear in newspapers, raising the purported Jewish issue with regard to any postwar arrangements. The culmination of this anti-Jewish mania was a military governor's ruling that disallowed travel by Jews, even within occupied Galicia, and forbade repatriation for those who wanted to return to homes outside occupied territories. Many Jews, like the Poles and Ukrainians, were forcefully deported to Russia.[18]

The year 1915 was difficult in many ways. A largely forgotten war episode, the so-called Carpathian campaign, took place not far from home. It was a brutal battle between Austro-Hungarian and Russian troops, fighting over mountain passes. Heavy snow, frostbite, and barbed wire inflicted additional wounds on

The Carpathian campaign in the winter of 1915.
(Wiener Bilder *April 11, 1915;* ÖNB, Vienna.)

both sides over a period of months. The horrific conditions were emphasized when reports started to trickle in of dead or injured soldiers falling prey to wolves. Austro-Hungarian troops started to falter, and only with the help of arriving Germans was the Russian offensive toward the south halted. The cycle of frequent offensives and counteroffensives, each costing lives and tens of thousands of captured prisoners, was to repeat itself over the next several months.

In early February, heavy fighting took place just south of Bohorodczany and other towns along the River Bystrzyca, with troops often fighting in snow above their waists. Then, one after another, groups of Russian soldiers, much less confident than they had been weeks before, retreated through Bohorodczany toward Stanislawow. The tide of events was changing; the Austro-Hungarian army was pushing the Russians back. On the morning of February 18, 1915, just a few mounted cavalrymen (called lancers) were spotted in the center of Stanislawow looking for marauding Cossacks. By noon, the full force of the Austrian

Stanislawow. The aftermath of the Russian artillery attack in February 1915.
The photograph shows destruction on Karpinski Street.

army was marching through the city streets; the rear guard of the Russian troops was gone.[19] To the disappointment of many, the local 58th Infantry Regiment, including Franciscus Sobolewski, was not part of this offensive.

With Stanislawow recaptured, hatred toward collaborators became quite apparent; a mob destroyed homes of those who had assisted the occupiers. But the battle for the city was not yet over. A barrage of Russian artillery fire rained down for five days, with 200 people reported dead or wounded. Even the Red Cross hospital operating on the city outskirts was shelled, with a few projectiles landing among its patients. In some parts of Stanislawow, gaping holes in buildings and shattered glass became common sights, although fortunately for the Regiec family, St. Joseph Street escaped major damage.[20]

After 11 days, the Russians counterattacked, reoccupying the city. Before they entered, however, up to a thousand civil administrators, mainly railway employees, had managed to escape with the retreating Austrians. But as far as we know, Joseph Regiec was among those who remained at home. Those who stayed behind would later recall that the returning Russian troops pillaged abandoned houses along city thoroughfares.[21]

With the front lines shifting back and forth, heavy fighting would continue in the surrounding region for the next few months. This was the backdrop as Helena gave birth to her second child. We do not know much about this little girl, who was most likely born early in 1915—not even her name. My grandmother only mentioned once that her older child, Irena, was quite persistent in seeking her mother's attention after the new baby arrived. Tragically, this second daughter lived for only a couple of years. There were frequent outbreaks of typhus, cholera, and dysentery —and, not surprisingly, young children were the most vulnerable.[22] Many decades later, when I asked whether she ever missed her younger child, my grandmother would hurriedly brush away my question, saying that the events of those days had not allowed her to feel sad for too long. The quickness of her response was, I felt, the response in itself. Hers was a generation that had become hardened quite fast and could not afford the luxury of self-pity. Without any doubt, however, this experience would make my grandmother intensely protective of her older daughter for the rest of her life.

WITH THE ARRIVAL OF spring, a new offensive by Austrian and German troops started in the Carpathian Mountains. This time, the objective was to inflict punishing damage to Russian lines at multiple points on the front. The brunt of the attack was concentrated on western Galicia, not far from the towns of Biecz and Nowy Sacz, which we visited when following the life of the Lösch family in more stable times. Even the highly censored newspapers warily announced, "BIG BATTLE BETWEEN VISTULA [RIVER] AND CARPATHIAN MOUNTAINS." Within days, news of a Russian retreat became known.

Chapter 9 — The Great War: A Tale of Conflict and Ordinary Life

Hrebenow after the spring offensive of 1915. Franciscus Sobolewski was taken prisoner in the vicinity of this bridge by the Russian forces. *(ÖNB, Vienna.)*

Along mountains and valleys at the eastern end of the front line, a push north was also moving ahead. Toward the end of April, the 58th Infantry Regiment was operating near one of the few passes that perilously connected Galicia and Hungary. A branch of the railroad wound through narrow valleys there, crossing mountain bridges and passing through a few tunnels. Whichever side controlled this artery could move troops in either direction. Austro-Hungarian troops maneuvered slowly, leaving behind peaks that rose from 2,000 to 3,200 feet. The grueling fighting continued, and progress was hard, as a company of soldiers commanded by the recently promoted lieutenant Franciscus Sobolewski pushed north.[23] On May 1, in one of the twists and turns of battle, Franciscus was taken prisoner near a village called Hrebenow. With the Great War fought on so many fronts over endless hundreds of miles, it is a cruel irony that he was captured so close to home; Hrebenow was barely 90 miles from Helena and the rest of the family. Under the circumstances, any sense of comfort that he might have felt at being there would have quickly evaporated. Instead, uncertainty over

Franciscus's future would cast a long shadow, and many years would pass before Helena and Franciscus would see each other again.

It is one of the paradoxes of war that an individual's fate does not always march in lockstep with the grand picture of the conflict. Clearly, the tide in eastern Galicia was quickly turning in favor of those who had been losing less than a year before. Soon, the Russian military command could no longer hide the fact that its army was retreating from the Carpathians under heavy attack.[24] The plan of the Austro-Hungarian and German forces was now clear: Their armies were moving steadily to encircle Lvov from the west, south, and east. The Russian press, in the face of defeat, would state nonchalantly that the capital of Galicia had no strategic importance. By mid-May, Austrians were already within 40 miles of Lvov, although the pincer of the encirclement was not yet ready to finish the job. Seeing the beginning of the end, the Russian military ordered forced deportation of the male population of Galicia from 18 to 50 years of age—to avoid their recruitment into the returning Austro-Hungarian army. In a perverse way, the Russians' anti-Semitic policies did at least some good; Jews were excluded from this draconian order.[25] On June 6, 1915, the first German military scouts, fighting as an advance of Austrian units, were spotted on the streets of Stanislawow; within days, the city had been liberated by Austro-Hungarian

Austrian cavalry units closing on Lvov in June 1915.
(Wiener Bilder *June 26, 1915*; ÖNB, Vienna.)

troops under the command of Archduke Joseph Ferdinand.[26] With any historical sensitivities brushed aside for the moment, most of the populace rejoiced at the entry of "our" troops.

Events were also unfolding rapidly in the rest of Galicia. The Austrian encirclement of Lvov was soon complete; inside the city, civil unrest, robbery, and arson would punctuate the next few days. Finally, on June 22, 1915, the capital city was declared free. The happy news traveled fast, and celebrations broke out all over the province. Even as far away as Vienna, the liberation of Lvov and Stanislawow was greeted with enthusiasm, as if the tides of war were finally turning. Within days, Franz Joseph, surrounded by his family, was waving to cheering crowds from the balcony of Schönbrunn Palace.[27]

The Russian army's retreat from Galicia in the summer of 1915.
(Wiener Bilder *August 8, 1915*; ÖNB, Vienna.)

In eastern Galicia, roads and eastbound trains were choked with hastily escaping Muscophiles and anyone from Russia, all fearful that the time of reckoning would soon arrive. Russian authorities, seeing their impending defeat, issued thousands of passports to their collaborators. At the same time, they also interned the top civil administrators of many Galician cities deep inside Russia; the idea was to create as much havoc as possible in the territories.[28] The throngs of escapees now seriously impeded any chance of an orderly military retreat, not to mention any deployment of fresh occupying forces. Those were needed to relieve Russian units in the many hot spots along the front line. Unable to move freely through congested roads, and fearful of capture by advancing Austrians and Germans, Russians abandoned their military hardware, leaving heavy artillery barely hidden in the forests. By the end of summer, the Great Retreat (as it would later be called) had left behind a devastated Galicia, with many of its citizens dead or missing—but at least it was free of the Russian army.[29]

The outlook in Galicia was far from bright. Crops had been left unattended or had simply not been planted during the military campaign; autumn brought food shortages. Prices were rising, and rationing of bread, sugar, and flour was introduced in Stanislawow. Deadly outbreaks of smallpox and cholera swept the province; local papers printed the names and addresses of those who succumbed to disease. Although Galicia was nominally free, it remained under military rule. Travel to and from Stanislawow was still limited, given the proximity of the city to the Russian border. Even worse, the Austro-Hungarian army had been depleted of men able to fight, so it clearly lacked the resources for any future actions. New waves of recruits, each time older than before, were repeatedly called up. Orders to turn over metal household items to be melted down for military purposes added to the general feeling that the war was not over.

Patriotic fervor among Galician Poles was whipped up by stories about the Polish Legions, military units fighting with the Central powers against Russia;

New recruits are drafted to the depleted Austro-Hungarian army in Galicia.
(Wiener Bilder *August 1, 1915*; ÖNB, Vienna.)

many viewed them as a first step toward future independence.[30] Fundraising efforts in support of the legions and of wounded soldiers recovering in local hospitals were widespread. There were many acts of generosity, both large and small. A remarkable Jewish woman donated a large sum of money to a charity run by the Roman Catholic Church, sending a simple message focusing on compassion. In return, the prelate of Stanislawow publicly expressed his gratitude to her. This was a powerful message that spoke volumes against the prejudices of the past. Wanda Regiec, Helena's sister, also made contributions, on a much smaller scale, to the legions. She was not wealthy, as music lessons were not the most sought-after activities in that time; nonetheless, she offered her small savings for a welcoming reception for the legionnaires, who passed through Stanislawow one day. Later, she donated money for Christmas gifts to be sent to the cherished unit. Helena was most likely involved, too; the packages from Stanislawow and Bohorodczany, containing food, clothing, and earmuffs, were sent on behalf of the Women's Leagues from both towns.[31]

For Helena and the entire Sobolewski clan in Bohorodczany, this was also a period of great anxiety, with no news of what had happened to Franciscus. The first question, whether he was dead or alive, would be answered by the Austro-Hungarian army, which had kept detailed records of the fallen. Luckily, his name was not among those who had died on the battlefield, though "missing in action" did not guarantee survival either. It would be months before Lieutenant Franciscus Sobolewski was mentioned by another prisoner of war who wrote home from an internment camp in the city of Astrakhan, near the Caspian Sea.[32]

Since there was no direct communication between the belligerent countries, short messages from captured soldiers were being managed by the Red Cross. This was truly "snail mail" but still better than none, with plain postcards often routed through other countries before they made their way home, months later.

Irena Sobolewska (1913–1998). This picture of Irena was sent to her father when he was held in a POW camp in Russia. On the back, the text written by Helena, Irena's mother, reads, "To Beloved Daddy from Kiki. February 18, 1916."

Franciscus was unharmed and would later end up in Samara, an industrial town deep in southeast Russia on the banks of the Volga River. The distance from Bohorodczany was frightening—more than 2,000 miles—but at home there was a sigh of relief at the knowledge that he was healthy and not being held in the even-more-feared Siberia. In time, Helena was somehow able to send him a letter with a small picture of "Irka," who was then two years old, dressed in a furry winter outfit and looking resolutely into the camera. A few copies of this picture have survived, including the one that belonged to Franciscus. The nickname of their daughter is inscribed on the back in my grandmother's handwriting, and a small pinhole remains at the top. One could imagine that it was affixed above Franciscus's cot for the next few years, somewhere deep in Russia.

The dawning of 1916 brought hope, once again, that the new year would decide the fate of Europe. It was almost impossible for anyone to believe that this war could last much longer. Some went even further, making unrealistic proposals for the elderly Franz Joseph to be crowned constitutional monarch of the future Kingdom of Poland which, along with the kingdoms of Hungary and Croatia, could be equal partners with Austria under the Habsburgs.[33] Time after time, however, the turn of events proved predictions utterly wrong.

༄

In eastern Galicia, some semblance of normalcy coexisted with constant fear of what might be next. In June, there were inklings that a new offensive in the east was imminent. In another case of bad timing, one sleepy Sunday morning, when a massive Russian offensive had already started (but news of it had not arrived yet), a newspaper in Lvov reported that the reorganization of the Russian army was complete, with the appointment of a new commander. This time correctly, a brief note concluded that a great offensive would be launched at the insistence of the western Allies, with the hope that opening another front in the east would resolve a deadly stalemate in France.

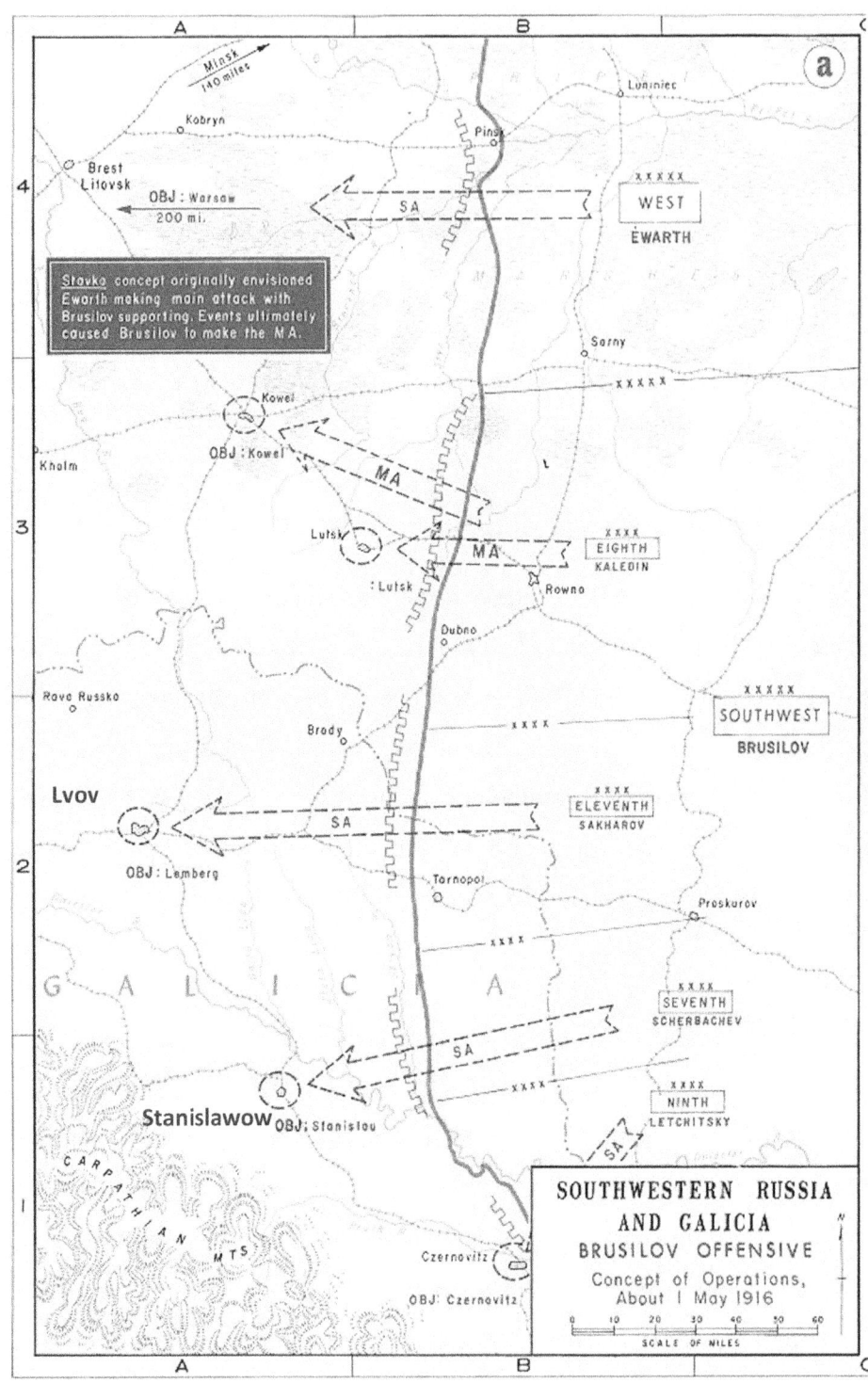

Map of the Brusilov Offensive of 1916. The planned direction of the attack is shown on this page. The actual front lines are depicted on the opposite page. Russian troops reoccupied Stanislawow and Bohorodczany in August 1916. The armed hostilities continued for months to the west of the two towns.

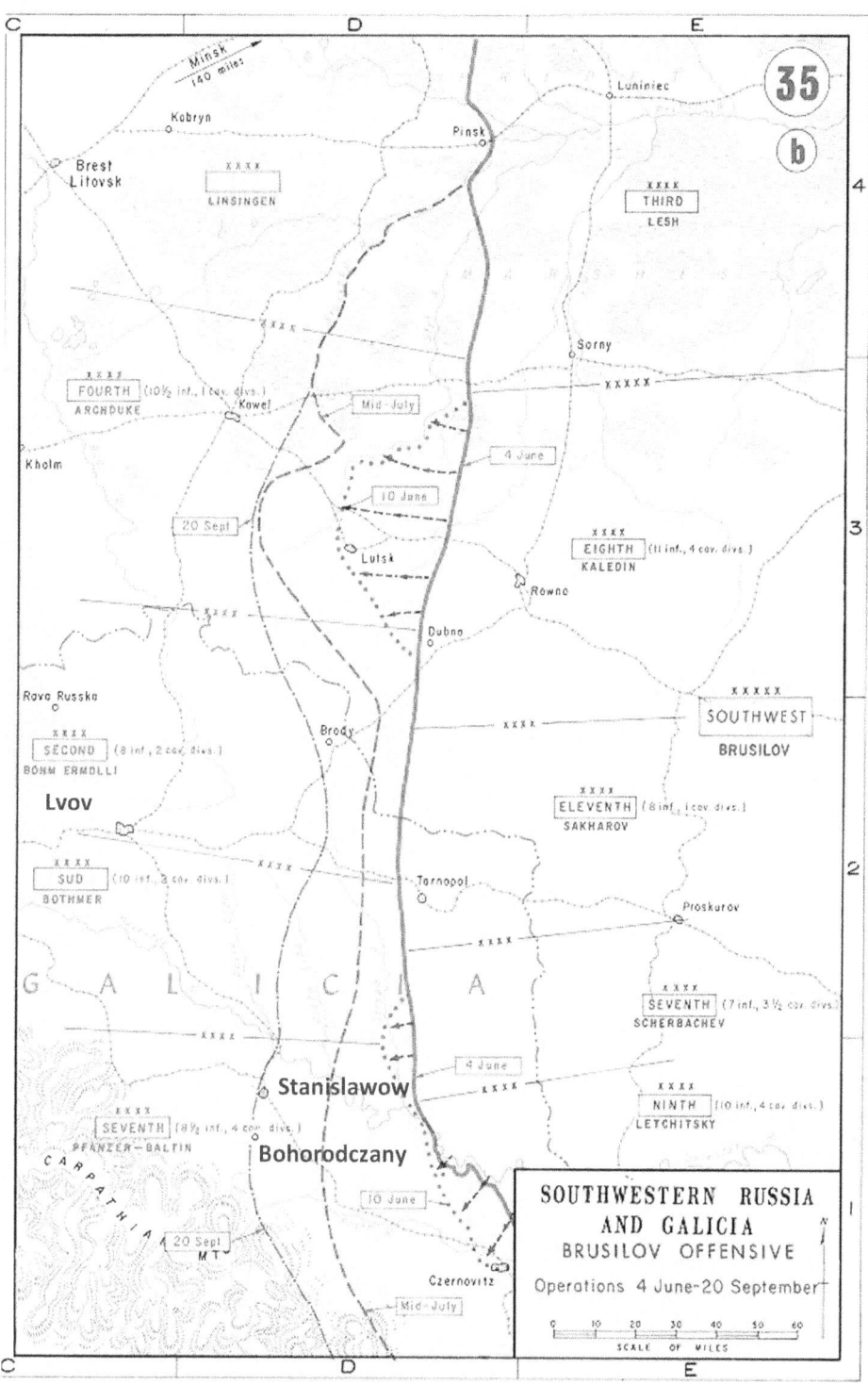

(Modified with permission of the Department of History, United States Military Academy.)

Indeed, the Russians' main attack did concentrate on the southern part of the eastern front, including Galicia. Its purpose was to inflict punishing damage on the Central powers at multiple points, and retake Lvov. The Russian commander, General Brusilov, who was experienced from the prior Galician campaign, envisioned brief curtain artillery fires followed by units of shock troops breaking through weaknesses in Austrian defenses. The mobility and speed of his troops were the essence of a new strategy. At first, the plan worked; Russians moved swiftly in the south, overrunning Czerniowce, the main town in Bukovina (where Joseph Regiec had worked years before), and soon reached the Carpathian Mountains. This was a bloody battle; in the aftermath, hundreds of dead bodies, rather than logs, floated down the River Prut.

By the end of June, the picture in Stanislawow was changing to a regrettably familiar one; hundreds crowded the train station awaiting what might be the last train to take them away from the coming invasion.[34] In Lvov, a terse statement, heavily underlined as though more emphasis was needed, was printed on the front page of the newspaper: "Based on information from a very competent military source, the current situation should not cause any concern for [the city of] Lvov and its citizens."[35] But fighting to the east was fierce, with hand-to-hand battles bringing attackers closer and closer to the outskirts of Stanislawow.

In that city, things did not look good; government employees, Jewish merchants, and refugees were moving west to safety. A few thousand Russian POWs were evacuated as well. Not long before, the Austrian military command had reassured the public that Stanislawow would not fall into enemy hands. But now onlookers saw long columns of infantry and then cavalry passing through the streets in a direction away from the distant boom of artillery fire. The signs were clear that an order for evacuation had come, but accidents plagued the withdrawal; several overcrowded trains even collided with each other.

By August 11, 1916, Stanislawow and Bohorodczany had fallen into Russian hands for the third time.[36] Just a few days later, the war was ratcheted up by the entry of neighboring Romania on the side of Russia. Whether this had any impact on the tsar's campaign would be debated by historians; but it is certain that with the arrival of additional German troops, the Russian invasion stalled and never reached Lvov. No doubt this was welcome news but, for the moment, those left in Stanislawow and Bohorodczany had the misfortune of being on the wrong side of the front. They would have to endure another period of uncertainty. The Brusilov Offensive, as this campaign would be called, damaged the Austro-Hungarian army's ability to fight on its own, without the support of Germany. The cost of this local spectacle in the global theater of war was staggering; both sides lost more than a million lives, and countless numbers of soldiers were wounded or captured.

On the third birthday of Irena Sobolewska, Helena's and Franciscus's daughter, there were most likely no celebrations at home. Despite the declaration that the big offensive was over, Bohorodczany continued to be in the path of stubborn fighting. The River Bystrzyca, the same one that flowed just behind the Sobolewski's ancestral home, separated the Central powers on the left bank from the Russian army on the right. Almost every day, skirmishes would break out between the opposing sides just beyond the town. Predictably, the Russians would report taking over a field post or breaking through barbed wire and taking a few prisoners, whereas the Austrian command would declare that the left bank of the river was well-defended, with attackers successfully being repelled. In the big scheme of the

Bohorodczany. The Dominican church and its archives suffered severe damage during military operations in 1916.

Bohorodczany. The church interior after the artillery shelling in 1916.

Great War, this was nothing, but it added to Helena's struggle to keep her family safe.[37] Even Christmas did not bring a resolution to the stalemate, with shooting and hand-to-hand combat, bayonets mounted, in neighboring Lachowce. The Dominican church, which had witnessed so many events celebrated by the Sobolewski family over the past 150 years, suffered heavy damage from artillery fire. But local tragedy and destruction were just another note in the newspaper when, in the closing days of 1916, the *New York Times* reported, "Russian troops, operating in the region of the River Bystritsa [sic], in Galicia,...broke through the barbed wire entanglements in front of the Austro-German advanced posts yesterday and penetrated into Bohorodczany Stare [Old], southwest of Stanislau."[38]

THE END IN SIGHT:

IS THIS TIME FOR REAL?

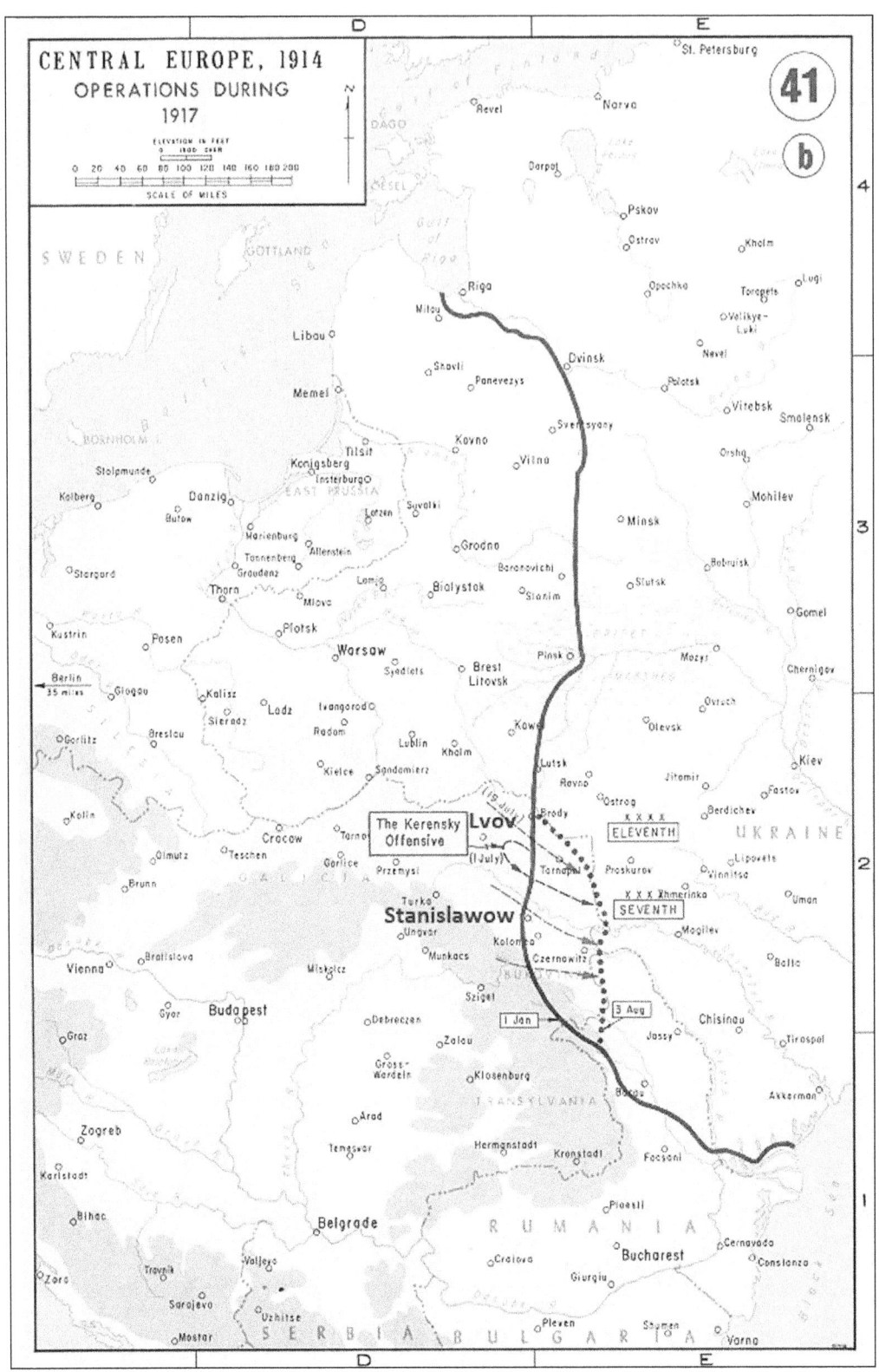

Map of the Kerensky Offensive of 1917. After the Russian offensive faltered, Stanislawow and Bohorodczany were recaptured by Austrian and German troops in July 1917.
(Modified with permission of the Department of History, United States Military Academy.)

$\mathcal{T}$HE SUMMER OF 1917 BROUGHT a new Russian offensive, true to the now almost predictable rhythm of recurring quiet periods followed by armed flareups. But its aim was more than a straightforward military one. The tsar had been overthrown earlier in the year, and the weak new government was hopeful that good news from the front would rally an increasingly restless society at home.

The very long front line spanned the territories of several countries from north to south; yet the stretch that really mattered in July 1917 was less than two miles from Stanislawow.[1] For more than a year, the Central powers to the west and the Russian forces to the east faced each other in the Black Forest, on the hills that guarded the passage toward Lvov. The aim of Russia's generals was to rout the weakened Austro-Hungarian army, as they had managed to do at the beginning of the war. As events unfolded, the outcome of that adventure would produce quite opposite results, setting the stage for calamitous changes in Russia that would bring the Bolsheviks to power.[2]

At first, everything seemed to go as planned; Russian infantry marched west through Stanislawow's streets to strengthen the coming offensive, and heavy guns were mounted in gardens and parks, ready to start bombardments in the direction of the nearby front. Even Russia's minister of war, Alexander Kerensky, arrived in the city to fire up his troops for battle. But a few more weeks of fighting again proved all predictions wrong, and the result became clearer with every report from the front: The Russian army had no will to fight and was rapidly disintegrating. The beginning of the end, of what was called the Kerensky Offensive, became quite apparent with a hasty retreat of Russian troops and the movement of large amounts of ammunition maneuvering east through Stanislawow. In the chaos, groups of Cossacks marauded through the city streets, unleashing their wrath, setting buildings on fire, and taking whatever they could find from stores, cellars, and private homes. Civilians were threatened, ambushed, robbed, and often stripped of their clothes. Explosions at ammunition depots in various parts of the city added to the sense that no one was in charge. The few remaining Russian officers, pleading for an orderly withdrawal, were simply ignored. After the turmoil in their own country earlier the same year, this was a very different army, in which orders were no longer to be obeyed. One Russian soldier mused that in the tsar's army, the officers had beaten soldiers, but soldiers could now beat their officers.[3]

In the midst of this mayhem, a unit of mounted lancers, all ethnic Poles serving in the Russian army, suddenly entered the city to thwart an imminent takeover by the Central powers. It did not take long for the trotting cavalrymen to realize who was causing the chaos in the city; without wasting time, they quickly directed their arms against the rampaging Cossacks. A strange sort of street fighting erupted, with lancers' sabers slashing unruly groups of looters and shots fired between two units of the same army with quite different missions in mind. The clashes continued into the night, and the Cossacks were finally reined in, saving the city from further carnage. But this was far from peace; at best, an uneasy order had been only temporarily restored.

Within a couple of days, what had been anticipated by everyone became a reality; German troops supporting the Austro-Hungarian army broke through Russian positions in several places and approached the same road that Helena had traveled so many times between Bohorodczany and Stanislawow. What happened next could be seen as a poorly executed battle or, as some later suggested, the revenge of Russian commanders for the lancers' efforts to restore order in the city. In a last-ditch effort to slow advancing troops before Stanislawow was fully encircled, the cavalry was ordered to attack the approaching Germans. The lancers galloped through the outskirts of Stanislawow toward a heavily armed infantry. Clearly, they were not a match for the well-dug-in German units; nonetheless, they charged six times at the enemy that afternoon. In the end, some were mowed down by machine-gun fire, with others injured when their horses tripped in fields treacherously dissected by old trenches and barbed wire.

Days later, old-fashioned military gallantry was on display when the field commanders on both sides of the front acknowledged the lancers' bravery. The German commander General Litzman, speaking with the city's mayor, would say, "Mr. Mayor, tell those lancers who attacked [my] Bavarian boys and now happen to be in our custody that the report I received spoke of their fearlessness and gallantry. Tell them that in our opinion they were courageous." The Russian soon-to-be commander in chief, General Kornilow, sent a telegram to the unit praising the lancers and according several of them the Cross of St. George, the

Commemorative medal with an inscription reading, "To Polish lancers for the defense of Stanislawow." It was issued in Vienna in recognition of the Polish lancers who saved Stanislawow from the chaos during the withdrawal of Russian troops in 1917.

highest military decoration in the Russian army. But pompous words and medals were useless to those who had fallen.⁴

⌘

"Traumatized and exhausted" was the best description of the general mood after German and Austro-Hungarian forces finally entered Stanislawow on July 25, 1917. There were no spontaneous celebrations in the streets, even though the defeat of the Russians was such a climactic event. When Charles I, Emperor Franz Joseph's successor, appeared in Stanislawow in a show of compassion toward Galicians, the visit was largely met with indifference. In stark contrast to its front-page coverage in the Viennese press, the young emperor's ride in an open car through the streets of Stanislawow was reported on the back pages of Galicia's main newspaper. No doubt this would have been viewed as a remarkable event in peaceful times.⁵ The new monarch toured damaged parts of the city, shook hands with troops (mainly German), and even promised compassionate treatment for those lancers who were now being held as POWs. As events would subsequently show, the latter pronouncement did not amount to much; pleas for the prisoners' release continued for months to come.⁶

Visit of the new emperor of Austro-Hungary, Charles I, to Stanislawow.
(Wiener Bilder *August 8, 1917*; ÖNB, Vienna.)

The Regiec family remained in Stanislawow during the last Russian occupation and witnessed the chaos of those eventful summer days. Again, a bit of luck was on their side; the fires and looting spared the short stretch of St. Joseph Street where they lived. Whether Joseph Regiec was able to receive his regular salary under the last Russian rule is unclear, although it is known that his department of the Railway Directorate was moved to the safety of a small town in Austrian Silesia (in today's northern Czech Republic).[7]

Somewhere around Stanislawow during the war. Wanda Regiec (left), Helena Sobolewska (middle) with Irena Sobolewska, and an unknown couple (right). The man is wearing an Austrian army uniform.

With the Russian army now pushed back far beyond prewar borders, and armed hostilities receding on the eastern front, Galicia was slowly regaining its bearings. This was not an end to the Great War, which still raged in other parts of Europe, with many Galician soldiers still under arms. Still, the fall of 1917 brought citizens' appeals to rebuild Galicia's civil society as quickly as possible. These calls reflected more than just a longing for life to return to normal; there was other subtext as well. The top administrators, mainly Polish and Jewish, had been evacuated to the safety of western Galicia during the last Russian occupation; and concerns had been raised by some that this could set up a dangerous status quo. The fear was that eastern Galicia would become dominated by the Ukrainian political organizations that had remained there. Who would ultimately control this part of the country? That was still an open question, but it was clear that whatever group dominated the schools, railroads, and city offices would have the upper hand in postwar arrangements. For those in Stanislawow and other cities in eastern Galicia, this anxiety colored demands for the old order to return quickly.[8]

In Stanislawow, the road to normal life was made difficult because of food shortages. With supplies of flour gone, there was no bread for 15 straight days in the winter of 1917; food was rationed and prices climbed. At some point, conditions were so dire that the intervention of Emperor Charles I was sought to improve delivery of basic nourishment to the starving populace. From time to time, the public had been riveted by stories of speculators being caught or the German army secretly shipping trainloads of food back home.[9]

Over a period of months, military restrictions on travel were lifted; then, slowly, some of the prewar civil administration offices reopened. Plans to bring the Railway Directorate back to Stanislawow were supposed to be executed as soon as possible. In reality, the return to a normally functioning state of affairs proved to be a challenge. The railway, often cited as the engine of employment in Stanislawow, was on the brink of collapse. Heavy equipment and even small tools were gone from the machine shops at the railroad yard; Joseph Regiec's elegant administrative offices downtown had been plundered and left empty by the departing Russians.[10]

But Joseph Regiec was a man who refused to be easily overtaken by life's adversities. Not long after all these events, he was publicly thanked in the main city newspaper for a donation to support elementary schools—help that was badly needed, given the devastation of war. On another occasion, Joseph was elected, along with the deputy mayor of Stanislawow, to a council of volunteers overseeing a boarding school that had fallen into disrepair. We can guess that only a few at that time knew the reasons education had such a special meaning to this railroad official.[11]

MY GRANDMOTHER'S LIFE IN Bohorodczany was not much easier. The town had suffered much damage due to its precarious location on the front line during the previous year. Helena and Franciscus's house was a casualty of the war, along with some of their belongings, taken by the retreating Russians.[12] With most buildings in ruins, the township office, post office, and district court had to relocate; this only added to feelings of abandonment among those who remained in town. The surrounding fields had lain bare for over a year for lack of agricultural supplies, and a despondent call from Bohorodczany indicated that even potatoes, the staple of the diet in hard times, were not available for planting in the coming year.[13]

Nonetheless, Helena considered herself lucky; she was physically unharmed. Some of her Jewish neighbors had been victimized even more during the Russian occupations; on at least one occasion, the dreaded Cossacks had brutally raped several Jewish women seeking refuge in a synagogue in Bohorodczany. This was a sad reminder that the heroes of one side, some of them proudly called the Eagles of the Tsar, were cruel thugs and murderers to the other.[14]

Despite the gloom of the situation, Helena's school reopened, allowing her to return to work. Soon, this young teacher was assessed by a district school inspector during a routine visit to the school. After observing the classroom, a short note was left in Helena's file: "Work quite satisfactory, teaching methods good, talent good, [class] behavior commendable."[15] We can be sure that

Helena felt relieved and happy with this outcome, which in some small measure may have compensated for the hardships of those times. With inflation spiraling out of control, teachers' salaries were considered painfully low; however, public pleas for bonuses and pay raises fell on deaf ears. The coffers of Galicia were empty.

The arrival of cold weather caused closings at Helena's school and others, as there was neither coal nor a sufficient supply of wood to heat the classrooms. In Stanislawow, temporary narrow-gauge tracks were placed on the streets to deliver logs from the surrounding mills as quickly as possible to the freezing population.[16] Despite these hardships, real hope surfaced in December 1917. An armistice had been agreed to between the Central powers (including Germany, Austro-Hungary, Bulgaria, and Turkey) and the weakened Russia, and on December 17, the eastern front fell silent along its thousand-mile stretch from the Baltic Sea to the Black Sea.

Irena Sobolewska during the war.

In fact, Bolshevik Russia, convulsed by its internal fight for survival, had asked for peace without territorial gains or demands for war reparations.[17] The mood was definitely more hopeful, and a playful message arrived from Galician troops enjoying a rare respite from fighting: "Greetings to Stanislawow's beautiful and ugly young ladies from the battlefield. The volunteers of the Riflemen Regiment."[18] For Helena, talk of restoring direct mail service between the adversaries was a helpful sign that news about Franciscus would become more frequent. Her ultimate hope was the promise of POW exchanges that seemed to be just around the corner.

For the first time in years, the annual cycle on the eastern front, with armies swinging back and forth, looked less likely to recur. Peace talks continued on and off, as events in Russia spiraled out of control. On February 9, 1918, full recognition of the Ukrainian National Republic by Austro-Hungary, and then by other powers sitting at the negotiating table, became the first in a series of agreements. That news was greeted with jubilation by Ukrainians living in Galicia, but Poles felt threatened. For the moment, the Ukrainian state encompassed only the territory lost by Russia in the war with the Central powers, an area that was clearly beyond the borders of Galicia. Still, many wondered whether, in time, eastern Galicia might become part of that emerging country. Poles had not been invited to the signing of the final peace treaty and felt left behind in their own quest for independence. Their anxiety was fueled by the resurgence of an old dispute about what territory ought to belong to which future state. Even the inclusion of a sliver of historically disputed land in the Ukrainian National Republic triggered massive street marches by Poles, with passionate speeches. It did not matter that before the war, that territory had been situated outside Galicia; the claims and counter-claims were setting the stage for dangerous conflict.

In Stanislawow, Polish railroad employees went on a short strike, and declarations of protest from the city council—signed by Mayor Nimhin and the teachers' association—followed. Approximately 12,000 people took to the streets there; similar protests happened in Lvov and other cities. With the war unfinished but becoming increasingly distant, public opinion was whipped up to another level of excitement by unfortunate phrases like "the fourth partition of Poland," even though such a country did not now formally exist. In Vienna, Polish parliamentarians protested and threatened to join the opposition, but to no avail.

It was clear that the sympathy of the Central powers was shifting toward settling the potentially explosive issue of eastern Galicia on terms less than favorable to Poles. Within a few weeks, there were more marches, this time in support of the new country and attended by throngs of Ukrainians living in the Stanislawow area. But Galicia was lucky; for the most part, these demonstrations remained peaceful, at least for the moment.[19] In the end, the Ukrainian National Republic turned out to be an unstable quasi-state besieged by Bolsheviks on one side and controlled by Germans on the other; but its creation brought back unresolved anxieties and xenophobia. It was only a matter of time before the next spark would start a fire.

Ukrainians demonstrating on the streets of Stanislawow after the announcement of formation of the Ukrainian National Republic. (Wiener Bilder *March 17, 1918;* ÖNB, Vienna.)

The formal peace treaty between Russia and the four Central powers was signed on March 3, 1918, in Brest-Litovsk (now Belarus). Russia was an undisputed loser, ceding a large territory to Germany that included Finland, the Baltic States, Ukraine, and all the former Polish lands it had governed since the partition of Poland in the eighteenth century. Under the explicit and humiliating terms of the agreement, Russia renounced any claims to the lost territories and abrogated any right to intervene in the affairs of the nations now firmly under German control.

In Galicia, reactions to the entire treaty were mixed at best. The cessation of major hostilities on the eastern front and the prospect that the Great War was finally coming to an end were welcome relief. The western front was far away, and the decisive impact of the United States on the war in favor of the Allies (the countries opposing the Central powers) was not appreciated as yet. To the contrary, some thought that Germany might now be in a strong position to negotiate a peace settlement in the west. The main reason for lack of jubilation on the streets, if not open hostility toward the treaty, was a sense of Austro-Hungary's wavering commitment toward keeping Galicia intact.

An even greater cause of anxiety was Germany, historically anathema to Poles, which was now unchallenged in its control of most Polish territory. A vague statement in the Treaty of Brest-Litovsk that "Germany and Austro-Hungary have the intention to resolve the future destiny of these lands in consultation with the people who live there" did not elicit much confidence. Speaking with visiting Poles shortly after the peace agreement, the German chancellor boasted about taking Paris in a few weeks, making it clear that they had no choice but to agree to limited autonomy now, before even those modest terms would be further diminished.[20] Again, it was a case of predictions never materializing; many now had to accept the unreliability of any talk about the future in their rapidly changing world.

Despite high hopes, there was no major breakthrough on POW exchanges after the agreement. A general declaration of intent deferred the details, which were supposed to be hammered out in separate talks.[21] In reality, the domestic wars that erupted in Russia prevented the release and transport of those who were interned somewhere in vast territories that often were not under the control of the central government.

Family portrait taken in Stanislawow. Wanda Regiec, Helena Sobolewska, and Irena Sobolewska.

The fall of 1918 brought a strange feeling in Galicia—that of living in a familiar atmosphere of public bickering but with an intense anticipation that things were about to change. Everyone was coping as best they could with the consequences of the war—and in a somewhat more relaxed atmosphere than had existed a few months before. As always, serious news was mixed with lighter fare. The city magistrate placed several ads in a local newspaper urgently calling for the owner of the stray cow that had been in the care of the city since 1916 to reclaim his property. Someone else wanted to buy six pillows and three quilts in good condition; several stores announced their openings. Indeed, these looked like hopeful signs.[22]

While visiting her family in Stanislawow, Helena, like many who had just emerged from the bleak war period, wanted to capture the moment in a few photographic images—as if to record that normal life had returned. These precious portraits are quite reassuring when viewed today, showing the resilience that would be typical of Helena in the years ahead. Looking at these pictures of her, always with Irka at her side and on occasion joined by her sister, Wanda, nobody would guess the turmoil they had all gone through at the center of a massive conflict. In Stanislawow, too, life was moving on; slowly, there were the openings of a few plays, concert performances, and movies. There, as in many other places, speculation continued about how much the central government in Vienna would contribute to the rebuilding of the city, despite the much bigger unknown of what would happen to all of Galicia.

※

The beginning of the end had come earlier in the year, with the announcement by U.S. President Woodrow Wilson of the Fourteen Points declaration. This clear statement, first presented to a joint session of the U.S. Congress, became a precondition for the suspension of hostilities as well as future peace negotiations between the Allies and the Central powers. At first, it was viewed as too idealistic by some "sophisticated" Europeans, yet this was the only comprehensive vision that existed on how to end the intractable Great War. Surprisingly,

Helena Sobolewska with her daughter, Irena. The photograph was taken in Stanislawow, circa 1918.

the censors of Austro-Hungary allowed the publication of the Fourteen Points, despite an unequivocal message they contained that did not bode well for the future of the empire's government.

It seemed that if the American proposal was accepted, that would guarantee the end of the old order. The document referred to the principle of self-determination for the peoples now under Habsburg rule. The intent was clear: The multiethnic Austro-Hungarian Empire was about to be broken apart. The specific call for the formation of an independent Polish state, encompassing "the territories inhabited by indisputably Polish populations," raised the hopes of Poles but added a greater sense of the unknown—namely, how people born in three very different countries would become one nation almost overnight.[23] Despite many lofty ideas and grand patriotic statements, in reality, no one from the current generation had ever participated in such a grand nation-building experiment. And there were other complications that would affect Galicia: ambiguities over where the borders of one country would end and another would begin. There was much serious talk mixed with recurring political gossip about the Austro-Hungarian government agreeing to split Galicia along the disputed ethnic lines; this meant great hope for some, and was viewed with fear or outrage by others.[24]

By October 1918, events were moving fast, with every day bringing headlines of almost historical proportions. Galicians immediately dismissed their government's meek assurances that the foundations of an independent Poland—which would include Galicia—were already in place. Talk of a union of this undefined future country with the Habsburg monarchy was derisively described in the press as a "too-late offer."[25] A few days later, a letter from Vienna to the government of the United States asked for immediate cessation of ground, sea, and aerial hostilities, and confirmed full acceptance by Austro-Hungary of President Wilson's plan. On October 16, Emperor Charles I, in a public manifesto, agreed that the Austrian territories that were considered historically Polish could join an independent Poland without any precondition or any union with Austria. On the world scene, there was a flurry of diplomatic missives; but in the end, the government of Austro-Hungary accepted all the demands conveyed to Vienna by the United States. By October 29, Austro-Hungary had suspended military activity on all fronts. The end seemed much closer now that Vienna had explicitly asked for peace, even if it was to be negotiated under a separate treaty from its ally Germany.[26]

On the surface, it looked as though the war in Galicia was finally over. The world would soon celebrate the end of the Great War, marked by the signing of an armistice agreement between the Allies and Germany on November 11, 1918. The official end of the war did not mean, however, that Galicia was to become peaceful. Days before the armistice, Poles and Ukrainians had openly declared competing sovereignty claims over the disputed territories.

Ukrainian politicians saw the imminent transfer of power—from a country that would soon cease to exist to one not yet formed—as a chance to proclaim eastern Galicia their own land. There they would have been a majority, particularly in the countryside. In a race to make this a fait accompli, the Ukrainian National Council was formed in Lvov. The self-proclaimed mandate of the council was to chart a separate Ukrainian state, which would include eastern Galicia, Bukovina, and the northern part of Hungary (the sub-Carpathian region). Surprisingly, this call was buried in the back pages of the leading papers.[27]

Not to be outdone, Polish politicians gathered in Cracow and formed the Liquidation Commission. Its mandate was to transfer power and state assets in Galicia, still nominally controlled by the crumbling Austro-Hungary, to Polish hands—in anticipation of an independent country to be formed soon. It was only a matter of days before the commission moved to Lvov to undertake similar action there, claiming all the territories of Austrian Galicia as Polish.

With no goodwill on either side, there was not the slightest prospect of compromise.[28] Even before the old conflict was completely extinguished, a new one was about to erupt. On November 1, Ukrainian troops from the military units of the Austro-Hungarian army entered Lvov, a city with a Polish majority. On the same day, the Ukrainian National Council proclaimed the founding of the West Ukrainian People's Republic, in order to preempt claims of Polish sovereignty over eastern Galicia. On November 3, 1918, Austrian general Rudolf Pfeffer formally surrendered military command of the city to the Ukrainians. Local garrisons were vetted for non-Ukrainian soldiers, who were quickly disarmed. Bloody street battles between Ukrainians and Poles, with much carnage inflicted by snipers, ensued. Even teenagers, later affectionately called "Eaglets," were armed by Poles for urban warfare. Daily heavy bombardments inflicted much damage and loss of life. After three weeks, with the arrival of Polish military reinforcements, a brief cease-fire between the warring sides allowed Ukrainian forces to retreat from the city.

However, there were no celebrations in Lvov, shocked by 200 dead and several hundred wounded. The situation remained tenuous, with snipers hidden on roofs still shooting at civilians. Fresh graves dotted many public squares; ironically, there was no longer any ethnic distinction between those being buried. The city center, including the seat of the former Galician *diet*, the main post office, and the train station, had been damaged, along with many other landmarks. Lvov remained under siege for weeks, with shelling by Ukrainian forces surrounding the city. For bringing in supplies, heavy armored trains with mounted machine guns were the only way to pierce the ring. The tracks carrying these trains were under frequent attack and became a symbolic lifeline between Lvov and the outside world. When the rail line into the city was temporarily overpowered by Ukrainians, Lvov was cut off from the rest of the world.[29]

What happened in the immediate aftermath of the Ukrainian withdrawal at the end of November was even more shocking. With senseless anger, a Polish mob went on a rampage against Jews in what would later be called Lvov's pogrom. For the next three days, Jews were viciously attacked, their synagogues set on fire and many of their shops robbed; later, an official commission would confirm that 150 Jews had been killed and 54 buildings burned. The situation was out of control, and the Polish military gave orders to shoot on the spot anyone armed and resisting arrest. With swift military justice, those found guilty of robbery or rape were summarily executed, and their names published in the next day's newspapers as a deterrent.[30] While the international opinion was shock and dismay, the reaction in Lvov was, sadly, mixed. Some editorials unequivocally condemned these acts of hatred, but others engaged in only qualified repudiation of the incidents.[31] Moral relativism was on full display when Ukrainians were blamed for the release of common criminals implicated in the riots; then Jews were accused of supporting the other side during the past weeks and even blamed for being at the helm of the Bolshevik Revolution in Russia.

Months later, Henry Morgenthau Sr., President Wilson's special envoy, arrived on a fact-finding mission. Over the next two months, he took part in hearings held in Lvov and other cities. Although the number of people killed was often in dispute, the American mission confirmed that murders had occurred and that various reprisals against Jews had caused great suffering.[32]

৵

Stanislawow, like many other cities of eastern Galicia, was also overrun by Ukrainian troops and their paramilitary forces, the Sich Riflemen. The atmosphere was tense in that city, but initially without major armed street battles. The local administration, still led by Mayor Nimhin, tried to run Stanislawow in a way that would avoid conflict. By the end of December 1918, the West Ukrainian People's Republic, unable to hold onto Lvov, moved its capital to Stanislawow and established its fledgling government in the same building that had housed Joseph Regiec's offices before the war. "Capital" was the grandiose term given to this city which, besides the confusion of having new masters again, was overwhelmed by thousands of former prisoners of war stranded there. The new hostilities that had engulfed eastern Galicia prevented many of these men from returning home, wherever their home was in the old Austro-Hungarian Empire.

Early in January 1919, the trickle of information from Stanislawow to the outside world described an apparently calm city, although nobody on the outside really knew whom to believe. News brought by travelers able to cross the front lines did not bode well for Joseph Regiec. In a tit-for-tat game, Polish railway employees refused to follow the orders of the Ukrainian administration, which brought an immediate suspension of their pay. At first, a former parliamentary deputy from Stanislawow, Edmund Rauch, was able to secure some financial help for railway employees after pleading with local banks; but this could not last for long. More serious consequences followed, with many of the employees irrevocably fired from their posts. We do not know how Joseph fared in those difficult months.[33]

But these events pale in comparison with stories of atrocities committed by both sides. Ukrainian paramilitary units were said to have attacked civilians and defenseless former soldiers trapped in Galicia.[34] Sadly, Jews again became easy targets of aggression. Stanislawow was spared the violent anti-Semitic outbursts reported in other places, although harassment of Jewish merchants by Ukrainian soldiers was reported in that city. Luckily, the situation there was brought under control by local police without escalating further. Elsewhere, Poles were accused of property confiscation and their share of brutality in the territories with Ukrainian majorities. Both sides engaged in misinformation campaigns to win domestic and foreign support; but over time, international sympathy began to slip away from the less well-known Galician Ukrainians.[35]

In reality, Helena and many like her were going through another difficult period. The government of the West Ukrainian People's Republic had demanded that civil employees take an oath of allegiance to the new regime. When that time came for the teachers of Bohorodczany, Helena refused. She paid dearly for this act of defiance, being promptly dismissed from her job at the beginning of 1919. In those harrowing times, there was no consideration of the fact that a mother with a young child was losing her only source of income.[36]

The fate of eastern Galicia was sealed by the military success of a new Polish army, which arrived in the spring. This new offensive pushed Ukrainian forces further east; Romania, determined to wrest control of Bukovina from the already weakened Ukrainians, was advancing from the south. Soon, a few Romanian infantry units passed Bohorodczany, marching toward Stanislawow. Romanian reconnaissance airplanes flew overhead, speeding the departure of Ukrainian troops. On May 25, 1919, Poles took control of Stanislawow, disarming any remaining Ukrainian soldiers; but the issue of who controlled the city was far from determined. The fear of a counterattack was palpable for days; Polish and Jewish high school students were sent to guard urban train stations, and many of

Polish paramilitary forces guarding the train station in Stanislawow.
One of the first pictures sent out from the tense city in early June 1919.
(Nowosci Illustrowane June 14, 1919.)

these young people were positioned in surrounding towns to forewarn the city of any impending attack. The danger was real; in some areas, groups of dispirited Ukrainian soldiers and peasants staged ambushes that often turned deadly. Although it was not widely reported, a few Romanian units temporarily entered Stanislawow to stabilize the situation before regular Polish army units could establish firm control.[37]

Regular army units enter Stanislawow. The military situation on the ground and the events in the Soviet Russia determined the fate of eastern Galicia for the next 20 years. (Nowosci Illustrowane *June 14, 1919.*)

By mid-June, the situation had become sufficiently stable in Stanislawow for a foreign military commission to visit the city. French and English officers taking part in a fact-finding mission were greeted by the new mayor, Antonius Stygar. He was a popular former deputy mayor who, in the previous year, had served with Joseph Regiec on a board overseeing one of the city's war-damaged schools.[38] The same day, the rail link between Stanislawow and Lvov was reestablished; but with the tenuous situation in conflict-ridden eastern Galicia, the press had to give repeated reassurances that the city was safe.

By the end of summer 1919, all of eastern Galicia was solidly in Polish hands, at least in the military sense. Debate in diplomatic circles continued for some time about how to resolve the issue of eastern Galicia; this only added to a lingering feeling of uncertainty, despite the fact that armed hostilities were officially over. To those living in and near Stanislawow, reports from the peace conference in Paris brought a string of confusing messages. First, it was reported that Galicia's fate would be decided in a plebiscite; then its eastern part was supposedly to remain under international oversight. Soon, other plans purportedly stipulated that Poland would hold jurisdiction over eastern Galicia for the next 25 years. It was said that maps were being redrawn, with borders that would split the east from the rest of the country under a so-called provisional solution.

In reality, however, "boots on the ground" and recent changes in Russia determined the future of the region. With the Bolsheviks suddenly gaining the upper hand against their domestic adversaries (the so-called White Russians, ardently supported by the Allies), there was no longer any reason to leave the eastern borders of Poland in an ambiguous state; the possibility of replacing the Bolsheviks with a more acceptable government was gone. By the end of December 1919, the decision was finally made at the peace conference that Galicia was not to be divided.[39]

༄

For Helena, this marked the end of a long journey, one that is difficult to put into a personal context today. In Stanislawow, the war had lasted off and on for five years, longer than it had in any other part of Europe. Eastern Galicia had had the misfortune of being the first to see invading troops in August 1914, and the last to witness the end of hostilities in July 1919. Although historians would never call the last armed conflict there part of the Great War, for ordinary people in the area, it was simply a continuation of the larger struggle they had been caught up in.

We can only wonder today how Helena could ever have adapted to the constant parade of friendly and hostile armies repeatedly entering the area, each time inflicting visible damage. So often in those years, she had had to put her own plans on hold simply to get by, rather than reach toward the higher aspirations that every young person has. Losing a young child who had never seen her own father, and raising another while coping with all the insecurities of the time—mostly alone, and not knowing when, if at all, she would see her husband again—must have added immeasurably to the strain of that experience.

The end of the war also brought a more subtle break between the present and the past. With the old order overturned and borders redrawn, the Kingdom of Galicia and Lodomeria, as it had been officially known for the past 140 years, ceased to exist. The familiar world of Helena's grandparents and parents, the Lösches and the Regiecs, and of her own youth, had simply slipped away. With a new country around her, it was not fashionable to look back. Helena's roots in Galicia, like those of thousands of others who eventually would move somewhere else, were not visible from the outside; but they remained within her.

A very private person, my grandmother did not like to talk much about herself; still, a bit of Galicia lingered on in her later life. In casual conversation, a listener might hear in her speech a few unique linguistic phrases. Her fluency in the multiple languages that had been heard in Galician towns was a giveaway; so were her stories, like the one about the best watermelons for hot summers (from the Caucasus, she said). Such hints did give away a bit of the long-gone past.

Chapter 11

WHERE TO GO?

OLD STORIES FADE AWAY AND

NEW ONES ARE BORN

Eastern front at the cessation of hostilities in December 1917 and after the Brest-Litovsk Treaty in March 1918. *(Modified with permission of the Department of History, United States Military Academy.)*

FRANCISCUS SOBOLEWSKI WAS NOW among hundreds of thousands of prisoners of war waiting to go home. When their journey would begin and how they would reach their destinations were topics of constant speculation; no one knew the answers. For several years, Franciscus had been held in the Russian city of Samara, on the banks of the Volga River, from where escape was virtually impossible. In Russia, train travel between provinces had always been under strict control; this was even more the case in wartime. There was no alternative transportation and no one could survive in that region for very long on foot. In reality, the vastness of the country was more effective in keeping Russia's prisoners of war in place than any fence with barbed wire and watchtowers. Even if one did manage to escape, not having the right papers at the right time meant beatings, arrest, and a ticket to a penal colony in Siberia. The few POWs lucky enough to be held in large cities were helped on rare occasions by the Danish consul, who represented the interests of Austro-Hungary. He mediated for the release of some desperate soldiers; but these diplomatic niceties could not work for the majority of them, stranded in the huge backyard of the Russian Empire.[1]

High hopes that the return of the former soldiers was just around the corner were raised by the Russian Revolution, and then by the Brest-Litovsk Treaty between the Bolsheviks and the Central powers. Unfortunately, as weeks turned to months, nothing happened. For Russia, breaking at her seams, there seemed to be no purpose in holding the men after hostilities on the eastern front had ended. Some wondered if this was a strategy, part of a Russian scheme to get the upper hand in future negotiations. Or perhaps it was a reflection of the legendary ineffectiveness of Russia's bureaucracy. These explanations and others were possible, but the chaos that reigned after the revolution was a more likely reason.

In September 1918, Franciscus Sobolewski and four other imprisoned officers made a decision to try their luck. Why they decided to escape then and not earlier will likely never be known, but it is certain that these restless POWs knew well that it would not be a leisurely trip. Many prisoners had hesitated, knowing the dangers along the way. One of those was an elderly high school teacher from Galicia, who taught with Franciscus in a school for displaced persons in Samara; his choice was to stay and to await more stable times.

The journey home, one that normally would take two to three days by train, took the five men almost three months and brought them, in Franciscus's own words, "through a land of anarchy and terror."[2] To reach Galicia, the escapees moved through lawless regions. Some were under the control of Bolsheviks; others were ruled by White Russians. Those who returned home told harrowing stories of overcrowded trains; unable to squeeze inside, many traveled on the roofs or steps of railway carriages for as long as they were moving west. The lucky ones who made it into train cars endured the ever-present smell of Russian tobacco (*machorka*) and horrible, unsanitary conditions.

The last leg of their journey to the border with Austro-Hungary took the escapees through eastern Ukraine. There, remnant German troops and Ukrainian national forces, in an alliance, were fighting Bolsheviks; soon, they directed their arms against Poles. A confusing puzzle of gigantic proportions was on display; making a wrong move could easily cost one one's life. The unpredictability of the journey was compounded by endless delays: Trains were stopped and held for days. Frequent changes in routes, sometimes based on news of what lay ahead but often at the whim of whoever was in control, were more the norm than the exception.[3]

When their train finally arrived at its final stop, with the border in clear sight, a strange scene ensued. The former POWs and interned persons each carried their meager belongings bundled up as best they could. All of them, young and old, dashed across the last stretch into Galicia. After years in captivity and the harrowing journey of the past few months, none of them felt safe enough to wait another minute on the "other side." The moment when Franciscus finally entered Galicia must have been a special one for him, after three long years in Russia. But nothing was straightforward in those times.

Ukrainian forces were then surrounding Lvov, with Stanislawow and Bohorodczany already under their control. The news from home was sketchy, but what little trickled out spoke of civil disobedience by Poles and a new regime putting its stamp on local affairs in Stanislawow. Further travel toward Bohorodczany was not possible or, at best, not advisable under the circumstances. Instead, Franciscus continued west to the safety of Cracow. Upon arrival he was ordered, like all former members of the Austro-Hungarian military, to report immediately to the newly formed Polish army. There was simply no time for reunions with families or even just a quiet period to enjoy freedom. Surely, any letter from Fraciscus, regardless of how brief it was, must have reassured Helena that her husband was safe although still far away.[4]

By December 28, 1918, Lieutenant Franciscus Sobolewski had been ordered to report to the town of Bedzin, located in a coal-rich region west of Cracow. His commission was as company commander of the 11th Infantry Regiment, which was just being born: a collection of men trying to resemble an army.[5]

The soldiers wore old German or Austrian uniforms, and their arms varied greatly. For Franciscus this became a busy time, filled with the training of new troops and short-term deployments to hot spots along the nearby borders with Germany and Czechoslovakia. We can only surmise that he was an effective officer, because on his first anniversary of rejoining the army, Franciscus would be promoted to the rank of captain (lieutenant commander). However, the real test of his character and skills would come in only a few months' time.

More than anywhere else in Europe, where the lines between old and new were not always clear, the border between Poland and Russia had remained unsettled after the Great War. The Bolsheviks, consumed by domestic troubles, had not been a party to the peace conference in Paris; and given general uncertainty about their survival, the Allies had waited before reaching an agreement with Russia on the border issue. There was no formal declaration of war, or any big battle marking the beginning of the new troubles. But skirmishes that began in early 1919 went on throughout the year, with Polish forces and the Soviet regime clashing from the Baltic countries through Belarus to Ukraine.[6]

At first, the situation did not look bad for Poles. The days of the Bolsheviks seemed to be numbered; the White Russians were marching on Moscow, and soon other rebel forces were closing in on St. Petersburg. Reports of panic and an impending collapse of the Soviets were read with relish throughout Europe, but again the fallacy of easy prediction became evident.[7]

By early 1920, what had started as a low-level conflict had escalated to a real war. Poland was pushing its forces east in the hope of helping smaller countries emerge along its eastern borders. If its plan succeeded, the chain of friendly nations would stretch from the Baltic Sea in the north to the border with Romania in the south, and then continue on to the shores of the Black Sea. At the core of this so-called Intersea Plan was the intent to contain any future Russia—Red or White—before her appetite for expansion resurfaced. Given the recent past,

Russia was not to be trusted, regardless of the outcome of its internal struggle. In reality, the situation was growing more complex; military cooperation between the forces of the Baltic countries and the Poles did not always materialize and, in some cases, quickly turned into bitter territorial disputes.[8]

In February 1920, the 11th Regiment was ordered to march to Cracow. After a few days of collecting military supplies, the troops boarded a train and journeyed east into a full-blown conflict between Poland and Russia. With his arrival at the front, Lieutenant Commander Franciscus Sobolewski became chief of operations and then commanding officer of the 2nd battalion of the 11th Infantry Regiment. With several hundred soldiers under his command, he took part in an offensive deep into the heart of Ukraine, which was by then overrun by the Soviets. This was a time of rapidly shifting alliances; the enemy of the past year, forces from the eastern Ukrainian National Republic, now fought alongside the Polish army to regain its territory. The grievances of the past were put aside for a common objective: to create an independent Ukraine between Poland and Russia.[9]

At first, it looked as if the Poles' plan would succeed; the Russians were driven from Kiev, the capital of Ukraine. Franciscus Sobolewski's unit was south of the city but still untested by major battles. The takeover of Kiev had symbolic meaning, but the sense of victory was short-lived. A Russian counteroffensive gathered strength, and the Polish army faltered. It began what would be called a retreat behind seven rivers—with each river marking what had been supposed to be an unbreakable line of defense. The situation became dire when Bolsheviks pierced through a long front and, in a rapid advance, entered the heart of Poland. In the summer of 1920, Cossacks appeared not too far from Warsaw. Russia was poised to take over the Polish capital.[10]

In the beginning of August 1920, heavy fighting continued, with daily loss of life. The stakes were extremely high; Russians were closing in on Warsaw, and the collapse of the southern front could mean only one thing: a Bolshevik invasion of Galicia and then a victorious swoop through the rest of Poland. The 11th Infantry Regiment was positioned to the south of the gaping hole in the front. This time, its mission was not a supportive role somewhere on the back lines; by now, these troops were under constant attack by Russian cavalry. The 2nd battalion, led by Franciscus, was in charge of defense along the River Bug, near the village of Dorohusk. The situation was fluid, with Russian attacks, Polish counterattacks, and frequent shifts of the front line from one side of the river to the other. Soldiers were dying not only from bullets; some drowned while trying to reach exposed positions on the east bank.

Writing from the battlefield to his superiors, the commanding officer of the 11th Infantry Regiment described events in crisp military style:

> On the morning of August 9, the enemy opened an artillery barrage on the trenches occupied by the 2nd battalion. At 7:30 a.m., Lieutenant Commander Sobolewski, the commanding officer of the 2nd battalion, received a report that the 8th company, located on the right flank of the battalion, was abandoning its positions; the Bolshevik cavalry had already been spotted nearby. Lieutenant Commander Sobolewski immediately rushed toward the right flank of his battalion. On his way, he noticed [at a distance] cavalry troops moving in formation west of the village of Dorohusk. He realized that this was the Polish [and not Bolshevik] cavalry, on which friendly artillery fire was already being opened. Realizing the mistake, he ran toward the artillery positions and stopped the deadly fire. Despite being wounded [in the line of fire], he maintained his composure, understanding the gravity of the situation. [Sobolewski] rallied the 8th company and led [the troops] back to previously abandoned trenches. In his action, Lieutenant Commander Sobolewski not only prevented bloodshed in our own [cavalry] units, but he rescued the entire battalion—as the adjacent companies, seeing the retreat of the right flank, began to withdraw![11]

Fortunately, Franciscus's wounds were not serious.

Major Franciscus Sobolewski decorated with the Silver Cross of the Virtuti Militari.
The photograph was taken in Bedzin, Poland, in 1922.

By early fall, the Poles, aided by French advisors and shipments of new arms, had been able to repel the Bolsheviks, averting a disaster that had almost ended their short-lived statehood.[12] Now they were in hot pursuit of a retreating Russian army, moving the front lines eastward again. At long last, with both sides exhausted, a cease-fire was signed in October 1920. A period of long negotiation followed, with troops remaining in their positions along the mostly quiet demarcation line.

Franciscus Sobolewski's certificate as recipient number 477
of the Order of the Virtuti Militari.

Franciscus remained at the front until the peace treaty with the Bolsheviks was signed in March of 1921. His conduct in battle had not gone unnoticed, and he was nominated for Poland's highest military decoration, the War Order of Virtuti Militari, a venerated award dating back to 1792. Lieutenant Commander—soon to be Major—Franciscus Sobolewski became an early recipient of the Silver Cross of the Virtuti Militari, awarded in unusual instances for acts of outstanding bravery and risk to life on the battlefield. In a broader sense, the award ceremony, which took place in November 1921, closed a circle of family tradition. In the distant past, a few Sobolewski men had earned titles for military valor; now Franciscus, a teacher turned soldier, had distinguished himself above and beyond the call of duty under fire.[13]

Chapter 11 — Where to Go? Old Stories Fade Away and New Ones Are Born

FOR HELENA, THE PREVIOUS year had also brought new challenges, but for quite different reasons. In February of 1920, her father, Joseph Regiec, had died of pneumonia at the age of 63. The general feeling, which would survive in a few scattered stories told many decades later, was that this was an unexpected and devastating loss of one who had held a central place in the lives and values of the entire Regiec family. And there were other issues for Helena as well. As war turned into peace, it became clear that Franciscus would not return to Bohorodczany. As my grandmother would later say, somewhat wistfully, "He went to a war from which he never came back." With their house destroyed during attacks on Bohorodczany and no more reason to await Franciscus's homecoming, Helena knew that her future would have to be built somewhere else.

For the moment, however, my grandmother was trapped with her daughter in a largely destroyed town. Taking matters into her own hands, she petitioned the school boards in Stanislawow and Nowy Sacz for work. Those places were, of course, natural choices that offered her some sense of familiarity. Going through the required bureaucratic channels, she submitted calmly written requests about her difficult situation. She attached all required professional credentials and even a short note by her husband in support of her application. Then she waited and waited. When the replies started to come, she must have felt deeply disappointed and insecure about the future. The recurring theme of these terse statements was that, due to a lack of funding, no position could be found.[14]

But Helena's patience and perseverance ultimately paid off. When the long-awaited "yes" response finally arrived, that must have been a bittersweet moment. The letter made it clear that this young woman with a small daughter was to journey to an unfamiliar place; she would have to leave her newly widowed mother and her sister, with no one awaiting her arrival in the faraway city.

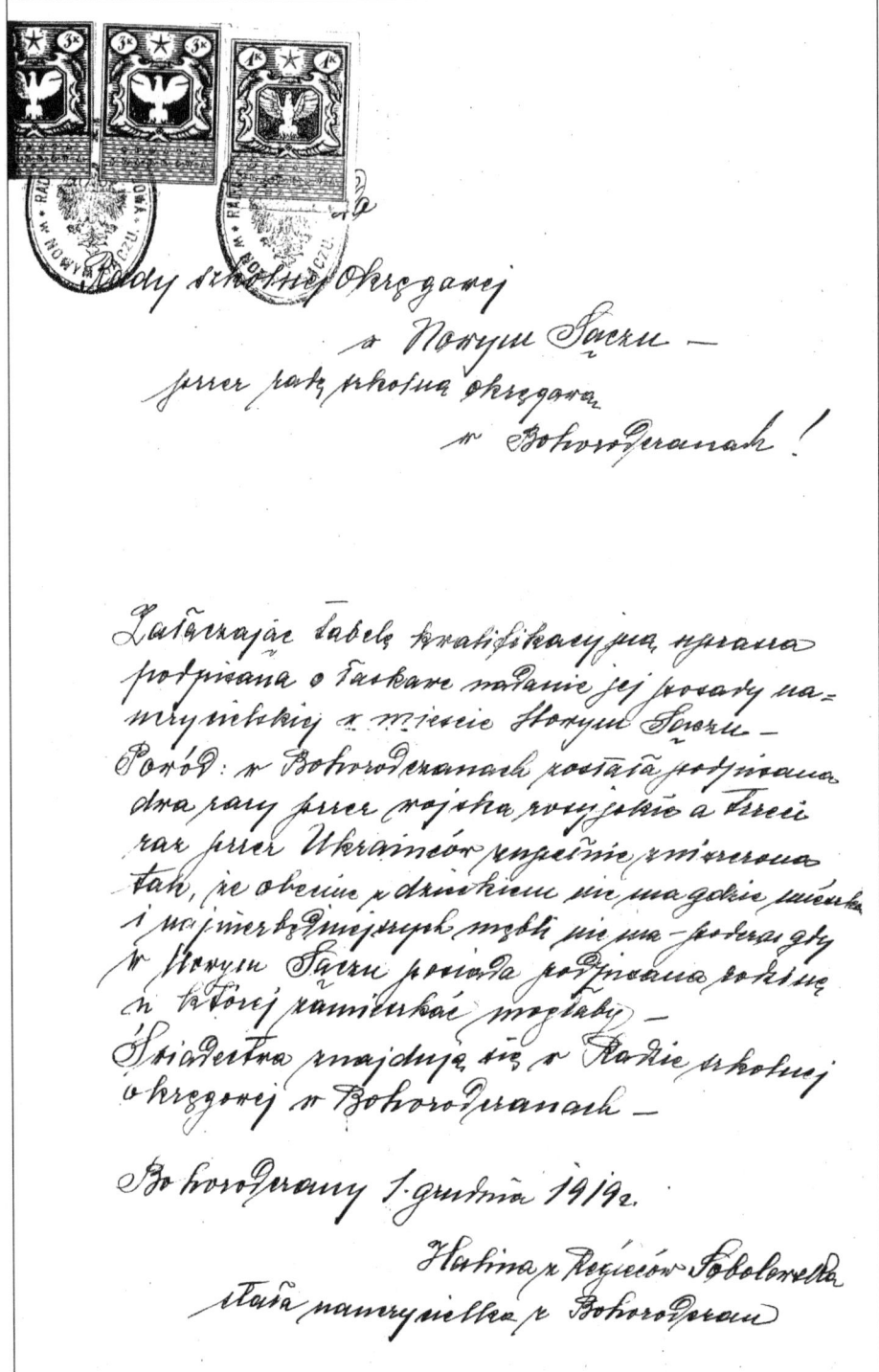

Helena (Halina) Sobolewska's handwritten petition seeking a teaching position in Nowy Sacz. In the text, Helena mentions property losses that she suffered during the past two Russian occupations in the course of World War I and during the most recent Polish-Ukrainian conflict. The document is dated December 1, 1919.

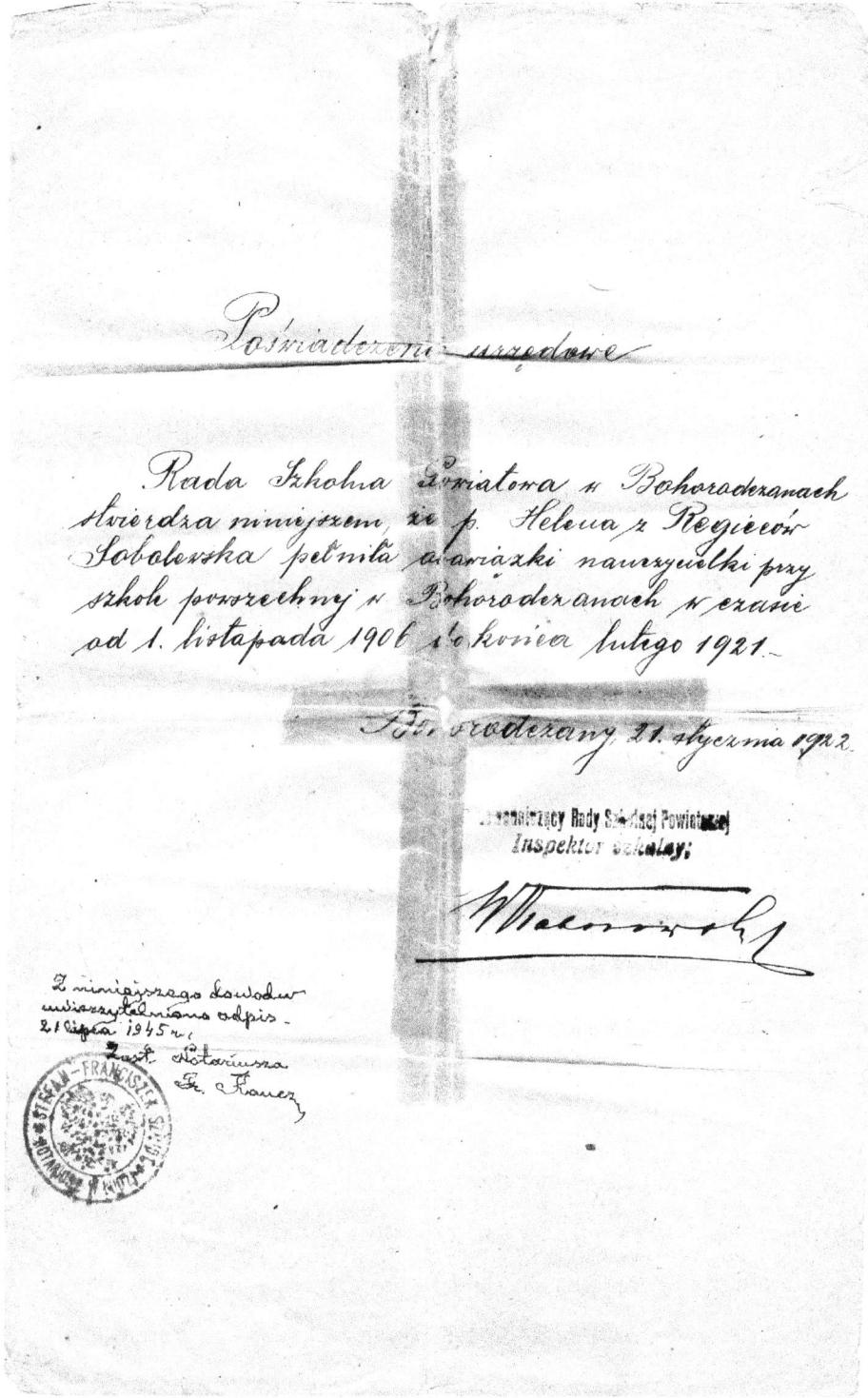

The School District of Bohorodczany issued this note attesting that Helena Regiec Sobolewska was "a teacher in Bohorodczany from November 1, 1906, to the end of February, 1921."
One era in Helena's life had ended, and a new one began.

But in the end, it was unlikely that she had many doubts. Helena was leaving behind just a few friends, including three women teachers who had been with her in Bohorodczany since before the war. Remarkably, all three had survived, but within a couple of years, they would be gone from the town as well.[15]

Then there was Helena's husband's family, which for generations had called no other place home. But times were changing; Sobolewski siblings and cousins were increasingly looking for opportunities elsewhere. Many of them had already left, and those who stayed behind would not remain in Bohorodczany for long. One was Wilhelmina, the youngest and prettiest of Franciscus's sisters, who was still there caring for her aging parents. In spite of the upheavals of war, she had married just a few years earlier. Wilhelmina and her recently born son (who will resurface later in our story) would become the very last in a long line of the family who began their lives in Bohorodczany before leaving behind the land and the rhythm of the past.[16]

When my grandmother left Bohorodczany in March 1921, her destination was the city of Lodz, in central Poland, where she had found work as a teacher. The reunion with Franciscus, if there was one, would not have been too long. His military career was on the rise, and with this came a postwar deployment back to the Silesia region, where his regiment was posted. A string of other deployments followed for him, all far away from what used to be home.[17] Not surprisingly, the marriage became strained, a long-distance relationship rather than what they both had hoped for.

Helena seldom talked about this period in her life, but the few hints she dropped gave away the story of what probably went wrong. Through no fault of their own, Helena and Franciscus had become stuck somewhere between two worlds, with different norms and spousal expectations. My grandmother, a professional woman who had been hardened by the experience of past years, could not accept a life of constant moving from one town to another, following her husband.

Chapter 11 — Where to Go? Old Stories Fade Away and New Ones Are Born   311

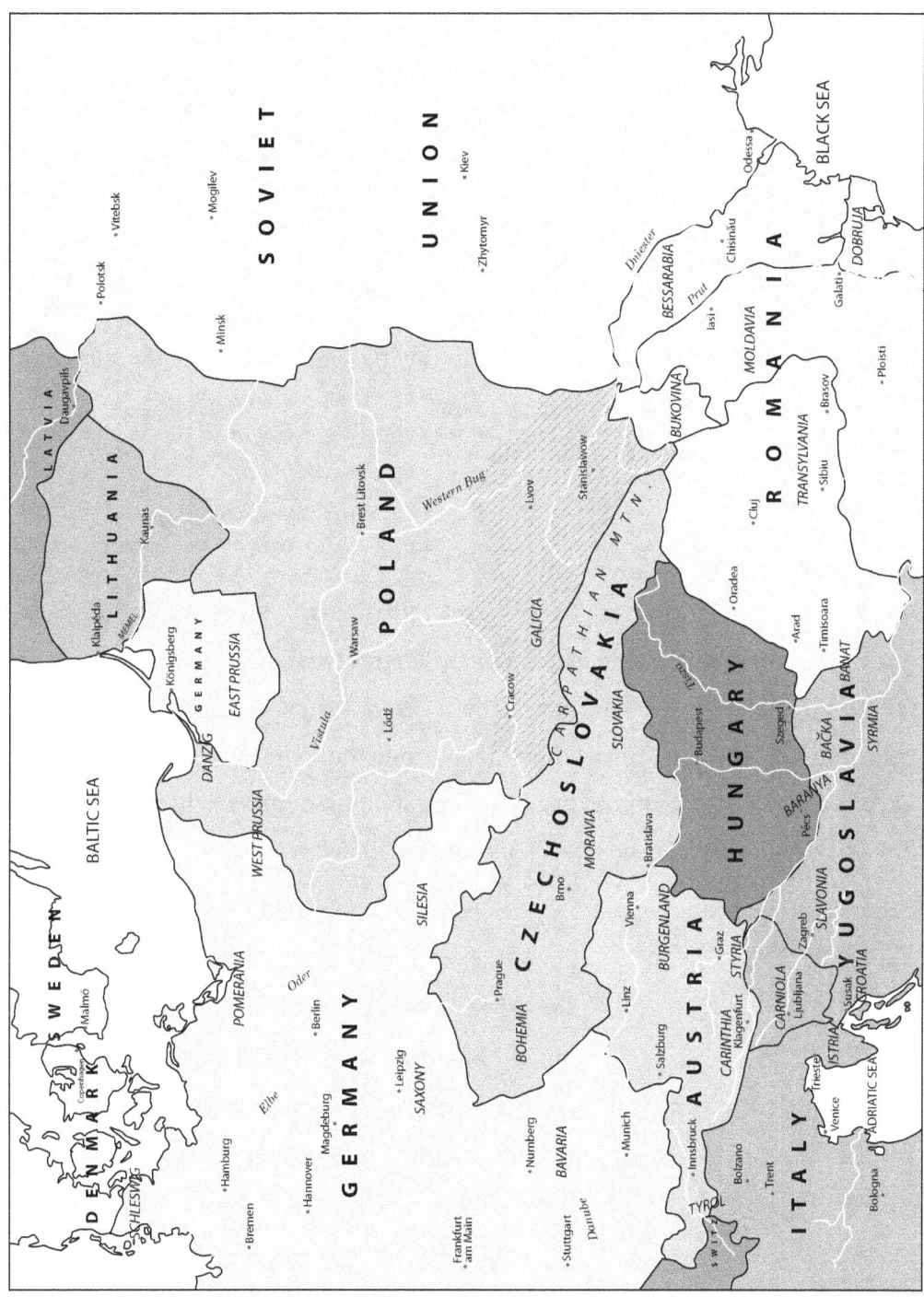

Map of central Europe circa 1921 with newly established borders of new countries in the post World War I arrangements. In March 1921, Helena Sobolewska moved from Bohorodczany and Stanislawow in former Galicia to the city of Lodz in central Poland.

Putting her teaching career, her hard-won ticket to independence, on hold was not an option for her. But this was not just about professional drive; it was also the way to provide stability and security for her young daughter. The experience of being a single mother in wartime for seven years had unalterably changed Helena; she was now, like it or not, a modern, very independent woman, sure of her skills and her ability to fend for herself.

Helena Sobolewska. The photograph was taken in the early 1920s.

My grandfather, on the other hand, was a military man used to giving orders rather than finding compromise; he could not have seen married life in a more different way. He was clearly looking for a traditional officer's wife, at his side regardless of where military life might take him. Rebuilding a life together, then, turned out to be quite difficult for this couple; and it became impossible to fill the gap in their married life. Helena and Franciscus separated in the late 1920s or early 1930s.[18]

Irena Sobolewska. The photograph was taken in Lodz in the 1920s.

For Helena, living alone with her daughter on a meager teacher's salary would be tough; but she coped as best she could, raising Irena without much help from her husband. Much later, my mother would recall, through the prism of a child's mind, a few lean years without a Christmas tree or the customary gifts. But despite all the challenges and personal disappointments, I would never hear my grandmother speak ill of Franciscus. Time after time, her quiet resilience gave her the strength to go through life without feeling sorry for herself.

Chapter 11 — Where to Go? Old Stories Fade Away and New Ones Are Born   313

Summer trip to Bohorodczany. The picture was taken in front of the old family house. Seated on the steps are Franciscus Sobolewski next to his mother, Anna Sobolewska, and his daughter, Irena Sobolewska. Above Franciscus (left to right) are Carolina Kubas, and Wilhelmina and Franciscus Durkalec with their son, "Bolek" Durkalec. Carolina and Wilhelmina were Franciscus's sisters. The photograph was taken in the late 1920s.

During Helena's first few years in Lodz, there were occasional trips back to what had been called Galicia. Perhaps a few weeks were spent on St. Joseph Street in Stanislawow during summer vacations, visiting Stephania and Wanda Regiec. There was also the opportunity for Helena and her daughter to see other towns with Galician-sounding names, like Ottynia and Zaleszczyki, which my mother would mention on a few occasions later in life. Then there would be one or two trips by Irena and her father to Bohorodczany. Irena, like any other teenager, must have felt awkward there at first; her memories of the place and the other Sobolewskis must have faded a bit. But the ice was broken quickly; she posed for a few photographs in front of the old

Stephania Regiec (1855–1930s). The only surviving photograph of Helena's mother toward the end of her life.

Summer trip to Ottynia. Seated are Helena Sobolewska (left) and Sophia Telesnicka Kühnberg (right). Standing in the middle is Irena Sobolewska next to her aunt, Wanda Regiec. The photograph was taken in August 1931.

family house before rediscovering the place with her younger cousin Bolek, with whom she would remain close for decades to come. But things were unmistakably beginning to change. After Stephania Regiec passed away in the 1930s, trips back to the former Galicia became less frequent for both mother and daughter. Within a few years, there was no one waiting in Bohorodczany; the remaining Sobolewski clan had moved away.

In the 1930s, a new generation was preparing to step into a broader world. While my grandmother continued to work in Lodz, Irena graduated from high school and then

Wanda Regiec. The photograph was taken in the 1930s in Stanislawow.

Helena Sobolewska. The photograph was taken in Lodz in the 1930s.

Irena Sobolewska. The picture was taken in the year of Irena's graduation from dental school, 1937.

moved to Warsaw. For women, times were changing. A wider spectrum of professions was becoming available and socially acceptable, although few women yet had family encouragement or the means to earn a university degree. Irena's choice was to study dentistry; but it was clear that she would never be able to afford the tuition if she was to be supported by her mother's salary alone. This time, however, Franciscus's past came to the rescue, as the law granted children of veterans with the Virtuti Militari decoration the right to an almost-free university education. Later, when Irena graduated with her dentistry degree, we can only guess at her mother's happiness and pride on seeing her daughter well-prepared for adult life.

※

By that time, Franciscus had retired from active military service. Not surprisingly, his transition into civilian life was not straightforward; but surviving pictures always show a debonair gentleman, this time in civilian clothes. Approaching his 50s, he struggled for a while to find an appropriate job before finally landing a civilian position linked with the army. In 1936, Franciscus Sobolewski remarried. In many families, this would break any remaining bonds with the first marriage, but not in this one. His second wife, Wanda, was a woman full of life, warm to everyone. But she was also a strong-willed person who liked things done her own way. Soon, she became relentless in her efforts to prod Franciscus into supporting his student daughter. As far as my mother recalled, Wanda's perseverance apparently paid off.

Over the years, Wanda and Helena developed a very natural relationship. They genuinely liked each other, and Wanda was always considered a close member of our family. If we advance, for the moment, a few decades, I may say that she was the only "aunt" I ever had growing up. For as long as I remember, it was Wanda, not Franciscus, who visited us often. When one year my grandmother became ill while my mother was away, Wanda was the first person I asked for help when I found myself, a hapless medical student, completely lost in the chore of cooking for my

Irena Sobolewska's high school diploma (issued on June 10, 1933, in Lodz, Poland).

KOPIA

DYPLOM

MY

REKTOR I RADA PROFESORÓW AKADEMII STOMATOLOGICZNEJ

W WARSZAWIE

OŚWIADCZAMY CO NASTĘPUJE:

Pani SOBOLEWSKA Irena Maria

rodem z Bohorodczan, woj. stanisławowskie, obywatelka polska,

po odbyciu przepisanych studiów w Akademii Stomatologicznej w Warszawie w latach od 1933 do 1937 i pomyślnym złożeniu obowiązujących egzaminów,

otrzymała stopień

LEKARZA-DENTYSTY,

stanowiący dowód ukończenia akademickich studiów lekarsko-dentystycznych i uprawniający do ubiegania się o stopień doktora, oraz do wykonywania praktyki lekarsko-dentystycznej w granicach ustaw, obowiązujących w Rzeczypospolitej Polskiej.

W dowód tego wydajemy na mocy uchwały Rady Profesorów niniejszy dyplom, opatrzony podpisami i pieczęcią Akademii.

W Warszawie, dnia 12 grudnia 1937 roku.

L. 388

REKTOR   m. p.   ZA RADĘ PROF

(—) *Prof. Dr J. Modrakowski*   (—) *Prof. Dr A. Meissner*

(—) *Prof. Dr M. Zeńczak*

Irena Sobolewska's dental school diploma (issued on December 12, 1937, in Warsaw, Poland).

Franciscus Sobolewski in civilian life in the 1930s.

grandma. If there was ever some awkwardness in that situation, I never felt it, and the thought of calling anyone else simply never crossed my mind. Wanda arrived a few days later, storming into the apartment and taking charge of everything within minutes.

Wanda had only one area about which she was shy, and that was her age. According to family gossip, she had managed to change the year of her birth in some documents.[19] At the beginning, this worked well; but many years later, Wanda realized to her chagrin that being "younger" meant working as a bookkeeper for a few years longer than was really needed, before her retirement pension would begin.

With the decade of the 1930s coming to a close, life had more surprises for Franciscus and those around him. Another war loomed on the horizon, and Lieutenant Colonel Franciscus Sobolewski was mobilized for the third time, proving that anyone's predictions about quiet civilian life were wrong again. In late August 1939, just days before the German invasion of Poland that marked the outbreak of World War II, he became the commander of air defenses and the military airport in Bialystok, a city in the northeastern part of the country.

By mid-September of 1939, German forces advancing from the west took Bialystok. To make matters worse, a few days later, the Soviets attacked Poland

Lieutenant Colonel Franciscus Sobolewski at the airfield in Bialystok, Poland. Franciscus is holding the hand of Zbigniew ("Zbyszek") Witkowski, his second wife's son. The picture was taken in 1937.

from the east, fulfilling their commitment in a secret pact with the Nazis that had been negotiated the previous summer. Franciscus hid his ceremonial officer's sword, Virtuti Militari decoration, and honorary certificate underneath the floor of the house where he lived. On September 22, 1939, he crossed the border into Lithuania, narrowly avoiding capture by the Soviet army. Whether this was pure luck or a premonition of what might happen next, we will never know; but it was a fateful decision for Franciscus. Several thousand other Polish officers, taken prisoner by the Soviets, were less fortunate; the majority would perish in a mass execution in the Katyn Forest just a few months later.

When the Soviet Union annexed Lithuania in June 1940, luck was on Franciscus's side again. In this war, he escaped deportation deep into Russia and remained unharmed in a Lithuanian displaced persons' camp until 1941, when the Germans overran the Baltic countries, waging an attack on their former ally, the Soviet Union.[20]

After the war, Franciscus returned to Bialystok to reclaim his personal belongings. The new owners of his former apartment apparently needed some strong convincing to allow him to remove pieces of the floor—revealing, to their bewilderment, carefully wrapped items that had lain beneath their feet for the past several years.

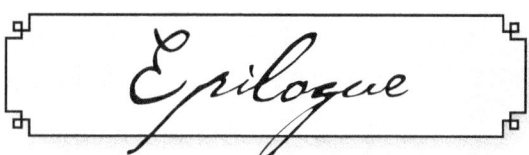

Epilogue

WITH WORLD WAR II OVERTURNING all plans again, Helena moved to Warsaw to live with her daughter. Years later, she told us that as she had waited for a train in Lodz, suitcase in hand, a German soldier approached. He barked some orders in her direction, but Grandma suddenly forgot all the German she knew; she could only wonder if her papers were in order and whether her modest luggage was arousing suspicion. It turned out to be something about waiting on the wrong platform, but the idea of being unable to reunite with Irena was what had truly frightened her. Besides the uncertainty of wartime, there was another reason she was anxious to be at her daughter's side; Irena had recently married, and Helena was soon to be a grandmother. Not long after her arrival in Warsaw, my brother George (Jerzy) was born. As my mother described it later, after a few days of watching the new parents, who were clueless about caring for a baby, Grandma stepped in and took charge.

There was another war story that somehow stuck in my memory. My grandmother recalled that a stray bullet had once entered through the kitchen

My grandmother is holding the future author. Behind her are my mother, Irena, and my brother, George. On the back of the picture, the dedication reads, "To our dear Grandma Wanda, the family; sister, niece, grandson George and grandson Andrew. October 1, 1952." As the picture was sent to the Soviet Union, with its intrusive censorship, my grandmother added beneath, asking her sister, Wanda Regiec, who remained in Stanislawow, "write whether you received?"

window, not far from where she was sitting holding George, and whizzed through the air, lodging in the door frame. Hearing this as a child, I ignored the part about her and George being in danger but kept inspecting the doorframe, where the mysterious bullet apparently remained.

After the war, Helena returned to Lodz, where she taught for a few more years before retiring in 1949. By that time, she had spent 43 years in various classrooms, teaching in different schools under at least three regimes. From the moment she retired, she focused her energy on helping Irena, who was practicing dentistry, to manage the household and raise both George and her second grandson, the author of this story.

THE POSTWAR PERIOD WAS a perilous time for the many who suddenly found themselves behind the "Iron Curtain." A typical case was that of Boleslaw ("Bolek") Durkalec, Franciscus Sobolewski's youngest nephew. When the Soviets occupied eastern Poland in September of 1939, Bolek Durkalec was forbidden to live in Stanislawow, as the Russification of these territories began in earnest. After the Germans took over in 1941, he survived by working in

Epilogue

construction battalions in the countryside, and was briefly in the anti-Nazi resistance in the underground Home Army. Even with the end of the war, he and thousands of others could not return to Stanislawow; the area had been annexed by the Soviet Union, and a massive exodus of Poles was in motion. Trying to restart his life, Bolek enlisted in the military of Communist Poland and became an officer with an exemplary record. But these accomplishments did not spare him from false accusations during one of the political purges of the Stalin years; having ties to a different political past was enough to put anyone in danger. Bolek's sins were wartime service in the underground Home Army, which had been aligned with the anti-Communist Polish government in exile; and then refusal to collaborate with Communist security forces at a time when a whisper of suspicion could end someone's career, lead to interrogation, or worse.

In 1951, Bolek was jailed and, after a secret trial on trumped-up charges, sentenced to prison. When he appealed, protesting this blatant miscarriage of justice, his time of imprisonment was only increased. He was released in 1954, in one of the amnesties common after Stalin's death. He left prison not only with an understandable bitterness at being falsely accused and never exonerated by the wicked system, but also severely ill with a case of tuberculosis that he had contracted while serving his sentence. After therapy, he luckily recovered and became a forest ranger. But it would be many decades before the unjust sentence was finally expunged from his records. I remember Bolek, in his later years, telling me once about his stamp collection; he was visiting my mother, who kept in close touch with her cousin.[1]

Boleslaw ("Bolek") Durkalec, Helena and Franciscus's nephew from Bohorodczany. The photograph was taken in the 1940s prior to his imprisonment by the internal security forces in Communist Poland.

Another who fell victim to a political witch hunt was my grandfather, Franciscus Sobolewski.[2] The story began when he and a few other former officers started meeting to discuss what might happen if the Communist regime should be overthrown. They certainly did not intend to do anything themselves, as none of these aging men had a single weapon. Instead, they wanted to be ready if and when the United States and NATO forces might restore Poland's independence. Over tea and cakes in their homes, they chatted about who among them would step forward and in which role, in order to fill the vacuum at such a moment of national emergency. At times, the meetings veered more toward where to get good tobacco (these ex-military men were all smokers), rather than how to create a new political order. When Franciscus once asked his friends about the political views of their organization, nobody really knew how to answer.

After several months, someone arrived from another city; the visitor was greeted at the train station and joined a conversation in Franciscus's apartment. The guest gave a few vague explanations of who he was and why he was there; then he nominated Franciscus for the rank of brigadier general. With a handshake, my grandfather was suddenly in "charge" of the southeastern military district, which was to include the territory of eastern Galicia that had been lost to the Soviets. He stood up and accepted the nomination but cautioned that he had left the military so long ago that he had no contacts among the army officers who would be needed to administer such a large territory. He was simply reassured not to worry about that and to be ready.

Two years after this underground organization began, the country's security forces got wind of it. In March of 1954, about 50 members were arrested in a sweep across Poland. Franciscus was grabbed from the streets of Lodz; that same day, his apartment was searched for evidence of crimes against the state. In the climate of paranoia that the Communist government perpetrated— with enemies believed to be lurking everywhere—these charges could have meant imprisonment, loss

Epilogue

of property, and even death, regardless of how ridiculous they might seem today. The photo of Franciscus that remained in the security archives shows not a dapper former officer but an old man with disheveled hair, dirty clothes, and a frightened look on his face. This was exactly how the regime wanted him to look and feel.

What followed were endless days of interrogations about the meetings—no more than five of them altogether—that had taken place in Lodz. Every testimony was stamped "STRICTLY SECRET." At the end, not much was needed for the security apparatus to brand Franciscus a member of the "central group," a sinister figure in the eyes of those who wanted to see a crime. He was kept in custody for months; his captors claimed that as an enemy of the state, he was too dangerous to be released. As if this was not enough, the authorities even planted an informer in Franciscus's prison cell who, after a few days, dutifully reported what my grandfather had said; but nothing earth-shattering was revealed. His former employees were also questioned, just to sniff out any anti-Communist leanings in the accused.

When the indictment came, the regime accused Franciscus and his "co-conspirators" of, among other crimes, plotting a terrorist attack using a car loaded with explosives in order to destroy the Communist Party headquarters. Nobody had bothered to mention that not only did none of them have any explosives, they also did not own, nor could they afford to buy, any vehicle; cars were considered a luxury in Poland at that time. On top of those charges, Franciscus and his co-defendants were accused of other serious crimes against the state, such as an alleged attempt to smuggle a document confirming the existence of the secret organization through an unidentified employee of the French embassy. Any due process was a fiction; that became obvious when Franciscus's defense attorney was still petitioning the military court for access to the evidence and the accused, a mere three days before the scheduled trial. Clearly, nobody in authority cared about such nuances.

Predictably, the "conspirators'" secret trial in front of a military court ended with Franciscus's conviction and a five-year prison term. On appeal, the sentence was shortened to two years; but by then, my grandfather's health had deteriorated to the point that he was admitted to the prison hospital. After spending one year behind bars, this almost 70-year-old man, bent by this experience, was released during a political thaw in 1955.[3] When a few months later he had the "audacity" to ask the regime to return his watch, another humiliation followed. Franciscus was sternly reminded that he had been sentenced to not just a prison term but also to the loss of his personal property; his old Swiss watch, apparently from 1910, now belonged to the state. He was more successful in retrieving 15 personal pictures that had been seized in his apartment. They were "magnanimously" returned in 1957.

In the early 1960s, amnesty was offered to many victims of the political prosecutions of earlier decades, but Franciscus refused to accept this and instead demanded a retrial. This time, in an open court, he was exonerated of all charges. The evidence showed clearly that internal security forces had used physical force and emotional intimidation to elicit testimonies from the accused. Even the star witness for the prosecution turned out to be an unreliable individual who had been committed for years to mental institutions and now refused to repeat any accusations, claiming he had lost his memories of all past events.

Was that the end of the saga that had begun with a few older men chatting among themselves, hardly conspiring to overthrow the regime? Not really. The security forces kept trawling through hundreds and hundreds of pages of old documents; they produced summaries of the alleged counterrevolutionary activities of Franciscus Sobolewski and his co-conspirators as late as 1973. Not surprisingly, these pages were again labeled "SECRET," even though all charges had been overturned 10 years before.[4]

Epilogue

MY GRANDMOTHER AND GRANDFATHER had a brief reunion when I was about 12. After making the necessary arrangements with his second wife, Wanda, my mother sent me to Lodz to bring Franciscus back to Warsaw for a week. He was already an elderly man, still straight and tall but showing a bit of forgetfulness; hence, he could not travel alone. When we arrived home, I knocked on the door with Franciscus standing at my side. My grandmother came to greet us and looked at her former husband for the first time in about 30 years. With a twinkle in her eye, she asked him as if surprised, "What are you doing here?"

Franciscus answered something, but after a bit of small talk, my grandma said, "You know, I am quite busy now; I have to prepare dinner for tonight." In just a few minutes, the former colonel was sitting in the kitchen with an apron around his waist, following an order to clean vegetables for the evening meal. My grandmother seemed happy moving around the kitchen, scolding Franciscus

Helena and Franciscus Sobolewski briefly reunited. The photograph was taken by a clumsy picture taker in Warsaw, circa 1960.

in good spirit when she felt he was mistaken about something from the past. A few days later, I took them for a little sightseeing and a walk in the park. I photographed them at various spots to document the occasion, but unfortunately, my old camera malfunctioned; still, a single picture survived. In the photo, they are smiling, unusual for those from a generation that never grinned when looking into the camera's lens. Although I quickly became bored with this excursion, it was obvious that they enjoyed each other's company, talking intensely for the entire time.

After Franciscus left, Wanda, on her visits, would say something to the effect that she was fine with sending him back for more than a week, to which my grandmother would answer with joy, "Well, you wanted him, so now you have to keep him." They both laughed heartily, along with everyone else. There were no more visits or direct contact between Helena and Franciscus.[5]

In those later years, another Wanda, whom we met earlier, continued to link Helena with long-gone Galicia. Wanda Regiec, my grandmother's younger sister, never married and managed to avoid mandatory resettlement to postwar Poland after World War II.[6] She led a modest life, making ends meet by playing an instrument in a touring ensemble. She visited us only once, sometime in the early 1960s. I do not remember much from that visit, only a few blurred images of a small, elderly woman who showed up unexpectedly one morning. To the chagrin of everyone, there had been some mixup with a telegram that had not arrived on time. Whether shy or a bit intimidated by living in what was then the Soviet Union, she did

Wanda Regiec, Helena's sister, in a picture taken in the 1960s in Ivano-Frankivsk, Soviet Union.

Epilogue

not want to accept any gifts, saying that she had everything she needed at home. But she managed to tell us about one of the cathedrals in the former Stanislawow (by then renamed Ivano-Frankivsk) that had been converted to an anti-religion museum. Although I did not fully comprehend that story at the time, I understand in retrospect how accurately it reflected what had happened there.

Wanda left for home after a few weeks, but the sisters continued to exchange letters. Now and then, she wrote us about visits or holidays with friends Helena knew from the past. A few years later, there would be a request from her for medication for heart failure, which my mother promptly sent; then the letters stopped, leaving my grandmother very worried about her sister. When one day a gray envelope stuffed with old photographs arrived from Ivano-Frankivsk, we knew immediately what had happened. Wanda Regiec was buried alongside her parents, Joseph and Stephania Regiec, in an old cemetery by Sapiezynska Street, not far from where they all had lived. Just a few years after she died, small signs were nailed to the old tress, informing passersby that the cemetery was to be liquidated. Soon the local Soviet government, with its

The grainy photograph documenting demolition of the old cemetery in Stanislawow (by then renamed Ivano-Frankivsk), ordered by the Soviets in 1980.

senseless ruthlessness, ordered bulldozers to obliterate the old monuments, erasing forever the names of those who were part of the history of this region. Any remaining trace of the Regiec family had vanished, and in a broader sense, another link to Galicia was taken away.

Toward the end of her life, Helena lived in a retirement community. My mother went to see her there every Wednesday; I wish I would have remembered to go more often. Whenever I visited her with my mother, she had cookies for us and wanted to hear our news, to be reassured that everything was fine. When the time came to say good-bye, my grandmother would insist on walking us to the bus stop, no matter what the weather. I remember seeing her from the window as we rode away, her small frame standing still until our bus turned the corner; only then would she start walking back home.

Reading was my grandmother's interest throughout her life, and when her eyesight faltered, that troubled her greatly. This was the only complaint I ever heard from her. Although she was a bit frail, she kept an interest in many things until the end. Ahead of her time, she helped educate the public about recycling before it became fashionable; at some point, this initiative of my grandma's was even discussed on a local radio station. My grandmother also arranged theater tickets and trips to museums for her fellow retirees. In the early 1970s, I remember stumbling to find a clear answer when she asked me, "What are those computers that I am hearing about?"

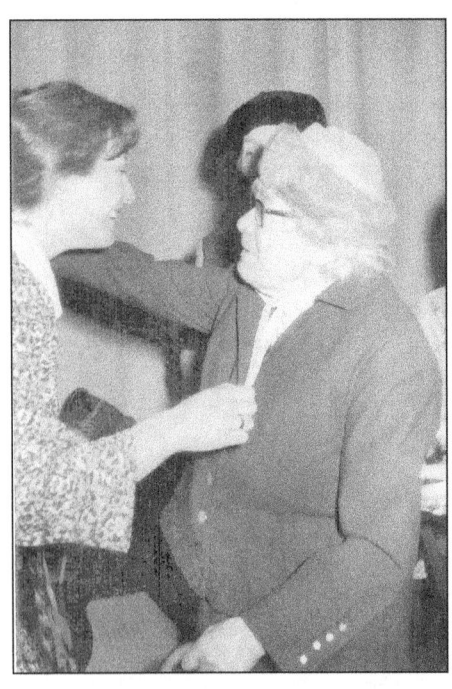

Helena Sobolewska at the age of 89, embracing my wife, Margaret, during our wedding on February 14, 1976.

Helena Sobolewska and Wanda Sobolewska chatting and having a good time.
The photograph was taken on February 14, 1976.

I was very fortunate that my grandmother lived long enough to meet my wife, Margaret, whom she was very fond of. Perhaps speaking a bit from her own experience, she once gave Margaret a gentle bit of advice: not to let me travel alone for too long. She lived until the ripe old age of 91. There is no right way to summarize it, other than saying that I was very fortunate to have Helena Regiec Sobolewska as my grandmother.[7]

"God Bless. Grandma." My grandmother wrote these words to Margaret and me, with difficulty, on the day of our wedding.

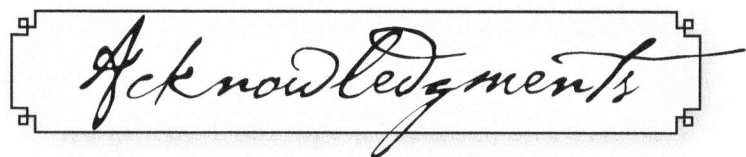

Acknowledgments

THIS BOOK WOULD NOT HAVE been possible without the support of my entire family. My wife, Margaret, endured months that turned into years of a husband who talked mostly about Galicia or the next piece of the puzzle he was eager to solve. There were weekends when she put up with my absence; I was in front of the computer or in a local family history center. Margaret became my sounding board, someone well-versed in the details of the families I follow in this story. My children, Ewa and Andy, thought for a while that their father had gone almost insane with this historical research, never before having been interested in his own family background. As one of them jokingly teased the other, "The issue is not a book but the fact that we will be quizzed on its contents." I hope that they will learn a bit about themselves reading these pages. Besides my own curiosity, this was a key incentive, driving me to probe further and deeper into the past.

My cousin, Mrs. Irena Szymczak, put her trust in me, sharing with me very personal material about her father, Boleslaw ("Bolek") Durkalec, along with precious family pictures of her father and the Sobolewski family, for which I am very grateful. Other cousins, Mr. Andrew Witkowski and Mrs. Magda Binder, contributed stories and pictures of Franciscus and Wanda Sobolewski. In my research I found my very distant cousin, Mr. Andrzej Fryś, who shared with me priceless memoirs of his own great-grandfather, and documents related to the Wilczek family that brought to light their long-forgotten story. His willingness to selflessly provide me with historical sources from his own collection was of great help and triggered preliminary thoughts about a possible next project. My only regret is that my late brother, George, could not see the final book, although in his laconic way, he commented once during my research, "So, it looks as though we had a large family."

I am very grateful to Mrs. Małgorzata Międzobrodzka from the History Department of the Salt Mines Museum in Wieliczka, Poland, who had the sharp eye of a historian in finding priceless information on the early years of the Lösch family. Mr. Jan Zielinski from Andrychow, Poland, shared with me early photographs of the town, and quickly identified ways to uncover traces of the Wilczek family. The State Archives in Cracow contributed old maps of Roztoka and Nowy Sacz. Mrs. Agnieszka Filipek from the branch of the archives in Nowy Sacz was instrumental in finding the forgotten story of Bronislawa Lösch, entirely unknown to me before then. Present-day school principals in the places where Bronislawa Lösch and Joseph Regiec taught graciously shared with me old documents preserved in school libraries, some in Bronislawa's and Joseph's handwriting, which shed light on their lives. The Regional Museum in Nowy Sacz contributed old postcards with views of the city from the nineteenth and twentieth centuries. Mr. Rajmund Piżanowski was always willing to share with me his encyclopedic knowledge of the history of Stanislawow. He has been a true gentleman who devoted a lot of time and personal resources to creating an excellent website dedicated to the history of this town. Our family friend, Mrs. Elwira Owczarska, facilitated many contacts with the archives in Poland; her help and patience were invaluable. Director Diana Peltz of the State Archives in Lviv provided me with the maps of Bohorodczany and copies of the old land census data where I could find many details about the Sobolewski family.

There were many other people who contributed to my research. I was very fortunate to come across excellent resources on the Internet that taught me basic methods of genealogical research and pointed to available sources of information on Galicia, including the monumental database on microfilm stored by the Mormon Church in Utah. I studied copies of those films in a family history center in Philadelphia. Many thanks go to Mrs. Geneva Roberts, who often braved sleet or rain to open the center's doors for those of us poring through those films. This was invaluable material that allowed me to reconstruct births, marriages, and deaths through the generations in amazing detail. The missing links were reconstructed from church archives in cities of the former Galicia, such as Cracow, Tarnow, and Jaslo, situated in today's Poland. There were emails and calls to the parishes to obtain not just dates of important events but other information recorded on the occasions of these ceremonies.

Many excellent digital libraries, with enough material for more than one book on Galicia, provided historical background. I was a frequent user of the Austrian National Library (ÖNB) website, which has a massive online collection of newspapers from Austro-Hungary, including Galicia. These tidbits of information provided context for the facts about people I was discovering. Other invaluable resources were the website of the Genealogical Society of Lesser Poland and the digital libraries of Jagiellonian University and the city of Tarnow, Poland. I am indebted to Mr. Tomasz Kozłowski from the History Meeting House in Warsaw, Poland, who provided outstanding illustrative material of Galician railroads and street scenes from Stanislawow.

There are probably numerous others who helped me in more indirect ways. But let us not forget the principals of this story, the members of the Lösch, Regiec, and Sobolewski families, who had exciting lives that allowed this narrative to flow. They truly deserve special acknowledgment.

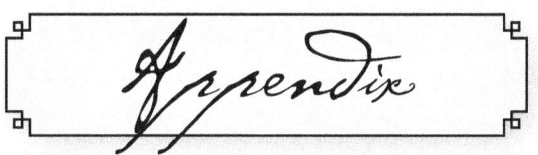

THE LÖSCH, REGIEC, AND SOBOLEWSKI FAMILY REGISTERS

THE LÖSCH FAMILY REGISTER

1st Generation.

1-1. Mathias Lösch born circa 1760, place unknown, and died March 15, 1818, in Wieliczka, Galicia. Mathias married **Anna Sedlaczek** before 1795, place unknown. Mathias settled in Wieliczka in 1809. Child of Mathias and Anna:

    i.   Christian Lösch born 1795 or 1798, place unknown.

2nd Generation.

2-1-i. Christian Lösch (son of Mathias and Anna) born 1795 or 1798, place unknown, and died May 25, 1871, in Wieliczka. Christian married three times:

a. **Antonina Pinkas** on November 14, 1819, in Wieliczka. Antonina was a daughter of Mathias Pinkas and Victoria de Baranski. She was born circa 1799 and died August 7, 1823, in Wieliczka. Children of Christian and Antonina (all born in Wieliczka):

    i.   **Andreas Lösch** born circa 1820 and died July 22, 1893, in Nowy Sacz, Galicia.

    ii.   Antonius Lösch born July 8, 1822, and died July 12, 1822.

    iii.   Antonius Christian Lösch born May 18, 1823, and died October 7, 1824.

b. Marianna Kwiatkowska circa 1824, place unknown. Marianna was born in 1807, place unknown, and died August 29, 1841, in Wieliczka. Children of Christian and Marianna (all born in Wieliczka):

    iv.   Christian Wilhelm Lösch born October 26, 1824.

    v.   Julius Gregory Lösch born April 17, 1828.

    vi.   Henricus Ignatius Lösch born June 28, 1829.

    vii.   Edward Franciscus Lösch born September 17, 1831.

c. Josepha Ferenz on February 25, 1843, in Wieliczka. Josepha was a daughter of Josephus Ferenz and Agatha Lacka. She was born circa 1822, place unknown, and died date and place unknown. Children of Christian and Josepha (both born in Wieliczka):

    viii.   Amalia Josepha Lösch born September 17, 1844.

    ix.   Stephania Lösch born July 10, 1845.

3rd Generation.

3-1-i. Andreas Lösch (son of Andreas and Antonina) born circa 1820 in Wieliczka and died July 22, 1893, in Nowy Sacz, Galicia. Andreas married **Eleonora Wilczek** on October 4, 1846, in Andrychow, Galicia. Eleonora was a daughter of Ignatius Wilczek and Thecla de Czerwinski. Eleonora was born January 5, 1819, in Andrychow, and died February 26, 1900, in Nowy Sacz, Galicia. Children of Andreas and Eleonora (all born in different towns of Galicia):

    i.   Bronislawa Valeria Lösch born August 9, 1848, in Jaslo.

    ii.   Wilhelmina (a.k.a. Guilhelmina) Lösch born circa 1852 in Andrychow.

    iii.   **Stephania Maria Lösch** born December 1, 1855, in Biecz, and died in the 1930s in Stanislawow, Poland.

4th Generation.

4-1-i. Bronislawa Valeria Lösch (daughter of Andreas and Eleonora) born August 9, 1848, in Jaslo, Galicia, and died September 10, 1912, in Nowy Sacz, Galicia. Bronislawa never married.

4-1-ii. Wilhelmina Lösch (daughter of Andreas and Eleonora) born circa 1852 in Andrychow, Galicia, and died date and place unknown. Wilhelmina married two times:

a. Roman Nowak date unknown in Andrychow. Roman died before 1879.

b. Vincentius Telesnicki Jr. on February 2, 1879, in Nowy Sacz, Galicia. Vincentius was a son of Vincentius Telesnicki Sr. and Euphrosinia Jahl. He was born in 1854 in Nowy Sacz and died on February 1, 1893, in Jaslo, Galicia. Children of Vincentius and Wilhelmina (all born in different towns of Galicia):

    i.   Sophia Telesnicka born October 7, 1883, in Tarnow. Sophia's married name was Kühnberg.

    ii.   Adamus Telesnicki born June 24, 1885, in Piwniczna.

    iii.   Janina Telesnicka born July 13, 1888, in Nowy Sacz.

    iv.   Mariannus Telesnicki born September 10, 1892, in Jaslo.

4-1-iii. Stephania Maria Lösch (daughter of Andreas and Eleonora) born December 1, 1855, in Biecz, Galicia, and died in the 1930s in Stanislawow, Poland. Stephania married **Joseph Regiec** (Regiec register 3-1-vii) on February 3, 1886, in Nowy Sacz, Galicia. The line **continues under the Regiec family register**.

THE REGIEC FAMILY REGISTER

1st Generation.

1-1. Josephus Regiec (a.k.a. Regetz or Regietz) born circa 1787, place unknown, and died March 28, 1847, in Gierowa, Galicia. Josephus married **Lucia Jarmula** in 1817 in Gierowa. Lucia was born circa 1793, place unknown, and died August 17, 1875, in Gierowa. Children of Josephus and Lucia (all born in Gierowa):

    i.   **Michaël Regiec** born August 12, 1817.

    ii.   Petrus Regiec born June 15, 1819, and died October 29, 1827.

    iii.   Marianna Regiec (a.k.a. Regetz) born August 28, 1821.

    iv.   Adalbertus Regiec born April 17, 1824.

    v.   Joannes Regiec born May 14, 1826, and died November 12, 1827.

    vi.   Catharina Regiec born August 7, 1828.

    vii.   Josephus Regiec (a.k.a. Regetz) born January 22, 1831.

2nd Generation.

2-1-i. Michaël Regiec (son of Josephus and Lucia) born August 12, 1817, and died date and place unknown. Michaël married three times:

a. **Thecla (a.k.a. Magdalena) Traczewska** on February 7, 1850, in Zakliczyn, Galicia. Thecla was a daughter of Valentino de Bogusz Traczewski and Anna Borzecka. She was born in 1827, place unknown, and died February 4, 1858, in Roztoka, Galicia. Children of Michaël and Thecla (all born in Roztoka, Galicia):

    i.   Ludovica Barbara Regiec born November 28, 1850.

    ii.   Marianna Cecilia Victoria Regiec born November 28, 1851.

    iii.   Theophilia Victoria born December 13, 1852.

iv. Eustachius Sigsmundus Vincentius Regiec born March 29, 1854.

v. Eleanora Sophia Regiec born May 16, 1855.

vi. Anna Julianna Regiec born June 28, 1856.

vii. Joseph Blasius Stanislaus Regiec born February 4, 1858, and died February 5, 1920, in Stanislawow, Poland.

b. Catharina Barbara Stoczynska on March 5, 1859, in Tuchow, Galicia. Catharina was a daughter of Valentino Stoczynski and Balbina Dunikowska. She was born in 1830, place unknown, and died date and place unknown. Children of Michaël and Catharina (all born in Roztoka, Galicia):

viii. Helena Ludovica Apolonia Regiec born January 26, 1860.

ix. Joannes Valentinus Regiec born January 23, 1862, and died January 29, 1862, in Roztoka.

x. Leon Valentinus Adalbertus Ignatius Regiec born February 7, 1863.

c. Josepha Catharina Stoczynska circa 1864. Josepha was a sister of Michaël's second wife and a daughter of Valentino Stoczynski and Balbina Dunikowska. Dates and places of birth and death unknown. Children of Michaël and Josepha (all born in Roztoka, Galicia):

xi. Franciscus Vincentius Regiec born March 14, 1865.

xii. Elisabetha Antonina Regiec born June 7, 1866, and died February 24, 1877, in Zakliczyn, Galicia.

xiii. Ludovica Rosalia Regiec born August 8, 1869, and died March 23, 1948, in Przemysl, Poland.

xiv. Josepha Marianna Regiec born July 19, 1871, and died July 25, 1871, in Roztoka, Galicia.

3rd Generation.

3-1-vii. Joseph Regiec (son of Michaël and Thecla) born February 4, 1858, in Roztoka, Galicia, and died February 5, 1920, in Stanislawow, Poland. Joseph married **Stephania Maria Lösch** (Lösch register 4-1-iii) on February 3, 1886, in Nowy Sacz, Galicia. Stephania was a daughter of Andreas and Eleonora. She was born December 1, 1855, in Biecz, Galicia, and died in the 1930s in Stanislawow, Poland. Children of Joseph and Stephania:

    i.   Helena Wanda Regiec born November 16, 1886, in Mszana Dolna, Galicia, and died June 19, 1977, in Warsaw, Poland.

    ii.   Wanda Julia Regiec born September 9, 1888, in Nowy Sacz, and died in the late 1960s in Ivano-Frankivsk, Soviet Union.

4th Generation.

4-7-i. Helena Wanda Regiec (daughter of Joseph and Stephania) born November 16, 1886, in Mszana Dolna, Galicia, and died June 19, 1977, in Warsaw, Poland. Helena married **Franciscus Sobolewski** (Sobolewski register 4-6-vi) July 17, 1912, in Kochawina, Galicia. The line **continues under the Sobolewski family register**.

THE SOBOLEWSKI FAMILY REGISTER

1st Generation

1-1. Ludovicus Sobolewski born before 1784, place unknown, and died June 6, 1835, in Lachowce, Galicia. Ludovicus married **Magdalena Krechowiecka** before 1794, place unknown. Children of Ludovicus and Magdalena:

    i.   Theresia Sobolewska born in 1794, place unknown.

    ii.   Mathias Sobolewski born in September 1797 in Lachowce.

    iii.   Adalbertus Sobolewski born May 1, 1802, in Lachowce.

    iv.   **Antonius Sobolewski** born in March 1805 in Lachowce and died May 16, 1873, in Bohorodczany, Galicia.

    v.   Martinus Sobolewski born before 1806, place unknown.

2nd Generation

2-1-iv. Antonius Sobolewski (son of Ludovicus and Magdalena) born in March 1805 in Lachowce and died May 16, 1873, in Bohorodczany, Galicia. Antonius married two times:

a. **Anastasia Kaszubinska** circa 1824, place unknown. She was born circa 1806, place unknown. Anastasia was a daughter of Basilius Kaszubinski and Justina Jacykiewicz. Children of Antonius and Anastasia:

    i.   Basilius Sobolewski born in August 1840 and died September 17, 1840, in Lachowce.

    ii.   Maria Sobolewska born before 1844.

    iii.   Nicolaus Sobolewski born circa 1846 and died June 24, 1908, in Bohorodczany.

    iv.   Catharina Sobolewska born before 1847.

v. Basilius Sobolewski born in 1847 and died March 17, 1920, in Bohorodczany.

vi. **Andreas Sobolewski** born in 1848 in Lachowce, Galicia, and died February 26, 1928, in Bohorodczany, Poland.

vii. Josephus Sobolewski born circa 1850 and died August 9, 1920, in Bohorodczany.

viii. Maria Sobolewska born before 1853 and died before 1887.

ix. Thomas Franciscus Sobolewski born December 18, 1853, in Bohorodczany.

b. Anna Ernest on June 14, 1855, in Bohorodczany, Galicia. Anna was born in March 1810 in Bohorodczany and died after 1873, place unknown. She was a daughter of Mathias Ernest and Catharina Nowicka. Anna was a widow after Joannes Stefanski died. Anna and Antonius did not have children.

3rd Generation.

3-4-vi. Andreas Sobolewski (son of Antonius and Anastasia) was born circa 1848 in Lachowce, Galicia, and died February 26, 1928, in Bohorodczany, Poland. Andreas married **Anna Machowska** on November 20, 1873, in Bohorodczany, Galicia. Anna was a daughter of Joannes Machowski and Carolina Krysztofek from Bohorodczany. She was born circa 1857 in Bohorodczany, Galicia, and died January 7, 1938, in Bohorodczany, Poland. Children of Andreas and Anna:

i. Antonius Sobolewski born February 23, 1875, in Bohorodczany, and died after 1954 in Cracow, Poland.

ii. Ladislaus Sobolewski born September 17, 1876, in Bohorodczany, and died after 1954, place unknown, Poland.

iii. Ludovica Sobolewska born August 23, 1878, in Bohorodczany, and died May 21, 1881, in Bohorodczany.

iv. Carolus Sobolewski born January 27, 1881, in Bohorodczany, and died date and place unknown.

v. Michael Sobolewski born November 19, 1883, in Bohorodczany, and died November 13, 1907, in Bohorodczany.

vi. **Franciscus Sobolewski** born November 17, 1885, in Bohorodczany, and died June 5, 1969, in Lodz, Poland.

vii. Carolina Sobolewska born February 20, 1888, in Bohorodczany, and died November 8, 1964 in Wroclaw, Poland.

viii. Theophilus Sobolewski born July 22, 1890, in Bohorodczany, and died after 1954, place unknown, Argentina.

ix. Wilhelmina Sobolewska born February 17, 1892, in Bohorodczany, and died May 10, 1971 in Jawor, Poland.

x. Ludovica Sobolewska born December 30, 1894, in Lachowce, and died November 1, 1898, in Bohorodczany.

xi. Joannes Bronislaus Sobolewski born July 5, 1898, in Bohorodczany and died April 8, 1899, in Bohorodczany.

xii. Mathilda Valeria Sobolewska born October 31, 1900, in Bohorodczany, and died May 24, 1902, in Lachowce.

4th Generation.

4-6-vi. Franciscus Sobolewski (son of Andreas and Anna) born November 17, 1885, in Bohorodczany, and died June 5, 1969, in Lodz, Poland. Franciscus married two times:

a. **Helena Wanda Regiec** on July 17, 1912, in Kochawina, Galicia. She was born on November 16, 1886, in Mszana Dolna, Galicia, and died June 19, 1977, in Warsaw, Poland (Regiec register 4-7-i). Helena was a daughter of Joseph Regiec and Stephania Lösch. Children of Franciscus and Helena:

i. **Irena Maria Sobolewska** born October 5, 1913, in Bohorodczany, Galicia, and died November 2, 1998, in Warsaw, Poland.

ii. Name unknown born circa 1915 and died date and place unknown.

b. Wanda Apolonia Rutkowska circa 1936 in Poland. Wanda was born in 1907 in Radomsko, Russia, and died October 11, 1982, in Lodz, Poland.

5th Generation.

5-6-i. Irena Maria Sobolewska (daughter of Franciscus and Helena) born October 5, 1913, in Bohorodczany, Galicia, and died November 2, 1998, in Warsaw, Poland. Irena married three times:

a. Name unknown in 1938 in Warsaw, Poland.

b. **Konstanty Joseph Müller** circa 1942 in Warsaw, Poland. He was a son of Joseph Müller and Francisca (maiden name unknown). Konstanty was born March 11, 1900, in Krauzberg, East Prussia. Konstanty died circa 1965 in Warsaw, Poland. Child of Irena and Konstanty:

    i.   George (Jerzy) Müller born April 27, 1943, in Warsaw, Poland, and died November, 25, 2010, in Los Angeles, California, U.S.A.

c. **Andrew Alfred Zalewski Sr. (a.k.a Alfred Hübner)** on May 7, 1951, in Warsaw, Poland. He was a son of Joachim Hübner and Regina Dub. Alfred was born October 13, 1911, in Brynce Cerkiewne, Galicia. During World War II, Alfred changed his name to Andrew Zalewski to survive the Holocaust. He died October 19, 1979, in Copenhagen, Denmark. Child of Irena and Andrew (Alfred):

    ii.   **Andrew Zalewski** born January 14, 1952, in Warsaw, Poland.

6th Generation.

6-1-i. George (Jerzy) Müller (son of Konstanty and Irena) born April 27, 1943, in Warsaw, Poland, and died November, 25, 2010, in Los Angeles, California, U.S.A. George married two times:

a. **Magdalena Całusinska** in July 1969 in Czestochowa, Poland. Magdalena is a daughter of Jan Całusinski and Lucja Emilia Malasiewicz. She was born June 29, 1948, in Czestochowa, Poland. Child of George and Magdalena:

    i.   **Barbara Anna Müller** born May 8, 1971, in Warsaw, Poland.

b. **Aleksandra Elżbieta Domagała** on August 16, 1980, in Warsaw, Poland. Aleksandra is a daughter of Roman Domagała and Celina Kowalewska. She was born July 4, 1957, in Warsaw, Poland. Child of George and Aleksandra:

ii. **Olaf Jerzy Müller** born April 15, 1981, in Warsaw, Poland.

6-1-ii. Andrew Zalewski (son of Andrew and Irena) born January 14, 1952, in Warsaw, Poland. He married **Margaret Kominek** on February 14, 1976, in Warsaw, Poland. Margaret was born October 17, 1951, in Wiciejow, Poland. She is a daughter of Joseph Kominek and Maria Morasicka. Children of Andrew and Margaret:

    i. **Ewa Margaret Zalewska** born December 19, 1978, in Warsaw, Poland.

    ii. **Andrew James Zalewski** born April 10, 1987, in Philadelphia, Pennsylvania, U.S.A.

7th Generation.

7-1-ii. Olaf Jerzy Muller (son of George and Aleksandra) born April 15, 1981, in Warsaw, Poland. He married **Sarah Elia Hernandez** May 29, 2011, in Los Angeles, California, U.S.A. Sarah was born April 23, 1974, in Los Angeles, California, U.S.A. She is a daughter of Rogelio Hernandez and Martha Gutierrez.

7-2-i. Ewa Margaret Zalewska (daughter of Andrew and Margaret) born December 19, 1978, in Warsaw, Poland. She married **Jason Todd Abrams** on September 6, 2008, in Philadelphia, Pennsylvania, U.S.A. Jason was born September 8, 1975, in Manhasset, New York, U.S.A. He is a son of Franklin S. Abrams and Leslie Aura Goldstein. Children of Ewa and Jason are the 9th generation in the line of Lösch and the 8th generation in the lines of Regiec and Sobolewski:

    i. **Eli Charles Abrams** born April 26, 2010, in New York City, New York, U.S.A.

    ii. **Theo Reid Abrams** born December 16, 2011, in Manhasset, New York, U.S.A.

    iii. **Zoe Leila Abrams** born December 16, 2011, in Manhasset, New York, U.S.A.

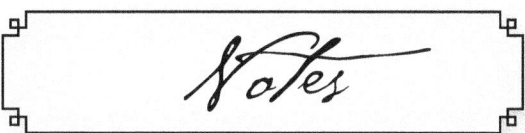

CHAPTER 1

1. *Slownik Geograficzny Krolestwa Polskiego i Innych Krajow Slowianskich*. Editors F. Sulimierski, B. Chlebowski, and W. Walewski. Warszawa 1881; vol. 2, pp. 445–477. This source offers a comprehensive description of the geography, history, and religions of historical and Austrian Galicia.

2. Paul R. Magocsi. "Galicia: A European Land" in *Galicia: A Multicultured Land*. University of Toronto Press Inc. 2005; pp. 6 and 18.

3. Paul R. Magocsi. *Galicia: A Historical Survey and Bibliographical Guide*. University of Toronto Press 1983; p. 67. Paul R. Magocsi. *The Roots of Ukrainian Nationalism: Galicia as Ukraine's Piedmont*. University of Toronto Press Inc. 2002; pp. 4–12.

4. The western part included Polish lands, while the eastern part contained large sections of historical Galicia. Most of old Lodomeria (with Volhynia and its main city of Volodymyr) remained under the rule of the Russian Empire. After Poland ceased to exist following the Third Partition, the Austrian administration of Galicia was temporarily divided into western (*Westgalizien*) and eastern (*Ostgalizien*) districts. The Duchy of Bukovina was initially a closed military district; it formally joined Galicia between 1787 and 1849, and was later separated into a distinct entity within Austro-Hungary. However, Bukovina retained strong administrative ties with Galicia. Its schools, railroads, and other offices were governed from there (based on annual books of the Galician civil service).

5. In 1773, Galicia had approximately 2,600,000 inhabitants. The 1869 census showed that the population had grown to 5,418,016.

6. *Continuato Edictorum et Mandatorum Universalium in Regnis Galiciae et Lodomeriae*. Leopoli 1774; pp.114–117. The law of October 1, 1774, included a liberal policy toward Protestants, Armenians, and others. It was issued by Maria Theresa and promulgated by Heinrich Auersperg, the third governor of Galicia.

7. After Joseph II became the sole emperor of Austria, he issued the subsequent edicts on September 17, 1781, and the Toleranzpatent on October 13, 1782.

8. Ludwig Schneider. *Das Kolonisationswerk Jozefs II in Galizien*. Posen 1939.

9. The term *Ruthenian* had been used in the Austrian Empire and later in the Austro-Hungarian Empire to describe the Ukrainian population. Ruthenia was an old Latinized name of a medieval East Slavic principality (termed *Rus*) that broke into two, with the eastern half forming the future Russia and the western part falling into Polish hands.

In the entire province of Austrian Galicia, 42 percent were Greek Catholic (Ruthenians), 47 percent were Roman Catholic (Poles, Germans), and 11 percent were Jewish. The eastern part was 62 percent Ruthenian (Austrian Census, 1910).

10. The term *Ruthenian* was also used to describe some of these smaller ethnic groups in mountainous regions of Galicia: the Hutsul, Lemko, and Boyko (www.halgal.com).

11. Paul R. Magocsi. "Galicia: A European Land" in *Galicia: A Multicultured Land*. University of Toronto Press Inc. 2005; p. 18. Shortly after the First Partition of Poland, there were only 172,000 Jews in all of Galicia. In the subsequent 140 years, their numbers grew, reaching 872,000 by 1910.

12. My paternal grandparents were Joachim Hübner (1878–1947) and Regina Dub. The family lived in Lvov, where they owned some real estate in the early twentieth century.

It is possible, but unproven, that Joachim's father or uncle was Alojzy Hübner. The newspapers of Lvov advertised the hardware business of Messrs. Hübner and Hanke, with a broad range of items for purchase or shipment. The store was located at 38 Market Square (*Kurjer Lwowski* July 12, 1885; and *Dziennik Polski* January 5 and 10, 1886). Later that year, the partners apparently split; Alojzy Hübner advertised a business located at 13 Charles Louis (*Carl Ludwig*) Street, whereas Joseph Hanke had his store at 38 Market Square. Their competition seemed to be intense, as the former partners placed competing ads in more than one national newspaper (*Dziennik Polski* November 9 and 11, 1886; and *Kurjer Lwowski* November 15, 1886). By 1894, however, Alojzy Hübner had likely acquired his competitor's business; his ads in the newspaper listed the address of the store at 38 Market Square (*Kurjer Lwowski* April 19, 1894).

13. The contract for construction of the Northern Railway was given to Salomon Myer von Rothschild. It is not surprising that initial plans did not include Cracow as the final stop on this link between Vienna and Galicia. Formally, the city of Cracow remained outside the borders of Austria from October 18, 1815, to November 16, 1846. After Austria reestablished its sovereignty over Cracow, the city received its first railroad connection with Austrian Silesia in 1847 and with the Emperor Ferdinand Northern Railway (*der Keiser Ferdinand Nordbahn*) in 1858.

14. Larry Wolff. *The Idea of Galicia: History and Fantasy in Habsburg Political Culture*. Stanford University Press 2010; pp. 132–198. Prince Leon Sapieha (1803–1878) and Alexander Fredro (1793–1876) joined forces on this project in 1844. The work on the entire route was completed in 1892, long after both men were dead. The railway extended east from Lvov to Tarnopol, terminating in the border town of Podwoloczyska at the border of the Russian Empire.

15. Since this was a state-owned enterprise, its name lacked the customary *k.k.* (the Imperial Royal prefix).

16. About U.S. $316 in 2009 (Consumer Price Index).

17. Karl Baedeker. *Austria Including Hungary, Transylvania, Dalmatia, and Bosnia*. Leipsic 1900; p. xii.

18. Jolanta T. Pekacz. *Music in the Culture of Polish Galicia*. University of Rochester Press 2002; p. 180. The quote was attributed to Stanislaw Szczepanowski, 1884.

19. The imperial patent of January 2, 1867, called for speedy elections to the regional legislatures. On December 21, 1867, the law signed by the emperor created the state council, consisting of the House of Lords and the House of Deputies. The House of Lords consisted of the members of the emperor's household, aristocrats with large landholdings throughout the country, high-level representatives of the clergy, and others nominated by the sovereign for their contributions in politics or art. The House of Deputies consisted of 203 members, with the three largest delegations from Czech lands (54), Galicia (38), and Moravia (22). On the same day, the governmental decree declared the emperor above the law and not accountable for his own actions. It also stipulated his role as the commander of the armed forces and other official functions.

20. Count Agenor Goluchowski (1812–1875) served as the supreme governor of Galicia three times. The first term (1849–1859) was prior to his post in the central government of the Austrian Empire (1859–1861). After returning from Vienna, he was reappointed governor of Galicia twice (1866–1868 and 1871–1875). The contribution of Count Goluchowski to reform in Galicia, which was transformed from a centrally governed province to a crown land enjoying a large degree of autonomy, was not fully appreciated even 25 years after his death. On the occasion of the unveiling of Goluchowski's monument in Lvov, press commentaries varied—from brief reports that it was more an official event than a national gesture of gratitude (*Kurjer Lwowski* June 27, 1901; and *Kurjer Stanislawowski* June 30, 1901) to articles underscoring Goluchowski's statesmanship (*Gazeta Narodowa* and *Gazeta Lwowska* June 27, 1901).

21. *Dziennik Polski* September 24, 1869. The reopening of the newspaper was accompanied by this front-page editorial. It referred to the seven-year period in which the newspaper had been forced to suspend publication, after harassment by police. The fall of the government of Anton von Schmerling in Vienna meant that attempts to reform Austria through a German-speaking bureaucracy had failed. Now the tone became more positive, focusing on a way to achieve maximal self-governance for Galicia within Austria.

22. Agnieszka B. Lance. *Literary and Cultural Images of a Nation without a State*. Peter Lang Publishing, Inc., 2008; p. 66. The first step toward autonomy came with the emperor's Fundamental Law of 1867, which provided Galicia with a local legislature and executive branch. In 1869, the Polish language was granted equal rights, and in 1873, the school board started providing full-time education in the local languages.

23. Daniel Unowsky. *The Pomp and Politics of Patriotism: Imperial Celebrations in Habsburg Austria, 1848–1916*. Purdue University Press 2005; pp. 57–69. The book provides a detailed description of the visit by Franz Joseph to Galicia.

Dziennik Polski September 12 and 14, 1880, reported on Franz Joseph's visit to Lvov, which was in stark contrast to his prior trips to Galicia. Symbolically, the degree of autonomy was also well-captured in a report by *Kronika*, the weekly paper of Stanislawow, in the issue of September 16, 1880. It described Franz Joseph's visit, with details of speeches at the welcoming ceremony.

The emperor returned to Lvov in September 1894. The official reason was his visit to a national fair. As before, Franz Joseph was greeted warmly, albeit with less fanfare. By now, it was almost business as usual. Consistent with the spirit of the cultural autonomy of Galicia, he sometimes signed his name in commemorative books using Polish rather than the German spelling (*Kurjer Lwowski* September 10, 1894).

24. William J. Showalter. "Partitioned Poland." *National Geographic* 1915; vol. 27, p. 88.

CHAPTER 2

1. Mathias Lösch was born around 1760 and married Anna Sedlaczek sometime before 1795. There is no evidence of Anna's presence in Wieliczka, which suggests that she had died before the Lösch family arrived there. Their son, Christian Lösch, was born about 1795. I suspect that he was born outside Galicia during his father's military service.

In an application by Christian Lösch to the administrators of the salt mines, there is a reference to Mathias's 27 years of service in the Austrian military (Salt Mine Museum, Wieliczka; March 19, 1817; Akta Salinarne sygn. 689; k. 208–209).

2. *Gazeta Krakowska* November 15, 1809, reprinted full text of the treaty signed on October 14, 1809. The article four of the Schönbrunn Treaty referred to French-negotiated division of Wieliczka between Saxon king and Austrian emperor.

An internal letter to an administrator of the mines indicates the continuous employment of Mathias Lösch as an inspector from 1809 until 1818 (Akta Salinarne sygn. 689, k. 208–209; and the annual *Schematismus der Königreiches Galizien und Lodomerien zuhr 1813–1818*, Lemberg). Mathias Lösch died on March 15, 1818, in Wieliczka.

3. *Gazeta Krakowska* November 26, 1809, described an eyewitness account of the visit to Wieliczka by Prince Joseph Poniatowski, a hugely popular commander-in-chief of military forces of the Duchy of Warsaw.

Marian Kallas. "Z dziejow Wieliczki w latach 1809–1813." In *Studia i Materialy do Dziejow Zup Solnych w Polsce*. Muzeum Zup Krakowskich. Wieliczka; vol. X, pp. 187–204. In reality, the joint administration was fraught with controversy. By 1812, the administrative powers had shifted entirely to Austria, and the Duchy of Warsaw ceased to exist by January 1813. In 1815, the gathering of victorious countries at the Congress of Vienna affirmed that Wieliczka was to remain in Galicia.

4. *Schematismus der Königreiches Galizien und Lodomerien für das Jahr 1815*. Lemberg 1815; p. 153. Christian Lösch is mentioned in the section "k.k. Administration der Salzwerkes zu Wieliczka, Buchbaltung Amtsdiener" (accounting clerk) for the first time in 1815. Actually, the promotion had taken place the previous year. In the same yearbook, Mathias Lösch is listed in the section "Berg-Inspection Visitationsbeamter" (inspector).

5. Andreas's mother, Antonina Lösch (maiden name Pinkas), died in 1823. Andreas's father remarried twice: in 1824 to Marianna Kwiatkowska, who died in 1841; and to Josepha Ferenz in 1843. Christian Lösch had nine children; at least two from his first marriage, to Antonina Pinkas, did not survive.

6. *Continuato Edictorum et Mandatorum Universalium in Regnis Galiciae et Lodomeriae*. Leopoli 1774; pp.104–105. The ruling was issued by Heinrich Auersperg, the third governor of Galicia, just two years after the First Partition. It likely applied to eastern Galicia, where small deposits of salt were also known.

7. Bayard Taylor. "The Salt Mines of Wieliczka, 1850" in Eva March Tappan, ed., *The World's Story: A History of the World in Story, Song and Art*. Boston 1914; vol. VI, pp. 370–377. Bayard Taylor (1825–1878), poet, journalist, and popular writer, was from Kennett Square in Chester County, Pennsylvania.

8. A report issued in 1832 of an inspection of the warehouse that was overseen by Christian referenced the return of a deposit in the amount of 600 florins placed by him at the beginning of his responsibilities in Turowka, near Wieliczka. This clearly exceeded his annual salary for years to come. The document contains Christian's signature (Akta Salinarne sygn. 1133, k. 205–228).

9. *Provinzial: Handbuch der Königreiche Galizien und Lodomerien für das Jahr 1850*, Lemberg, p. 196, listed Christian Lösch as the official in charge (*einnehmer*) of the office of transportation in Turowka.

There is no single method that accurately translates past values into today's economic realities. Bayard Taylor's 1850 estimate is equivalent, in 2010 dollars, to $28,800,000 using the Consumer Price Index, $203,000,000 using the unskilled wage index, $433,000,000 using the production worker index, and $5,680,000,000 using the share-of-GDP method.

10. To the east of Cracow, preparations for the railway construction started in 1850. Once completed, this route would be known as the Imperial Royal Galician Railway of Archduke Charles Louis (*k.k. priv. Galizische Carl Ludwig Bahn*). It would give rise to a dead-end extension to Turowka. Beyond Turowka, the last stretch of the railroad was financed by the company; it used horses between the mine shafts and the storehouses until approximately 1889 (courtesy of Mrs. Małgorzata Międzybrodzka; History Department; The Salt Mines Museum in Wieliczka, Poland).

11. This salary information was based on records of the salt mines of Wieliczka from 1861. The highest-paid employee was Johann Geramb, director of the mines, earning 2,158 florins. The salary difference of less than three times between Christian Lösch and Johann Geramb was trivial compared to the compensation spread in today's corporate environment (courtesy of Mrs. Małgorzata Międzybrodzka; History Department; The Salt Mines Museum in Wieliczka, Poland).

12. The names of the employees are from *Handbuch des Statthalterei-Gebietes in Galizien für das Jahr 1865*; Lemberg; pp. 210–212. Unfortunately, Christian Lösch did not enjoy his retirement for too long. He died on May 25, 1871, in Wieliczka.

13. *Schematismus der Königreiche Galizien und Lodomerien für das Jahr 1843–1847*. Lemberg. Adam Kwiatkowski worked in the district office in Tarnow alongside Andreas. In earlier years, Adam was employed in the governmental office in Wadowice (1840–1841), where he could easily have come into contact with the Wilczek family from the nearby town of Andrychow. This could have been one of many opportunities for Andreas Lösch to be introduced to his future wife, Eleonora Wilczek.

14. *Schematismus der Königreiche Galizien und Lodomerien für das Jahr 1846*. Lemberg; p. 50. Andreas Lösch was transferred to the district office in Jaslo, where he was listed as *kreiskanzlisten*.

15. Christian Lösch married Josepha Ferenz in 1843. As with the family of his first wife, the father of the bride was also employed in the mines of Wieliczka. Joseph Ferenz was the head of the transportation department of the Turowka mines, the same position that Christian would occupy in a few years' time. During the uprising of 1846, Amalia Josepha was less than two years old and Stephania was aged only a few months, having been born in the fall of the previous year.

Gazeta Lwowska March 12, 1846, and *Gazeta Krakowska* March 17, 1846, printed report of the Lieutenant Colonel Benedek of the Austrian army who entered Wieliczka on February 26, 1846. Earlier in the day, heavy fighting with street battles erupted in the town of Gdow only about 9 miles east of Wieliczka. The advancing Austrians, supported by the peasants, killed 150 rebels and took about 60 prisoners there, with the rest of the insurgents retreating toward Wieliczka and Cracow. Despite bad weather, with the fields and roads covered with mud, the Austrians were in hot pursuit. The same day, Benedek's unit entered Wieliczka; his report spoke of four people shot dead and the impending house searches for the rebels hiding in town. The hotbed of insurgency, the city of Cracow, was taken over by Austrian troops on March 3, 1846.

16. *Gazeta Lwowska* March 3, 1846, reported that a few hundred insurgents from approximately 70 villages had gathered around Tarnow on February 18. With the complicity of von Wallerstern, the peasants attacked the antigovernment forces, killing many and taking hundreds of prisoners.

17. Agnieszka B. Nance. *Literary and Cultural Images of a Nation without a State*. Peter Lang Publishing, Inc., New York 2008; pp. 62–64. The planning of the nobles' uprising was leaked to Austrian officials in Galicia, leading to preemptive arrests of several would-be leaders. Ultimately, it was merely a nine-day event that sparked a backlash of peasant hostility.

18. Stefan Dembinski. *Rok 1846 Kronika Dworów Szlacheckich*. Jaslo 1896; pp. 170–172. In addition, *Gazeta Lwowska* March 3 and 12, 1846, confirmed unrest in the Jaslo district and in Wieliczka. The report stated that the peasants refused to support the insurgents and actively fought against them.

19. Eleonora Barbara Wilczek had been born in Andrychow, western Galicia, on January 5, 1819. Her parents were Ignatius (Ignaz) Wilczek and Thecla Czerwinski. She had at least two siblings, Antonina Marianna, born in 1814, and Ferdinandus Antonius, born in 1816.

It is possible that Joannes Bochenski was the man connecting the Lösches with Eleonora's father, a magistrate official in Andrychow. Bochenski, a secretary in the Wieliczka magistrate, had served as a witness at Andreas's parents' wedding and was a godparent to one of his siblings. An alternative explanation is that the bride's father had come across the Lösches while arranging the purchase of salt for his municipality.

20. Families with the name "Wilczek" originated in Silesia, near the town of Kosel (Kedzierzyn-Kozle in today's Poland). Those with noble titles built castles and palaces in Königsberg (Klimkovice in today's Czech Republic); Konczyce Wielkie (near Cieszyn in today's Poland); and Hultschin (Hlučin, in today's Czech Republic), which straddled the territory of Silesia, divided between Austria and Prussia in the eighteenth century. Some Wilczeks distinguished themselves as government officials serving the Austrian empress Maria Theresa and the emperors of Austria Joseph II, Leopold II, and Francis I. Among lesser-known members of the extended family was Jacob Wilczek, a physician (*kreisarzt*) working in several towns of western Galicia at the turn of the nineteenth century (*Schematismus für die Königreich Westgalizien 1798–1806*), and Joseph Wilczek, professor of theology in Jagiellonian University in Cracow in the 1850s.

21. The Foundation of Franciscus Wilczek Sr. was established in September of 1826, approximately six months before the death of its benefactor. Franciscus Wilczek Sr. left 62.5 percent of the proceeds from the sale of one of his houses to his son-in-law (Jan Kanty Fryś), who was married to Franciscus's daughter (Magdalena Fryś, maiden name Wilczek) to provide seed money for funeral expenses and religious services in the memory of the Wilczek family, to be arranged in perpetuity by the Fryś family and their descendants. Other instructions stipulated "weekly donations to beggars," and a lump sum was to be paid to his loyal servant after Franciscus's death. When, two generations later, the payments lapsed, the civil authorities of Galicia took descendants of the original trustees of the foundation to court for breach of contract. In 1875, an agreement was reached and a sum of money was deposited by Antonina Piwowarczyk (maiden name Fryś) to restore the intent of the benefactor's will. The Foundation of Franciscus Wilczek Sr. was renamed the Fund for the Poor and was listed in the annual administrative books of Galicia (*Schematismus*) from 1883 to 1896. [The information on the life of Franciscus Wilczek Sr. was derived from the memoirs of his grandson, Piotr Fryś, written shortly after 1862. Copies of legal documents concerning Wilczek's professional activities and the charitable foundation were provided by Mr. Andrzej Fryś of Andrychow, Poland (the great-great-grandson of Franciscus Wilczek Sr.).]

22. Franciscus Wilczek Sr. had four sons and three daughters. Among them was Eleonora's father, Ignatius (Ignaz) Wilczek (1792–1862), who was the magistrate assessor (*ehrenbeisitzer*) in Andrychow from about 1831 until 1855. During the Spring of Nations of 1848, he was elected to the national council that formed in Andrychow. Around 1855, Ignatius Wilczek became a merchant (*mercator*). He returned to public life, becoming the mayor of Andrychow (1861–1862). Ignatius died in office in 1862. His older brother, Eleonora's uncle, was Franciscus (Franz) Wilczek Jr. (1783–1847), who was a teacher from 1808 to 1823 and then became a magistrate employee there from 1824 to 1831.

Romualdus Wilczek of Andrychow, a contemporary of Eleonora, was born in 1830. He went to the gymnasium in Teschen (Cieszyn), where he studied for six years before moving to Vienna to study medicine (1848–1855). While at Joseph's Academy there, he enlisted in the military (1852) and became a surgeon who served in many places throughout the empire.

23. *Provinzial Handbuch der Köngreiche Galizien and Lodomerien für Jahr 1846*. Lemberg 1846; p. 50. Andreas Lösch worked with several members of the Winkler and Telesnicki families.

24. While in Jaslo, Eleonora delivered another child, who did not survive (December 1, 1853).

25. *Provinzial-Handbuch des Krakauer Verwaltungs-Gebietes für das Jahr 1856*. Krakau 1856; pp. 43–44. His position was listed as the county commissioner (*bezirks-adjunkt*).

26. Romualdus Wilczek started his career in the military hospital in Vienna (1852). The string of assignments that followed brought him to Verona (in today's Italy), Ratstatt (in today's Germany), Brzezany (in today's Ukraine), Carlsburg (in today's Romania), and finally Budapest (in Hungary). There are two confirmed visits by Dr. Wilczek to his hometown; the first took place for a few months in 1855 during cholera epidemics (based on the military service record) and the second around 1862. The latter visit is documented in the memoirs of Piotr Fryś, who was seeking advice on how to obtain deferment from military service.

Romualdus took part in two campaigns on the Italian front, in 1859 and 1866. In 1866, he received the Golden Cross of Merit with Crown, for his wartime service during the battle of Custoza, where Austrians prevailed over Italian forces. Dr. Wilczek's last military post in the rank of major (*stabsarzt*) was in the garrison hospital in Budapest, Hungary (1881–1883).

27. *Szematyzm Krolestwa Galicyi i Lodomeryi z Wielkim Ksiestwem Krakowskim na Rok 1875*. Lwów 1875; p. 42.

28. Church records from the village Wielka Wies, dated from 1845, mention a Michael Regiec born in Hungary (unrelated to the Michaël Regiec described later in this narrative).

In my search for any information about my line of Regiecs, I was looking for records from the village of Roztoka. The fact that at least six villages with that identical name could be found in a radius of approximately 40 miles around Nowy Sacz greatly complicated my efforts at first. The records of one village after another showed, disappointingly, no one with the name of Regiec. After many searches, the very last place on the list yielded long-awaited details, helping us to solve the mystery.

29. Tatars settled mainly in the eastern parts of Poland and Lithuania between the thirteenth and sixteenth centuries. Interestingly, reviewing the eighteenth-century church records from Bohorodczany, I noticed a few converts to Catholicism from "Secta Mahometica," which most likely represented Tatars living in the area. By the nineteenth century, most Tatars had become Polonized.

30. Based on church records, I have estimated that Joseph was born in 1787 and Lucia in 1793. Lucia's maiden name is not entirely clear. Some later church records identify her as a daughter of Michael Kaminski; other entries list her pre-marriage name as Jarmula. Nonetheless, both names were common around the village of Gierowa.

A land and tax census was conducted in 1787 throughout the empire on the orders of Emperor Joseph II. A census document, dated September 14 of that year, provides detailed descriptions of the village of Janowice and the smaller hamlets of Gierowa and Podbrzeze. In the year of the census, no one with the name of Regiec lived there. Other details about Janowice quoted later in the text are from *Gemeindelexikon der im Reichsrate Vertretenen Königreiche und Länder*; *Galizien*; Wien 1907; vol. XII, p. 696.

31. Michaël Regiec was 18 when the baptism of Laurentius Pajuz took place. The event occurred in 1836, before the official end of serfdom in Galicia in 1848.

32. The parish books show one attempt by Catharina Regiec to record her signature, with misspellings of both her first and last names. How Michaël, the son of a shepherd, learned how to read and write is a mystery. I suspect, though I have no proof, that the young Michaël, while working on the estate of the Jordan family in the village of Roztoka, was educated alongside the master's children.

33. S. Dembinski. *Rok 1846 Kronika Dworów Szlacheckich.* Jaslo 1896; p. 371. The story refers to the village of Wroblowice.

34. Thecla Traczewska's parents were Valentinus de Bogusz Traczewski and Anna Borzecka. It is unclear why their domicile address was listed as Janowice, while their land was in the village of Gierowa.

35. Jerzy Sewer Hr. Dunin-Borkowski. *Spis Nazwisk Szlachty Polskiej*. Lwów 1887; p. 464. In addition, Zbigniew Leszczyc; *Herby Szlachty Polskiej*; Poznan 1908; vol. 1, p. 6; provided a detailed description of the Traczewskis' coat of arms.

36. *Skorowidz Wszystkich Miejscowosci Polozonych w Krolestwie Galicyi i Lodomeryi*; Lwów 1855; pp. 151, 183, and 213; still listed the Jordans as the owners of the neighboring villages of Olszyny, Roztoka, and Sukmanie. Since at least the sixteenth century, the Jordan family had been the main landowners in the area. After the death of Franciscus Jordan in 1841 at the age of 48, parts of the landholding were sold.

From the late 1840s, Michaël was the head administrator of the Roztoka estate. He was not simply leasing a piece of land for a fee paid to the owner, but was obligated to turn a fixed amount of profit over to the hereditary owners. The rest of the profit belonged to him. He was described as the "owner" of the estate without the right of passing property to his heirs (*possesori allodi* in Latin). The owners of large estates from neighboring towns would befriend Michaël, later becoming godparents of his children. Among the guests at these celebrations in Roztoka we can find Adolph Jordan, one of the original owners of the Jordan estate.

37. Based on church records, 1850–1879, from the parish of Olszyny, to which Roztoka belonged.

38. Angela Traczewska married in 1856, and Catharina Regiec in 1859. They both left Roztoka to join their husbands in neighboring towns.

39. *Dominus* means master, owner; whereas *Domina* means lady, mistress of the family. Other inhabitants of Roztoka are listed with their occupations, such as farmers or servants, without additional titles. The parish of Olszyny (Roztoka) records, 1850–1871.

40. Catharina Regiec had the out-of-wedlock baby in 1856. It is unclear whether the man who married her three years later was the father of the boy. Valentinus Traczewski, the hereditary owner of property in Gierowa or Janowice, was listed as the main witness during the marriage ceremony. As the wedding took place one year after Thecla's death and just a few days before Michaël's second marriage, it suggests an ongoing close relationship between Catharina and the family of her late sister-in-law.

Surveying church records from several villages and small towns around Roztoka and, further east, in and around Bohorodczany, I found several records of out-of-wedlock births but not in the families of local estate-owners or nobility.

41. Church records of Olszyny (Roztoka) parish. His name was Michael Babiarz.

42. Kochanowski family members were godparents to one of the Regiec girls. In 1860, they are listed as the owners of an estate in the neighboring village of Olszyny. By 1888, they become the owners of a large property in Roztoka. *Slownik Geograficzny Krolestwa Polskiego i Innych Krajow Slowianskich*. Editors B. Chlebowski and W. Walewski. Warszawa 1888; vol. IX, p. 802.

43. The right of citizens to free basic education was established in a decree signed by Franz Joseph on December 21, 1867. In addition, this decree laid out the principle of educational instruction in native languages (articles 17 and 19). This progressive law, however, faced the enormous challenge of financing schools, particularly in small towns and rural areas. In later years, the situation became even more complex with heated budgetary debates, complicated by rising tensions between Poles and Ruthenians. Both groups remained vocal and adversarial.

44. Josepha and Mary (Marya) Regiec were midwives in the district town of Sanok from 1874 to 1878.

45. *Slownik Geograficzny Krolestwa Polskiego i Innych Krajow Slowianskich*; Editor B. Chlebowski; Warszawa 1893; vol. XIII, p. 358; provided a contemporary description of Wieloglowy. Wieloglowy and Janowice were only 25 miles from each other.

Unfortunately, there is no information on where Joseph went to school and who supported him. The nearest teachers' college was likely in Tarnow; nearby Nowy Sacz still lacked such an institution in the mid-1870s.

46. *Dziennik Polski* January 1, 1887, provided a stark picture of educational needs in Galicia. The literacy rates were 58 percent and 52 percent in Cracow and Lvov, respectively. In the remaining parts of the crown land, literacy was estimated at 25 percent or less; particularly appalling rates of under 5 percent were noted in the mountainous areas. In Galicia, containing 27 percent of the Austrian population of Austro-Hungary, there were only 33 high schools. Galicia had two universities and a polytechnic school.

In the decade between 1875 and 1884, there was an unprecedented rise in the number of Jewish students in high schools, by 81 percent. This signaled a growing emphasis on education in Jewish communities, with the dropping of prior barriers that had limited their access to it, as well as the fact that many Jewish families were embracing assimilation as a new way of life.

47. A copy of the school *Chronicle* received courtesy of Mr. Janusz Bielec, principal of the Wieloglowy School Network (2011).

48. Bronislawa Lösch became a teacher-in-training in a girls' school in Nowy Sacz in 1879. She was appointed a permanent teacher, together with her lifelong friend Klotylda Kowalska, in 1885 (*Kurjer Lwowski* July 4, 1885).

49. The Winkler family had been well-acquainted with the Lösches since Andreas's career began in Tarnow more than 40 years before. Wilhelm Winkler, the son of Andreas's friends, would likely help to transfer Joseph Regiec to Nowy Sacz a few years later.

Vincent Telesnicki Jr. was a stationmaster in Piwniczna, a small town in the region. Employment records from *Szematyzm Krolestwa Galicyi i Lodomeryi z Wielkim Ksiestwem Krakowskim na Rok 1886*; Lwów 1886; pp. 489 and 491. Vincent Jr. was Stephania's brother-in-law, having married her older sister Wilhelmina in 1879. His father, Vincent Telesnicki Sr., was a long-serving secretary in the commissioner's office, working under Andreas Lösch.

50. *Slownik Geograficzny Krolestwa Polskiego i Innych Krajow Slowianskich*. Editors F. Sulimierski, B. Chlebowski, and W. Walewski. Warszawa 1885; vol. VI, pp. 781–782.

51. There were other bearers of the Regiec name who showed similar upward mobility: Ludwik Regiec started as an assistant lecturer in Lvov's Polytechnic School (1886), became district engineer in Tarnobrzeg (1900–1903), and assumed the position of head engineer in the Commission of Vistula River in Cracow (1907–1913). Jan Regiec was a physician in Cracow (1901–1907). Zygmunt Regiec was a doctor of law in Cracow (1913).

52. The town census listed separate households under the families of Andreas Lösch (house 270) and Joseph Regiec (house 478) in 1890, whereas Wilhelmina lived in Stary Sacz with her family (house 349).

53. Wanda Julia Regiec was born in Nowy Sacz on September 9, 1888. The records indicate her father's employment with the railway. Soon after, *Kurjer Lwowski*, on January 1, 1889, listed Joseph Regiec among newly appointed railroad employees. The subsequent annual records of civil administration listed Joseph Regiec as clerk (1890 and 1893–1894) or assistant to the stationmaster (1891–1892) in Nowy Sacz.

54. *Slownik Geograficzny Krolestwa Polskiego i Innych Krajow Slowianskich*. Editors B. Chlebowski and W. Walewski. Warszawa 1889; vol. X, pp. 354–360. Detailed descriptions of the history of Nowy Sacz and an overview of the city center, the school, and recreational areas at the time the Regiec family lived there.

55. *Kurjer Lwowski* July 11, 1885.

56. Toward the end of her life, Bronislawa lived at 39 Jagiellonian Street.

57. Tadeusz Aleksander. *Zycie spoleczne i przemiany kulturalne Nowego Sacza w latach 1870–1990*. Oficyna Literacka, Krakow 1993; p. 37. The women's teachers' college opened in 1903; the high school for girls began admissions in September of 1907.

58. The Folk School Association. Minutes of the meeting on November 24, 1905.

59. *Mieszczanin* February 1, 1904, described festivities during the carnival ball that was organized by Bronislawa's association in January of that year. Information about Bronislawa's work with the Folk School Association comes from the minutes of the meeting of April 23, 1908.

60. The Folk School Association. Bronislawa raised this topic many times but finally succeeded on November 10, 1908, when the executive committee agreed to progress with printing the postcards.

61. *Kurjer Lwowski* June 24, 1909, reported on the teachers' retreat and the Folk School Association: the minutes of the meeting on September 3, 1911, were the last recorded by Bronislawa Lösch. This was also her last public appearance. In November's minutes, there is a reference to Miss Lösch's absence due to illness.

62. Bronislawa Lösch died at the age of 64, in September 1912; the cause was listed as tuberculosis. Her funeral was arranged by her friend Klotylda Kowalska, the principal of St. Elisabeth School for Girls.
Sprawozdanie z Dzialnosci Towarzystwa Szkoly Ludowej za Rok 1912. Krakow 1913; pp. XXVIII and 55*–56*. Included a tribute to Bronislawa and a mention of the opening of the school bearing her name.

63. Vincent Telesnicki Jr. married Wilhelmina Lösch on February 2, 1879, in Nowy Sacz. The parents of the groom were Vincent Telesnicki Sr. and Euphrosina Jahl. Based on the records of the civil administration in Galicia, Vincent Telesnicki Jr. worked in the following towns: Tarnow (1884), Stary Sacz (1887–1892), and Jaslo (1892–1893).

64. *Sądeczanin* May 1, 1897, reported on the competition between the only two professional photographers in Nowy Sacz. Mr. Michael Friedman, the Jewish owner of the first photography shop, encouraged the public to use his services by lowering his prices, to the outrage of supporters of the Janina studio, owned by Mr. Alfred Wierosz Silkiewicz. Disingenuous arguments about undermining professional standards were laced with anti-semitic implications in a local newspaper that waged a campaign against the Friedman studio. In spite of strong words, the public seemed to ignore appeals to boycott Friedman.

65. In these early cameras, when the lens cap was taken off, the subject had to stand still for several minutes, allowing for the long exposure of silver-coated plates. These were wooden, box-like cameras standing on tripods.

66. The press praised Mr. Winkler for his composure during the tragedy. Although the first name was not cited in the reports, this might have been the same Wilhelm Winkler who had been witness at Joseph's and Stephania's wedding and brought Joseph Regiec to his initial post in Nowy Sacz.

67. *Kurjer Lwowski* April 19, 20, and 21; special edition of *Kurjer Lwowski* April 23, 1894; and *Pogon* April 22, 1894. The fire received wide coverage in the regional and national press. By coincidence, it broke out on the fourth anniversary of a similar but smaller disaster in Nowy Sacz. There was no doubt about the extent of damage; the reports uniformly blamed the city administration for mismanagement, as no action had been taken to make the city better prepared to deal with such easily erupting blazes.

At the time of the fire, Bronislawa and Eleonora Lösch occupied house 270, just across the street from the royal castle, further away from the central square. Andreas Lösch was not around to see the big fire; he had passed away a year before.

68. The entries refer to the school year 1898–1899. In 1899, the list of honor students also identified Janina Telesnicka, the youngest daughter of Wilhelmina and the late Vincent Telesnicki Jr.

69. *Kurjer Stanislawowski* June 24 and 28, 1894, described the preparations for the opening of the Railway Directorate in Stanislawow, scheduled for July 1 of that year. This new administrative center was responsible for the area from Stanislawow to the Russian border in the east and through Bukovina in the south. *Kurjer Stanislawowski* January 6, 1895, announced the hiring of Joseph Regiec by the Railway Directorate and his annual pay of 600 guldens. (At the time, Dr. Nimhin, who served as de facto mayor of Stanislawow, was earning 1,200 guldens per year.) This new position explains why subsequent civil administration records listed Joseph Regiec in Buczacz, in eastern Galicia, in 1895; in Nowosielica from 1897 to 1899; and in Czerniowce in 1900.

70. Kai Struve. "Gentry, Jews, and Peasants" in *Creating the Other: Ethnic Conflict and Nationalism in Habsburg Central Europe.* Edited by Nancy M. Wingfield. Austrian Studies. Berghahn Books 2003; vol. 5, pp.116–118. For years, the relationships between Galician peasants and Jews had been growing increasingly confrontational. Stanislaw Stojalowski, a former priest, encouraged self-education, financial independence, and abstinence from alcohol among the impoverished peasants. With time, however, his political views became enmeshed with overt and vile anti-Semitic messages, in which Jews were blamed for everything wrong in the countryside. In this climate of constant agitation, not much was needed to trigger unrest.

Dziennik Polski June 21, 1893, reported on the trial of Stojalowski held in Cracow. The indictment listed several prior verdicts against him by civilian courts and ecclesiastical tribunals for the incitement of violence among peasants and dereliction of duties as a priest.

Pogon June 18, 1898. The weekly published in Tarnow, in the center of the unrest, condemned violence by Stojalowski and his supporters. The paper blamed the anti-Jewish attacks on false charges that Jews had poisoned the well of a local priest, leading to the deaths of many villagers. Attacks on Jewish-owned businesses had followed.

71. *Kurjer Lwowski* June 20, 26, and 30, 1898; and July 2, 1898.

72. *The New York Times* September 29, 1898. The article refers to excommunicated Roman Catholic priest Stanislaw Stojalowski.

73. *Kurjer Lwowski* February 23, 1893.

CHAPTER 3

1. A. Szarlowski. *Stanislawow i Powiat Stanislawowski*. Stanislawow 1887; pp. 20–27. The original village that gave rise to the future town of Stanislawow was most likely called Zablotow (loosely translated as "behind the marsh"). In the nineteenth and twentieth centuries, one part of the modern city was still called the Zablotow district. The town could trace its origin to 1662, when Count Potocki issued the Magdeburg Rights to its population (an example of a document laying out internal rules of a town by its ruler). These were confirmed by King Casmir the Great in the following year. The younger Stanislaw Potocki died while defending Vienna from an Ottoman attack in 1683.

2. *Kurjer Stanislawowski* September 17, 1911, described the origin of the name "Stanislawow" in preparation for the 250th anniversary of the city, to be celebrated the following year.

3. A. Szarlowski. *Stanislawow i Powiat Stanislawowski*. Stanislawow 1887; pp. 59–62 and 157. By 1704, the Armenian community numbered only 460 in Stanislawow.

4. Ulrich van Werdum. *Das Reisejournal des Ulrich von Werdum, 1670–1677*. P. Lang Frankfurt am Mein, New York 1990 (Helicon series).

5. *Haslo* March 29, 1874, referred to the attacks on Stanislawow by Tatars aligned with the Ottoman Turks in 1676, a domestic war that engulfed the town in 1712, and the Russian invasion of 1739.

6. *Continuato Edictorum et Mandatorum Universalium in Regnis Galiciae et Lodomeriae*. Leopoli 1774; pp. 9–10, 19–22, and 66–69. The laws were issued in 1773 by Maria Theresa, who governed with a co-regent, her son Joseph II. The edicts were implemented by Count Anton Pergen, the first governor of Galicia.

7. A. Szarlowski. *Stanislawow i Powiat Stanislawowski*. Stanislawow 1887; pp. 158–159.

8. *Kurjer Stanislawowski* May 24, 1896, indicated that Catharina Kossakowska (maiden name Potocka) was the owner of the Stanislawow dominion since 1771. The article described her troubles with civil administration and the feisty language she used after losing her battle to keep Stanislawow. The content of the letter is adapted to the English language.

9. *Kurjer Stanislawowski* March 20, 1904; and April 10, 1904; provided details of the devastation.

10. *Kronika* September 16 and 19, 1880, described the visits of Franz Joseph in 1880. The first was a 15-minute visit of the imperial train on the way to other cities of eastern Galicia; three days later, the train made a similar stop there before leaving Galicia for Hungary. It seems a strong possibility that someone from the Sobolewski family from nearby Bohorodczany witnessed the emperor's visit. Franz Joseph also visited Stanislawow in 1851.

11. The building was erected on Fish Square, donated by the city of Stanislawow. Planning began in 1893, and the synagogue opened in 1899. The final plans were drawn up by the Viennese architect Wilhelm Stiassny. As reported by *Kurjer Stanislawowski* on May 26, 1895, the mysterious stone apparently had been placed during construction of an old Orthodox church on the same site in 1670. Across the street from the newly built synagogue was a theater that opened in 1891.

12. *Haslo* January 4, 1874, indicated that gas lighting for a few businesses and private homes would be in service later that year. In reality, the service was initiated two years later. *Kurjer Stanislawowski* February 17, 1901; December 8, 1901; and November 29, 1903; described the expansion of the service, contrasting Stanislawow with other cities of Galicia.

13. *Kurjer Stanislawowski* July 24, 1904.

14. *Kurjer Stanislawowski* August 2, 1903, reported strikingly low annual mortality rates for Stanislawow, compared to Lvov and Cracow. Similarly, the rates of mortality for tuberculosis were lower in Stanislawow. *Kurjer Stanislawowski* June 10, 1906, provided a detailed report of hospital activities. Actually, the city had three hospitals: the military hospital serving the local garrison, the city or public hospital, and the Jewish hospital.

Kurjer Stanislawowski June 23, 1918, announced that Anna Frankel, the town's first female physician, had opened a practice.

15. *Kurjer Stanislawowski* December 4, 1904; and M. Orlowicz, *Ilustrowany Przewodnik po Galicyi*, Lwów 1919, pp. 134–135.

16. *Kurjer Stanislawowski* February 20, 1910, quoted *Stanislauer Nachrichten* (the Yiddish weekly), which threatened a boycott of high schools using the Polish language if the demands for a separate school for Jewish students were not met. The term *Maskilin* denotes leaders of the Haskalah movement among European Jews, which advocated secular studies and wider involvement in the secular world.

17. *Kurjer Lwowski* December 3, 1900; and January 13, 1909.

18. *Kurjer Stanislawowski* April 2, 1905, described a heated debate in the city council. Nimhin's commission found that a real Catholic priest had been passing through the streets, and the gossip had been propagated by those claiming that the man had a beard, which was not true. Hasty conclusions had been reached by the Catholic leaders who made the unsubstantiated charges.

19. *Kurjer Stanislawowski* November 7, 1909, reported on the verdict of the case. In response to the petition by a lawyer from Czerniowce in Bukovina, the court ruled that Jews in Western and Eastern Europe used different languages. Hence, Yiddish, used only in the east, could not be considered a language of the minority. Subsequent to this decision, Dr. Nimhin and Edmund Rauch, a Jewish parliamentarian from Stanislawow, appealed to the Jewish population in a public letter on the occasion of the upcoming census (*Kurjer Stanislawowski* January 1, 1911).

Kurjer Stanislawowski April 9, 1911, celebrated the 25th anniversary of the paper. The front page included recollections of Arthur Nimhin. Others provided glimpses of his inclusiveness.

20. *Kurjer Stanislawowski* January 20 and March 17, 1901, provided somewhat inflated numbers, as they included military personnel stationed in the city. It was estimated that with inclusion of the municipality called Knihin, home to many employed in the city who took advantage of affordable housing there, the population of "greater" Stanislawow would rise to 54,000. A few years later, this was one of the major criticisms of Arthur Nimhin by the opposition weekly, *Rewera*, which would blast the mayor for failing to push through this change.

Kurjer Stanislawowski February 19, 1911, provided census data broken down by religious affiliation from 1870 through 1910.

21. *Kurjer Stanislawowski* March 10, 1901; and November 20 and 27, 1910; listed phone statistics and subscribers.

22. *Kurjer Stanislawowski* March 17, 1901; and October 6 and 13, 1901. Despite many plans, electrical trams did not start operating until after World War I. This was one of the later criticisms of Mayor Nimhin.

23. *Kurjer Lwowski* June 30, 1901, reported on the protest of the pharmacists trying unsuccessfully to thwart competition.

24. *Kurjer Lwowski*, March 6 and 14, 1893, described city commitments to attract the Third Railway Directorate to Stanislawow. They included guarantee of suitable housing for the staff (15 buildings, with each providing 10 apartments) and guaranteed rent control for the next 10 years. In addition, the city was to build future administrative offices.

25. *Kurjer Stanislawowski* June 9, 1901.

26. *Kurjer Lwowski* January 17, 1901; and *Kurjer Stanislawowski* January 20, 1901.

27. *Gazeta Stanislawowska* July 22, 1893, announced the opening of the women's teachers' school. The article mentioned that there were only three similar schools in all of Galicia. Originally, it was located on Halicka Street, off the central city square. *Kurjer Stanislawowski* August 9, 1903; and July 10, 1904; continued the topic of women's education. Another high school for girls opened in 1904; it would not be until 1912 that the first female student would receive her high school diploma in a local school for girls, as opposed to passing the required exit examination in one of the schools for boys, as my grandmother had done (*Kurjer Stanislawowski* June 9, 1912). The current value of school tuition was calculated based on the Consumer Price Index.

28. *Kurjer Stanislawowski* November 17, 1901.

29. *Kurjer Stanislawowski* July 3, 1904; July 2, 1905; and July 15, 1906.

30. M. Orlowicz. *Ilustrowany Przewodnik po Galicyi*. Lwów 1919; pp. 134–135.

31. *Kurjer Stanislawowski* January 1, 1905; and July 3, 1910.

32. *Kurjer Stanislawowski* July 31, 1910.

33. Yearbooks of civil administration indicated Joseph's positions as adjunct, commissioner, and then superintendent in the departments of accounting and revenue between 1901 and April 1913. The building housing his office was designed by Ernest Baudisch in 1893, and the construction was carried out by the company of Ludwik Radwanski. The directorate remained on Karpinski Street from 1894 until 1914, when the offices of the railway administration moved to a newly completed building, with a richly decorated interior, on Grunwaldzka Street.

34. *Kurjer Stanislawowski* October 26, 1902. It is unclear which member of the Strauss family conducted, though it was certainly not Johann Strauss Jr., the most famous waltz composer, who had died a few years before.

35. *Kurjer Stanislawowski* October 25, 1908; and January 24, 1909.

36. *Kurjer Stanislawowski* August 18, 1901; January 11, 1903; and November 27, 1904. The ads for new shows were published weekly until 1910, when they started to disappear.

37. *Kurjer Stanislawowski* April 17, 1904. The first performances were in a theater for dramatic arts. *Kurjer Stanislawowski* July 30, 1905, had a short announcement of the summer outdoor performances.

38. In the United States, the first movie theater was Vitascope Hall in New Orleans, which opened in 1896. By 1910, there were three movie theaters in Stanislawow: the Urania, the Olympia, and the Apollo. *Kurjer Stanislawowski* March 31, 1912, announced that the first movie produced in Galicia was to begin distribution in April of that year.

39. *Kurjer Lwowski* December 1, 1911.

40. *Kurjer Lwowski* January 11, 1901.

41. *Kurjer Stanislawowski* September 3, 1905; and February 24, 1907. In New York City, the first taxicabs with meters were the French-built Darracqs; 65 of them hit the streets in 1907 (*The New York Times* May 4, 2011). *Kurjer Lwowski* January 4, 1911, reported that the first metered taxicabs in Lvov were to start service the same year.

42. *Kurjer Lwowski* January 23, 1908.

43. *Kurjer Stanislawowski* February 17, 1907.

44. *Kurjer Stanislawowski* January 1, 1905, reported on a visit to the city by Ernest Baudisch of Vienna, the main architect of the ambitious reconstruction. The work was to begin later that year and also include the building of an additional post office.

Kurjer Lwowski December 24, 1909, described new multilingual tickets being sold in Stanislawow.

45. *Kurjer Stanislawowski* July 26, 1908.

46. *Kurjer Stanislawowski* August 11 and 25, 1907.

47. *Kurjer Stanislawowski* May 27, 1906.

48. Karl Baedeker. *Austria Including Hungary, Transylvania, Dalmatia, and Bosnia.* Leipsic 1900; pp. 25, 31–40, and 71–72. This travel book described various tourist attractions awaiting visitors in Vienna. It also provided detailed information on the train journey between Galicia and the capital of the empire, the route traveled by the Regiec family.

49. The Viennese Giant Wheel had opened in 1897 and was based on an original built only four years earlier by John Ferris Jr. for the World Expo in Chicago. In 1916, the *Wiener Riesenrad* was scheduled for demolition, but because no funds were available, the plans were never carried out. It has remained in its original place and is still working today. For several decades, it was the largest Ferris wheel in the world.

50. *Skorowidz Przemyslowo-Handlowy Krolestwa Galicyi*; Lwów 1906; pp. 76–79; and *Kurjer Stanislawowski* June 18, 1905.

51. *Kurjer Stanislawowski* January 6, 1907.

52. *Kurjer Stanislawowski* January 22, 1905, provided an early description of the just opened Gartenbergers' Passage and its main attraction, the elegant Cafe Edison. Two Gartenberger brothers owned several buildings downtown. The shopping arcade was situated between Sapiezynska, Karpinski, and Kosciuszko streets; the buildings on the Karpinski Street side were largely destroyed during World War I.

Kurjer Stanislawowski April 7, 1907, published what appeared to be a paid advertisement on the benefits of owning one of the American typewriters available in Gartenbergers' Passage.

53. *Kurjer Stanislawowski* February 25, 1906; and May 6, 1906; described the construction boom that swept the city that year and the high hopes of Stanislawow's public.

54. *Kurjer Stanislawowski* July 22, and 29, 1906; and August 5, 1906. The estimated value of the revenues was calculated based on the Consumer Price Index.

55. *Kurjer Stanislawowski* February 16, 1908.

56. *Kurjer Lwowski* January 8, 1908; and *Kurjer Stanislawowski* January 12, 1908. Joseph Regec (sic) from Stanislawow is listed as promoted to rank VIII. There is no single metric that precisely measures the relative value of wages over time. For calculating the value of Joseph's salary, so-called economic and income value metrics were used.

57. *Kurjer Lwowski* December 1–3, 1908. *Kurjer Stanislawowski* November 29, 1908; and December 6, 1908; provided descriptions of local celebrations.

Szematyzm Krolestwa Galicyi i Lodomeryi z Wielkim Ksiestwem Krakowskim na Rok 1912; Lwów; p. 873 mentioned that two commemorative decorations had been presented to Joseph Regiec in preceding years.

58. A reference to Joseph Regiec's professional success can be seen in the history of the small school in Wieloglowy where he had taught; as already noted, it was written by another teacher approximately 20 years after Joseph had left.

59. The annual report listed Joseph Regiec as a member of the association in 1904. *Kurjer Stanislawowski* March 20, 1910, reports on the election of Joseph Regiec to the executive committee. *Kurjer Stanislawowski* October 26, 1912, lists Regiec among the contributors.

60. *Kurjer Stanislawowski* July 11, 1909, reports that Joseph Regiec joined a civic association supporting an orphanage and paid his annual dues.

CHAPTER 4

1. *Slownik Geograficzny Krolestwa Polskiego i Innych Krajow Slowianskich*. Editors F. Sulimierski, B. Chlebowski, and W. Walewski. Warszawa 1880; vol. I, p. 287. The description of Bohorodczany and surrounding villages in the original text has been altered in a few places for linguistic clarity; it was supplemented by additional information from the period, including Austrian census data (*Gemeindelexikon der im Reichsrate Vertertenen Königreiche unf Länder; Galizien*; Vienna 1907; vol. XII, pp 40–43 and 824).

2. At that time, Bohorodczany and Lachowce were owned by a man named Jan from the village of Buczacz, who became a royal official.

3. Pinkas Hakehillot. *Encyclopedia of Jewish Communities, Poland*. Vad Yashem, Jerusalem 1980; vol. II, pp. 71–72.

4. *Szematyzm Krolestwa Galicyi i Lodomeryi z Wielkim Ksiestwem Krakowskim na Rok 1885*. Lwow; p. 642.

5. M. Hasten. *Mark My Words*. Brotchin Books 2003. The description of the synagogues refers to the beginning of the twentieth century.

6. *Kurjer Stanislawowski* October 11, 1903, reported on the history of the *ikonostas* and a visit to Bohorodczany by the metropolitan Szeptycki, the highest official in the Greek Catholic Church in Galicia. The artwork originated in the Skit Maniawski monastery, which belonged to the Russian Orthodox Church. That order was dissolved by decree of the emperor Joseph II of Austria in 1785. In 1782 or 1785, the famous *ikonostas* was moved to the Greek Catholic church in Bohorodczany.

7. *Handbuch des Statthalterei-Gebietes in Galizien für das Jahr 1861*. Lemberg; p. 340. Several Potockis founded churches for the Dominican order in the Stanislawow district. Besides Constantia Potocka and the church in Bohorodczany, Jacob Potocki established a church in Jezupol in 1600, Stephan Potocki founded one in Potok in 1608, and Nicolaus Potocki set up another in Tysmienica in 1631.

8. Grand hetman was a highly prestigious military title; *Palatinus* referred to an overseer of the province (*voivodeship*), a title bestowed by the crown.

9. Two of Sophia's children, Ignatius and Stanislaus, were baptized in Bohorodczany in 1722 and 1723. (Based on the baptismal records of Bohorodczany.)

10. The infant boys, Adalbertus and Nicholaus Leszczynski, were sons of Jacob and Alexandra Leszczynski. The godparents included several members of the Potocki family (based on the baptismal records of Bohorodczany).

A. Szarlowski. *Stanislawow i Powiat Stanislawowski*. Stanislawow 1887; pp. 76–80. Joseph Potocki's wife was Victoria Leszczynski, claimed by some to be a sister of King Stanislaus Leszczynski of Poland, whereas others believed she was his more distant relative. Victoria married Joseph Potocki at the age of 14.

11. The brick church was established by Stanislaus Kossakowski, the son-in-law of the original founder of the church. By 1775, it was consecrated in the name of the Blessed Virgin Mary. The church was reconstructed in 1904 but suffered significant damage in 1916, during World War I. It was rebuilt between 1928 and 1933.

12. Franz Stadion held the post of governor of Galicia for two years (1847 and 1848); his younger brother Rudolph was the governor of Moravia (1845–1847).

13. The land was bought by Franz Stadion (1808–1853). By 1849, ownership had passed to his younger brother Rudolph. By 1876, Rudolph Stadion's daughters, Rudolphine and Gisela, would own other real estate in the neighboring town of Łysiec. The last owner of the family's Bohorodczany and Lachowce estates was George Stadion, who was listed as the owner of the still largest property in Bohorodczany in the waning days of World War I (J. Bigo; *Najnowszy Skorowidz Wszystkich Miejscowosci z Przysiolkami*; Lwów 1918; pp. 13 and 86).

14. *Kurjer Stanislawowski* November 29, 1903. The advertisement section contained a call for applications to manage forests in Bohorodczany. It listed the address of the management offices in today's Czech Republic.

15. Overall, the entire district of Bohorodczany contained two smaller towns, 37 rural settlements, seven special self-governing tracts of land, and 47 smaller administrative units. In 1880, the district numbered 51,892 people.

16. *Skorowidz Przemyslowo-Handlowy Krolestwa Galicyi*. Lwów 1906. The publication provided detailed listings of shop owners. The lumberyards selling firewood were owned by Abraham Leib Karliner, Jakob Kern, Löwi Kern, Naftali Schultz, and Gabryel Schwalb. Among the owners of tanneries, Hersz and Majer Schreyer, Mechel Rieger, and others were listed.

17. One of the midwives would be needed in due course when my mother was born a few years later.

18. *Slownik Geograficzny Krolestwa Polskiego i Innych Krajow Slowianskich*; editors F. Sulimierski, B. Chlebowski, and W. Walewski; Warszawa 1880; vol. I, p. 287; and *Gemeindelexikon der im Reichsrate Vertertenen Königreiche unf Länder, Galizien*; Vienna 1907; vol. XII, pp. 40–43 and 824.

19. The village name has been Pidhirja (Підгір'я in Ukrainian) since 1963. It was known as Bystryca from 1944 to 1963, and Lachowce prior to that.

20. Jan, the first known owner of Lachowce (previously mentioned), agreed to the payment of 300 grzywna. The grzywna was a measure of weight, mainly of gold and silver, used throughout medieval central Europe. The grzywna was also a unit of exchange, used as money.

21. *Slownik Geograficzny Krolestwa Polskiego i Innych Krajow Slowianskich*; editors F. Sulimierski, B. Chlebowski, and W. Walewski; Warszawa 1884; vol. V, p. 54; provides a description of the village and the census data from 1880. *Gemeindelexikon der im Reichsrate Vertertenen Königreiche unf Länder, Galizien*; Vienna 1907; vol. XII, pp. 40–43 and 824; gives detailed statistics from the beginning of the twentieth century.

22. *Slownik Geograficzny Krolestwa Polskiego i Innych Krajow Slowianskich*. Editors B. Chlebowski, W. Walewski, and F. Sulimierski. Warszawa 1890; vol XI, pp. 267–268. The name is still in use today. Current maps indicate a distance of 11 miles from Bohorodczany.

23. *Dziennik Polski* August 12, 1885. The article dismissed the idea of exporting oil to China but lamented that barriers to supplying oil existed within Austro-Hungary itself. Interestingly, the biggest imports of oil to China were then coming from Russia and America.

CHAPTER 5

1. Wiktor Wittyg. *Nieznana Szlachta Polska i Jej Herby*. Krakow 1908; p. 299. It is unclear whether Jarosz Sobolo(e)wski, who paid the tax in 1564, was the earliest recorded member of the family. The records provide conflicting information about his coat of arms, which might have been used for identification beyond the similar last name. Nonetheless, Janowice was the village where Thecla Regiec, Joseph's mother, was from.

2. Jerzy Sewer Dunin-Borkowski. *Spisk Nazwisk Szlachty Polskiej*. Lwów 1887; p. 52. This source listed Kula Sobolewski from the village of Sobolów as a knight in Cracow's official roster of 1633.

3. Swietoslaw Sarnecki. *Zwiazek Nierozdzielny*. Krakow 1679. The pamphlet includes an entry by Michael Cyrus Sobolowski, who was listed as a student; the family of Cyrus Sobolowski was mentioned in the poem.

4. Oswald Zaprzaniec, *Elektorow Poczet*, Lwów 1845, p. 338, listed several Sobolewskis, including Joseph Sobolewski from Cracow province, an elector of Stanislaus Augustus Poniatowski in 1764.

5. Kasper Niesiecki. *Herbarz Polski*. Published by Jan Nep. Bobrowicz. Leipzig 1841; vol. VIII, p. 438.

6. Zbigniew Leszczyc. *Herby Szlachty Polskiej*. Poznan 1908; vol. 2, table XLIX. There was another family of Sobolewskis that originated in central Poland and was distinguished by a different coat of arms, called Slepowron.

7. On the occasion of the births of Franciscus and Sophia, Simon Sobolewski, of unknown profession, and his wife, Anna, were mentioned in the church baptismal books of Stanislawow (1723 and 1725). Among other early entries were Nicolaus Sobolewski, born in 1738; he was the son of Stanislaus Sobolewski, a member of the military, and his wife, Anna.

8. M. Vishnitzer. *The Memoirs of Ber of Bolechow (1723–1805)*. Oxford University Press 1922; pp. 96–100. The book provides graphic descriptions of attacks on the Jewish community.

9. A. Szarlowski. *Stanislawow i Powiat Stanislawowski*. Stanislawow 1887; pp. 137–143. When Oleksa Dobosz, who had plundered Bohorodczany, was killed, a cross studded with diamonds was found sewn into his clothes. This was returned to Stanislaus Kossakowski. In 1754, the next leader of *opryshky* was caught in the area. After interrogation and torture, he was sentenced to death.

10. A quill pen was the writing instrument of the time; goose feathers were most commonly used. Dip pens were introduced approximately 50 years later.

11. *Continuato Edictorum et Mandatorum Universalium in Regnis Galiciae et Lodomeriae*. Leopoli 1783; pp. 20–25 and 35–37. The initial laws requiring the registration of nobility were issued in 1775 and were followed by the edict of 1782, in which all hereditary classes were joined together by Emperor Joseph II. This was an attempt to dilute the power of the large, landowning families of the old Poland. It is surprising to see that the Sobolewskis applied much later. The same year, Joseph II issued a progressive edict that abolished free labor and established the right of former serfs to marry and relocate at will, without permission of their estate owners. This edict was largely ignored in Galicia and was later rescinded by Joseph's brother.

12. *Poczet Szlachty Galicyjskiej i Bukowinskiej*. Lwów 1857; p. 331. The entries by the three Sobolewski men are listed.

13. There are no known birth records of any of the three Sobolewski men whom we assume were brothers. Using a sometimes imprecise way of estimating their years of birth from their ages entered in marriage or death records, we can calculate that Ludovicus was born in 1728, Ignatius in 1729, and Joannes in 1748. The accuracy of these estimates is clearly questionable. The first written record attesting to their physical presence in Bohorodczany dates back to 1787, when Ignatius Sobolewski's son Adalbertus was born. Of note, there is no record of the birth of Adalbertus's older sister, Catharina, in Bohorodczany. Earlier entry from 1752, referring to the birth of Anna Sobolewska, did not specify location of the Sobolewski's home, other than stating that her parents resided in "the county of Bohorodczany."

Surprisingly, there is no record of the marriage between Ludovicus Sobolewski and Magdalena Krechowiecka in Bohorodczany parish. The ceremony likely took place sometime before 1794, when their first child was born. In 1800, Joannes Sobolewski, from Kosmacz, married a woman we assume was a relative of Magdalena's, Helena Krechowiecka, from the village of Rozulna.

14. The Emperor Francis census from 1820 specified the size of lands owned by the inhabitants of Bohorodczany, including that of the Sobolewski family, living in house 26.

15. The Josephine land census conducted in Lachowce and Bohorodczany in March 1787, and certified in 1788, did not list any members of the Sobolewski family as landowners. This is surprising, since the birth of Adalbertus Sobolewski, the son of Ignatius, was recorded as taking place in house 25 in Bohorodczany on April 9, 1787. Instead, the census identifies Johannes and Sophia Balcer as the owners of the large country house and land spanning Lachowce and Bohorodczany. It is possible that the land title was not transferred to the Sobolewski family in time to be reflected in the census documents, despite evidence that they were already living there.

16. The Josephine land census conducted in 1787 provided detailed descriptions of the land and crops grown in Bohorodczany. The agricultural area of the town was divided into gardens (vegetables and orchards), pastures, and farming fields with meadows.

17. Given his age, this Joannes was likely the one requesting certification of his noble status with Ignatius and Ludovicus. Another Joannes Sobolewski was younger (born in 1770) and lived in house 27. On a contemporary map of Lachowce, there was a large compound labeled "SJB," standing for "Sobolewski Joannes Bonorum"; that could denote house 27.

18. The church records provide date, house number, and name and age of the deceased. Sophia was listed as 112 years old at her death, and Ludovicus as 107 years old. Joannes's age is more appropriate at 74 years. Sophia's and Ludovicus's ages most likely represent errors made by Dominican friars, who were precise when recording information about families but sometimes inaccurate when giving the exact ages of the deceased.

19. Several marriages of German-speaking *colonista* took place in Bohorodczany. On January 29, 1839, a rare dual marriage ceremony took place: Herman Wilhelm Kaendel (or Kändel) from the German settlement of Landestreu married Franciska Palczynska, and Josephus Andreas Feitner from Hotzenplotz tied the knot with Joanna Schimke from Moravia (today's Czech Republic, then part of Hungary). In 1860, Franciscus Sobolewski was the witness at the marriage of his neighbors, *colonista* from Horocholina.

20. There are many examples of members of the Sobolewski family marrying in the eastern rites of the Greek Catholic Church. At times, the differences between Roman Catholics and Greek Catholics were blurred even further. A good example was the marriage of Anna Sobolewska, a Roman Catholic, to a Greek Catholic theologian or priest (*theologus*), which took place in the Dominican church of Bohorodczany in November of 1840. In contrast to Roman Catholic priests, who had to observe celibacy, Greek Catholic priests were free to marry. As Anna was only 17 years old at the time of her wedding, her father, Adalbertus Sobolewski (house 25), signed permission with his full name in the church books.

21. In 1830, Adalbertus Sobolewski was a witness at the marriage of Magdalena Heymann from Hradisch, Moravia.

22. This event was not simply a reflection of the lack of Protestant churches in the area. Although the construction of a Protestant church was finished in neighboring Stanislawow only in 1885, it is certain that other Protestant churches had existed near there since the early years of the nineteenth century. They were to be expected in some of the German rural settlements.

23. *Kurjer Stanislawowski* October 24, October 31, and November 7, 1909, printed a series of articles providing an account of events. The Austrian garrison left Stanislawow in early June 1809. However, Bohorodczany and Stanislawow had been retaken by the Austrian army by the end of July of that year. This description was based on the diary of an eyewitness, first published in 1869.

24. Alexandre Rembowski. *Sources Documentaires Concernant L'histoire du Regiment des Chevau-Legeres de la Garde de Napoleon I.* Varsovie 1899; p. 469.

25. Unlike Joseph Regiec's mother, Anastasia probably did not die as a result of childbirth. Her son, Thomas Franciscus, was born on December 18, 1853, but then there is a gap in the records. We can surmise that Anastasia passed away early in 1854, followed by the customary one-year mourning period before Antonius remarried in June 1855. Antonius Sobolewski died of pneumonia in May 1873, in the same house (number 26) where he and his children had been born and his grandmother and parents had also died. He was 63. The record simply identifies his profession as farmer (*agricola*).

26. Andreas Sobolewski never knew his grandfather Ludovicus, who had died in 1835, before Andreas's birth in 1848. The names of the children of Andreas and Anna Sobolewski were Antonius, Ladislaus, Ludovica, Carolus, Michael, Franciscus, Carolina, Theophilus, Wilhelmina, Ludovica 2nd, Joannes, and Mathilda. Of their 12 children, the four who died very young were Ludovica, Ludovica 2nd, Joannes, and Mathilda.

27. *Kurjer Stanislawowski* March 29, 1903, published reports of intentionally set fires in Bohorodczany. Tensions between the Ruthenian and Polish populations were on the rise, with large agrarian strikes against landowning Poles erupting over the next few years.

28. Michael Sobolewski's life came to untimely end when he died at the age of 23 in November 1907. The cause of death was attributed to typhus. Before his illness, Michael was likely a clerk (*dictarius*) in a local district office in Bohorodczany.

29. *Szematyzm Krolestwa Galicyi i Lodomeryi z Wielkim Ksiestwem Krakowskim na Rok 1908.* Lwów 1908; pp. 415 and 740.

30. *Kurjer Stanislawowski* July 10, 1904, listed Franciscus and Stanislaus Sobolewski as graduates of the all-male teachers' school.

31. Reported in *Kurjer Stanislawowski* on July 17 and October 2, 1904, and in the national *Kurjer Lwowski* and *Gazeta Narodowa* on July 13 and 16, and September 27, 1904. The reports in the newspapers were clearly pro-Sobolewski. Nobody seemed to have remembered that the reverse had happened just a few years before. In an earlier language-related incident, the Greek Catholic church had complained about receiving a minor communication from the district offices in Bohorodczany written in Polish. Subsequently, official directives were issued in Lvov reminding officials in eastern Galicia about the requirement to use Ruthenian when dealing with Greek Catholic institutions (*Kurjer Stanislawowski* January 22, 1899).

32. *Kurjer Lwowski* January 11, 1908, reported on the number of emigrants leaving Galicia.

33. The advertisement sections in *Kurjer Stanislawowski* March 4, 1906, and November 24, 1907, and in *Kurjer Lwowski* December 7, 1911, listed several routes and ship services. Not much is known about Theophilus's life in Argentina. In 1954, he was still living there, as recalled at the time by his brother Franciscus Sobolewski.

34. *Kurjer Lwowski* August 9, 1905, described the teachers' conference in Bohorodczany.

35. Prior to 1802, military duties had been for life, interrupted by frequent furloughs. Over the years, the service had become more tolerable; at that time, it was shortened to 10 years, and after 1862, it was further reduced to 3 years. Typically, service began when the recruit was 20 or 21 years old. In 1912, the service was further reduced to 2 years.

36. *Kurjer Stanislawowski* October 9, 1910.

37. Details of Franciscus Sobolewski's military service were derived from his own biographical sketch (Polish Central Military Archives).

38. *Szematyzm Krolestwa Galicyi i Lodomeryi z Wielkim Ksiestwem Krakowskim 1905–07, 1911–13.*

CHAPTER 6

1. *Kurjer Stanislawowski* September 23, 1900, described the changes in the law but stated that women were allowed to run pharmacies only after obtaining special permission from a government ministry.

2. *Kurjer Stanislawowski* May 26, 1907.

3. *Kurjer Stanislawowski* October 28, 1906.

4. Helena's new home was in house 75. Looking at a map of the town, we see that it was situated behind the market square and near the courthouse.

5. *Schematismus für das Königreich Ostgalizien 1799*, Lemberg 1799, p. 214, and *Schematismus für die Königreiche Ostgalizien und Lodomerien sammt einem Schreibkalender und Namen-Register für das Jahr 1802*, Lemberg, p. 233. Listed under the German-Jewish schools is S. Bland as a local teacher in Bohorodczany. The last teacher was M. Minzchelez, listed in *Schematismus für die Königreiche Galizien und Lodomerien sammt einem Namen-Register für das Jahr 1806*, Lemberg 1806, p. 253.

6. *Szematyzm Szkol Ludowych*, Lwów 1865, p. 34, detailed compensation of the teacher from Bohorodczany. Additional information about the number of children of school age is derived from *Handbuch des Statthalterei-Gebietes in Galizien für das Jahr 1861*, Lemberg 1861, p. 269.

7. *Kurjer Lwowski* January 16, 1901.

8. *Kurjer Stanislawowski* May 31, 1903, described the construction of the school, which cost 40,000 kronen. The paper raised concerns about the use of shoddy building materials. The citizens of Bohorodczany complained that the bricks had been purchased from a local brickyard (one that belonged to the Stadion family), and apparently their quality was not appropriate for the two-story building.

9. *Szematyzm Krolestwa Galicyi i Lodomeryi z Wielkim Ksiestwem Krakowskim na Rok 1908*. Lwów; pp. 529–531. Since 1899, the district cities had been required to appoint regional school boards that included county officials, representatives of the teachers, and clergy from all religious denominations with more than 1,000 congregants.

10. The monthly salary has been calculated based on the total compensation that Helena is known to have received during her years spent in Bohorodczany. It is more than likely that her income in the first few years as a teacher-in-training was even lower. Teachers were paid little, and their income would later be eroded by the inflation that became rampant during the Great War.

11. *Kurjer Stanislawowski* February 20, 1910, described the opening of the public omnibus route. On May 7, 1911, it reported the arrival of an "automobile omnibus" with two classes of service, shuttling between towns south of Stanislawow. The first vehicles carried up to 12 passengers and traveled at the "amazing" speed of 11 miles per hour. A ticket cost 6 to 8 kronen.

12. *Kurjer Stanislawowski* February 27, 1898, published a report of carnival entertainment that took place about eight years before Helena's arrival in Bohorodczany. It is likely that similar evening parties were organized in later years.

Kurjer Stanislawowski February 17, 1907, in an article signed by "two dancing female observers," decried the declining manners of the men attending carnival balls. They also made a point that the evening entertainment was becoming less formal, with gatherings increasingly organized in private homes or even restaurants.

13. I recall my grandmother telling me that she spoke Ukrainian but had some difficulty with Russian. Of note, both languages use the Cyrillic alphabet.

14. *Szematyzm Krolestwa Galicyi i Lodomeryi z Wielkim Ksiestwem Krakowskim na Rok 1909*. Lwów 1909; p 604.

15. Mark Hasten. *Mark My Words!* Brotchin Books 2003; pp. 7–9. The author went to school in Bohorodczany about 30 years after Helena was a teacher there. He provides a vivid description of the early education of Jewish children.

16. *Kurjer Stanislawowski* February 14, 1909. This was the first time I had heard that my grandmother played the violin, apparently quite well. The teacher who sang a few songs was Marya Krzyzanowska, who had joined the school as a teacher-in-training that year. The cytra that provided accompaniment was a stringed instrument then popular in Austria.

17. *Sprawozdanie z Dzialalnosci Towarzystwa Szkoly Ludowej*; Kraków 1911; pp. 39, 242, 269, and 347; and Kraków 1912; p. 28*. Edward Sobolewski was the secretary, and Antonius Sobolewski was a member of the executive committee and deputy treasurer in 1910.

18. Today, Kochawina is known as Hnizdyczow, Ukraine. Approximately one month after the wedding, an unrelated celebration was held there for a famous painting of the Madonna that had hung in the church for several centuries. At that time, the place was visited by several church dignitaries, and received papal letters and blessings. An estimated 100,000 pilgrims attended. (The railway employees of Stanislawow were known to make frequent excursions to that oft-visited place.)

19. Wilhelmina Telesnicka (older sister of Stephania) could have attended; she and her children still likely lived in Nowy Sacz. Unfortunately, Bronislawa Lösch was not among the crowd of well-wishers. She was gravely ill, and passed away in September of 1912.

20. *Rewera* March 29, 1913, described extreme views from the larger city of Lvov; a lecturer from there suggested that although young women were often more successful in school than boys, they were not to be encouraged to pursue higher education, as they were considered less capable of "brainy" pursuits. This was a remarkable ghost of past attitudes, which from time to time reemerged in that society.

21. I suspect that Antonius was the oldest brother of Franciscus and Andreas, one of many cousins. Their grandfather, Antonius, was long dead, and it would have been unusual to have Franciscus's father, Andreas, as a witness.

22. I remember my grandmother as a tiny woman with soft gray hair, although my mother often said she had looked very different as a younger person.

23. *Kurjer Stanislawowski* September 7, 1907. The fire had consumed about 30 Jewish shops and small warehouses; property losses were estimated at 30,000 kronen.

24. *Kurjer Stanislawowski* July 21, 1895, described the busy atmosphere from the early morning hours to nightfall in Bohorodczany. The correspondent complained that Jewish businesses ignored the local ordinance requiring stores to remain closed on Sundays. In reality, however, Christian and Jewish neighbors worked alongside each other regardless of the day of the week.

25. Czortkow was also home to many Hassidic Jews and famous Rebbes. Some of them held Hassidic court, providing various rulings that were sought by Jews from Galicia, including those from Bohorodczany. An interesting story about the Czortkow Rebbe who provided advice on dealing with trespassing Dominican friars is described in M. Hasten's book *Mark My Words*, Brotchin Books 2003.

CHAPTER 7

1. Paul Robert Magocsi. *The Roots of Ukrainian Nationalism: Galicia as Ukraine's Piedmont*. University of Toronto Press, Inc. 2002. My comments on the Ukrainian movement and aspirations are based on pages 19–24.

2. *Rzeczpospolita* January 3, 1914.

3. *Kurjer Lwowski* July 31, August 1, and August 5, 1902, began its series of reports in a conciliatory tone, commenting that the protests were legal. However, the tone changed over time, speaking about landowners' financial losses and daily skirmishes between strikers and troops. *Kurjer* provided daily reports by district; Bohorodczany was not mentioned throughout the summer. Toward the end of the strike, *Gazeta Narodowa* August 14, 1902, published a front-page, inflammatory article painting the events of the past few weeks as the beginning of conflict between Ruthenians and Poles, alluding also to problems at Lvov's university.

In Bohorodczany, Ruthenian gatherings included between few hundreds to several thousands of protesters who demanded equality in election laws and threatened to join future agrarian strikes. The yellow-blue flags of Ukrainian national movement were on display (*Kurjer Stanislawowski* January 7, January 28, and May 13, 1906).

4. Until 1873, deputies to the lower house of the national parliament in Vienna were elected by provincial *diets* from various crown lands, like the one in Galicia. Then the elections became direct, but deputies were chosen from a system of four *curiae* (large landowners, trade and industry, large cities, and rural communities). The representation was heavily skewed toward the first *curia*. Despite changes in national election law in 1907, the representatives to the provincial legislature (*diet*) continued to be chosen based on the curial system.

5. *Gazeta Narodowa* July 5, 6, and 7, 1907, reported on the so-called "Galician Discussion" in the national parliament in Vienna. Debate focused on critical issues like the potential division of Galicia into two parts, alleged election fraud, and voter intimidation. The conservative paper reprinted the speech by the internal affairs minister of Austria, with reactions from various parliamentary groups.

6. *Kurjer Lwowski* July 29, 1907, devoted its front-page article to the subject. The controversy over election laws for the provincial Galician legislature spilled far beyond the ethnic parties representing Poles and Ruthenians. In fact, there was vigorous debate among Poles themselves. The conservative press (*Gazeta Narodowa*) advocated preservation of the curial system in the election of deputies to the local legislature. Other, more populist newspapers (such as *Kurjer Lwowski*) demanded introduction of a plurality vote, like the one newly in use for the election of deputies to the national parliament. To preserve at least some advantage for Polish conservative landowners in Galician politics, a thought was floated about a bicameral body with an upper house based on non-proportional representation.

7. *Kurjer Stanislawowski* December 15, 1901.

8. *Kurjer Lwowski* April 13, 1908. A special edition provided detailed eyewitness accounts.

9. *Kurjer Lwowski* April 16, 1908, and *Kurjer Stanislawowski* April 19, 1908, referred to news of the assassination reaching Stanislawow that Sunday. *Kurjer Lwowski* April 14, 1908, described the first reactions in Vienna on the day of the event. *The New York Times* reported news of the assasination on April 13, 1908.

10. *Kurjer Lwowski*'s evening edition on April 14, 1908, detailed funeral events attended by the minister-president of Austria, Baron von Beck; the minister of internal affairs, Baron Bienerth; and the minister of the treasury, Dr. Korytkowski. The governors of Moravia, Bukovina, Lower Austria, and Austrian Silesia were also in attendance.

11. *Kurjer Stanislawowski* May 31, 1908, reported on the memorial services in Bohorodczany.

12. *Kurjer Lwowski* April 14, 1908, reprinted excerpts from *Neue Wiener Tagblatt* and *Neue Freie Presse*.

13. *Kurjer Lwowski* April 15, 1908, quoted from *Wiener Allgemeine Zeitung* and *Arbeiter Zeitung*.

14. *Kurjer Lwowski* July 1, 1908.

15. *Kurjer Lwowski* July 5, 1908, quoted *Neue Freie Presse*, which described the letter from Countess Potocka to the emperor.

16. *Kurjer Lwowski* June 22, 1909, described the proceedings of the highest court, and on July 14, 1909, provided commentary about the emperor's ruling on Siczynski's sentence.

17. *Kurjer Stanislawowski* August 1, 1909.

18. *Kurjer Stanislawowski* August 20, 1911.

19. *Kurjer Lwowski* broke the news on November 10, 1911. Additional details were described in *Kurjer Lwowski* on November 11 and 12, 1911. *Kurjer Stanislawowski* November 12 and December 17, 1911, wrote about the suspected whereabouts of Mr. Siczynski.

20. *Kurjer Stanislawowski* May 3, 1914, reported that Siczynski was living in the United States, where he occasionally contributed short articles to Ukrainian-language publications. *Kurjer Stanislawowski* October 24, 1915, quoted U.S.-based reports that confirmed the whereabouts of the fugitive.

21. *Kurjer Lwowski* December 21, 1908, reported that the prior governor, Count Potocki, a few months before his assassination, had communicated to the university senate a secret mandate from the government in Vienna to form two departments (chemistry and law) with Ruthenian faculty.

22. *Kurjer Lwowski* December 13, 1908.

23. *Kurjer Lwowski* December 14, 1908, and *Kurjer Stanislawowski* December 20, 1908.

24. *Kurjer Lwowski* July 1 through 3, 1910, described events in detail.

25. *Kurjer Stanislawowski* July 26, 1910, refers to the official inquiry.

26. *Kurjer Lwowski* December 21, 1908. The article referred to a declaration by the academic senate stating that Polish had been established as the language of civil administration in 1879 and as the language of academic instruction in 1882.

27. *Rzeczpospolita* January 9, 1909. The article implied that the additional funding for the Ruthenian departments could have been introduced only with tacit agreement of the governor of Galicia. In a sense, this was an excuse for the unrest and the attack on Dr. Bobrzynski that had taken place the month before.

28. *Rzeczpospolita* June 11, 1910. This article, written shortly before the incident at the university, viewed Lvov as an unacceptable site for the Ruthenian university. Instead it suggested Halicz, a historical capital of Galicia but by then a small provincial town.

29. *Kurjer Stanislawowski* May 19, 1912, reported that the city council had passed a resolution supporting the idea of a Ruthenian university. *Kurjer Lwowski* December 30, 1912, provided a detailed description of the agreement hammered out in Vienna.

30. *Kurjer Lwowski* January 20, 1913, reprinted a draft of the emperor's declaration.

CHAPTER 8

1. *Kurjer Lwowski* July 7, 1904, and January 10, 1905. Among many stories from Asia, *Kurjer* reprinted the report from the British *Daily Mail* about the Japanese army's alleged practice of a "new style war," full of concern for the native population. It was apparent that the campaign of misinformation on the part of the Japanese was working well in Europe.

2. *Kurjer Stanislawowski* January 8, 1905. The newspaper described what appeared to be a spontaneous demonstration that included marching through the streets of Stanislawow. In Japanese, "Banzai!" is a traditional exclamation meaning "ten thousand years."

3. *Wiener Bilder* April 20, 1910.

4. *Wiener Bilder* June 1 and June 8, 1910. *Kurjer Lwowski* June 1, 1910, reported that the emperor received ovations and tributes in Sarajevo.

5. *Kurjer Lwowski* October 13, 1912; and *Kurjer Stanislawowski* October 20, 1912; referred to the possibility that a conflict between Austria and Russia might engulf Galicia. *Kurjer Stanislawowski* October 20 and December 1, 1912, printed, respectively, Governor Bobrzynski's plea to the public and his other reassurances about banks' solvency.

6. *Kurjer Lwowski* January 3, 1913. Ultimately, the Treaty of London was signed, restoring a short-lived peace between the warring countries on May 30, 1913. The Second Balkan War broke out on June 29, 1913. This time, Bulgaria attacked its former allies, Serbia and Greece. Withn a few weeks, other countries had entered the fray. The Ottomans also exploited the situation, reclaiming a small portion of European territory that has more or less remained part of modern Turkey.

7. *Kurjer Stanislawowski* September 7, 1913, described the welcome ceremony.

8. The mayor could expect a more lenient view of his policies from *Kurjer Stanislawowski*, where he had once served as an editor.
Rewera October 12, 1912, published a satirical article that criticized the entire city and, by extension, the mayor's administration. There were also frequent personal diatribes against Dr. Nimhin, sometimes exploiting his Jewish background. The feud between *Rewera* and the mayor continued, even with charges that his supporters promoted the distribution of pornography (March 21, 1914).
Kurjer Stanislawowski December 22, 1912, reported on the election of Dr. Nimhin, who had won by a wide margin despite a hard-driven campaign by his opponents.

9. *Kurjer Stanislawowski* March 9 and October 12, 1913. In a reversal of public opinion, the usually pro-mayor *Kurjer Stanislawowski* for November 28, 1913, criticized the mayor for his handling of the fiscal crisis.

10. *Kurjer Stanislawowski* October 5, 1913.

11. *Kurjer Stanislawowski* October 26, 1913, and February 15, 1914.

12. *Kurjer Stanislawowski* November 9 and December 21, 1913. The second play, *Aszantka*, was unusual as it featured a young man from a wealthy family who became entangled with a simple woman who aspired to become the best prostitute in town. The relationship between the main characters quickly changes, and the man becomes totally dependent on the woman in both emotional and financial terms.

13. *Kurjer Stanislawowski* November 23, 1913. The electric lights that confused the hapless balloonists were at the train station.

14. *Kurjer Lwowski* January 1, 1914. The new year's leading article cautiously raised the prospect of calm in the region and, by extension, in Galicia.

15. *Kurjer Stanislawowski* October 26, 1913, had published an unusually open idea about the need to enrich the school curriculum with studies of the Ukrainian language.

16. *Kurjer Lwowski* July 28, 1914, analyzed the causes of tensions in an unemotional way. Other factors included the dependence of landlocked Serbia on Austro-Hungary for export of its agricultural products.

17. *Kurjer Stanislawowski* July 5, 1914, described the arrival of the news and the subsequent events in the city.

18. *Rzeczpospolita* July 11, 1914; *Kurjer Stanislawowski* July 12, 19, and 26, 1914; and *Rewera* July 11, 1914.

CHAPTER 9

1. *Kurjer Lwowski* July 29, 1914, and July 31, 1914.

2. *Kurjer Lwowski* August 7, 1914. Not only was the war much longer than anticipated, but unresolved problems stemming from its conclusion eventually caused World War II rather than a long period of harmony.

3. *The European Powers in the First World War: An Encyclopedia*. Edited by Spencer A. Tucker. Routledge 1996; p. 173. Over the course of the entire war, Austro-Hungary mobilized 7,800,000 of its citizens, whereas Russia had the staggering number of 12,000,000 men under arms.

4. *Kurjer Lwowski* August 1 and 2, 1914. The mobilization order was issued on July 31, 1914.

5. *Kurjer Lwowski* August 17, 1914, reported from Stanislawow about the state of preparations, in clear anticipation that the city would likely receive many wounded.

6. *Kurjer Lwowski* August 18, 1914. This was a common theme of the many speculations in the newspapers. The idea that improved lines of communication and the massive cost of war would limit the conflict's duration soon proved tragically false.

7. *Kurjer Lwowski* August 17, 1914, reported on the situation in Stanislawow. The issue of *Kurjer Stanislawowski* dated August 23, 1914, just days before Russians entered the city, provided a list of 136 people arrested under suspicion of being Muscophiles, i.e., Russian sympathizers.

8. *Kurjer Stanislawowski* October 17, 1915, described the panic and evacuation of bank assets on August 27, 1914. *Kurjer Stanislawowski* September 19 and 26, 1915, described the Russian takeover of Stanislawow the year before.

9. *Kurjer Lwowski* August 29–30, 1914, had big headlines but lacked details of the battle; an extra edition of *Kurjer Lwowski* on September 3, 1914, provided the public appeal dated September 2, issued by the remaining members of the city council.

10. *Nowosci Illustrowane* October 10, 1914, described and printed pictures of the evacuation of civilians from Cracow. The report stated that the military had declared Cracow a fortress to be defended if attacked. Several districts of the city had already been ordered to evacuate, and food rations were distributed to those who remained. Other reports indicated that up to 100,000 Galicians had reached Vienna, mostly refugees from the areas occupied by Russians.

Nowosci Illustrowane October 3, 1914, reported that a few units of the Cossack advance force had crossed into Hungary. Even under military censorship, the report noted panic among the rural population and victims of the attacks.

11. *Kurjer Lwowski* September 20, 1914, reported that the first military governor, Colonel Sergei Szeremetiev, agreed to open Polish schools. By September 23, 1914, he was replaced by a nationalistic governor, Count Georgiy Bobrinski, who was much less interested in reconciliation with Poles. *Kurjer Lwowski* October 7, 1914, printed the order of the governor regarding censorship.

12. *Kurjer Stanislawowski* March 5, 1916, printed an article about the harsh period of the Russification of Galicia in the years 1914 to 1915.

13. *Kurjer Lwowski* November 8, 1914, published "The Voice of a Country Teacher," a sorrowful plea by a teacher displaced by the war. *Kurjer Lwowski* January 1, 1915, implied that the schools had already been closed for some time. As indicated by a front-page article in *Kurjer Lwowski* January 4, 1915, the dire financial situation of teachers continued into the next year. *Kurjer Lwowski* March 2, 1915, reported from the Russian press that teachers from St. Petersburg would be arriving in Galicia soon.

14. *Gazeta Narodowa* January 31, 1915, printed an anonymous report from Stanislawow that mixed facts with propaganda. After the Russian takeover of the city on September 3, 1914, the military governed there until October 2, 1914, when civil administration started to function. The report was critical of the mayor and his fiscal policies.

15. *Kurjer Stanislawowski* September 26 and October 3, 1915, reprinted the report of the eyewitness, who served as a nurse at the hospital in Stanislawow. The 3rd Infantry Regiment of Polish Legions had been transferred to the easternmost part of the Carpathian Mountains to protect the passes from Russian advances toward Hungary. The nurse described a previously unknown episode of their surprise counterattack. She was said to have witnessed an unusual bond between the Cossack and the boy soldier, and claimed that the Russian took care of him afterward.

16. *Kurjer Lwowski* October 1, 1914, reported that the metropolitan archbishop Sheptytsky (a.k.a. Szeptycki) had been deported by a military convoy to Kiev. He was falsely accused of prior illegal entries to Russia and subversive activities. *Kurjer Lwowski* October 6, 1914, wrote about a resolution from St. Petersburg calling for confiscation of Greek Catholic Church property and members' conversion to the Orthodox faith.

17. *The New York Times* May 22, 1915. The title read, "Though Slavs, They Are Not Russians, but Ukrainians."

18. *Kurjer Lwowski* November 5, 1914, listed the languages that were allowed for use in private correspondence. The list excluded Yiddish, which was spoken by the majority of the Jewish population in Galicia. *Kurjer Lwowski* February 20, 1915, printed a short announcement by Count Bobrinski severely restricting the movements of Jews.

19. *Kurjer Stanislawowski* February 20, 1916, described in detail the entry of Austro-Hungarian troops into Stanislawow, on the first anniversary of the event. There is some disagreement about the exact date when Austrian forces recaptured Stanislawow; *Kurjer Stanislawowski* October 3, 1915, mentioned February 18, 1915, whereas *Kurjer Lwowski* March 12, 1915, had the date as February 19.

20. *Kurjer Stanislawowski* September 19, 1915, featured a front-page article on the Red Cross hospital and included details of its operations during the Russian artillery attack on the city.

Kurjer Stanislawowski October 10 and 31, 1915, provided a list of damaged properties that concentrated on Pelesza, Copernicus, and Kaminski streets.

21. *Kurjer Lwowski* March 10, 12, and 13, 1915, reported from the Russian perspective on the battle in and around Stanislawow. *Kurjer Stanislawowski* September 19, 1915, offered additional details, including damage to the Red Cross hospital and the consequences of the Russian bombardment.

22. *Kurjer Stanislawowski* September 12 and 19, 1915. This outbreak of serious communicable diseases, mainly cholera, in the Stanislawow area was reported in several newspaper articles during the fall of 1915. The public hospital became overcrowded and was temporarily closed to new admissions. A special isolation ward opened on Kazimierzowska Street.

23. *Kurjer Lwowski* April 29, 1915, provided detailed descriptions of the Carpathian passes, including the one leading to the place where Franciscus was fighting.

24. *Kurjer Lwowski* May 3, 1915, reprinted a military communiqué from the Russian command, stating that the tsar's forces had been forced to retreat from the Carpathian Mountains.

25. *Kurjer Lwowski* June 4 and 7, 1915.

26. *Kurjer Stanislawowski* May 21, 1916, reported on the first anniversary of the event, placing the day of liberation at June 8, 1915.

27. *Nowosci Illustrowane* July 3 and 10, 1915. This weekly magazine, published in Cracow, described official celebrations there and in Vienna. On the front page of the July 10 issue, the headline read, "Lvov's Dark and Bright Days." Beneath it, two photographs depicted the very first unit of Russian forces that entered the city in 1914, and the populace greeting the Austrian general who liberated Lvov in 1915.

28. *Nowosci Illustrowane* July 10, 1915. The weekly reported that 10,000 passports had been allegedly issued by the retreating Russians. *Kurjer Stanislawowski* November 21, 1915, reported that Carol Fiedler, who had served as deputy mayor during the Russian occupation of Stanislawow, was deported by the Russians as they left. By the end of November, a simple postcard routed through Denmark arrived in Stanislawow. Mr. Fiedler was alive and interned in Siberia. He would return in March 1918 (*Kurjer Stanislawowski* March 10, 1918).

29. *Kurjer Lwowski* July 26, 1915, reported that for Galician collaborators ("Muscophiles") who escaped east, the government of Russia had waived the required five-year period of residency—granting them full citizenship.

Kurjer Stanislawowski September 19, 1915, announced rewards for citizens who reported abandoned military hardware to the authorities.

30. The term *Central powers* described the military alliance of the German Empire, the Austro-Hungarian Empire, the Ottoman Empire, and the Kingdom of Bulgaria, fighting against the Allied powers (also known as the Entente powers).

Kurjer Lwowski August 17, 1914, reported on the appeal of Polish members of the Austrian parliament who, with tacit agreement from Vienna, called for immediate formation of Polish Legions to fight under Austro-Hungarian command. Two military units were formed on August 27, 1914. In 1916, command of the legions was transferred to Germany. They were later dissolved, their soldiers either demoted or interned after the units refused to swear allegiance to German Kaiser Wilhelm.

31. *Kurjer Stanislawowski* November 28, 1915, reprinted the thank-you letter of the church prelate, with the Jewish donor remaining anonymous. *Kurjer Stanislawowski* November 7, 1915, and January 1, 1916, listed Wanda Regiec among donors. In the issue dated January 1, 1916, an article described packages from Bohorodczany prepared by the Women's League.

32. *Kurjer Stanislawowski* January 16, 1916, reported that in a surprising letter written by someone from the area, two names of other POWs, including my grandfather's, were mentioned.

33. *Kurjer Stanislawowski* January 1, 1916, and *Kurjer Lwowski* January 1, 1916. The union of four monarchies under the titular rule of the emperor and king Franz Joseph was proposed by a Hungarian parliamentarian. The new country was to be called the Danube Empire.

34. *Kurjer Lwowski* June 21 and 24, 1916, reported events in Czerniowce, including fires lighting the sky at night, refugees streaming through town, and artillery fire. A passenger passing through Stanislawow described throngs of people at the station.

35. *Kurjer Lwowski* June 16 and 19, 1916. There was growing panic in Lvov that the Russians would sweep through eastern Galicia as they had in 1914. The reassuring official press reports about halting them and capturing huge numbers of POWs were not always convincing.

36. *Kurjer Lwowski* August 12, 13, and 14, 1916, provided information about the military evacuation of Stanislawow. Later, more detailed information referred to a subdued atmosphere in Lvov. The view of Russia was expressed in "The Capture of Stanislavoff [*sic*] by a Russian Correspondent"; *The New York Times Current History*; *The European War*; New York 1917; vol. VIII, pp. 245–247. The report described brutal battles before Russians entered the city, but it should be read with some caution as it very likely contained a good measure of propaganda.

37. *Kurjer Lwowski* October 4 and 7, 1916, cited military communiqués on fighting around Bohorodczany, with details of battles reported by both sides.

38. *The New York Times* December 21, 1916, from the eastern front of the Great War. Other reports about fighting in Łysiec and Lachowce around Bohorodczany were reported in *Kurjer Lwowski* December 27, 1916.

CHAPTER 10

1. *Kurjer Lwowski* July 20, 1917, described three possible directions for the Russian attack on Lvov, indicating that the Russians had decided to take the longer southern route, which would take them west of Stanislawow.

2. The term *Bolshevik* (meaning "majority") denoted the political party that came to power during Russia's October Revolution in 1917.

3. *Kurjer Lwowski* July 31, 1917, described the lack of discipline in the Russian army during the last occupation of Stanislawow, and provided the quote of an unnamed Russian soldier.

4. *Kurjer Lwowski* July 28, 1917, reprinted a communiqué of the Russian command, indicating battles around Łysiec on July 25, 1917. Łysiec was situated halfway between Bohorodczany and Stanislawow. There were reports of street fighting during the takeover of the city by German forces. *Kurjer Lwowski* July 31, 1917, recorded that the lancers arrived on July 22, 1917, and the city fell on July 25.

Kurjer Stanislawowski March 17, 1918, reported that 32 lancers had been killed and more than 50 wounded in the battle of Krechowce, south of Stanislawow. The same issue quoted the German and Russian generals praising the bravery of the lancers.

5. *Kurjer Lwowski* July 31 and August 2, 1917, reported on the visit of Emperor Charles I to Stanislawow and other towns of the region on July 29, 1917.

6. *Kurjer Stanislawowski* February 17, 1918, reported that only two of the lancers held in Austrian internment had been released; the remaining soldiers were still being held by the Germans more than seven months after Charles I made the promise. Additional releases were announced in *Kurjer Stanislawowski* on July 21, 1918.

7. *Kurjer Lwowski*, January 4, 1917; *Kurjer Stanislawowski* November 18, 1917, and January 13, 1918. Russian military campaigns with frequent changes of the front line had necessitated the transfer of several administrative departments from eastern Galicia west to Cracow and other towns. It would be no sooner than April and May of 1918 that all departments of the Railway Directorate would return to Stanislawow.

8. *Kurjer Lwowski* February 14, 1918, reported that most of Galicia was transitioning back to civil administration.

9. *Kurjer Stanislawowski* November 25 and December 2, 1917, reported on the dire conditions in the city. For days, local bakeries could not make bread due to the chronic lack of flour.

Kurjer Stanislawowski March 10, 1918, provided a front-page report on secret transports to Germany of large quantities of meat, grain, and other food products, sometimes concealed in train cars designed for the transfer of oil.

10. *Kurjer Lwowski* January 1, 1917, reported that the Russians had removed all the furniture from the directorate offices and devastated the machine shops.

11. *Kurjer Stanislawowski* March 3, 1918, printed a personal thank-you note by the treasurer of the association to Mr. Joseph Regiec for a donation of 20 kronen. *Kurjer Stanislawowski* March 24, 1918, described the dire conditions of the boarding school that provided vocational (handicraft) training. The council was elected to revitalize the institution. The deputy mayor, Antonius Stygar, was elected its chairman; Joseph Regiec was secretary. Later in the year, Joseph became involved in the revival of another boarding school, one for peasants' children in Stanislawow (*Kurjer Stanislawowski* July 21, 1918).

12. *Kurjer Lwowski* January 1, 1917, reported from Bohorodczany that furniture and other valuables of the town's inhabitants had been confiscated by the Russians. *Kurjer Stanislawowski* April 28 and May 19, 1918, confirmed the extensive damage to the town of Bohorodczany. The documents discovered in the State Archives in Ivano-Frankivsk Oblast revealed financial losses suffered by Helena Regiec Sobolewska.

13. *Kurjer Stanislawowski* May 18, 1918, described bare fields in and around Bohorodczany.

14. *Pinkas Hakehillot: Encyclopedia of Jewish Communities, Poland*. Yad Vashem. Jerusalem 1980; vol. II, p. 71. There is no independent report of these atrocities. However, Jews were often silent victims; their experiences were seldom reported in local Polish or Austrian newspapers. "The Eagle of the Tsar" by Ludovic H. Grondijs in *The European War*; New York 1917; vol. X, pp. 694–695; described the Cossacks in much more positive terms, focusing on their almost mythical perseverance.

15. Notes from school inspections in April 1916 and June 1918 were retrieved from the State Archives in Ivano-Frankivsk Oblast.

16. *Kurjer Stanislawowski* December 9 and 16, 1917, reported the lack of heating in Stanislawow and the school closings. The narrow-gauge railroad was responsible for a number of accidents and was dismantled, as reported in *Kurjer Stanislawowski* September 15, 1918.

17. *Kurjer Lwowski* December 17, 19, and 27, 1917, described conditions of the cease-fire signed on December 15, 1917. The final peace treaty would not be signed until March 3, 1918.

18. *Kurjer Stanislawowski* February 17, 1918.

19. *Kurjer Lwowski* February 13, 1918, summarized the agreement pertaining to the formation of the first modern Ukrainian state. The main marches took place in Lvov and in Stanislawow on February 18, 1918. *Kurjer Stanislawowski* February 24, 1918, described the march. The protests were over the inclusion in the Ukrainian state of a territory considered part of a future Poland, which had been governed by Russia prior to the war.

20. *Kurjer Lwowski* March 16, 1918, described under the title "German Ultimatum" the visit of Polish politicians from Warsaw to Germany. The chancellor refused to discuss the borders of a future self-governing Poland, but he indicated that conditions were steadily changing in favor of the Central powers. Poles were advised to sign the agreement quickly, as their bargaining power was becoming smaller and smaller.

21. *Kurjer Lwowski* March 5, 1918, provided the content of the peace treaty in detail.

22. *Kurjer Stanislawowski* September 15 and 22, 1918.

23. *Kurjer Lwowski* January 11, 1918, printed the Fourteen Points in their entirety, despite censorship. However, the Central powers started to weigh the Points' acceptance only in October 1918. The lands that were considered Polish were not clearly defined, but they loosely covered the territory that had been partitioned between Austria, Prussia, and Russia at the end of the eighteenth century.

24. *Kurjer Lwowski* March 9, 1918, reported on the demands of Polish parliamentarians for a guarantee from Vienna that Galicia would not be split into two administrative regions (western, predominantly Polish; and eastern, predominantly Ukrainian). *Kurjer Lwowski* October 19, 1918, described the plan of the Austrian prime minister to establish Ukrainian sovereignty in the eastern part of Galicia.

25. *Kurjer Lwowski* October 3 and 5, 1918, printed a speech by the prime minister of Austro-Hungary in parliament and the reactions of parliamentarians. The speech referred to the feeble negotiations of a few Poles with Germans about the transition of power, and self-governance as a basis for a quasi-independent Poland.

26. *Kurjer Lwowski* October 6, 1918, reprinted the original diplomatic note. *Kurjer Lwowski* October 19, 1918, announced on its front page the manifesto signed by the emperor and the prime minister. *Kurjer Lwowski* October 29, 1918, announced the cease-fire, with the Austrian foreign minister accepting all additional demands from the United States.

27. *Kurjer Lwowski* October 20 and 21, 1918, described proceedings of the Ukrainian National Council that gathered for the first time in Lvov. Its members included all Ukrainian legislators from the upper and lower houses of the national parliament and the Galician *diet*. In addition, representatives of other political parties were invited. Polish and Jewish representatives from the claimed territories were invited to join the council in the future.

28. *Kurjer Lwowski* October 30 and 31, 1918, reported on the meetings of the commission, which announced that all Polish lands within the territory of Austro-Hungary (i.e., Galicia) had ended their alliance with the central government.

29. *Gazeta Lwowska* November 3, 1918, provided a brief description of the first day of fighting, with major strategic buildings guarded by the Ukrainians. This was the last issue before the paper was shut down for several weeks. *Gazeta Lwowska* January 9, 1919, described the transfer of power in Lvov on November 3, 1918. *Kurjer Lwowski* resumed its publication after Polish forces retook Lvov. The issue of November 23, 1918, described damage to many buildings in the city, allegedly set on fire by escaping Ukrainian troops. Reports of artillery fire falling on Lvov continued for weeks. In *The European War*; New York 1921; vol. XX, pp. 63–64; the perilous state of Lvov's defenses was described.

30. *Kurjer Lwowski* November 23, 24, and 25, 1918, reported on big fires in Jewish districts. The attackers allegedly were wearing military uniforms. The public was warned that military courts were empowered to issue only death sentences against those caught. There were reports of 1,000 to 1,500 arrested during the three days of these attacks.

31. *Gazeta Lwowska* November 28, 1918, unequivocally condemned the anti-Jewish attacks with no excuses or obfuscation. In contrast, *Kurjer Lwowski* December 1, 1918, expressed regret over the events but provided a skewed view of alleged Jewish transgressions during the past weeks. The *New York Times* on November 10, 1919, returned to the Jewish massacre in Lvov. *Gazeta Lwowska* December 28, 1918, provided a preliminary assessment of a fact-finding commission sent to Lvov by the Ministry of Foreign Affairs of Poland.

32. *Goniec Krakowski* June 19, 1919, reprinted the request from the prime minister of Poland to the president of the United States to appoint an American mission to investigate anti-Jewish events in Poland. Henry Morgenthau Sr., who was chosen to lead the investigation, was a highly respected lawyer and former United States ambassador to the Ottoman Empire. After visiting Lvov and taking part in hearings concerning anti-Jewish atrocities, Morgenthau's report was submitted to the International Commission to Negotiate Peace, which was in Paris deliberating the fate of the warring nations. The report itself was an objective review of the historical context of Jewish life in Poland, and the chaos that had reigned in Lvov and many other cities in the aftermath of the 1918 collapse of Germany and Austro-Hungary. The Polish side in Lvov and elsewhere did not deny these atrocities but viewed them as isolated cases unrelated to the fact that the victims were Jews. Instead, the victims' alleged sympathy with the Bolsheviks was often cited as the cause of the violence.

33. *Goniec Krakowski* December 28, 1918, brought the news of retaliations against the railway employees of Stanislawow by the Ukrainian administration. The article mentioned the initiative of Mr. Rauch and other influential citizens of the city.

34. *Kurjer Lwowski* December 2, 1918, and *Gazeta Lwowska* December 22, 1918, described thousands of POWs stranded in Stanislawow. *Gazeta Lwowska* January 10, 1919, mocked the reports of alleged calm in Stanislawow. *Goniec Krakowski* May 30, 1919, referred to alleged crimes against civilians and POWs committed by Ukrainian troops in eastern Galicia.

35. The Kiev-based Ukrainian National Republic (in today's eastern Ukraine) entered the conflict with a poorly disciplined army, one that was sometimes responsible for pogroms. For example, *Goniec Krakowski* June 7, 1919, summarized their crimes against Jews, committed in 56 towns in eastern Ukraine, alleging the killing of 5,000 in Zytomierz. In later years, some contrasted the Kiev-based Ukrainian National Republic with the more disciplined military force of the Stanislawow-based West Ukrainian People's Republic (in today's western Ukraine). However, propaganda efforts by Poland painted all Ukrainians as savages. *Gazeta Lwowska* July 11, 1919, reprinted a report from the Ukrainian newspaper *Narod*, March 30, 1919, about attacks by soldiers on Jewish stall owners in Stanislawow.

Paul Robert Magocsi; *A History of Ukraine: The Land and Its People*; University of Toronto Press Inc. 2010; p. 550; provides a description of the successful military campaign by the West Ukrainian forces in the early months of 1919 but notes that Poles were favored by the Allies.

36. Documents retrieved from the State Archives in Ivano-Frankivsk Oblast list Helena among three female teachers who refused the oath. She was reinstated when a Polish administration was established in May or June of 1919.

37. *Goniec Krakowski* May 30, 1919; and *Gazeta Lwowska* May 31 and June 12, 1919; provided vague descriptions of the underground military organization that had orchestrated the Polish takeover of Stanislawow. *Gazeta Lwowska* and *Goniec Krakowski* June 7, 1919, reprinted a delayed communiqué of the Romanian army approaching Bohorodczany. *Goniec Krakowski* June 26 and 28, 1919, gave an eyewitness report from the town of Tłumacz, about 17 miles east of Stanislawow. It was about two weeks before the regular units of the Polish army took control of the area. Other papers tried to deny the presence of Romanian troops in Stanislawow, noting that only a single Romanian liaison officer was stationed there.

Gazeta Lwowska June 15, 1919, described inhabitants' fears of roaming Ukrainian peasants. The newspaper gave an example of the self-defense force organized in tense Stanislawow. Even on June 19, 1919, *Gazeta Lwowska* tried to reassure the public that Stanislawow was safe. In the same issue, it was announced that railroad traffic between Lvov and Stanislawow had resumed.

38. *Gazeta Lwowska* June 14, 1919, reported the welcome ceremony for the foreign military mission and the hearing at City Hall, attended by Poles and Ukrainians.

39. *Kurjer Lwowski* December 29 and 30, 1919, reported from Paris that the Council of Four Powers (Great Britain, France, Italy, and the United States) had reversed its prior decision granting Poland only temporary administration of eastern Galicia. France was the main proponent of the changes, convincing Great Britain that, given recent victories of the Bolsheviks over the White Russians, a decision in favor of Poland should be made. Even the Polish press was aware that it was geopolitical factors, rather than ancient claims to the territories, that had tipped the balance.

CHAPTER 11

1. *Kurjer Lwowski* March 15, 1918, described the return of prisoners released by the Russians. The efforts by the Danish consul in Kiev and the journey through Ukraine to the border with Galicia were described.

2. Franciscus recorded these words in his biographical sketch, which was submitted years later to the military authorities. There, he included the name of the teacher, Professor Antonius Talar, who was from the city of Przemysl, in Galicia. The handwritten document was obtained from the Central Military Archives in Poland.

3. *Kurjer Lwowski* March 17 and 21, 1918, continued the story of the horrific travel conditions endured by released POWs. The article described the journey from Kiev that normally would take 1 day but instead took 10. Of note, Kiev was much closer to Galicia than was Samara, where Franciscus had been interned.

4. *Kurjer Lwowski* November 2, 1918, printed an order from the Cracow military headquarters of the nascent Polish army commanding all former Austro-Hungarian officers and soldiers up to age 35 to report for duty. The exact date Franciscus reached Galicia remains unknown, but he resurfaced in Cracow sometime in December 1919.

5. Roman Knauer, *Zarys Historii Wojennej 11-go Pulku Piechoty*, Warszawa 1930, described the history of the 11th Infantry Regiment. Franciscus was there at the inception of this unit, as the first daily order was issued by the regiment's commanding officer on January 17, 1919.

6. In 1918, the Soviet Russian Republic (or Soviet Russia for short) was formed; it evolved into the Soviet Union after the 1922 conclusion of domestic wars on its territories. During the years 1918 to 1922, the terms *Bolsheviks* and *Soviets* were used interchangeably.

7. *Kurjer Lwowski* October 12 and 26, 1919, cited press reports from the capitals of Europe that alleged anti-Bolshevik unrest in Moscow and St. Petersburg. The White Russian army was spotted less than 20 miles from St. Petersburg. Within a few days, however, the Bolshevik army claimed victory over the White Russians (*Kurjer Lwowski* November 6, 1919).

8. The Polish-Lithuanian relationship was strained. The Lithuanian government was concerned about Polish aggression and territorial claims to Vilnus. Polish-Latvian cooperation was more in evidence; their joint armed forces conducted operations against the Bolsheviks in 1919 and 1920.

9. Forces of the Kiev-based Ukrainian National Republic, under the command of the nationalist general Symon Petlura, had fought Bolshevik Russia and Poland during the war in Galicia in 1919. They should not be confused with the forces of the West Ukrainian People's Republic, which had been defeated by the Polish and Romanian armies in the summer of that year. After Petlura's forces were repelled from most of Ukraine by the Bolsheviks, he and his remaining troops fled to the territory of their former enemy, Poland. By April 1920, General Petlura had signed the Treaty of Warsaw, aligning his army with Poles in a common fight against Russia.

10. *Gazeta Lwowska* August 17, 1920, reported that Russian units had briefly taken over a town approximately 18 miles east of Warsaw. In the same issue, the military press office described heavy fighting in the region where the 11th Infantry Regiment was positioned.

11. The handwritten report was filed by Lieutenant Colonel Alexander Zawadzki, commanding officer of the 11th Infantry Regiment, while recommending Lieutenant Commander Sobolewski for the highest military decoration. It was sent via military field mail on December 27, 1920 (recovered from the Central Military Archives in Poland).

12. *Gazeta Lwowska* August 8, 11, and 17, 1920, reported that French troops and officers were on their way to Poland. In addition, supplies of tanks and ammunition were arriving there. France also led efforts on the diplomatic front, lobbying in support of Poland with the governments of the United States, Hungary, and England. The bleakest time in the conflict came when Russian troops were only a few miles from Warsaw. At that time, the Polish government issued desperate appeals, calling for courage among soldiers and the inhabitants of the threatened city.

13. *Gazeta Lwowska* July 19, 1919, provided information on proposed legislation to reintroduce the Virtuti Militari. There were five classes; some were for commanders and some were for individual acts of bravery. By 1923, there were 6,589 recipients of the Virtuti Militari; Franciscus Sobolewski's medal was number 477.

14. Based on documents retrieved from the State Archives in Ivano-Frankivsk Oblast, my grandmother petitioned the school boards in Stanislawow and Nowy Sacz in December of 1919. Her application seeking a teacher's position in Stanislawow was accompanied by a short note by her husband. Franciscus pleaded with the authorities to grant his wife a job. In case of difficulties, he offered to resign from his position as a teacher in Bohorodczany (which was awaiting his return), indicating that he had no plans to return to his former civilian role. The official replies trickled in throughout 1920 and 1921. The last negative reply came from Stanislawow in April 1921. That answer was forwarded to Lodz, where Helena had luckily been able to secure a teaching post at last.

15. Josepha Kiernik, Helena Niemczewska, and Jetti Seinfeld, along with Helena, were still employed at the school in Bohorodczany in 1919 to 1920. Josepha was the school principal (based on documents from the State Archives in Ivano-Frankivsk Oblast). By 1924, none of them could be found there. This was probably to be expected, as the town was hardly livable (based on S. Lehnert; *Spis Nauczycieli Publicznych Szkol Powszechnych i Panstwowych Seminarjow Nauczycielskich Oraz Spis Szkol*; Lwów 1924; p. 76).

16. Boleslaw ("Bolek") Durkalec was born March 16, 1920, in Bohorodczany. His parents were Wilhelmina Sobolewska and Franciscus Durkalec. Franciscus was a policeman in town. They stayed in Bohorodczany until the late 1920s, when they moved to Stanislawow, where two of Wilhelmina's brothers, Antonius and Ladislaus, already lived.

17. Franciscus returned to Bedzin with the 11th Infantry Regiment. He subsequently served in different positions: commander of the 2nd and 3rd battalions, quartermaster, and briefly commander of the entire regiment (1926). Other deployments included stays in various towns, such as Sosnowiec (1923), Pszczyna (1926), and Zawiercie (1927). From 1928 to 1930, he was the deputy commander of the 83rd Infantry Regiment in Kobryn (today's western Belarus) and the commandant in Piotrkow. He retired from the military in 1933 (based on records retrieved from the Central Military Archives in Poland).

18. By 1934, Franciscus Sobolewski was already divorced (based on a job application found in the Central Military Archives in Poland).

19. Her birth year was "miraculously" altered during the confusion of World War II. During that period, her documents were lost and new ones had to be issued, leading to accidental and intentional mistakes. My mother always jokingly said that nobody knew Wanda's real age. After she died, it turned out that she had been born in 1907.

20. In August 1939, Germany and the Soviet Union had signed an agreement in which, under secret clauses, they divided up spheres of influence in Poland and the Baltic states. A month later, German forces relinquished power in Bialystok to their ally, the Soviets. The Katyn massacre claimed the lives of 26,000 Polish nationals, including 8,000 officers, who were executed by U.S.S.R. forces in March 1940. Soon Lithuania, which was to remain under the agreed-upon Soviet sphere of influence, was forced to accept a large contingent of the Russian army stationed on their soil. In June 1940, the U.S.S.R. annexed Lithuania, launching a campaign of terror and deportations. Almost exactly a year later, the German army occupied the Baltic states.

In Lithuania, Franciscus spent three months in the internment camp for Polish officers and then was transferred to a civilian camp for war refugees. During the Soviet occupation, he lived in Vilnus. When Germans entered Lithuania in the summer of 1941, Franciscus was able to return to central Poland (occupied by Germans) to be reunited with Wanda (based on Franciscus Sobolewski's testimony to the internal security agents in 1954 in Warsaw, Poland).

EPILOGUE

1. His original trial took place before a naval military court, which sentenced Captain Boleslaw Durkalec to a three-year prison term. On appeal in 1952, his sentence was increased to five years, with no witnesses examined. The court verdict was expunged from Bolek's records only in 1977. He retired in 1982 and continued to live in Jawor, Poland. Documents detailing his ordeal were shared with me by his daughter, Irena Szymczak of Jawor.

2. The information about Franciscus Sobolewski's prosecution was obtained under a Polish freedom-of-information-like act that allows family members to access documents of the former internal security forces. The declassified documents from Lodz and Warsaw that I examined included transcripts of Franciscus's interrogations, his indictment, and the verdicts of the secret trials that followed (in total, about 1,200 pages).

3. Franciscus Sobolewski's trial, with his five "co-conspirators," took place before the regional military court in Warsaw from November 22 to 26, 1954. The prosecutor asked for a seven-year prison term for Franciscus. The appeal was heard in front of the high military court in Warsaw on March 10, 1955. Franciscus was conditionally released from prison on March 23, 1955.

4. The verdict overturning all charges against Franciscus Sobolewski and two co-defendants was announced on April 5, 1963. Most ridiculous was the continued fascination with this affair on the part of the internal security forces; the last police document I discovered had been written four years after Franciscus's death.

5. Franciscus Sobolewski died on June 6, 1969, at the age of 83. He was buried in Lodz, Poland. Wanda Sobolewska died unexpectedly on October 11, 1982. She was also laid to rest in Lodz, alongside her son from her first marriage, Zbigniew Witkowski.

6. There were two waves of expulsion of ethnic Poles from the eastern territories of prewar Poland that had been incorporated into the Soviet Union after World War II. The first cycle of deportations took place between 1944 and 1946, and the second wave occurred between 1955 and 1959.

7. Helena Regiec Sobolewska passed away on June 19, 1977. She is buried in Warsaw alongside her daughter Irena, who died on November 2, 1998.

Index

A

Abdank, coat of arms, 55

Andrychow (Andrychów), 42-43, 46, 48, 334, 339, 353, 354

Argentina, 176, 177, 346, 368

Armenians, 6, 11, 23, 94, 103, 106, 185, 349, 360

armistice, 282, 289

Astrakhan, 266

Austria, 5-10, 13, 15, 16, 20-21, 24, 27-29, 32-33, 36, 39, 44, 46, 94, 129, 158, 167, 178, 215, 235, 242, 248, 267, 289, 350, 351, 352, 354, 363, 364, 370, 371, 373, 379,

Austro-Hungary, ix, 122, 150, 177, 220, 235, 241, 242, 247-249, 252-253, 278, 282, 283, 285, 288, 289, 299, 300, 335, 349, 356, 365, 374, 375, 379, 380

B

Balkan Wars, 235, 236, 241, 373

Balkans, 6, 234-6, 241, 247

balloonists, 240, 373

Baltic states, 284, 383

Baumann, 165

Bedzin (Będzin), 301, 305, 383

Belarus, 284, 302, 383

Bialystok (Białystok), 318-320, 383

Biecz, 45, 88, 260, 339, 340, 343

Binder, Magda, 334

Black Forest, 185, 275

Black Sea, 5, 94, 282, 302

Bland, S., 189, 369

Bobrzynski, Michael, governor, 19, 222-224, 372, 373

Bochnia, 16

Bogusz, 55, 341, 355

Bohemia, province of, 10, 14, 21, 41, 113, 140, 164, 165

Bohorodczany, 12, 131-145, 156-180, 183-208, 214, 218, 239, 301, 307, 310, 313-314, 323, 344-347, 355, 364-370, 371, 381

    district court, 141, 145, 281

    churches, 135-136, 138, 142-143, 165-166, 169, 206, 271-272, 364, 367

    Jewish heritage, 134-135, 141, 144-145, 189, 203, 370

    maps, 132, 142-143, 161, 186-187, 269

    Millbrook (Mühlbach or Młynówka), 162

    Old, 110, 139, 145-146, 188, 204, 272

    schools, 189-191, 293, 309, 310, 383

    shops, 141-145, 202-204

    synagogues, 135, 281

    teachers, 179, 189-190, 194, 310, 369, 370, 383

    World War I, 249-251, 255-256, 258, 265, 266-267, 269, 270-272, 277, 281, 377, 378

Bolshevik(s), 275, 282, 284, 291, 295, 300, 302-306, 378, 380, 381, 382

Bosnia, 234, 236, 241

Boyko, 350

Brest-Litovsk Treaty, 284-285, 298, 300

Brusilov, 270
  Offensive, 268-269, 271

Buczacz, 358, 364

Budapest, 123, 222, 251, 355

Buenos Aires, 177

Buffalo Bill's Wild West Show, 126-128

Bug, river, 304

Bukovina, district of, 8, 18, 84-85, 94, 109-110, 122, 134, 214, 251, 270, 289, 293, 349, 358

Bulgaria, 234, 282, 373, 377

Bystrzyca, river, 120, 133, 145, 146, 147, 162, 185, 188, 258, 271

Canada, viii, 176

Carpathian
  campaign, 257-258
  Mountains, 6, 8, 15, 18, 133, 165, 212, 252, 260, 270, 376
  passes, during World War I, 253, 261, 376

cars, 119, 120, 184, 238, 325, 362, 369

Casmir the Great, king, 5, 94, 226, 360

Caucasus, 212, 296

cavalry, 29, 39, 86, 167, 185, 207, 258, 262, 270, 276, 277, 304

census data, 106, 107, 134, 135, 147, 349, 350, 355, 361, 367

Central powers of World War I, 264, 270, 271, 275, 276, 282, 283, 284, 285, 287, 300, 377, 379

Charles I, emperor, 278, 280, 288, 378

Charles Louis, Galician Railway, 17, 123, 353

Chrzanow, 46

Cieszyn, see Teschen

Cisleithania, 19

colonista(s), 11, 164, 367

Cossacks, 168, 252, 253, 256, 258, 276, 281, 309, 379

Cracow (Kraków), 8, 15, 16, 22, 28, 35, 39, 41, 46, 63, 123, 153-155, 219, 252, 289, 301, 303, 345, 350, 353, 354, 356, 357, 359, 361, 366, 375, 377, 378, 382
  map of the Free City of, 36-37, 39, 41

crown land(s), 4, 8, 10, 20, 21, 23, 62, 140, 146, 351, 356, 371

curiae (curial voting blocks), 215, 371

Custoza, battle of, 355

cytra, 195, 370

Czerniowce, 85, 109, 122, 207, 208, 270, 358, 361, 377

Czortkow (Czortków), 207, 370

Dorohusk, 304

Drohomirczany, 185, 186-187

Duchy of Warsaw, 28, 31, 352

Dunajec, river, 52, 53, 54, 58, 71

Durkalec family, 313, 383
  Boleslaw ("Bolek"), 313-314, 322-323, 333, 383, 384

Eagles of the Tsar, 281

Eaglets, 290

East Slavs, 4-6, 212

Emperor Ferdinand Northern Railway, 16-17, 123, 350

Ernest, 165

Ernest, Anna, 169, 345

Ferdinand, emperor, 16,

Ferenz, Joseph, 339

Ferenz, Josepha, 339, 352, 353

Feyerl, 165

Fiedler, Carol, 377

Filipek, Agnieszka, 334

Folk School Association, 73-76, 130, 195, 357, 358

Foundation of Franciscus Wilczek Sr., 42, 354

Fourteen Points, 287-288, 379

Franz Ferdinand, archduke, 241, 242

Franz Joseph, emperor, 17, 19, 21, 24, 86, 124, 128-129, 179, 197, 218, 220, 227, 233, 234, 236, 242, 356, 377
  visits to Galicia, 22-23, 100, 351, 360
  World War I, 247, 263, 267

Fredro, Alexander, 17, 350

Friedman, Michael, see Nowy Sacz, photography

Fryś, Andrzej, 334, 354

Fryś, Antonina, 354

Fryś, Jan Kanty, 354

Fryś, Magdalena, 354

Fryś, Piotr, 354, 355

Galicia, viii, 3-24
  autonomy, 20-23, 62-63, 211, 232, 351
  maps, 26, 48-49, 88-89, 268-269, 274
  railways, 16-18, 46, 70, 71, 84-85, 109, 121, 122-123, 350, 353

Galician Slaughter, 39-41, 53, 86, 169

gentry, 6, 9, 39, 40, 156, 159, 167

German kaiser, 247, 377

German settlers, 11

Gierowa, 50, 52, 59, 341, 355, 356

Goluchowski, Agenor, 19, 20-21, 22, 351

Granz, Leopolina 59

Great Retreat of 1915, 264

Great War, the, 248-249, 261, 272, 279, 285, 287, 289, 295, 302, 377

Greek Catholic,
  Church, 12, 14, 256, 364, 367, 368, 376
  churches 15, 22, 101, 107, 115, 136, 142-143, 146, 185, 188
  metropolitan Szeptycki, 364, 376

Habsburg(s), viii, 3, 7-9, 12, 13, 23, 28, 267, 288

Halawaj, 165

Halpern, 104, 144

Halychyna, 4, 98

Hebrew, 104, 189, 190

Herman, 165

Homberg, Herz, 189-190

Horocholina 10, 139, 150, 164, 367

Horowitz, 104, 219

Hrebenow, village of, 261

Hungary, 8, 18, 19, 21, 41, 46, 50, 253, 261, 267, 289, 355, 360, 367, 375, 376, 382

Hutsuls, 12, 85, 188, 350

Hübner family, 14, 257, 347, 350

ikonostas, 135-136, 364

Infantry Regiment,
  11th, 301, 303, 304, 382, 383
  58th, 178, 236, 250, 259, 261

Intersea Plan, 302

Italy, 46, 177, 266, 355, 381

Ivano-Frankivsk (Stanisławów), 328, 329, 343
  see also Stanislawow

Jahl(s), 44, 340, 358

Janowice, 63, 153, 355, 356, 366

Japan, 116, 231, 233

Jaremcze, 121-122

Jarmula (Jarmuła), Lucia, 341, 355

Jaslo (Jasło), 18, 38, 39, 44, 77, 335, 339, 340, 353, 354, 355, 358

Jews, 6, 9, 13-14, 70, 94, 98, 105-107, 141, 144, 146, 147, 156, 175, 176, 189, 211, 219, 232, 257, 262, 291, 292, 350, 358, 359, 361, 370, 376, 379, 380,
  massacre in Lvov, 290-291, 380

Jordan(s), 53, 55, 59, 355, 356

Joseph II, emperor, 7, 10, 11, 95, 98, 350, 354, 355, 360, 364, 366

Joseph Ferdinand, Archduke, 263

Joseph's Academy in Vienna, 354

Jubilee Cross of 1908, 128, 179

Kaszubinska, Anastasia, 165, 169, 344
Kerensky, Alexander, 276
  Offensive, 274, 276
Kiev, 4, 136, 226, 235, 303, 376, 380, 382
Kingdom of Galicia and Lodomeria, 8, 9, 15, 20, 31, 38, 50, 62, 84, 95, 296
Kochanowski, 62, 356
Kochawina, 200, 343, 346, 370
Korea, 233
Kornilow, General, 277
Kossakowska, Catharina, 95, 98, 360
Kossakowski, Dominic, 136
Kossakowski, Stanislaus, 157, 364, 366
Kosterkiewicz, the owner of Wielopole, 65
Kowalska, Klotylda, 357, 358
Kozłowski, Tomasz, 335
Kraków, see Cracow
Krechowce, 185, 187, 378
Krechowiecka, Magdalena, 159, 344, 367
Kreczko, Ambrosius, Dominican friar, 158
Kubas, Carolina, 205, 207, 313
Kubas, Franciscus, 205, 207
Kühn, 165
Kurjer Stanislawowski, weekly, see Stanislawow
Kwiatkowska, Marianna, 338, 352
Kwiatkowski, Adam, 38, 41, 353

Lachowce, 139, 146-150, 152, 159, 160, 161, 162, 163, 272, 344, 345, 346, 364, 365, 367, 377
  maps, 147, 148-149, 163, 186-187
Łada, coat of arms, 155-156, 157
lancers, 258, 276-278, 378
Landestreu, 11, 164, 367
legionnaires, Polish, 265
legions, Polish, 264, 265, 376, 377
Leszczynski, Stanislaus, king, 138, 364

Leszczynski, Victoria, 138, 364
Lincoln, Abraham, 24
Liquidation Commission, 289
Liszki, 45-46
Lithuania, 155, 319, 355, 383
Litzman, German general, 277
Lodz (Łódz), 310-314, 316, 321, 322, 324, 325, 327, 346, 383, 384
Lösch, Andreas, ix, 31, 38-41, 44-47, 48-49, 67, 69, 71-72, 76, 77, 80, 83, 87, 90, 338, 339, 340, 343, 352, 353, 354, 357, 358
Lösch, Bronislawa (Bronisława), 22, 44, 66, 69, 72-77, 80, 90, 121, 130, 183, 195, 197, 334, 339, 357, 358, 370
Lösch, Christian, 28-35, 38-39, 46, 338, 339, 352, 353
Lösch, Eleonora, ix, 44-47, 48-49, 72, 77, 80, 83, 86, 87, 90, 339, 340, 343, 358
Lösch, Mathias, ix, 11, 28-29, 167, 338, 352
Lösch, Stephania, x, 45, 66-67, 69-71, 78, 81, 88-89, 90, 110, 111, 116, 119, 125, 129, 183, 199, 201, 205, 208, 255, 313-314, 329, 339, 340, 343, 346, 357, 358, 370
Lösch, Wilhelmina, 44, 339, 357, 358
Lysiec (Łysiec), 185, 186-187, 188, 364, 377, 378
Lvov (Lwów), 11, 17, 22-23, 46, 63, 93, 101, 105, 116, 121, 122, 135, 141, 146, 175, 196, 197, 212, 224, 231, 237, 252, 262-263, 267, 270, 271, 275, 283, 289, 290-291, 294, 301, 350, 351, 356, 361, 362, 368, 370, 377, 378, 379, 380, 381
  University of, 216, 222-227, 371, 372
Lwów, see Lvov

M

Machowska, Anna, 169-170,
Manchuria, 231
manor house, 40, 53, 56-57, 58, 65, 139, 140, 146, 150, 156, 188
Maria Theresa, empress, 8, 9, 95, 349, 354, 360
Martyniec, 165
Międzybrodzka, Małgorzata, 334, 353
Milowka (Milówka), 54

Moravia, province of, 10, 28, 41, 42, 50, 139, 165, 252, 351, 364, 367, 371

Morgenthau Sr., Henry, 291, 380

Mszana Dolna, 18, 67-69, 343, 346

Müller, Barbara, 347

Müller, George (Jerzy), 321, 322, 334, 347

Muller, Olaf, 348

Muscophiles, 212, 251, 264, 375, 377

N

Napoleon of France, 28, 39, 107, 167, 168

Napoleonic Wars, 9, 28, 35, 167, 168

New York, 118, 177, 218, 362

Nimhin, Arthur, 105-106, 109, 237-238, 243, 255, 283, 291, 358, 361, 373

Nowosielica (Nowosielitza), 84, 85

Nowy Sacz (Sącz), 18, 46-47, 52, 64, 66, 67, 69-72, 73, 75-76, 78-83, 85-97, 88-89, 195, 260, 307, 308, 334, 338, 339, 340, 343, 355, 356, 357, 357, 370, 383

   city fire of, 78-80

   map of downtown, 81

   photography in, 78, 358

   St. Elisabeth School of, 358

O

oath of allegiance, 95, 293

Old Ruthenians, see Ruthenians

Olszyny, 50, 61, 356

opryshky, 156-157, 366

Ostgalizien, 349

Ottoman Empire, 9, 104, 234-236, 360, 377, 380

   Ottomans, 93, 360, 373

Owczarska, Elwira, 334

P

partitions of Poland, 6-7, 9, 32, 95, 146, 156, 226, 284, 349, 350, 352

Petlura, Symon, 382

Pfeffer, Rudolph, 290

Pinkas, Antonina, 31, 338, 352

Piwowarczyk, Antonina, 354

Piżanowski, Rajmund, 334

Poland, 3, 4, 41, 50, 167, 251, 288-289, 295, 302-305, 310, 311, 316-317, 318-319, 322-328, 334, 335, 339, 340, 342, 343, 345, 346, 347, 348, 349, 355, 366, 379, 380, 381, 382, 383, 384

   Kingdom of, 5, 8, 93, 95, 136, 153, 155, 267

Poles, 4-6, 12, 22, 28, 85, 94, 103, 107-108, 136, 165, 173, 176, 202, 211- 213, 215, 219, 221, 224-227, 232, 235, 241, 256-257, 264, 276, 283-285, 288-290, 292-293, 301-303, 323, 350, 356, 368, 371, 375, 379, 380, 381, 384

polonaise, dance of, 75, 192

Poniatowski, Joseph, 29, 352

Poniatowski, Stanislaus August, king, 7, 155, 366

Port Arthur, 232, 233

Potocka, Constantia, 136, 364

Potocka, Cristina, 219, 220, 371

Potocka, Victoria, 138, 364

Potocki, Andreas (founder of Stanislawow), 94, 360

Potocki, Andreas (governor of Galicia), 217-219, 372

Potocki, Joseph, 136-138, 156, 157, 364

Potocki, Stanislaus (Stanisław), 94, 360

POWs, World War I, 266, 283, 285, 292, 299-301

Prut, river, 85, 270

Przeslakiewicz (Prześlakiewicz), 190

R

railways,

   Galicia, 16-18, 46, 70, 71, 84-85, 109, 121, 122-123, 350

   Wieliczka, 34-35, 353

Rauch, Edmund, 292, 361, 380

Red Rus (Ruthenia), 4-5, 8

Regiec, Adalbertus, 52, 59, 62, 341

Regiec, Apolonia, 59

Regiec, Catharina, 52, 58, 60, 61-62, 341, 355

Regiec, Franciscus, 63

Regiec, Helena, see Sobolewska, Helena

Regiec, Joseph (father of Michaël), 50-53, 341, 355

Regiec, Joseph (brother of Michaël), 58, 341

Regiec, Joseph (son of Michaël and father of Helena), ix, 60-71, 74, 78, 79, 80, 83-85, 88-89, 90, 101, 109-116, 121-122, 128-130, 179, 183, 185, 201, 205, 208, 255, 260, 270, 279-280, 292, 294, 307, 329, 342, 343, 356, 357, 358, 362, 363, 378,

Regiec, Michaël, 52, 56-57, 169, 341, 355, 356

Regiec, Stephania, 66, 68-71, 78, 85, 88-89, 90, 110, 111, 116, 119, 125, 129, 199, 201, 205, 208, 255, 313-314, 329, 340, 343, 358,

Regiec, Wanda, 70, 85, 93, 113, 117-118, 125, 201, 208, 239-240, 265, 279, 286, 287, 313-314, 322, 328-329, 343, 357, 377

Rewera, weekly, see Stanislawow

Romania, 8, 46, 84, 85, 271, 293, 302

Roosevelt, Theodore, 233-234

Rothschild, 17, 350

Roztoka, 50, 52-62, 88-89, 341, 342, 343, 355, 356

  maps, 54, 56-57, 88-89

Russians, 231, 252, 254, 255, 256, 258, 259, 264, 270, 271, 278, 280, 281, 303, 375, 376, 378, 382

  White, 295, 300, 302, 381, 382

Ruthenians (see also Ukrainians), 6, 11-12, 85, 94, 108, 135, 144, 165, 173, 175, 176, 189, 195, 202, 212-216, 219, 220, 221, 225-227, 256, 350, 356, 371

  Old Ruthenians, movement, 212, 219

Samara, 267, 299-300, 382

salt mines in Wieliczka, 28-35, 334, 352, 353

Sapieha, Leon, 17, 350

Saxony, 28

Schönbrunn Palace, during World War I, 263

Schönbrunn Treaty, 29, 352

Schüssel, 165

secret trials, 323-326, 384

Sedlaczek, Anna, 28, 338, 352

Seinfeld, Jetti, 194, 383

Semianow, 165

Serbia, 234, 241, 247, 248, 373, 374

serfdom, 159, 355

serfs, 9, 39-40, 52147, 366

Sich Riflemen, 291

Siczynski, Miroslaw, 217, 219-222, 372

Silesia, 8, 41, 44, 46, 73, 123, 134, 279, 310, 350, 354, 371

Slovakia, 8, 45, 50

Sobolewska, Anna, 157-158, 169-170, 171, 205, 313, 367

Sobolewska, Carolina, 205, 313, 346

Sobolewska, Helena, vii, x

  childhood, 68-69, 78-83, 85, 343

  teenage years , 93, 110-111, 118, 122-124, 125

  Bohorodczany and WWI, 133, 183-207, 219, 239, 241, 249-251, 254, 255, 260-262, 265, 266-267, 271, 279, 281-282, 286, 287, 292-296, 301, 346, 369, 370, 378, 380, 383

  interwar period, 307-315

  later years, 321-322, 327-332, 343, 384

Sobolewska, Irena ("Irka"), 206, 260, 266, 271, 279, 282, 286, 287, 312, 313, 314, 315-316, 321, 322, 346, 347, 384

Sobolewska, Sophia, 160

Sobolewska, Theresia, 165, 344

Sobolewska, Wanda, 315, 318, 327, 328, 331, 384

Sobolewska, Wilhelmina, 192, 205, 207, 310, 313, 346, 383

Sobolewski, Adalbertus, 162, 366, 367

Sobolewski, Andreas, 169-171, 199, 201, 205, 345, 368, 370

Sobolewski, Antonius (grandfather of Franciscus) 167, 169, 171, 368

Sobolewski, Antonius (brother of Franciscus) 172, 173-175, 201, 345, 368, 370, 383

Sobolewski, Fabian, 155

Sobolewski, Franciscus, x, 171-173, 178-180, 191, 193, 196, 198-202, 206, 219, 241, 250, 259, 261-262, 266-267, 282, 299-307, 310, 312-313, 315, 318-320, 322, 324-328, 334, 343, 346, 368, 376, 382, 383, 384

Sobolewski, Ignatius, 159, 162, 164, 366, 367

Sobolewski, Joannes, 157-158, 159-160, 164, 367

Sobolewski, Ladislaus, 207-208, 345, 368, 383

Sobolewski, Ludovicus, 159-160, 162, 164, 170, 344, 366, 367, 368

Sobolewski, Martinus, 162

Sobolewski, Michael, 172-173, 346, 368

Sobolewski, Stanislaus, 171, 178

Sobolewski, Theophilus, 176-178, 346, 368

Sobolów, 153, 366

Sobolo(e)wski, Albertus, 154

Sobolo(e)wski, Michael, 155

Soviet Union, 319, 322, 323, 328, 382, 383, 384

St. George, the Cross of, 277

St. Petersburg, 248, 302, 375, 376, 382

Stadion,
  family, 139, 140, 144, 147, 188, 190, 214, 369
  Franz, 41, 139, 364
  Rudolph, 139, 146, 148-149, 190, 364

Stanislawow (Stanisławów),
  churches, 99, 106, 107
  entertainment, 116-119, 124-128, 193-194, 238-239
  Gartenbergers' Passage, 125, 126, 363
  history, prior to World War I, 93-101, 167-168
  Jewish heritage, 94, 98, 103-107
  Kurjer Stanislawowski, weekly, 237
  maps, 96-97, 112, 186-187, 268-269, 274, 311
  railway directorate, 83, 116, 128, 279, 280, 358, 361, 362, 378
  Rewera, weekly, 237, 373
  schools, 110-113, 115, 171-172
  synagogues, 99, 100-101, 103, 112, 116, 219
  theater, 117, 239-240

World War I, 250-252, 255-271, 274-281, 283-287

Starunia, 150, 204

Stocki, Alexander, 155

Stojalowski (Stojałowski), Stanislaw, 358, 359

Stygar, Antonius, 294, 378

Sukmanie, 54, 356

Swirski (Świrski), Alexander, 171, 202

Szeptycki, see Greek Catholic metropolitan

Szymczak, Irena, 333, 384

Talar, Antonius, prisoner of war, 382

tango, 192, 238-239

Tarnow (Tarnów), 38, 39, 41, 52, 77, 335, 353, 356, 357, 358, 359

Tatars, 50, 93, 355, 360

Taylor, Bayard, 33-34, 352

Telesnicka (Teleśnicka), Wilhelmina 69, 77-78, 340, 357, 358, 370

Telesnicki (Teleśnicki), Julianus, 69

Telesnicki (Teleśnicki) Jr., Vincent, 66, 77-78, 339. 357, 358

Telesnicki (Teleśnicki) Sr., Vincent, 67, 340

Teschen (Cieszyn), 354

Tlumacz (Tłumacz), 381

Toleranzpatent, 10, 35

Traczewska, Angela, 58, 356

Traczewska, Thecla, 55, 341, 355

Traczewski, Valentinus, 355, 356

Transleithania, 19

Transversal Railway, Galician, 18, 70, 71, 123

Trieste, 177

Trzopinski, Joannes, 200

Turowka (Turówka), 32-35, 352, 353

U

Ugartshal, 164
Ukraine, 3, 4, 84, 284, 300, 302, 303, 355, 370, 380, 382
Ukrainian National Council, 289-290, 379
Ukrainian National Republic, 283-284, 303, 380, 382
Ukrainians (see also Ruthenians), 11, 212, 213, 241, 257, 283, 284, 289-293, 376, 380, 381
Ukrainophiles, 212
University of Lvov, see Lvov

W

Wadowice, 353
Wallerstern, Joseph Breinl R., 39, 353
Warsaw, 303, 315, 317, 321, 327, 379, 382, 384
West Ukrainian People's Republic, 290-292, 380, 382
Westgalizien, 349
Wieliczka,
   maps, 36-37, 48-49
   railroads in, see railways
   salt mines of, see salt mines of Wieliczka
   unrest of 1846, 39, 353
Wielka Wies (Wieś), 355
Wieloglowy (Wielogłowy), 63-67, 74, 356, 357, 363
   maps, 64, 88-89
Wielopole, 64-65, 80
Wilczek, Eleonora 41-44, 48-49, 339, 353, 354
Wilczek, Franciscus (Franz) Jr., 43, 354
Wilczek, Franciscus (Franz) Sr., 42, 43, 354
Wilczek, Ignatius (Ignaz), 354
Wilczek, Jacob, 354
Wilczek, Joseph, 354
Wilczek, Magdalena, 354
Wilczek, Romualdus, 44, 46, 355
Wilson, Woodrow, 24, 287, 288, 291
Winkler, Wilhelm, 66, 67, 79, 357, 358
Witkowski, Andrew, 334
Witkowski, Zbigniew, 319, 384

V

Venice, 122
Vienna (Wien), 9, 10, 16, 17, 18, 20, 21, 23, 24, 27, 28, 44, 46, 75, 95, 100, 109, 116, 117, 122-124, 128, 177, 211, 212, 215, 217, 218, 220, 222, 227, 231, 234, 235, 237, 350, 351, 363, 371
World War I, 252, 255, 257, 263, 277, 283, 288, 289, 375, 377, 379
Virtuti Militari, 305, 306, 315, 319, 383
Volhynia, 5, 349

Y

Yiddish, 23, 104, 106-107, 134, 141, 150, 194, 257, 361, 376

Z

Zakliczyn, 54, 55
Zawadzki, Alexander, 382
Zielinski, Jan, 334

www.ingramcontent.com/pod-product-compliance
Lightning Source LLC
Chambersburg PA
CBHW080419230426
43662CB00015B/2151